XHTML

New
Riders

Other Books by New Riders Publishing

Inside XML
  Steven Horner, 0-7357-1020-1

Designing Web Usability
  Jakob Nielsen, 1-56205-810-X

Web Application Development with
PHP 4.0
  *Tobias Ratschiller and Till Gerken,
  0-7357-0997-1*

<creative html design.2>
  *Lynda Weinman, 0-7357-0972-6
  Available February 2001*

XML, XSLT, Java, and JSP: A Case
Study in Developing Web Applications
  *Westy Rockwell, 0-7357-1089-9
  Available March 2001*

Berkeley DB
  *Sleepycat Software, Inc. 0-7357-1064-3
  Available March 2001*

Vi iMproved (VIM)
  Steve Qualline, 0-7357-1001-5

MySQL
  Paul DuBois, 0-7357-0921-1

A UML Pattern Language
  Paul Evitts, 1-57870-118-X

Constructing Superior Software
  Paul Clements, 1-57870-147-3

Python Essential Reference
  David Beazley, 0-7357-0901-7

KDE Application Development
  Uwe Thiem, 1-57870-201-1

Developing Linux Applications with
GTK+ and GDK
  Eric Harlow, 0-7357-0021-4

GTK+/Gnome Application
Development
  Havoc Pennington, 0-7357-0078-8

DCE/RPC over SMB: Samba and
Windows NT Domain Internals
  Luke Leighton, 1-57870-150-3

Linux Firewalls
  Robert Ziegler, 0-7357-0900-9

Linux Essential Reference
  Ed Petron, 0-7357-0852-5

Linux System Administration
  *Jim Dennis, M. Carling, et al,
  1-556205-934-3*

XHTML

New Riders

201 West 103rd Street,
Indianapolis, Indiana 46290

Chelsea Valentine
Chris Minnick

XHTML

International Standard Book Number: 0-7357-1034-1

Library of Congress Catalog Card Number: *00-104521*

05 04 03 02 01   7 6 5 4 3 2 1

Interpretation of the printing code: The rightmost double-digit number is the year of the book's printing; the right-most single-digit number is the number of the book's printing. For example, the printing code 01-1 shows that the first printing of the book occurred in 2001.

Composed in *Quark 4.0* and MCPdigital by New Riders Publishing

Printed in the United States of America

Trademarks

Warning and Disclaimer

Publisher
David Dwyer

Associate Publisher
Al Valvano

Executive Editor
Stephanie Wall

Managing Editor
Gina Brown

Product Marketing Manager
Stephanie Layton

Publicity
Susan Nixon

Development Editor
Katherine Pendergast

Media Developer
Michael Hunter

Project Editors
Jake McFarland
Keith Cline

Copy Editor
Evelyn Hayes

Indexer
Chris Morris

Manufacturing Coordinator
Jim Conway

Book Designer
Louisa Klucznik

Cover Designer
Brainstorm Design

Proofreader
Jessica McCarty

Composition
Amy Parker

LANWrights Project Editor
Mary C. Burmeister

Contents

1 **Introducing XHTML**   1

What Is XML?   2

XHTML Is XML   4

XHTML History and Antecedents   5

The XHTML 1.0 Specification   6

About Backward Compatibility   9

The Argument for Adopting XHTML   10

For More Information   11

2 **All About Markup**   13

The Purpose of Markup   13

The Importance of Well-Formed and Valid Documents   17

Of Elements, Attributes, Entities, and More   18

How XML Changes HTML to XHTML   25

Making XHTML Work for You   26

For More Information   27

3 **Overview of Element Structure**   29

Common Attributes   29

Alphabetic Listing of Elements   31

For More Information   103

4 **Converting HTML to XHTML**   105

Differences Between HTML and XHTML   105

Compatibility Issues and Browser Requirements   109

Mechanical Translation from HTML to XHTML   110

Working with HTML Tidy   115

For More Information   119

5 **Working with Web Development Tools**   121

Dancing on the Bleeding Edge   121

Who's Hip to XHTML?   122

Other Tools, Other Rules   134

For More Information   134

6   Adding Style with CSS   135

Why Use CSS?   **135**

CSS for Today   **142**

CSS Basics   **143**

Property Categories   **151**

Adding CSS to XHTML Documents   **158**

Adding CSS to XML Documents   **160**

For More Information   **160**

7   Adding Style with XSL   161

What Is XSL   **162**

Transforming Your Pages with XSLT   **168**

Associating Style Sheets with Your Documents   **182**

Adding CSS to Your Transformed Documents   **183**

XSLT Tools   **183**

For More Information   **184**

8   Understanding XForms   185

The History of Web Forms   **185**

Why Use Forms at All?   **186**

Using Forms Today   **187**

Present-Day Limitations   **189**

What Exactly Are XForms?   **190**

For More Information   **192**

9   Calling Scripts and Other Objects   193

Working with Media Types in XHTML   **194**

The Document Object Model   **196**

Creating Dynamic XHTML Pages   **200**

object Element   **206**

Using Java Applets   **209**

Providing Alternatives   **211**

For More Information   **212**

10   Working with Multimedia and Graphics   213

SVG Takes on Graphics   **214**

Moving Beyond Static Images   **221**

Working with Audio   224
Making Movies   226
For More Information   227

11 Advanced Linking Techniques   229
History and Theory of Linking   229
XLink Basic Concepts   233
Linking Elements with XLink   236
The Role and Reason for XPointer   243
XPointer and References   243
Understanding XPath   246
Bringing XLink, XPointer, and XPath Together   253
The State of XLink Today   254
For More Information   255

12 The Benefits of Extensibility   257
When Structure Matters Most   260
Let the Data Drive Your Development   261
Of DTDs and Schemas   265
XML Schema   275
Adding to the Base Namespace   276
Incorporating XML Applications   278
For More Information   282

13 Where the Future Leads, XHTML Follows   283
Upcoming Design Trends   284
XHTML 1.1 Goes Modular   288
Tracking Key Working Groups and Specifications   291
Emerging Development Efforts   294
Incorporating Legacy Web Sites with the Future   296
For More Information   297

 **A XHTML 1.0: The Extensible HyperText
    Markup Language   299**
A Reformulation of HTML 4 in XML 1.0
W3C Recommendation 26 January 2000   299
Abstract   300
Status of This Document   300
1. What Is XHTML?   300

2. Definitions   **303**

3. Normative Definition of XHTML 1.0   **304**

4. Differences with HTML 4   **308**

5. Compatibility Issues   **311**

6. Future Directions   **311**

Appendix A: DTDs   **312**

Appendix B: Element Prohibitions   **313**

Appendix C: HTML Compatibility Guidelines   **313**

Appendix D: Acknowledgements   **317**

Appendix E: References   **317**

B   XHTML Elements and Attributes   319

C   CSS Properties Listed Alphabetically   345

**D   A Compendium of HTML, XML,
and XHTML Resources   363**

The Standards   **364**

Online Resources   **364**

Tools   **367**

Books   **370**

Magazines   **370**

E   Glossary   371

F   Contents on the CD-ROM   377

What You Will Find   **377**

What You Need to Get Started   **378**

How to Get Started   **378**

CD Contents   **378**

Software Included   **379**

About the Authors

Chelsea Valentine is a Web master, writer, and trainer at LANWrights, Inc., where she maintains the company Web site and related training sites, oversees LANWrights online training efforts for Austin Community College, and pitches in on books as her busy schedule permits. So far, she's contributed to numerous books since returning to LANWrights in early 1999, including *Hip Pocket Guide to HTML 4.01* (IDG Books Worldwide, 2000); *XML for Dummies, 2nd Edition* (IDG Books Worldwide, 2000); *HTML 4 for Dummies, 3rd Edition* (IDG Worldwide, 2000); and *XHTML for Dummies* (IDG Books Worldwide, 2000). In her spare time, when she's not listening to her boyfriend Sam perform, or acting as his muse, Chelsea's idea of a good time is sitting (yeah, that's right, just sitting), with nothing at all on her mind. Contact Chelsea at chelsea@lanw.com.

Chris Minnick is the founder and president of Minnick Web Services (www.minnick-web.com). Minnick Web Services specializes in developing database-driven Web applications and application services for small- to medium-sized businesses, and project-oriented Web applications for large consultancies and law firms. Chris has been writing and teaching about Web applications since 1996. He has co-authored several books, and he is a contributing editor for *Software Development Magazine* and a judge for the annual Jolt Product Excellence and Productivity Awards. In his spare time, Chris trains in martial arts, writes fiction, produces television shows for Austin's cable access channels, and publishes an online humor and travelzine (www.motelmag.com) with his wife, Margaret.

About the Technical Reviewers

These reviewers contributed their considerable hands-on expertise to the entire development process for *XHTML*. As the book was being written, these dedicated professionals reviewed all the material for technical content, organization, and flow. Their feedback was critical to ensuring that *XHTML* fits our reader's need for the highest quality technical information.

Simon St. Laurent is a Web developer, network administrator, computer book author, and XML consultant living in Ithaca, New York. His books include *XML: A Primer* (IDG Books Worldwide, 1999), *XML Elements of Style* (McGraw-Hill, 1999), *Building XML Applications* (McGraw-Hill, 1999), *Cookies* (McGraw-Hill, 1998), and *Sharing Bandwidth* (IDG Books Worldwide, 1998). He is a contributing editor to *xmlhack* and an occasional contributor to *XML.com*.

Andrew J. Indovina is currently a software developer for NetSetGo Inc., located in Rochester, New York. With a degree in computer science, he has a wide programming background including assembly, C, C++, Visual Basic, Java, XML, and ASP. In addition, he develops games in his spare time.

Acknowledgments

Chelsea Valentine: I'd like to thank MomMom and PopPop, the most memorable people in the world.

I'd also like to thank Ed Tittel for giving me the opportunity to work on this book, Chris Minnick for being a great co-author, and Mary Burmeister for keeping me in line and making me sound good. And yes Sam, I'm still going to marry you.

Chris Minnick: I would like to thank Mary Burmeister and Ed Tittel for their support and guidance. I also would like to thank my wife and business partner Margaret for her words of encouragement, her brilliant advise, and her sometimes brutally honest (but always correct) critiques.

Tell Us What You Think

As the reader of this book, you are the most important critic and commentator. We value your opinion and want to know what we're doing right, what we could do better, what areas you'd like to see us publish in, and any other words of wisdom you're willing to pass our way.

As the Executive Editor for the Networking team at New Riders Publishing, I welcome your comments. You can fax, email, or write me directly to let me know what you did or didn't like about this book—as well as what we can do to make our books stronger.

Please note that I cannot help you with technical problems related to the topic of this book, and that due to the high volume of mail I receive, I might not be able to reply to every message.

When you write, please be sure to include this book's title and authors' names as well as your name and phone or fax number. I will carefully review your comments and share them with the authors and editors who worked on the book.

Fax: 317-581-4663
Email: nrfeedback@newriders.com
Mail: Stephanie Wall
          Executive Editor
          New Riders Publishing
          201 West 103rd Street
          Indianapolis, IN 46290 USA

Introduction

XHTML is a re-creation of the enormously popular and widely used Hypertext Markup Language (HTML), based on the Extensible Markup Language (XML). In essence, XHTML restates HTML's simple and usable markup and syntax, and makes it play by the XML rules for describing and handling markup.

If you've worked with HTML, you will find much of XHTML instantly familiar and readily usable. However, there are parts of XHTML that are derived from XML that may be unfamiliar and perhaps a bit harder to understand. Much of what this book provides is the kind of explanation and exploration that will help its readers become familiar and comfortable with the X in XHTML. For now, it suffices to say that the X in XHTML helps you create a Web-content delivery vehicle that is much easier for computers to understand and render. In addition, XHTML's rules and behaviors are far better documented and understood than was ever possible with old-fashioned HTML.

For those pondering the arrival of XHTML on the Web scene, two questions nearly always come up. To the first question, "Will XHTML replace HTML?" the authors reply that it may very well do so for new Web sites some day in the not too distant future. But given the billions of existing HTML documents already on the Internet, HTML itself is in no danger of disappearing entirely from the scene. This nearly always leads to a second question, "If HTML isn't going to disappear, why should I (or my organization) use XHTML instead of HTML?" The long answer to that question motivates most of the content for this book, not to mention numerous other sources of information about XHTML. The short answer is, "Because XHTML is easier to create, manage, and control, especially with the help of a new, emerging generation of tools for creating Web content."

Some of the most interesting appeal for XHTML comes from its extensibility, which enables new markup to be defined and added to the HTML-derived markup that makes up XHTML's core. All the problems that caused HTML to go through four-plus versions since the early 1990s, and caused Web-browser vendors to create proprietary (and sadly, incompatible) markup during the so-called browser wars of the 1990s, can be completely avoided by using markup extensions that carry their syntax definitions with them wherever they go. Any browser capable of interpreting those definitions will be able to interpret the related markup. This makes the need to continually upgrade and refine specifications less necessary, and takes the browser vendors out of the driver's seat when it comes to deciding what markup content developers really need. In short, XHTML is a big win for anybody who's involved with creating, delivering, or displaying Web content online.

About This Book

We wrote this book to address the needs of working Web professionals to learn what XHTML is and how best to use it, and to help those who are contemplating making the switch from HTML to XHTML (and possibly, other XML applications as well) decide if and when to take the plunge. Both of this book's authors not only write and teach about this technology, they also consult and implement this technology as part of their workaday routines. Thus, we've benefited not only from our own experience in researching, absorbing, and digesting the information that we must master to understand XHTML, but also have benefited from sharing this information with students and Web professionals. In this latter situation, we've learned much from our audiences about what people most need to know, and what kinds of examples and illustrations work best to illuminate that information. That collective wisdom drives this book throughout.

XHTML is more than just a new kind of HTML, although that is indeed a large part of what XHTML represents. In this book, therefore, we try to connect those parts of XHTML with HTML where that is appropriate. However, we also stress the differences and resulting new capabilities that XHTML possesses, but that HTML does not, at every possible opportunity. We do this because we believe these new features and capabilities will help you justify the work involved in switching your existing content from HTML to XHTML, and using XHTML to develop new content going forward. Then again, you may be asked to justify this switch to your organization, so this information should arm you to explain why this may be beneficial, despite additional requirements for learning and effort.

Our main goals in this book are the following:

- Explain the relationship between XHTML and HTML, and XHTML and XML, to help readers understand not only what makes XHTML similar to HTML, but also what makes it different from HTML.

- Explain how to implement standard, static Web content in XHTML with the same facility and capability as in HTML.

- Explore and expose the underlying XML structure of XHTML so that it may be properly stated in XHTML documents and so that structure can be as fully exploited as possible. Because this enables XHTML to provide functions and manage text in ways that HTML never could, this is a crucial point to understand.

- Describe how to convert HTML to XHTML, both by hand (which is essential for you to understand this process) and by computer (for this is the only reasonable approach when dealing with large collections of existing HTML documents).

- Acquaint you with the mechanisms available to XHTML to control how Web documents appear when rendered in a browser—which may be accurately described as page presentation—using both Cascading Style Sheets (CSS) and the Extensible Stylesheet Language (XSL).

- Describe how you can include nontextual information in XHTML documents, such as multimedia and graphics.

- Explore various methods for accepting input through XHTML documents and for adding interactivity to such documents, including user input to forms (XForms), calling scripts, creating dynamic pages, and so forth.

- Explore the benefits of XML-derived functionality in XHTML documents, particularly when it comes to using advanced linking techniques and creating and using customized markup or other previously defined XML applications in the context of an XHTML document.

- Acquaint you with emerging trends in Web design, Web development tools, and emerging XML/XHTML specifications that may impact your Web activities in the future.

Audience

This book is aimed primarily at Web content developers of all kinds, and Web-site administrators who also must understand content creation and delivery issues. Secondary audiences include managers responsible for and anyone interested in learning about current trends in Web-content creation or delivery. Even though this book aims primarily to inform and educate Web professionals, much of what's covered herein will appeal to all of these audiences.

What Version?

As we're completing this book, XHTML 1.0 is the current W3C Recommendation that governs this markup language and XML application. A second version of the specification, called XHTML 1.1, is currently under development, as are efforts to modularize XHTML so that related groups of markup can be used separately and independently for basic text, lists, image maps, graphics, and so on. Likewise, efforts also are underway to define an XForms specification to handle user input into Web documents.

Despite the many efforts underway to better organize XHTML, and to extend its capabilities, XHTML 1.0 is ready to use today and offers significant improvements to content creation and delivery by itself. Therefore, we focus the bulk of this book on the concepts, syntax, and markup for XHTML (and as much underlying XML as is necessary to understand and use XHTML's capabilities to its fullest). Nevertheless, XForms, advanced linking tools, and coming attractions are covered in several chapters in this book as well.

Today, in fact, many organizations still use HTML 4.0 or 4.01. Although it is possible to delay the adoption of XHTML indefinitely, we hope that you'll find what XHTML has to offer to be interesting and compelling enough to merit your consideration, if not your immediate adoption. The improved syntax and mechanical validation for documents that XHTML supports and its capability to incorporate well-defined extensions will make the strongest case for those holdouts who resist XHTML and reconsider their decisions. Our prediction is that while most personal and the smallest of commercial Web sites may remain resistant to wiles and lures of XHTML (and XML as well), most serious Web professionals and most commercial Web sites of any size will begin the process of migrating from HTML to XHTML and XML before the end of 2001.

Hopefully, by the middle of this decade, most such organizations will be fully (and happily) committed to the markup languages, applications, and services XHTML and XML can deliver. The best advice we can give to those sitting on the fence (or still firmly in the HTML camp) is to carefully consider how important it is to share your organization's content and other data, and to reconsider in the light of XHTML's (and XML's) superior capabilities to capture, present, and deliver such information to your users.

Please refer any comments and/or questions to

Chelsea Valentine	Chris Minnick
LANWrights, Inc.	Minnick Web Services
2207 Klattenhoff Drive	PO Box 270266
Austin, TX 78728-5410	Austin, TX 78727-0266
`chelsea@lanw.com`	`cminnick@minnickweb.com`

Organization of This Book

XHTML thoroughly covers the concepts, terminology, mechanics, and markup for XHTML. For those unfamiliar with this subject matter, we begin with an introduction of XHTML's history and antecedents and also explain markup languages (such as HTML or XHTML) in general. This book also covers the complete syntax and semantics for all defined XHTML elements, along with issues involved in converting from HTML to XHTML. It also provides discussion and copious examples of topics related to creating and delivering Web content using XHTML that range from page presentation, to adding interactivity, to incorporating images and multimedia, to working with and incorporating extensions or existing XML applications. In addition, at the end of every chapter, we include a "For More Information" section, which provides additional resources that you can use to learn about the topics covered in the individual chapters.

The book is organized to provide a logical progression between topics. It contains 13 chapters and 5 appendixes.

Chapter 1, "Introducing XHTML," presents an overview of XHTML. This overview includes XHTML's origins and history, and the specification that governs its current form and functions. It also includes a discussion of XML and the intimate relationship between XML and XHTML.

Chapter 2, "All About Markup," explains the concepts and terminology involved in using markup languages, and specifically, how these apply to XHTML. From a syntactical perspective, this chapter also explains what's involved in converting HTML to XHTML, and how to take advantage of XHTML's more advanced capabilities in converted and new Web documents.

Chapter 3, "Overview of Element Structure," contains the entire set of XHTML elements, their common and specific attributes, and lays out the entire lexicon of predefined markup available to XHTML. Each element is covered in alphabetic order, with all of its attributes, plus information about valid contexts for use along with examples of such use. We also let you know which elements are deprecated.

Chapter 4, "Converting HTML to XHTML," covers the interesting and sometime intricate details involved in converting HTML to XHTML, both from a manual and a mechanical perspective. It also covers issues related to Web browsers, markup compatibility, and a variety of helpful translation tools.

Chapters 5, "Working with Web Development Tools," demonstrates that it's not only possible, but also desirable, to create or manage XHTML documents within the embrace of any of a set of powerful and capable Web development tools. Some of the tools covered include Web authoring packages such as Dreamweaver, and XML-oriented editing tools such as Clip! and XMetaL. Although it's not an exhaustive catalog of all the possibilities, this chapter shows that a good XHTML (or XML) tool is worth using.

Chapter 6, "Adding Style with CSS," shows how to use the Cascading Style Sheets language to manage presentation and display of XHTML documents. It begins by establishing a rationale for using CSS, and then covers how to work with inline and external CSS style rules, and covers issues involved when using CSS together with either XHTML in particular or XML in general.

Chapter 7, "Adding Style with XSL," shows how to take a more purely XML-based approach to managing presentation and displaying XHTML documents. It begins by explaining the XSL, and continues on to explore XSL's capabilities to convert XHTML and other forms of XML to native, plain-vanilla HTML for delivery to Web consumers, while maintaining the underlying content in a more structured and manageable form.

Chapter 8, "Understanding XForms," covers the current (draft) state of the XForms specification, to explain how it will ultimately provide the same capabilities to define forms within Web pages, and ultimately, capture their contents for delivery and interpretation once such forms are filled in.

Chapter 9, "Calling Scripts and Other Objects," explains how to capture and navigate the contents of XHTML documents, and explains what's involved in creating and using dynamic XHTML pages. It also explains how to embed executable objects in XHTML documents, including applets and scripts, and how to exploit the capabilities that such executable objects can deliver.

Chapter 10, "Working with Multimedia and Graphics," exposes the syntax, semantics, and politics of using multimedia and complex or moving images within XHTML documents. It covers the use of sound, video, and animation using XHTML so that you can take advantage of multimedia in your XHTML-based Web documents.

Chapter 11, "Advanced Linking Techniques," deals with advanced XML-derived linking mechanisms that support hyperlinks with multiple targets and allow objects residing at multiple locations to be accessed transparently by Web users.

Chapter 12, "The Benefits of Extensibility," explains how creating custom markup to add to basic predefined XHTML constructs can improve your ability to capture and represent structured data on the Web. Because XHTML is inherently self-describing, formal descriptions of custom markup move with the document that contains it, making it much easier for Web browsers to handle arbitrary extensions to your documents. Understanding how this can be a big win for your documents is one key to understanding the true value and power of XHTML.

Chapter 13, "Where the Future Leads, XHTML Follows," covers emerging trends in Web design and development tools that are sure to impact your Web site at some point in the future. Here, you learn more about upcoming design trends, development tools and applications, and modularization of XHTML. You also learn how to tune in on the ongoing development of the future of XML and XHTML, and how to incorporate legacy Web documents and materials alongside the latest and greatest future whizbangs.

Appendix A, "XHTML 1.0: The Extensible HyperText Markup Language" is a copy of the XHTML 1.0 Specification from the W3C Web site for you to use as a reference.

Appendix B, "XHTML Elements and Attributes," is a compact list of XHTML's predefined markup, with syntax information, and related definitions. It should make a handy reference tool while creating or investigating XHTML markup.

Appendix C, "CSS Properties Listed Alphabetically," summarizes the elements, attributes, and syntax of CSS. For those who use CSS to manage XHTML document presentation, this also makes a handy reference tool.

Appendix D, "A Compendium of HTML, XML, and XHTML Resources," presents the "best of the best" resources online for HTML, XML, and XHTML topics that include markup, applications, tutorials, and a plethora of examples. For those who want to investigate these topics further, we provide any number of great points from which to launch such investigations.

Appendix E, "Glossary," lists of all the terms we thought you might need more information on.

Appendix F, "Contents on the CD-ROM," lists the contents of the CD-ROM, including all the software tools we could get permission to include with the book.

Conventions Used in This Book

This book uses the following conventions:

- *Italics.* Used to emphasize new terms and important ideas when they're first introduced.

- `Constant width.` Represents markup—in other words, elements, attributes, attribute values, and so on. Also represents URLs.

- *Constant-width italics.* When used in code, italicized text represents a place-holder. For example, in `href="url"`, you would insert a Uniform Resource Locator (URL) such as `http://www.lanw.com` where *url* appears.

Abbreviations and acronyms are used freely throughout, but each is written out when it is first introduced—for example, Uniform Resource Locator (URL).

1

Introducing XHTML

XHTML STANDS FOR EXTENSIBLE HYPERTEXT MARKUP LANGUAGE, and it is the future of HTML. It brings the veteran standard for building Web pages, the Hypertext Markup Language (HTML), and the new standard for describing data, the Extensible Markup Language (XML), together. Whether you're an established Web developer or new to the Web world, you will most likely be using XHTML to build your Web pages very soon.

The current version of XHTML, 1.0, isn't much different from HTML 4.01, and it isn't difficult to learn. However, XHTML plays by the set of rules imposed by XML; therefore, you need to be more careful and syntactically correct as your build your Web pages with XHTML than you do with HTML.

This chapter introduces you to the basics of XHTML—what it is and what it isn't—and explains what it has to do with XML and your Web development activities. You also get a quick tour of the XHTML 1.0 Specification, your official guide to XHTML, and learn more about the backward-compatibility issues associated with adopting XHTML. (For a complete look at the XHTML 1.0 Specification, see Appendix A, "XHTML 1.0: The Extensible HyperText Markup Language," or the W3C site at www.w3.org/TR/xhtml1/.)

What Is XML?

So what do you need to know about XML to use XHTML? The good news is you don't need to know much about the specifics and syntax of XML to begin using XHTML. You do, however, need to know what XML is in a general sense, why it came to be, and what its relationship to XHTML is.

XML is a set of rules and syntax conventions you can use to build your own sets of markup elements, which you can then use to describe your content. XML was developed because HTML wasn't designed to describe the many different kinds of data that people want to send across the Web. HTML isn't designed to describe financial data, software installation guidelines, mathematical equations, or any of the other myriad data types you find on the Web.

Although HTML was originally designed to be a true markup language (one that describes content and is independent of display), it has become a tag-based language that developers use to guide the look and feel of information presented in a Web page. There are, however, many issues beyond look and feel when you're dealing with the dissemination of data, and HTML isn't the proper tool to address those issues.

XML was developed to provide flexibility and consistency that you can't achieve with HTML. Because you can use XML to write your own sets of markup elements, you don't have to try to make your content fit within the limited element set provided by HTML. The true purpose of a markup language is to describe the pieces and parts of a document without any concern for how the document will be rendered or displayed. Markup gives structure to data, and then that data can be used in a variety of ways, from display on a cellular phone to storage in and retrieval from a database.

What You Need to Know About XML, Technically Speaking

To use XHTML, you need to understand the very basic rules and syntax that form the foundation of XML. XHTML must play by these basic XML rules, and if you've done Web development with HTML, they may take a bit of getting used to. Chapter 2, "All About Markup," explains the XML rules and syntax conventions you need to be familiar with to use XHTML.

Sets of XML elements designed to describe a particular kind of information are called XML applications, or vocabularies. A large number of XML vocabularies have already been developed by industry groups to describe everything from chemical reactions (the Chemical Markup Language, or CML), to financial data (the Open Financial Exchange, or OFX), to genealogical data (the Genealogy Markup Language, or GedML). Solution developers and business-to-business tools use XML to describe data. Database developers, such as Oracle and Microsoft, are developing XML utilities that help build XML documents from data stored in databases.

The trend in information management and storage is for all data to be stored in a common format that can easily be ported to any computer running an operating system, and often any software package. Because the documents you build with markup languages are text documents, they are 100 percent portable across all platforms and can be read by any application. In a nutshell, XML provides a standard mechanism for describing any kind of data in documents that are highly portable and reusable.

Learning More About XML

The best way to start learning the ins and outs of XML and how to build XML solutions is to visit the resources identified at the end of every chapter in the "For More Information" sections. Books on XML in general are popping up left and right, as a quick search for XML at www.amazon.com or www.barnesandnoble.com shows. The two best Web sites for learning more about the basics of XML are the W3C's XML pages at www.w3.org/XML/ and www.xml.com, a site sponsored by both Seybold and O'Reilly. The W3C's site is highly technical and contains the most up-to-date information about the current state of XML and its related technologies. If you're looking for short tutorials, introductory articles, and topic-specific information turn to XML.com.

Because XML and its related technologies and vocabularies are changing regularly and quickly, you'll find that identifying a few key resources that are continually updated is an important step in learning about XML and staying caught up with its changes.

XHTML Is XML

XHTML is an XML vocabulary. It was built according to the rules of the XML 1.0 Specification; XHTML documents are XML documents. XHTML is really nothing more than a reformulation of HTML 4.01 according to the rules of XML. The following list describes what this reformulation of HTML into XHTML really means for the users of XHTML:

- XHTML documents must adhere to a stricter set of rules that includes always putting quotation marks around attribute values and nesting elements correctly.
- XML is case sensitive; therefore, XHTML also is case sensitive. The XHTML 1.0 Specification uses lowercase text to describe all elements and attributes; therefore, you also need to do the same in your XHTML documents.
- Because XML documents are designed to separate content from markup, XHTML is moving away from formatting elements such as the `font` element and toward using style sheets to drive the display of your documents.

In general, the many manipulations and quirky combinations of markup that developers have grown accustomed to using to carefully guide the display of a Web page aren't acceptable in the XML world. XHTML moves Web development away from manipulating markup and more toward using it consistently so that your documents will be more portable and more accessible.

There is a method to the madness of building Web pages that adhere to a standard and don't rely on markup to drive the display of the content in the Web browser. The entire driving force behind the Web is that the same content should be accessible to anyone with a browser that displays HTML, or in this case XHTML. Granted, the final display may be somewhat different, but the content will still be there. The browser is supposed to build the display of the document based on the description of content by markup, as well as other factors, such as the size of the user's screen and the user's preferences. Using markup to drive display means that some Web pages are totally inaccessible to some users.

In reality, XHTML is designed to return HTML to its roots and make it a set of markup that describes a particular kind of content—paragraph and tabular for the most part—without concern for how that content will be displayed.

Because XHTML is an XML vocabulary, it can benefit from the many technologies and tools that are being developed specifically to work with XML. XHTML documents have the benefit of XML's extensibility, but they still work with the current Web browsers. Later in this chapter, in the "About Backward Compatibility" and "The Argument for Adopting XHTML" sections, you can further explore the issues of the practicality of using XHTML here and now, and more importantly, why you might want to do so.

XHTML History and Antecedents

To quote the W3C (www.w3.org/Markup/), "XHTML 1.0 is the first major change to HTML since HTML 4.0 was released in 1997. It brings the rigor of XML to Web pages and is the keystone in W3C's work to create standards that provide richer Web pages on an ever-increasing range of browser platforms including cell phones, televisions, cars, wallet-sized wireless communicators, kiosks, and desktops."

The development of HTML began in the early 1990s and has continued at varying paces since then. The official versions of HTML include 2.0, 3.2, 4.0, and 4.01. Along the way, Microsoft and Netscape developed their own elements that only their browsers support. These elements include, for Internet Explorer 3.0, the bgsound element for embedding sound files in a document, and for Navigator 4.0, the layer element for building bits of content that overlap each other on a Web page. In fact, many elements that began as proprietary browser elements eventually appeared in later HTML specifications. The two most notable are the table family of elements and the frame family of elements.

It became evident early on that adding element set after element set to HTML was not practical. Vendor-developed elements brought Web developers new functionality but made it difficult to build cross-browser- and cross-platform-compatible Web pages.

As mentioned earlier, XHTML is simply a reformulation of HTML 4.01 under the rules of XML. Any elements that are available in HTML 4.01 are available in XHTML 1.0. HTML 4.01 represents the final iteration of HTML as a standalone markup language. All future developments of HTML will be done under the banner of XHTML.

XHTML 1.0 became a W3C Recommendation in January 2000 and XHTML 1.1 is already under development. Look for it to appear early in 2001. In addition, several subsets of XHTML are already being developed to meet specific information-dissemination needs and XHTML is becoming a family of XML vocabularies. The following list details some of the XHTML family members currently under development:

- **XHTML Basic.** A stripped-down version of XHTML designed for use with mobile phones, personal digital assistants (PDAs), and other interfaces that can't reasonably support the full range of XHTML elements.

- **XForms.** The next generation of Web-based forms. XForms supports better integration with scripting and helps developers build smarter and more effective forms to improve interactivity.

- **XHTML Modularization.** A mechanism for extending the functionality of XHTML without building entirely new XML vocabularies. The developers of XHTML recognize that people will want to continue to extend XHTML and that all the extensions need to work together in a cohesive framework. Modularization of XHTML provides a formal mechanism for extending XHTML within the bounds of XML syntax and conventions. XHTML 1.1 will be a collection of XHTML modules built according to the modularization specification.

The modular approach to the future development of XHTML will be the key to allowing users and organizations to build on the XHTML Specification without needing to build proprietary markup or versions of the specification. The continued move of XHTML away from format-oriented markup toward descriptive markup and style sheets to guide display makes it much easier to extend XHTML and not worry if a browser supports the extension. As long as you build a style sheet to support your extension, browsers that support modular XHTML will be capable of, in theory, displaying your XHTML documents correctly.

Much work is being done in the XHTML world to ensure that it remains a viable tool for building Web pages while ensuring that XHTML can keep up with the many changes occurring in XML technology. The W3C's markup page at www.w3.org/Markup/ details all that is being done in the world of XHTML. The HTML Roadmap, available at www.w3.org/TR/xhtml-roadmap/, outlines the next several development activities slated for HTML/XHTML.

The XHTML 1.0 Specification

The XHTML 1.0 Specification is a relatively manageable document and is the official set of guidelines for building an XHTML document. As you work with XHTML, you'll invariably find that you need to visit the specification to troll for information. Note that you also should visit the HTML 4.01 Specification. As mentioned in the "XHTML History and Antecedents" section earlier, XHTML is simply a reformulation of HTML 4.01 under the rules of XML; therefore, any elements that are available in HTML 4.01 are available in XHTML 1.0. Visit www.w3.org/TR/html4 to find information about what an element or attribute does or is used for.

This section provides you with an overview of what you'll find in the specification so it will be easier to work with the first few times you sift through its somewhat technical design.

The XHTML Specification at Your Fingertips

You'll reference the XHTML 1.0 Specification more times than you might expect. However, you might not always have an Internet connection that allows you to zip over to the specification on the W3C's Web site. For this reason, we include a copy of the specification in Appendix A of this book for your reference.

The XHTML 1.0 Specification is comprised of six main sections:

- **Section 1: What Is XHTML?** An overview of what XHTML is and how it fits under the XML umbrella. This section serves as an introduction to the specification and addresses other issues, such as what HTML 4 and XML are, and why you need XML.

- **Section 2: Definitions.** A list of terms and definitions used in the specification. If you aren't sure what a term means, check in this section of the specification. Some terms are defined in very technical terms; but most, if not all, reference other W3C documents that provide more clarity.

- **Section 3: Normative Definition of XHTML 1.0.** Addresses what both XHTML documents and XHTML processors must do to conform to the XHTML Specification. This section is really just a list of rules that governs document conformance, how to use XHTML markup within other XML documents via namespaces, and how a user agent (Web browser or other display tool) must behave to conform to the XHTML Specification. The information in this section will help you create conforming XHTML documents as well as evaluate browsers to see if they conform to the specification. The namespace information (Section 3.2) is particularly useful if you want to use bits and pieces of XHTML in other XML documents described with different XML vocabularies. Chapter 2 discusses both conforming documents and namespaces in more detail.

- **Section 4: Differences with HTML 4.** Lists all the differences between XHTML 1.0 and HTML 4.01. The key differences are addressed in Chapter 2; but a cursory glance through this section of the specification shows that XHTML documents must be well-formed, elements must be written in lower-case, empty elements (such as the `img` element) must be handled in a special way, scripts need special treatment, and a few other odds and ends. If you've worked with HTML extensively, take some time to familiarize yourself with these differences so you can get comfortable with the new ways of doing things in XHTML.

- **Section 5: Compatibility Issues.** Addresses the need, or lack thereof, for XHTML documents to be compatible with existing browsers. Although in practice XHTML documents don't necessarily need to work with the current browsers and older browsers, this is almost a necessity for a real-world XHTML solution.

- **Section 6: Future Directions.** Summarizes the future development work slated for XHTML and provides a brief roadmap of what to expect in coming versions of XHTML.

The specification also includes five appendixes that include some of the most valuable and most frequently used content in the entire specification.

- **Appendix A: DTDs.** XHTML supports three different flavors—Strict, Transitional, and Frameset—each represented by a different Document Type Definition (DTD). Each DTD defines which elements belong to which flavor of XHTML. The Transitional DTD includes all the elements in HTML 4.01 and is the most flexible. The Frameset DTD specifically includes elements for building sets of frames, and the Strict DTD includes only elements that describe content, not those that describe formatting. Chapter 2 describes these three flavors of XHTML in more detail and provides guidelines for when to use which one.
- **Appendix B: Element Prohibitions.** Although the way you can combine elements is liberal, for most elements in the XHTML Specification, the following five elements have special prohibitions placed on them:

  - a
  - pre
  - button
  - label
  - form

  The prohibitions for each element simply state which other elements you can't nest inside of these five elements, on any level. Take a couple of minutes to review these prohibitions to make sure you don't inadvertently violate them.
- **Appendix C: HTML Compatibility Guidelines.** Describes how to build XHTML documents that work with the current HTML browsers. This section of the specification is meant only to be informative. You don't have to build XHTML documents that can be viewed with the current browsers, although it makes sense to do so. The next section of this chapter, "About Backward Compatibility," discusses these guidelines and the backward compatibility of XHTML documents in more detail.
- **Appendix D: Acknowledgements.** Contains a list of people who worked on the XHTML Specification.
- **Appendix E: References.** Includes a list of W3C and other documents relevant to the specification. Reference lists at the end of specifications are usually great resources for further reading and explanations.

Compared to some of the other W3C specifications, the XHTML Specification is fairly easy to read and includes a lot of information that you can use right away to build XHTML documents. Before you begin any serious XHTML development, be sure to take the time to read through the specification at least once to familiarize yourself with what it contains. Whereas other references about XHTML are valuable, the specification is the official guide to XHTML and is the final word on XHTML document syntax and requirements.

About Backward Compatibility

Although a theory often sounds good and promises to bring needed change and functionality, the real-world implementation of that theory is of immediate concern to those who want to adopt it. XHTML doesn't escape this dilemma and there are some issues with real-world implementation that you need to consider as you work with XHTML.

XHTML is backward compatible with existing browsers, including the earlier 2.0 browsers that don't support tables or frames. In general, a browser simply ignores any element that it doesn't recognize and often displays the content within the tags without any formatting. XHTML's backward compatibility with earlier browsers isn't perfect, however, and there are a few things you need to consider as you build XHTML documents that you know will be viewed by older browsers.

- Technically, a conforming XHTML document must start with an XML processing statement that identifies the document as an XML document, (for example, `<?xml version="1.0" encoding="UTF-8"?>`). Some older browsers, however, don't recognize this as an HTML element and will display it in the browser window. (Note that Macintosh Internet Explorer browsers up to version 4.5 fall into this category.) Currently, the only solution to this problem is to not include the processing instruction in your XHTML documents. Therefore, your documents won't strictly conform, but they will work. As XHTML-compatible browsers begin to appear, you can add the processing instruction back in.

- Empty elements in XHTML are denoted with a space and a slash before the greater than sign (for example, `<br />`). Be sure to put a space between the end of the tag name and the slash so that older browsers can recognize the tag.

- Both scripts and style sheets may generate errors in XML processors because of the particular characters used in the scripting languages and the style sheet's syntax conventions. Whenever possible, save both style sheets and scripts in external files. Chapter 6, "Adding style with CSS," and Chapter 9, "Calling Scripts and Other Objects," discuss the backward-compatibility issues associated with style sheets and scripts, respectively.

In general, it isn't too difficult to build XHTML documents that work with older browsers. Your best solution for ensuring that your XHTML documents function well in older browsers is to simply test a sample XHTML document in a variety of browsers. Appendix C of the XHTML Specification includes more specific guidelines for making your XHTML documents compatible with older browsers, but the three issues listed previously are the primary ones to think about as you build your XHTML documents.

The Argument for Adopting XHTML

Even though XHTML is backward compatible with current browsers and it isn't much different from HTML 4.01, many developers are still resisting making the move to XHTML because they aren't sure where the added value is in moving to a tool with stricter set of syntax conventions.

The biggest benefit of moving from HTML to XHTML is that XHTML is an XML vocabulary. If you choose to make the move from HTML to XHTML, you get all the power associated with XML. The XHTML Specification contains a list of reasons why switching to XHTML is a good thing, including the following:

- Because XHTML documents are XML documents, they can be edited and processed by XML tools.
- XHTML documents are built according to a standard process and do not include proprietary elements that work only on some platforms and with some browsers.
- XHTML documents work with both the HTML Document Model and the XML Document Model. Chapter 9 discusses object models in more detail.
- Documents built according to the specifications in the XHTML family all work well together.

In addition to these particular benefits listed at the W3C, XHTML has all the benefits provided by XML and can work with all the new technologies being developed to support XML, such as the following:

- Advanced linking
- Style sheets that convert documents from one XML vocabulary to another
- Detailed queries of XML documents

Many of these benefits are directly related to using XHTML as a true markup language, a topic discussed at length in Chapter 2. If XHTML is your first introduction to XML, you may not be familiar with the benefits of XML. Take some time to peruse the XML resources listed earlier in the chapter to explore the benefits of XML in depth and begin to think about how they might improve your Web development activities. If you're already familiar with XML and its inner workings, simply think of XHTML as another XML vocabulary that acts like any other XML vocabulary.

In general, XHTML is the best of both the HTML world and the XML world. It provides you with a mechanism for using XML right here and now with existing processing tools (browsers) to deliver XML documents to users immediately. You adopt a new technology, but you're still able to serve your customers, who use a variety of tools to access your data. You can use the latest technologies without the many pitfalls that often accompany the unique status of early adopters.

Because XHTML is an XML vocabulary, it's a true markup language and needs to be used as such. In Chapter 2, you learn more about the details of markup theory that you need to master before you can use XHTML effectively.

For More Information

- **XHTML 1.0 Specification.** www.w3.org/TR/xhtml1
- **XHTML Basic.** www.w3.org/TR/xhtml-basic
- **XForms.** www.w3.org/MarkUp/Forms/
- **Modularization of XHTML.** www.w3.org/TR/xhtml-modularization/
- **XHTML 1.1.** www.w3.org/TR/xhtml11/

2

All About Markup

UNDERSTANDING AND USING MARKUP CORRECTLY IS ONE of the keys to implementing an XHTML solution. Although HTML processors, such as Web browsers, are fairly lenient about the accuracy of HTML markup, XHTML is a subset of XML; therefore, any documents you create using XHTML must adhere closely to a predefined set of XML rules. This chapter describes the very specific role of XHTML markup, discusses the basic components of that markup, and looks at how you can use it effectively to disseminate information.

The Purpose of Markup

If you've been using HTML for awhile, you may wonder why you need a refresher course in markup and how to use it. The simple reason is that HTML lets you break many of the basic rules of markup. If you don't unlearn some of the bad habits you might have inadvertently picked up, you may have problems creating XHTML documents that work correctly, if at all. In fact, because of the way some Web browsers interpret HTML, many Web developers have found that they can break the rules to get a specific result in a particular browser. For example, list item elements are not designed to be used outside of a list; however, because some browsers indent list items, some developers may use list item elements to create indented text.

Markup Describes Content

Markup is intended to describe the part of content that makes up a document. In its purest form, markup does not comment at all on how a given element in a document should be displayed. In fact, markup is designed to totally separate content from markup so that a single document can be displayed in any environment that can read it. In addition, markup should help outline the structure of the document.

Using markup to describe content and structure is driven by a need to create documents that are highly portable across various devices and platforms, but that still include information about the content of the document. To that end, markup tags, written in plain ASCII text, are embedded within the text document. Because text is the universal language of computers, markup documents can be ported to any platform. The final interpretation of the markup and processing of the content it describes (for display or any other purpose) depends entirely on the application that processes it.

Whereas markup is most commonly used to describe content for display, you can also use markup to describe a set of instructions that guide a computer's activities. For example, the Open Software Description (OSD), an XML vocabulary designed by Microsoft, uses markup to guide the automatic installation of software packages over a network.

To reiterate, the main purpose of markup is to describe content. Processing applications process the content based on descriptions. In the case of XHTML, a Web browser or some other display mechanism bases the display of a document on the XHTML markup elements that describe the content in that document.

Separating Markup from Display

Even when a document is designed to be displayed, markup should not include explicit instructions for that display (like the `font` element does). Because markup is designed to be portable across devices, as well as across platforms, you don't want to include any information in the markup that might tie the document to one display mechanism. Instead style sheets (discussed in detail in Chapter 7, "Adding Style with XSL") guide the display of a document on a device based on the markup *and* the device's capabilities and parameters.

An XHTML document displayed in a Web browser on a screen with a display size of 800 × 600 looks very different than one displayed on a personal digital assistant screen. By removing all display instructions (for example, absolute font sizes and the `font` element) from the markup and using style sheets for display instructions, it's possible to build a single XHTML document that can be displayed on several devices using a series of style sheets specific to each device.

XHTML 1.0 Includes Formatting Elements

Although an XML vocabulary technically should not include elements that guide display, XHTML 1.0 represents the transition of HTML into the family of XML vocabularies, and as such includes the HTML formatting-oriented elements. Although you'll still find formatting elements such as `font`, and formatting attributes such as `bgcolor` in XHTML, the future version of XHTML (XHTML 1.1) will deprecate formatting elements in favor of style sheets. To help with the transition from using HTML to drive display to using XHTML to describe content, XHTML 1.0 has three different flavors:

- **XHTML Transitional.** This includes all the elements found in HTML 4.01 and is designed to enable developers to take advantage of XML technologies, such as advanced linking and style sheets, but still be backward compatible with older browsers. If you want to adopt XHTML slowly and still serve users with older browsers, XHTML Transitional provides you with the necessary flexibility while still allowing you to use XML.

- **XHTML Strict.** This does not include any of the HTML 4.01 elements or attributes that are designed to guide the display of a page in a Web browser. Even if you initially use XHTML Transitional to describe your documents, you should eventually plan to move to a combination of XHTML Strict and style sheets and use markup only to describe your content.

- **XHTML Frameset.** This includes the HTML 4.01 elements and is designed to divide a display into one or more frames. You don't need to use this version of XHTML unless you plan to use frames in your documents.

Motivations for Using Markup to Describe Only Content

XHTML doesn't prevent you from using markup to describe content, and Web browsers will certainly continue to support formatting elements and attributes. Web browsers and other devices don't support style sheets very well yet, and frankly, developers are accustomed to using markup to guide display. So why change now, especially, if you're only building Web pages? Here are some reasons for you to ponder:

- **Markup that guides display limits accessibility.** The traditional use of markup to describe Web pages relies heavily on manipulating elements to guide the display of a page in a Web browser. This approach to design has served only to generate Web pages that work well in one or two browsers, but not in all. In addition, these pages are often inaccessible to those using text-only browsers or very old browsers. This rift in accessibility has frustrated both designers and users. The best solution to building documents that are available to the widest possible audience is to use markup to simply describe content, not to guide display.

- **XHTML documents can be converted to other documents.** As described in Chapter 1, "Introducing XHTML," XML is a set of rules for building customized markup languages. Already, a wide variety of markup languages have emerged, and there are many more to follow. For example, the Extensible Stylesheet Language Transformations (XSLT) is an XML technology that allows you to convert documents from one XML markup language to another. This is particularly useful if you need to share content or convert it for multiple uses (Web display, wireless display, print, and so on). By using XHTML to describe your content and not including display information in the markup, your content can be more easily converted from XHTML to any other XML vocabulary.

- **Style sheets give you more style power.** In reality, HTML 4.01 Transitional (and consequently XHTML 1.0 Transitional) includes a fairly limited set of formatting elements. To make up for this, designers have instead used convoluted collections of table and other elements to strictly guide the display of their pages. Style sheets provide more features than XHTML, and will provide you with more control over the look and feel of your pages. The browser vendors, so often ahead of the curve, have actually been slow to implement style sheet support, but have finally realized its benefits. You should see improved support for style sheets fairly soon, so now is the time to begin using them. Take our word for it, once you work with style sheets, you're hooked, and a handful of markup elements just can't compete.

- **XHTML isn't the only XML vocabulary.** XHTML may be your first exposure to XML, which seems to be taking over the Internet and Web worlds, but it won't be your last. More than likely, you'll run into other XML vocabularies that you'll want to take advantage of as part of future solutions. These new vocabularies won't include formatting elements, so you'll need to use style sheets. XML is the future of information description, so it's beneficial for you to learn about it now.

There are many arguments for separating content from display and simply using markup to describe your information. However, we know that you're probably not going to rework legacy documents into perfect XHTML documents that use style sheets to guide display. Instead, we suggest that you follow the guidelines of well-formed markup and start using style sheets more often, transitioning from the old ways of HTML to the new ways of XHTML and XML. XHTML Transitional makes the change less painful, and your documents backward compatible, so you have nothing to lose. And in this case, change is good.

The Importance of Well-Formed and Valid Documents

As you do more work with XHTML and XML in general, you'll hear the terms *well-formed* and *valid* thrown around quite a bit. Both of these terms are important to the development of functional XHTML documents. A well-formed XHTML document is one that plays by all of XML's syntactical rules. The rules really aren't that difficult to adhere to, as you'll see in the section "Of Elements, Attributes, Entities, and More" later in the chapter, and these rules ensure that all XML documents have the same basic structure.

For an XHTML document (or any XML document for that matter) to be processed on any platform and by any XML-compatible processor, the processor needs some sort of guarantee that certain syntax and structures are present in the document. Well-formed documents have these structures and can be processed easily by any XML-compliant processor. Documents that aren't well formed generally cause a processor to generate an error.

The lack of a well-formedness requirement for HTML documents has, in some ways, contributed to the ability of Web developers to tweak their HTML to generate specific output from a Web browser. The problem, of course, is that other browsers don't always process a "broken" HTML document the same way. Therefore, the results across browsers and platforms of pages designed this way are questionable. The well-formedness requirement in XML is included specifically to ensure that all documents have the same basic structure so that processors have a stable base to work from.

A *valid* XHTML document is a well-formed XML document that also adheres to the rules set down in the XHTML vocabulary. This means that an XHTML document that uses list item elements outside of a list is invalid. The three different flavors of XHTML all have different validity requirements. For example, if you use a formatting element such as the `font` element in your document, it will be valid under XHTML Transitional, but not under XHTML Strict.

Once again, the lack of a validity requirement for HTML documents has led to all kinds of HTML combinations that produce unpredictable results from browser to browser. Although not all XML documents (and XHTML documents by extension) must be valid, the developer of a processor (such as a Web browser) can choose to require that a document be valid before the processor will interpret it and display the results.

We don't think the new generations of Web browsers will require that XHTML documents be valid; but by committing to building valid documents, as a developer, you're committing to using a vocabulary as it was designed to be used. A vocabulary not only sets which elements you can use to describe markup, but also how you can use them together. By adhering to the rules of a vocabulary, you increase the chances that your documents will be processed correctly.

Many of the development tools described in Chapter 5, "Working with Web Development Tools" are specifically designed to make sure you build both well-formed and valid XHTML documents. If your favorite tool won't check for well formedness or validate your document, there are a host of tools that will, as described in Appendix D, "A Compendium of HTML, XML, and XHTML Resources."

Of Elements, Attributes, Entities, and More

If you're going to use markup to describe content, which is what you'll be doing with XHTML, you need to know a bit about the different components of markup. If you've worked with HTML before, you should be familiar with the different constructs. If you're new to the Web world and markup in general, the constructs may seem a bit odd at first, but they'll become familiar soon enough.

XML in general, as well as XHTML specifically, has several key components that you use repeatedly to build XHTML documents. The next several sections discuss these different constructs in detail. They are as follows:

- **Document Type Definitions (DTDs).** Documents that identify the elements, attributes, and entities that are part of any XML vocabulary. A DTD is essentially a roadmap to an XML document.

- **Elements.** The building blocks of markup that describe document content at the most basic level. Elements are made up of tags and can either be a tag pair with both a start tag and an end tag, or an empty element, which only has a start tag. The key to using any set of markup is to know which element to use to describe which chunk of information.

- **Attributes.** Additions to elements that provide more information about a given instance of an element. Attributes keep a markup language from becoming unreasonably large and enable a single element to apply to a wide variety of data and still provide detailed information about a single chunk of that data.

- **Entities.** Virtual storage units that hold everything from multimedia files to information about non-ASCII characters. Entities play a much larger role in XML than they do in HTML.

- **Namespaces.** Links to resources that provide more information about a particular XML vocabulary. Namespaces account for the fact that markup elements may be reused from vocabulary to vocabulary and that processors may need more information to help them figure out how to deal with a given set of markup (and the content it describes). When you build an XHTML document, you need to identify its namespace as the XML namespace.

- **XML declaration.** Identifies an XHTML document as an XML document. Without this declaration, a processor may not know what to do with an XHTML document.

This book is specifically about one XML vocabulary, XHTML, so we can't go into all of the wonderful, but gory, details about how XML works. To use XHTML to build Web pages, you don't need to know much more about XML than what you'll find in this book. If, however, you want to use XHTML as part of a larger XML solution, you need to learn more than we can present in this book.

DTDs

A DTD is a roadmap to an XML vocabulary. A DTD does all of the following:

- Identifies the elements in a vocabulary
- Specifies which attributes you can use with which elements
- Dictates how the elements can be used together
- Identifies entities and the information they hold or represent

The preceding isn't an exhaustive list of what a DTD can do; it's just an example of its key elements. The XML specification explains how to write the DTDs that describe vocabularies, and how to use the constructs in those DTDs to create documents.

You can actually build an XML document without a DTD, but a DTD helps put all of your elements and attributes into perspective and shows how they work together. The three different flavors of XHTML are each defined by a DTD, as follows:

- **XHTML Transitional.** `http://www.w3.org/TR/xhtml1/DTD/xhtml1-transitional.dtd`
- **XHTML Strict.** `http://www.w3.org/TR/xhtml1/DTD/xhtml1-strict.dtd`
- **XHTML Frameset.** `http://www.w3.org/TR/xhtml1/DTD/xhtml1-frameset.dtd`

Documents are validated against a DTD, so if you want to build a valid XHTML document, you need to choose a DTD and build your document according to its rules. You specify the DTD that your document uses in the `DOCTYPE` declaration at the beginning of an XHTML document. The three possible `DOCTYPE` declarations for an XHTML document are as follows:

- **XHTML Transitional.**

```
<!DOCTYPE html
    PUBLIC "-//W3C//DTD XHTML 1.0 Transitional//EN"
            "DTD/xhtml1-transitional.dtd">
```

- **XHTML Strict.**

```
<!DOCTYPE html
    PUBLIC "-//W3C//DTD XHTML 1.0 Strict//EN"
            "DTD/xhtml1-strict.dtd">
```

- **XHTML Frameset.**

```
<!DOCTYPE html
    PUBLIC "-//W3C//DTD XHTML 1.0 Frameset//EN"
            "DTD/xhtml1-frameset.dtd">
```

Chapter 3, "Overview of Element Structure," describes the DOCTYPE declaration in more detail, and Chapter 12, "The Benefits of Extensibility," discusses DTDs in more detail.

Elements

Elements describe content in an XHTML document. An XML vocabulary such as XHTML sets down the specific elements you can use to describe a document using that vocabulary. You can expect to see two different kinds of elements in XHTML documents:

- Standard elements that describe data. These elements have a start and an end tag. For example:

  ```
  <p>This is a paragraph</p>
  ```

- Empty elements that don't describe data, but instead include information in the document. The empty elements you see in XHTML embed something in a document, such as an image or a line break. Unlike HTML elements, XHTML empty elements must include a slash (/) before the final greater than sign (>) to specify that the element is empty. For example:

  ```
  <img src="mypicture.gif" />
  ```

If the DTD specifies that an element is empty, it's a good idea to format it as an empty element.

XML is case sensitive and you must build elements in an XML document using the case specified in the DTD. All three XHTML DTDs use lowercase for all elements and attributes, so you should build your entire XHTML document using lowercase elements and attributes.

Part of an element's definition in a DTD includes specific information called a *content model*, which describes how the element can be used with other elements. Content models can be very specific and can closely control how you can and can't (and in some cases must) use combinations of elements to describe your content. For example, the `html` element must contain exactly one `head` element and one `body` element.

The content model for a particular element only applies to the elements nested one layer down within it. Therefore, although you can only include one `head` element and one `body` element within the `html` element, you can include a variety of other elements within both the `head` and `body` elements.

The element descriptions in Chapter 3 provide content information for each and every element in all three XHTML DTDs. Consult Chapter 3 if you have questions about which elements you can, can't, or must use with other elements. A validation tool such as the ones discussed in Chapters 4, "Converting HTML to XHTML," and 5, "Working with Web Development Tools," will also check if your use of elements together violates any content models in a DTD. For a document to be valid, it must adhere to the content models set in the DTD.

Attributes

Attributes provide more information about elements, which makes elements more flexible in the kind of information they can describe. The XHTML `img` element is a good example of an element that greatly benefits from an attribute. You can use the `img` element to embed literally hundreds of images in a single document. (Okay, you shouldn't embed hundreds of images in a single document, but technically you still could.)

Each instance of the element refers to a different image, identified with the `src` attribute. The element is a generic identifier that describes the kind of information (an image in this case) and the attribute provides more specific information about each use of the element.

The combination of elements and attributes makes DTDs smaller and more manageable. Without attributes, DTDs would need to define elaborate element nesting schemes to provide a way to describe information in greater detail.

Using Uppercase Tags

For those developers who are attached to uppercase tags, you can still build your documents using uppercase tags. However, you'll need to run your documents through a conversion tool to convert the uppercase elements and attributes to lowercase. For more information on conversion tools, see Chapter 4.

One of the basic rules of XML is that all attribute values must be quoted. In HTML a few values, usually URLs, must be quoted, but others don't necessarily need to be. This isn't true in XML, so be sure to put quotation marks around all attribute values in your XHTML documents. (You can use single or double quotation marks.) It doesn't matter; however, we suggest you pick one or the other and be consistent. Tools that check a document for well formedness will warn you if you forgot a quotation mark or two. Also, the tools discussed in Chapter 5, which are designed specifically for building XHTML or XML documents, will often automatically generate quotation marks around attribute values for you.

Attribute values take several different forms in XHTML. For some attributes, you supply a value; for others, you select from a predefined list of values. Some attributes are required for each instance of an element, whereas others are optional. For a document to be valid, you need to use attributes with elements as described in the DTD. The element definitions in Chapter 3 include all the information about the attributes you can use with any given element, including identifying required elements and any predefined values that are set up in the DTD for the attribute.

Entities

An *entity* in XML is a virtual storage unit that can hold all kinds of information, including multimedia files, frequently used bits of text (such as footers and copyright statements), and even large chunks of information described with markup. If you haven't worked with XML very much and come from the HTML world, you'll be surprised at the role entities play in XML documents as you do more XML development.

However, because older Web browsers (and even some XHTML processors) don't know what to do with XML entities, you'll mainly use entities to identify non-ASCII characters such as the copyright symbol (©). XHTML 1.0 supports several different sets of non-ASCII and special characters. The following list includes links to documents at the W3C that identify the characters in each set and the entities that go with them:

- **Latin-1 characters.** www.w3.org/TR/xhtml1/DTD/xhtml-lat1.ent
- **Special characters.** www.w3.org/TR/xhtml1/DTD/xhtml-special.ent
- **Symbols.** www.w3.org/TR/xhtml1/DTD/xhtml-symbol.ent

All the characters can be represented by either a set of letters, called a *character entity,* or by a set of numbers, called a *numeric entity.* Entity references in XHTML are the same as those in HTML:

- **Character entities.** These begin with an ampersand (&) and end with a semicolon (;). For example:

  ©

- **Numeric entities.** These begin with an ampersand and pound sign combination (&#) and end with a semicolon. For example:

  ```
  &#169;
  ```

Whereas XHTML supports these different character sets, you may find that some older Web browsers (and even some newer ones) do not. Numeric entities are more widely supported than character entities. If a browser doesn't display a character entity correctly, try using its numeric counterpart.

Namespaces

Although anyone can use XML to define any kind of element or attribute (including `<blahblahblah smurf="blue" />`), chances are that most developers are going to build elements that are not only computer readable, but also human readable. (Note that these elements should also provide some sort of structure to the document.) This means there will most likely be a variety of DTDs and documents that use elements with the same names to describe different information. Although the person building the DTD and document may know exactly what the purpose behind an element or attribute is, an XML processor might not.

In addition to the issue of duplicate element names confusing processors, with XML, you can incorporate elements from multiple DTDs into your documents as needed to describe your content accurately. Whereas you could build a DTD that is a hybrid of a variety of DTDs, it's easier to associate a set of markup with its original DTD.

Consequently, the confusion about duplicate markup and multiple DTDs drove the W3C to develop the namespaces specification to complement the XML Specification. A namespace is nothing more than a link to a resource, often a DTD, that provides more information about a set of markup elements. To identify your XHTML document as referencing the XHTML namespace, you need to reference the XHTML namespace declaration in the `html` element of your document, as follows:

```
<html xmlns="http://www.w3.org/1999/xhtml">
```

Note that you can actually use XHTML markup within other XML documents as well, simply by pointing at the XHTML namespace. Section 3.1.2 of the XHTML Specification at `www.w3.org/TR/xhtml1/` includes more information about how to do this.

XML Declarations

An XML declaration simply states that your document is an XML document and identifies the version of XML that it adheres to. Currently, the only full version of XML is 1.0. Because XHTML documents are fully qualified XML documents, you must include an XML declaration as the first line of each document, as follows:

```
<?xml version="1.0"?>
```

Note that some older Web browsers may not recognize the XML declaration as something they shouldn't display and will actually display the declaration as part of the Web page. If you want to ensure that the declaration doesn't show up in your Web document, you can remove it from your documents, making them malformed. If you're committed to well-formed XHTML documents, however, you can use a script on your Web server to determine which browser is requesting a page. Therefore, you can send older browsers an HTML document (without the declaration) and newer ones the XHTML document (with the declaration).

Encodings

You can also use the XML declaration to include encoding information. If you're working with documents in encodings other than ASCII, UTF-8, or UTF-16, you should use the XML declaration for the encoding declaration (for example, `<?xml version="1.0" encoding="ISO-8859-1"?>`).

How XML Changes HTML to XHTML

The main difference between HTML and XHTML is that XHTML uses the syntax of XML and is designed to guide the development of well-formed and valid XML documents. XHTML is a true vocabulary of XML, whereas HTML is a markup language related to XHTML. The differences between HTML and XHTML are best illustrated by the basic rules of XML, to which all well-formed documents adhere. The basic rules are as follows:

- All elements, except empty elements, must have a start and an end tag. For example:

  ```
  <title>This is a document title.</title>
  ```

- All empty elements must have a slash (/) before the closing greater than sign (>), as follows:

  ```
  <br />
  ```

  Remember to put the space before the slash to make your empty tags readable to older browsers.

- All attribute values must be enclosed in quotes (single or double, just be consistent), as follows:

  ```
  <a href="http://www.w3.org/XML">The W3C's XML Pages</a>
  ```

- You can't use markup tags or entity starting characters, such as > or &, in your text; use entities to represent these characters. For example:

  ```
  <p>Both the less than sign (&lt;) and the ampersand (&amp;) must be
      represented by entities if they're not used in markup.</p>
  ```

- You must nest elements properly. Always close the element first that you opened last, as follows:

  ```
  <p><strong>This is a strongly emphasized paragraph.</strong></p>
  ```

All XML really does is make HTML documents more standard and guarantee that they play by a predefined set of rules. In addition to the basic requirements of a well-formed XML document, all XHTML documents must meet a few criteria (if they are to strictly conform to the rules of XHTML):

- They must be valid documents that adhere to one of the three XHTML DTDs.
- They should begin with an XML declaration.
- Their `html` element must hold all other markup and text. In XML terms, `html` is the root element.
- They must include an XHTML namespace declaration.
- They must include a `DOCTYPE` declaration that identifies one of the three XHTML DTDs.

Given all of these rules, the two key things you need to do to build XHTML documents are as follows:

- Create well-formed XML documents.
- Use one of the XHTML DTDs to build a valid XHTML document.

If you want to convert an existing HTML document to XHTML, you need to do the same things: make the document valid and well formed. Chapter 4 is devoted to converting documents from HTML to XHTML; it addresses issues of browser compatibility and identifies some of the conversion tools already available to make the process easier, less time consuming, and more accurate.

Making XHTML Work for You

XHTML is the new kid on the block, so you may be approaching it with trepidation and may not be totally convinced of why you should make the switch from HTML to XHTML. As you've learned in this chapter, the biggest difference between HTML and XHTML documents is that XHTML documents are valid XML documents. Herein lies the strength of XHTML and is the single best reason for making the move from HTML.

XHTML isn't alone. A whole collection of related technologies have emerged to support XML, providing a variety of advanced data functions, such as the following:

- Advanced hyperlinks (the XML Linking Language, XLinks) that can include more than one document, combine information from several documents into one, and facilitate the development of link catalogs for easier link management.

- An advanced style sheet mechanism (XSLT) that you can use to convert documents from one set of markup to another. An XSLT style sheet makes information easier to share and convert, but works only with well-formed XML documents.

- A query language (XML Query) for drilling down into markup-based documents.

- A more sophisticated approach to the development of user-input forms (XForms) that better integrates scripting and other technologies to increase user interaction with content.

XHTML documents that can take advantage of any and all technologies associated with XML, as well as new tools and technologies, are appearing almost daily. XML has also become a major player in information-dissemination solutions. You can use a custom XML vocabulary to describe your content accurately and then use a style sheet to convert your data to XHTML for display in a Web browser.

The following three chapters help you get a handle on both developing XHTML documents from scratch and converting HTML documents to XHTML. That's the easy part. You begin to make XHTML work for you when you treat your XHTML documents as XML documents. Chapters 6 through 12 of the book focus on the technologies that support XML and how you can use them with XHTML, as well as the benefits of using an extensible tool such as XHTML to build Web pages.

For More Information

As always, there's a wealth of information available on the Web. For more information on XHTML and XML, check out the following sites:

- **The XHTML Specification.** www.w3.org/TR/xhtml1/
- **The XML FAQ.** www.ucc.ie/xml/
- **What Do XML. Documents Look Like?**
  www.xml.com/pub/98/10/guide2.html
- **XHTML Part 3: What's New.** www.webreview.com/pub/1999/07/16/
  feature/index3.html

3

Overview of
Element Structure

XHTML IS AN XML LANGUAGE THAT uses HTML as its vocabulary. For this reason, XHTML uses the same 90-plus elements that HTML 4 uses. In the following sections, we identify each element, define it, name its attributes, and provide a usage example.

Some elements have been deprecated, which means that the World Wide Web Consortium (W3C) plans to leave them out of the next version of XHTML. This is already in the works. When you look at the XHTML 1.1 working draft, you see that all the deprecated elements from XHTML 1.0 are not included in XHTML 1.1 (see www.w3.org/TR/xhtml11/changes.html#a_changes). For this reason, we do not define the deprecated elements in detail. Most of the time, we point you to style sheets to achieve the same results as the deprecated elements. See Chapters 6, "Adding Style with CSS," and 7, "Adding Style with XSL," for more information on style sheets.

Common Attributes

There are several attributes that can be applied to almost all XHTML elements. Instead of defining them individually for every element, we list them here. They are commonly referred to as the *common attributes*. See the following section, "Alphabetic Listing of Elements," to see what the letters in brackets stand for. Here are the common attributes:

```
id="name" [CS]
```

Used to assign a unique name to an element (the name must be unique within the document).

```
class="name" [CS]
```

Used to assign a class or set of classes for an element. Used in conjunction with Cascading Style Sheets (CSS) style rules to define presentation properties for a given subset of elements.

```
lang="language-code" [CI]
```

Specifies the language to be applied to the element and its contents.

```
dir="ltr|rtl" [CI]
```

Specifies the direction of text for content that is directionally ambiguous.

```
title="text" [CS]
```

Used much like the title element; however, the title attribute applies only to a specified element, rather than an entire document. Behavior of this attribute is not defined by the specification; browsers can interpret this attribute as they want.

All elements except base, basefont, head, html, meta, param, script, and title can use this attribute.

```
style="style" [CN]
```

Enables the author to use CSS style rules as attribute values and defines presentation for the specified element.

All elements except base, basefont, head, html, meta, param, script, style, and title can use this attribute.

Event handlers, or *intrinsic events*, enable authors to incorporate scripting into their Web pages. For a complete discussion of intrinsic events, see Chapter 9, "Calling Scripts and Other Objects." When an element uses these attributes, we just say "all intrinsic events" instead of listing each one. Here are the intrinsic events supported by XHTML:

```
onload="script" [CT]
onunload="script" [CT]
onclick="script" [CT]
ondblclick="script" [CT]
onmousedown="script" [CT]
onmouseup="script" [CT]
onmouseover="script" [CT]
onmousemove="script" [CT]
onmouseout="script" [CT]
onfocus="script" [CT]
onblur="script" [CT]
onkeypress="script" [CT]
onkeydown="script" [CT]
onkeyup="script" [CT]
onsubmit="script" [CT]
onreset="script" [CT]
onselect="script" [CT]
onchange="script" [CT]
```

Alphabetic Listing of Elements

In the following sections, we list all XHTML elements alphabetically. The following information is described for all elements that are not deprecated:

- **The element name.** The name of the element is listed; however, we do not include the XML syntax that surrounds the element name. Keep in mind that when you use elements in an XHTML document, you must use the following syntax: `<element>...</element>` or `<empty-element />`. Also note that all placeholders are italicized. Deprecated elements have (Deprecated) next to them, and empty elements have (Empty) next to them.

- **Element definition.** The element definition tells you what the element is used for or provides a brief description.

- **Attribute names and definitions.** In the attribute section of the element, we provide the specific attributes as well as a list of the common attributes, if there are any. Each specific attribute is listed with four parts:

  - **The attribute name.** The name of the attribute.

  - **Possible attribute values.** If the attribute value is in italics, it's a placeholder. If the attribute value is a list of terms separated by a pipe bar, those are the value choices.

    Note that the attribute name and possible attribute values appear on one line.

  - **Case information.** [CI] means that the value is not case sensitive, [CN] means that the value, (which is numbers or characters) is not subject to case changes, and [CT] means that case sensitivity is noted in the definition.

  - **Attribute definition.** Provides a description of the attribute.

  When we list the common attributes, we just give you their names because we defined them in the "Common Attributes" section at the beginning of this chapter.

- **Context.** This is the element relationship listing. The possible parents and children for each element are listed in this section.

- **Example.** Because of space issues, the examples we show are not full, well-formed XHTML documents. We just show you what's necessary for you to grasp how the markup should be used.

As you read through this section, be sure to note the empty elements because they require special syntax, `<empty-element />`.

a

The anchor (or hyperlink) element indicates a portion of text or object that when activated by the user, triggers the browser window to go to another URL.

Attributes

Specific attributes:

```
accesskey="character" [CN]
```

Identifies the character to be used as a keyboard shortcut. The value can be any alphanumeric character from a browser's character set.

```
charset="character-encoding" [CI]
```

Identifies the character encoding of the linked Web resource. The default is ISO-8859-1.

```
coords="coordinates" [CN]
```

Defines the coordinates that correspond with the value of the shape attribute.

```
href="uri" [CT]
```

Identifies the Uniform Resource Identifier (URI) to be loaded when the hyperlink is triggered. You can also reference an email address using the following as the value: mailto:name@domain.com. Note that a URL is a type of URI.

```
hreflang="language-code" [CI]
```

Identifies the base language of the resource identified by the href attribute. See www.w3.org/TR/html4/struct/dirlang.html#adef-lang for more on the various language codes.

```
name="text" [CS]
```

Defines a name for a given region on a page. This value is used in conjunction with the value of the href attribute, thereby allowing the browser to jump not only to a page, but also to a given section of that page.

```
rel="text" [CI]
```

Defines the relationship between the current document and the resource specified by the href attribute. This attribute is not widely used.

```
rev="text" [CI]
```

Defines a reverse link from the resource specified by the href attribute to the current document. This attribute is not widely used.

```
shape="rect|circle|poly|default" [CI]
```

Specifies the shape of a region.

```
target="window|_blank|_parent|_self|_top" [CI]
```

Used within a frameset where a frame is named as an attribute of the frame element. Defines how the resource should be loaded. This is what each value means:

- *window* loads the resource into the named targeted window.
- *_blank* loads the resource into a new window.

- **_parent** loads the resource into the parent of the current document.
- **_self** loads the resource into the same window.
- **_top** loads the resource into the body of the window.

`tabindex="`*`number`*`" [CN]`

Tabbing allows the author to give focus or access to an element by using a standard keyboard sequence. The sequence order is normally defined by the order of the elements. The `tabindex` attribute allows the author to establish a different order by identifying the position of the current element in the tabbing order. The value must be a number between 0 and 32767. The tabbing order specifies the order of attention for elements when navigated by the user.

`type="`*`content-type`*`" [CI]`

Provides the MIME type of the URL, or resource.

Common attributes: `id`, `class`, `lang`, `dir`, `title`, `style`, and all intrinsic events.

Context

Can contain the following:

```
a, abbr, acronym, b, bdo, big, br, button, cite, code, dfn, em, i, img, input,
kbd, label, map,object, q, samp, script, select, small, span, strong, sub, sup,
textarea, tt, var
```

Can be used in the following:

```
a, abbr, acronym, applet, b, basefont, bdo, big, blockquote, body, button,
caption, center , cite, code, dd, dfn, div, dt, em, fieldset, font, form, i,
iframe, kbd, label, legend, li, noframes, noscript, object, p, pre, q, s, samp,
small, span, strike, strong, sub, sup, td, th, tt, u, var
```

Example

```
<a href="http://www.lanw.com">Text for the link</a>
<a href="http://www.w3.org" target="_blank">When triggered, the W3C Web site will
open in a new window</a>
<a href="http://www.w3.org/TR/html4/struct/links.html#edef-A">When triggered, the
referenced page will replace the current page and will jump to the section
containing the "edef-A" anchor name</a>
```

abbr

The `abbr` element identifies contained text as an abbreviation, (for example, W3C and ISBN). We suggest using the `title` attribute to provide the expanded word or phrase.

Attributes

Specific attributes: None.
Common attributes: id, class, lang, dir, title, style, and all intrinsic events.

Context

Can contain the following:

a, abbr, acronym, b, bdo, big, br, button, cite, code, dfn, em, i, img, input, kbd, label, map, object, q, samp, script, select, small, span, strong, sub, sup, textarea, tt, var

Can be used in the following:

a, abbr, acronym, applet, b, basefont, bdo, big, blockquote, body, button, caption, center, cite, code, dd, dfn, div, dt, em, fieldset, font, form, i, iframe, kbd, label, legend, li, noframes, noscript, object, p, pre, q, s, samp, small, span, strike, strong, sub, sup, td, th, tt, u, var

Example

```
<p>The <abbr title="World Wide Web Consortium">W3C</abbr> is the place to look for
information on XHTML.</p>
```

acronym

This element identifies contained text as an acronym, (for example, WWW and HTTP) an abbreviated form in which the first letter of each word is used. We suggest using the title attribute to provide the expanded phrase.

Attributes

Specific attributes: None.
Common attributes: id, class, lang, dir, title, style, and all intrinsic events.

Context

Can contain the following:

a, abbr, acronym, b, bdo, big, br, button, cite, code, dfn, em, i, img, input, kbd, label, map, object, q, samp, script, select, small, span, strong, sub, sup, textarea, tt, var

Can be used in the following:

a, abbr, acronym, applet, b, basefont, bdo, big, blockquote, body, button, caption, center , cite, code, dd, dfn, div, dt, em, fieldset, font, form, i, iframe, kbd, label, legend, li, noframes, noscript, object, p, pre, q, s, samp, small, span, strike, strong, sub, sup, td, th, tt, u, var

Example

```
<p>The <acronym title="World Wide Web">WWW</abbr> is where you publish all your
XHTML pages.</p>
```

address

This element identifies information about the author. The `address` element is generally used at the beginning or end of a document and most browsers render it in italics. This element is commonly used as a footer.

Attributes

Specific attributes: None.
Common attributes: `id`, `class`, `lang`, `dir`, `title`, `style`, and all intrinsic events.

Context

Can contain the following:

```
a, abbr, acronym, b, bdo, big, br, button, cite, code, dfn, em, i, img, input,
kbd, label, map, object, p, q, samp, script, select, small, span, strong, sub,
sup, textarea, tt, var
```

Can be used in the following:

```
applet, basefont, blockquote, body, center dd, div, fieldset, form, iframe, li,
noframes, noscript, object, pre, td, th
```

Example

```
<address>
Jane Doe<br />
1111 One Drive<br />
North Pole<br />
</address>
```

applet (Deprecated)

This element and all its attributes are deprecated in favor of the `object` element.

area (Empty)

First created for client-side image maps, the `area` element specifies destinations for hot spots of an image using an HTML encoding system. The `shape` and `coords` attributes identify the dimensions of a geometric shape and the `href` attribute identifies the hyperlink destination. The author can use an arbitrary number of `area` elements within a given map.

Attributes

Specific attributes:

```
accesskey="text" [CN]
```

Identifies the character to be used as a keyboard shortcut. The value can be any alphanumeric character from a browser's character set.

```
alt="text" [CS]
```

Specifies alternative text to be displayed as a substitute for nonvisual browsers. This is an important attribute for accessibility reasons. The language of the alternative text can be set using the lang attribute.

```
coords="coordinates" [CN]
```

Defines a hyperlink region by specifying the coordinates, in pixels, that are appropriate for the geographical region identified by the shape attribute. The shapes that can be defined are as follows:

- **Rectangle (rect).** coords="left-x, top-y, right-x, bottom-y"
- **Circle (circ).** coords="center_x, center_y, radius"
- **Polygon (poly).** coords="x1,y1,x2,y2,...xn,yn"

```
href="uri" [CT]
```

Identifies the URI to be loaded when the hyperlink is triggered. You can also reference an email address using the following as the value: mailto:name@domain.com.

```
nohref="nohref" [CI]
```

Specifies that a region is not to reference any resource. Remember, the href and nohref are contradictory and cannot be used together.

```
shape="rect|circ|poly|default" [CI]
```

Identifies the shape of a region. The shapes are as follows:

- **rect** defines a rectangular region.
- **circ** defines a circular region.
- **poly** defines a polygonal region.

```
tabindex="number" [CN]
```

Tabbing allows the author to give focus or access to an element by using a standard keyboard sequence. The sequence order is normally defined by the order of the elements. The tabindex attribute allows the author to establish a different order by identifying the position of the current element in the tabbing order. The value must be a number between 0 and 32767. The tabbing order specifies the order of attention for elements when navigated by the user.

```
target="window|_blank|_parent|_self|_top" [CI]
```

Used with a frameset where a frame is named as an attribute of the `frame` element. Defines how the resource should be loaded. Here's what each value means:

- *`window`* loads the resource into the named targeted window.
- *`_blank`* loads the resource into a new window.
- *`_parent`* loads the resource into the parent of the current document.
- *`_self`* loads the resource into the same window.
- *`_top`* loads the resource into the body of the window.

Common attributes: `id`, `class`, `lang`, `dir`, `title`, `style`, and all intrinsic events.

Context

Can contain the following:

`Empty`

Can be used in the following:

`map`

Example

```
<map name="clientsidemap">
   <area shape="rect" coords="100,100,0,0"
         href="http://www.mydomain.com/file.htm" />
   <area shape="circle" coords="95,100,5"
         href="http://www.mydomain.com/file.htm" />
   <area shape="poly" coords="5,100,10,110,0,110" nohref="nohref" />
</map>
```

b

This is an inline style element that renders text in boldface.

Attributes

Specific attributes: None.
Common attributes: `id`, `class`, `lang`, `dir`, `title`, `style`, and all intrinsic events.

Context

Can contain the following:

`a, abbr, acronym, b, bdo, big, br, button, cite, code, dfn, em, i, img, input, kbd, label, map, object, q, samp, script, select, small, span, strong, sub, sup, textarea, tt, var`

Can be used in the following:

`a, abbr, acronym, applet, b, basefont, bdo, big, blockquote, body, button, caption, center, cite, code, dd, dfn, div, dt, em, fieldset, font, form, i, iframe, kbd, label, legend, li, noframes, noscript, object, p, pre, q, s, samp, small, span, strike, strong, sub, sup, td, th, tt, u, var`

Example

```
<p>Sometimes you want to <b>bold</b> your text.</p>
```

base (Empty)

The base element defines a document's base URI. This element must occur as a child of the head element and establishes a base URL for all relative references.

Attributes

Specific attributes:

```
href="uri" [CT]
```

Identifies the URI that is loaded when the hyperlink is triggered.

```
target="window|_blank|_parent|_self|_top" [CI]
```

Used with a frameset where a frame is named as an attribute of the frame element. Defines how the resource should be loaded. Here's what each value means:

- **window** loads the resource into the named targeted window.
- **_blank** loads the resource into a new window.
- **_parent** loads the resource into the parent of the current document.
- **_self** loads the resource into the same window.
- **_top** loads the resource into the body of the window.

Common attributes: None.

Context

Can contain the following:

```
Empty
```

Can be used in the following:

```
head
```

Example

```
<head>
<title>Document Title</title>
<base href="http://www.lanw.com/" />
</head>
```

basefont (Empty) (Deprecated)

The basefont element is deprecated in favor of using style sheets.

bdo

The bidirectional override (`bdo`) element defines the default algorithm used for language and display direction.

Attributes

Specific attributes:

```
dir="ltr|rtl" [CI]
```

The `dir` attribute is mandatory. It specifies the base direction of the contained text.
Common attributes: `id`, `class`, `title`, and `style`.

Context

Can contain the following:

> *text*, a, abbr, acronym, applet, b, bdo, big, br, cite, code, dfn, em, font, i,
> img, iframe, kbd, map, object, q, s, samp, script, small, span, strike, strong,
> sub, sup, tt, u, var

Can be used in the following:

> a, abbr, acronym, applet, b, basefont, bdo, big, blockquote, body, button,
> caption, center, cite, code, dd, dfn, div, dt, em, fieldset, font, form, i,
> iframe, kbd, label, legend, li, noframes, noscript, object, p, pre, q, s, samp,
> small, span, strike, strong, sub, sup, td, th, tt, u, var

Example

```
<p>We read plain old English, but some may read <bdo lang="IW"
dir="rtl">Hebrew</bdo>.</p>
```

big

This is an inline style element that renders text larger than the base text.

Attributes

Common attributes: `id`, `class`, `lang`, `dir`, `title`, `style`, and all intrinsic events.

Context

Can contain the following:

> *text*, a, abbr, acronym, applet, b, bdo, big, br, cite, code, dfn, em, font, i,
> img, iframe, kbd, map, object, q, s, samp, script, small, span, strike, strong,
> sub, sup, tt, u, var

Can be used in the following:

> a, abbr, acronym, applet, b, basefont, bdo, big, blockquote, body, button,
> caption, center, cite, code, dd, dfn, div, dt, em, fieldset, font, form, i,
> iframe, kbd, label, legend, li, noframes, noscript, object, p, pre, q, s, samp,
> small, span, strike, strong, sub, sup, td, th, tt, u, var

Example

```
<p>Sometimes you want text to render <big>larger</big> than the rest.</p>
```

blockquote

This element is used to set off a long quotation.

Attributes

Specific attributes:

```
cite="uri" [CT]
```

Designates a URL that identifies a source document or message about the quotation.
Common attributes: id, class, lang, dir, title, style, and all intrinsic events.

Context

Can contain the following:

```
address, basefont, blockquote, dir, div, dl, fieldset, form, hr, isindex, ol,
menu, noframes, noscript, p, pre, table, ul
```

Can be used in the following:

```
a, abbr, acronym, applet, b, basefont, bdo, big, blockquote, body, button,
caption, center, cite, code, dd, dfn, div, dt, em, fieldset, font, form, i,
iframe, kbd, label, legend, li, noframes, noscript, object, p, pre, q, s, samp,
small, span, strike, strong, sub, sup, td, th, tt, u, var
```

Example

```
<body>
<blockquote cite="http://www.url.com/source.html">This is a quote from a very
famous person and the source document is found at the URL identified in the value
of the cite attribute.</blockquote>
</body>
```

body

The body element must be a child of the html element. It contains the document's
content.

Attributes

Specific attributes: All specific attributes of the body element are deprecated in favor
of using style sheets (see the "Example" section).
Common attributes: id, class, lang, dir, title, style, and all intrinsic events.

Example

```
<html xmlns="http://www.w3.org/1999/xhtml">
<head>
<title>Document title</title>
<style type="text/css">
body {color:black; font-size:12pt;}
</style>
</head>
<body>
...
<body>
</html>
```

br (Empty)

This element inserts a forced line break.

Attributes

Specific attributes: The `clear` attribute is deprecated in favor of using the `clear` property in style sheets.
Common attributes: `id`, `class`, `title`, and `style`.

Context

Can contain the following:

```
Empty
```

Can be used in the following:

```
a, abbr, acronym, applet, b, basefont, bdo, big, blockquote, body, button,
caption, center, cite, code, dd, dfn, div, dt, em, fieldset, font, form, i,
iframe, kbd, label, legend, li, noframes, noscript, object, p, pre, q, s, samp,
small, span, strike, strong, sub, sup, td, th, tt, u, var
```

Example

```
<body>
<p>Sometimes you want to<br />
force a line break.</p>
</body>
```

button

The `button` attribute creates a push button to be used as a child of the `form` element. Similar to the standard `submit` and `reset` buttons.

Attributes

Specific attributes:

```
accesskey="text" [CN]
```

Identifies the character to be used as a keyboard shortcut. The value can be any alphanumeric character from a browser's character set.

```
name="cdata" [CI]
```

Defines the field when passed to the form-processing application.

```
value="cdata" [CI]
```

Represents the value of the control.

```
type="submit|button|reset" [CI]
```

- **submit** creates a submit button that sends the data of the form to the server. This is the default value.
- **reset** creates a reset button that restores the form to the original state.
- **button** creates a push button that calls a script.

```
disabled="disabled" [CI]
```

When used, this attribute disables the control for user input.

```
tabindex="number" [CN]
```

Tabbing allows the author to give focus or access to an element by using a standard keyboard sequence. The sequence order is normally defined by the order of the elements. The `tabindex` attribute allows the author to establish a different order by identifying the position of the current element in the tabbing order. The value must be a number between 0 and 32767. The tabbing order specifies the order of attention for elements when navigated by the user.

Common attributes: id, class, lang, dir, title, style, and all intrinsic events.

Example

```
<form method="post" action="http://www.lanw.com/cgi-bin/application">
...
<button type="submit" name="submitbutton">
<img src="submit.gif" alt="Submit Button" />
</button>
</form>
```

caption

The text contained by the `caption` element describes the corresponding table. If present, the `caption` element must occur immediately after the `table` start tag. There may only be one `caption` element for a given table.

Attributes

Specific attributes: The `align` attribute is deprecated in favor of using style sheets.
Common attributes: `id`, `class`, `lang`, `dir`, `title`, `style`, and all intrinsic events.

Context

Can contain the following:

```
a, abbr, acronym, b, bdo, big, br, button, cite, code, dfn, em, i, img, input,
kbd, label, map, object, q, samp, script, select, small, span, strong, sub, sup,
textarea, tt, var
```

Can be used in the following:

```
table
```

Example

```
<table>
<caption>The caption goes here</caption>
<thead>...</thead>
<tfoot>...</tfoot>
<tbody>...</tbody>
</table>
```

center (Deprecated)

The `center` element is deprecated in favor of using style sheets. Shorthand for `<div align="center">`.

cite

The `cite` element contains a citation or reference to another resource.

Attributes

Specific attributes: None.
Common attributes: `id`, `class`, `lang`, `dir`, `title`, `style`, and all intrinsic events.

Context

Can contain the following:

```
a, abbr, acronym, b, bdo, big, br, button, cite, code, dfn, em, i, img, input,
kbd, label, map, object, q, samp, script, select, small, span, strong, sub, sup,
textarea, tt, var
```

Can be used in the following:

```
a, abbr, acronym, applet, b, basefont, bdo, big, blockquote, body, button,
caption, center, cite, code, dd, dfn, div, dt, em, fieldset, font, form, i,
iframe, kbd, label, legend, li, noframes, noscript, object, p, pre, q, s, samp,
small, span, strike, strong, sub, sup, td, th, tt, u, var
```

Example

```
<body>
<p>As <cite>Mark Twain</cite> once said...</p>
</body>
```

code

This element contains a computer code fragment.

Attributes

Specific attributes: None.
Common attributes: id, class, lang, dir, title, style, and all intrinsic events.

Context

Can contain the following:

```
a, abbr, acronym, b, bdo, big, br, button, cite, code, dfn, em, i, img, input,
kbd, label, map, object, q, samp, script, select, small, span, strong, sub, sup,
textarea, tt, var
```

Can be used in the following:

```
a, abbr, acronym, applet, b, basefont, bdo, big, blockquote, body, button,
caption, center, cite, code, dd, dfn, div, dt, em, fieldset, font, form, i,
iframe, kbd, label, legend, li, noframes, noscript, object, p, pre, q, s, samp,
small, span, strike, strong, sub, sup, td, th, tt, u, var
```

Example

```
<body>
<code>
&gt;html&lt;
</code>
</body>
```

col **(Empty)**

The `col` element defines a table column within the `colgroup` element.

Attributes

Specific attributes:

```
align="left|center|right|justify|char" [CI]
```

Specifies the alignment of data in a cell. The values are as follows:

- **left** specifies that the data is left-justified. This is the default value for table data.
- **center** specifies that the data is centered in the cell. This is the default value for table headers.
- **right** specifies that the data is right-justified.
- **justify** specifies that the data is double-justified.
- **char** specifies that the text aligns around a specific character.

```
char="character" [CN]
```

You use this attribute to designate a specific character that will be used as a point to which to align data from each cell in the column.

```
charoff="length" [CN]
```

Sets the offset within the cell where the alignment character will be placed.

```
span="number" [CN]
```

Defines the number of columns the `col` element spans (and thereby shares its attributes with the columns).

```
valign="top|middle|bottom|baseline" [CI]
```

Specifies the vertical alignment of data within a cell. The values are as follows:

- **top** specifies that the cell data should align with the top of the cell.
- **middle** specifies that the cell data should be centered vertically within the cell. This is the default value.
- **bottom** specifies that the cell data is aligned with the bottom of the cell.
- **baseline** specifies that all cells in the same row should have their data positioned so that the first text line occurs on a common baseline.

```
width="multi-length" [CN]
```

Identifies a default width for all columns spanned by the `col` element.

Common attributes: id, class, lang, dir, title, style, and all intrinsic events

Context

Can contain the following:

`Empty`

Can be used in the following:

`colgroup, table`

Example

```
<table border="1" cellpadding="5" width="75%">
<colgroup>
   <col width="20" />
</colgroup>
<colgroup>
   <col width="50" />
   <col />
   <col />
</colgroup>
<caption>Table Caption</caption>
<thead>
  <tr>
   <th>cell</th>
   <th>cell</th>
   <th>cell</th>
   <th>cell</th>
  </tr>
</thead>
<tbody>
  <tr>
   <td>cell</td>
   <td>cell</td>
   <td>cell</td>
   <td>cell</td>
  </tr>
  <tr>
   <td>cell</td>
   <td>cell</td>
   <td>cell</td>
   <td>cell</td>
  </tr>
  <tr>
   <td>cell</td>
   <td>cell</td>
   <td>cell</td>
   <td>cell</td>
  </tr>
</tbody>
</table>
```

colgroup

This element contains the `col` elements and allows the author to specify default properties for the contained columns. This element should be listed before the standard table elements (`tr`, `thead`, `tbody`, and/or `tfoot`).

Attributes

Specific attributes:

```
align="left|center|right|justify|char" [CI]
```

Specifies the alignment of data in a cell. The values are as follows:

- **left** specifies that the data is left-justified. This is the default value for table data.
- **center** specifies that the data is centered within the cell. This is the default value for table headers.
- **right** specifies that the data is right-justified.
- **justify** specifies that the data is double-justified.
- **char** specifies that the text aligns around a specific character.

```
char="character" [CN]
```

You use this attribute to designate a specific character to be used as a point with which to align data from each cell in the column.

```
charoff="length" [CN]
```

Sets the offset within the cell that the alignment character will be placed.

```
span="number" [CN]
```

Specifies the number of columns contained by the column group. If the `span` element is not included, each `colgroup` element defines a column group containing one column.

```
valign="top|middle|bottom|baseline" [CI]
```

Specifies the vertical alignment of data within a cell. The values are as follows:

- **top** specifies that the cell data should align with the top of the cell.
- **middle** specifies that the cell data should be centered vertically within the cell. This is the default value.
- **bottom** specifies that the cell data is aligned with the bottom of the cell.
- **baseline** specifies that all cells in the same row should have their data positioned so that the first text line occurs on a common baseline.

```
width="multi-length" [CN]
```

Identifies the width of the column group.

Common attributes: `id`, `class`, `lang`, `dir`, `title`, `style`, and all intrinsic events.

Context

Can contain the following:

    col

Can be used in the following:

    table

Example

See col example.

dd

The dd element identifies a list of terms and definitions and is a child of the dl element.

Attributes

Specific attributes: None.
Common attributes: id, class, lang, dir, title, style, and all intrinsic events.

Context

Can contain the following:

    text, a, abbr, acronym, address, applet, b, basefont, bdo, big, blockquote, br,
    cite, code, dfn, dir, div, dl, em, fieldset, font, form, hr, i, iframe, img,
    isindex, kbd, map, menu, noframes, noscript, object, ol, p, pre, q, s, samp,
    script, small, span, strike, strong, sub, sup, table, tt, u, ul, var

Can be used in the following:

    dl

Example

```
<dl>
<dt>XHTML</dt>
<dd>A markup language used to create documents for the Internet.</dd>
<dt>XML<dt>
<dd>A metalanguage used to create markup languages, such as XHTML.</dd>
</dl>
```

del

This element allows authors to mark revised text. The `del` element marks text that has been deleted from a previous version of the document.

Attributes

Specific attributes:

```
cite="uri" [CT]
```

Identifies a source document or message.

```
datetime="datetime" [CS]
```

Specifies the date and time when the change was made. The values can be as follows:

```
YYYY-MM-DDThh:mm:ssTZD
```

- **YYYY.** Four-digit year
- **MM.** Two-digit month
- **DD.** Two-digit day of the month
- **hh.** Two-digit hour
- **mm.** Two-digit minutes
- **ss.** Two-digit seconds
- **TZD.** Time zone designator

Common attributes: id, class, lang, dir, title, style, and all intrinsic events.

Context

Can contain the following:

```
text, a, abbr, acronym, address, applet, b, basefont, bdo, big, blockquote, br,
cite, code, dfn, dir, div, dl, em, fieldset, font, form, hr, i, iframe, img,
isindex, kbd, map, menu, noframes, noscript, object, ol, p, pre, q, s, samp,
script, small, span, strike, strong, sub, sup, table, tt, u, ul, var
```

Can be used in the following:

```
body
```

Example

```
<body>
<del>
...Deleted text...
</del>
</body>
```

dfn

The dfn element identifies the first instance of a term used in a document. Most browsers render contained text in italics.

Attributes

Specific attributes: None.
Common attributes: id, class, lang, dir, title, style, and all intrinsic events.

Context

Can contain the following:

    a, abbr, acronym, b, bdo, big, br, button, cite, code, dfn, em, i, img, input,
    kbd, label, map, object, q, samp, script, select, small, span, strong, sub, sup,
    textarea, tt, var

Can be used in the following:

    a, abbr, acronym, applet, b, basefont, bdo, big, blockquote, body, button,
    caption, center, cite, code, dd, dfn, div, dt, em, fieldset, font, form, i,
    iframe, kbd, label, legend, li, noframes, noscript, object, p, pre, q, s, samp,
    small, span, strike, strong, sub, sup, td, th, tt, u, var

Example

```
<body>
<dfn>The World Wide Web Consortium</dfn> was created in 1994 to...
</body>
```

dir (Deprecated)

The dir element is deprecated in favor of using an unordered list (ul).

div

The div element is a generic style container used for block formatting. When used with the id or class attribute, the div element offers a powerful mechanism for adding style to structured blocks. The most common use for the div element is when using style sheets.

Attributes

Specific attributes: The align attribute is deprecated in favor of using style sheets.
Common attributes: id, class, lang, dir, title, style, and all intrinsic events.

Context

Can contain the following:

> *text*, a, abbr, acronym, address, applet, b, basefont, bdo, big, blockquote, br, cite, code, dfn, dir, div, dl, em, fieldset, font, form, hr, i, iframe, img, isindex, kbd, map, menu, noframes, noscript, object, ol, p, pre, q, s, samp, script, small, span, strike, strong, sub, sup, table, tt, u, ul, var

Can be used in the following:

> applet, basefont, blockquote, body, center dd, div, fieldset, form, iframe, li, noframes, noscript, object, pre, td, th

Example

```
<div class="content">This content will be styled by using a Cascading Style Sheet
style rule. Without the style rule, the presentation of this text will follow the
browser's default styles.</div>
```

dl

The dl element is a container for a list of terms and definitions. The dt and dd elements are children and contain the actual content for the definition text.

Attributes

Specific attributes: The compact attribute is deprecated in favor of style sheets.
Common attributes: id, class, lang, dir, title, style, and all intrinsic events.

Context

Can contain the following:

> dt, dd

Can be used in the following:

> applet, basefont, blockquote, body, center dd, div, fieldset, form, iframe, li, noframes, noscript, object, pre, td, th

Example

```
<dl>
<dt>term</dt>
<dd>term definition</dd>
<dt>term</dt>
<dd>term definition</dd>
</dl>
```

dt

This element contains the term in a definition list.

Context

Can contain the following:

```
a, abbr, acronym, b, bdo, big, br, button, cite, code, dfn, em, i, img, input,
kbd, label, map, object, q, samp, script, select, small, span, strong, sub, sup,
textarea, tt, var
```

Can be used in the following:

```
dl
```

Example

```
<dl>
<dt>term</dt>
<dd>term definition</dd>
<dt>term</dt>
<dd>term definition</dd>
</dl>
```

em

This element specifies emphasis on contained text.

Attributes

Specific attributes: None.
Common attributes: id, class, lang, dir, title, style, and all intrinsic events.

Context

Can contain the following:

```
a, abbr, acronym, b, bdo, big, br, button, cite, code, dfn, em, i, img, input,
kbd, label, map, object, q, samp, script, select, small, span, strong, sub, sup,
textarea, tt, var
```

Can be used in the following:

```
a, abbr, acronym, applet, b, basefont, bdo, big, blockquote, body, button,
caption, center, cite, code, dd, dfn, div, dt, em, fieldset, font, form, i,
iframe, kbd, label, legend, li, noframes, noscript, object, p, pre, q, s, samp,
small, span, strike, strong, sub, sup, td, th, tt, u, var
```

Example

```
<p>Sometimes you will want to <em>emphasize</em> text.</p>
```

fieldset

The `fieldset` element groups related `form` elements and controls.

Attributes

Specific attributes:

```
accesskey="text" [CN]
```

Identifies the character to be used as a keyboard shortcut. The value can be any alphanumeric character from a browser's character set.

The `align` attribute is deprecated in favor of using style sheets.

Common attributes: id, class, lang, dir, title, style, and all intrinsic events.

Context

Can contain the following:

```
text, a, abbr, acronym, address, applet, b, basefont, bdo, big, blockquote, br,
cite, code, dfn, dir, div, dl, em, fieldset, font, form, hr, i, iframe, img,
isindex, legend , kbd, map, menu, noframes, noscript, object, ol, p, pre, q, s,
samp, script, small, span, strike, strong, sub, sup, table, tt, u, ul, var
```

Can be used in the following:

```
applet, basefont, blockquote, body, center dd, div, fieldset, form, iframe, li,
noframes, noscript, object, pre, td, th
```

Example

```
<form method="post" action="http://www.mydomain.com/cgi-bin/application">
<fieldset>
<input type="text" name="Email" value="email" />
<button type="submit" name="Submit" value="submit">
<img src="file.gif" />
</button>
</fieldset>
</form>
```

font (Deprecated)

This element and its attributes are deprecated in favor of using style sheets; namely, the font properties in CSS.

form

This element is used to indicate an interactive form.

Attributes

Specific attributes:

```
accept="content-type-list" [CI]
```

Specifies the MIME types separated by commas that the form processing server and script should recognize.

```
accept-charset="charset list" [CI]
```

Specifies the character set, or character encodings, for input data that the server must accept.

```
action="uri" [CT]
```

Identifies the form processing application. When the user clicks the Submit or Reset button, the browser locates the application and sends the data to that application. This attribute is required.

```
enctype="content-type" [CI]
```

Specifies the content type used to submit the form to the server. The default value is `application/x-www-form-urlencoded`.

```
method="get|post" [CI]
```

Identifies how the browser should interact with the application identified by the `action` attribute. The default value is `get`. If `get` is selected, the browser sends a query URL that contains all the form name/value pair information to the application indicated in the `action` attribute. The information looks like this:

```
URL?name=value&name=value&name=value.
```

If `post` is selected, the contents of the form are encoded and sent as a data block that is easier to read.

```
name="cdata" [CI]
```

Provides the element with a name so it can be referred to by scripts and/or style sheets. Although this element is not deprecated, it's better practice to use the `id` attribute to identify elements.

```
target="window|_blank|_parent|_self|_top" [CI]
```

Used with a frameset where a frame is named as an attribute of the `frame` element. Defines how the resource should be loaded. This is what each value means:

- *window* loads the resource into the named targeted window.
- **_blank** loads the resource into a new window.
- **_parent** loads the resource into the parent of the current document.
- **_self** loads the resource into the same window.
- **_top** loads the resource into the body of the window.

Common attributes: `id`, `class`, `lang`, `dir`, `title`, `style`, and all intrinsic events.

Context

Can contain the following:

> *text,* a, abbr, acronym, address, applet, b, basefont, bdo, big, blockquote, br,
> cite, code, dfn, dir, div, dl, em, fieldset, font, hr, i, iframe, img, isindex,
> kbd, map, menu, noframes, noscript, object, ol, p, pre, q, s, samp, script, small,
> span, strike, strong, sub, sup, table, tt, u, ul, var

Can be used in the following:

> applet, basefont, blockquote, body, center dd, div, fieldset, form, iframe, li,
> noframes, noscript, object, pre, td, th

Example

```
<form method="get" action="http://www.mydomain.com/cgi-bin/application"
enctype="application/x-www-form-urlencoded">
...
</form>
```

frame (Empty)

The `frame` element is used within the `frameset` container. A `frame` element calls a document using the `src` attribute to be used to fill the content of that frame. Note that the `frame`, `frameset`, and `noframes` elements will not be supported in XHTML 1.1. Try using tables rather than frames for presentation. In the future, you'll most likely use CSS for positioning.

Attributes

Specific attributes:

> name="*text*" [CI]

Specifies a target name for the frame.

> longdesc="*uri*" [CT]

Identifies a resource that contains a long description of the frame.

> src="*uri*" [CT]

Calls and displays the source file for the frame.

> noresize="noresize" [CI]

Prevents the user from being able to resize the frame.

> scrolling="yes|no|auto" [CI]

Specifies the scrolling behavior for a frame.

> frameborder="1|0" [CN]

If 1 is selected, the browser renders a border around the frame. If 0 is selected, no border is displayed.

```
marginwidth="pixels" [CN]
```

Specifies the amount of space, in pixels, between the frame's content and the left and right margins.

```
marginheight="pixels" [CN]
```

Specifies the amount of space, in pixels, between the frame's content and the top and bottom margins.
Common attributes: id, class, title, and style.

Context

Can contain the following:

```
Empty
```

Can be used in the following:

```
frameset
```

Example

```
<html xmlns="http://www.w3.org/1999/xhtml">
<head>
<title>Document Title</title>
</head>
<frameset rows="20%,*">
<frame src="frame1.htm" name="navigation" />
<frame src="frame2.htm" name="body" />
</frameset>
</html>
```

frameset

Used in place of the body element, the frameset element is required when creating a framed document display. The frameset sets the structure for the frames and is the container for the frame, noframes, and other frameset elements. Note that the frame, frameset, and noframes elements will not be supported in XTHML 1.1.

Attributes

Specific attributes:

```
rows="multi-length-list" [CN]
```

Specifies the layout of horizontal frames. The value can be a comma-separated list of pixels, a percentage, or a relative length.

```
cols="multi-length-list" [CN]
```

Specifies the layout of vertical frames. The value can be a comma-separated list of pixels, a percentage, or a relative length.

Common attributes: `id`, `class`, `title`, `style`, `onload`, and `onunload`.

Context

Can contain the following:

```
frame, frameset, noframes
```

Can be used in the following:

```
html
```

Example

```
<html xmlns="http://www.w3.org/1999/xhtml">
<head>
<title>Document Title</title>
</head>
<frameset cols="20%,*">
<frame src="frame1.htm" name="navigation" />
<frameset rows="50%, *">
<frame src="frameA.htm" name="bodyA" />
<frame src="frameB.htm" name="bodyB" />
</frameset>
</frameset>
</html>
```

h1-h6

Identifies heading levels. There are six heading levels: `h1`, `h2`, `h3`, `h4`, `h5`, and `h6`. Most browsers render `h1` with the largest and boldest font and `h6` with the smallest font. The heading elements should be used to add structure and not solely as formatting tools.

Attributes

Specific attributes: The `align` attribute is deprecated in favor of using style sheets.
Common attributes: `id`, `class`, `lang`, `dir`, `title`, `style`, and all intrinsic events.

Context

Can contain the following:

```
a, abbr, acronym, b, bdo, big, br, button, cite, code, dfn, em, i, img, input,
kbd, label, map, object, q, samp, script, select, small, span, strong, sub, sup,
textarea, tt, var
```

Can be used in the following:

```
applet, basefont, blockquote, body, center dd, div, fieldset, form, iframe, li,
noframes, noscript, object, pre, td, th
```

Example

```
<body>
<h1>
<h1>The heading with the most importance</h1>
<h2>A second level heading</h2>
<p>Text content for the rest of the page</p>
</body>
```

head

This top-level element (found in every XHTML document) contains information about the document, including the title, meta-information, links to other documents, and index information.

Attributes

Specific attributes:

```
profile="uri" [CT]
```

Specifies location of a meta-data profile for the current document.
Common attributes: lang and dir.

Context

Can contain the following:

```
base, isindex, link, meta, script, style, title
```

Can be used in the following:

```
html
```

Example

```
<html xmlns="http://www.w3.org/1999/xhtml">
<head>
<title>Document Title</title>
<link rel="stylesheet" type="text/css" href="stylefile.css" />
</head>
<body>
...
</body>
</html>
```

hr (Empty)

This element creates a visual horizontal rule between sections of text.

Attributes

Specific attributes: The `align`, `noshade`, `size`, and `width` attributes are deprecated in favor of using style sheets.
Common attributes: `id`, `class`, `lang`, `dir`, `title`, `style`, and all intrinsic events.

Context

Can contain the following:

```
Empty
```

Can be used in the following:

```
applet, basefont, blockquote, body, center dd, div, fieldset, form, iframe, li,
noframes, noscript, object, pre, td, th
```

Example

```
<body>
<p>This section of text <hr />
is set off from this section of text.</p>
</body>
```

html

The `html` element is the document element (also called the root element). Remember, all XML-compliant documents (this means XHTML documents too) must have a root element. For XHTML, that root element must be `html` and it must also be the first element to occur after the `DOCTYPE` declaration.

Attributes

Specific attributes:

```
xmlns="http://www.w3.org/1999/xhtml"
```

Although `xmlns` is not technically an attribute but is a namespace, we include the `XHTML` namespace because it's a required piece of information in the `html` element. The namespace uniquely identifies the elements as belonging to the XHTML vocabulary. You will not find a document at `www.w3.org/1999/xhtml`, because it's used as a symbolic last name. For more information on namespaces, see Chapter 12, "The Benefits of Extensibility."

The `version` attribute contains redundant information also found in the `DOCTYPE` declaration and is therefore deprecated.
Common attributes: `lang` and `dir`.

Context

Can contain the following:

    body, frameset, head

Can be used in the following:

    N/A

Example

```
<?xml version="1.0" encoding="UTF-8"?>
<!DOCTYPE html
    PUBLIC "-//W3C//DTD XHTML 1.0 Strict//EN"
    "DTD/xhtml1-strict.dtd">
<html xmlns="http://www.w3.org/1999/xhtml" xml:lang="en" lang="en">
  <head>
    <title>Document Title</title>
  </head>
  <body>
    <p>Text of document.</p>
  </body>
</html>
```

i

The i element is an inline style element that renders italicized text.

Attributes

Specific attributes: None.
Common attributes: id, class, lang, dir, title, style, and all intrinsic events.

Context

Can contain the following:

    a, abbr, acronym, b, bdo, big, br, button, cite, code, dfn, em, i, img, input,
    kbd, label, map, object, q, samp, script, select, small, span, strong, sub, sup,
    textarea, tt, var

Can be used in the following:

    a, abbr, acronym, applet, b, basefont, bdo, big, blockquote, body, button,
    caption, center, cite, code, dd, dfn, div, dt, em, fieldset, font, form, i,
    iframe, kbd, label, legend, li, noframes, noscript, object, p, pre, q, s, samp,
    small, span, strike, strong, sub, sup, td, th, tt, u, var

Example

```
<p>Sometimes you want text to render in <i>italics</i>.</p>
```

iframe

This element specifies an inline subwindow.

Attributes
Specific attributes:

```
name="text" [CI]
```

Specifies a target name for the frame.

```
longdesc="uri" [CT]
```

Identifies a resource that contains a long description of the frame.

```
src="uri" [CT]
```

Calls and displays the source file for the frame.

```
noresize="noresize" [CI]
```

Prevents the user from being able to resize the frame.

```
scrolling="yes|no|auto" [CI]
```

Specifies the scrolling behavior for a frame.

```
frameborder="1|0" [CN]
```

If 1 is selected, the browser renders a border around the frame. If 0 is selected, no border is displayed.

```
marginwidth="pixels" [CN]
```

Specifies the amount of space, in pixels, between the frame's content and the left and right margins.

```
marginheight="pixels" [CN]
```

Specifies the amount of space, in pixels, between the frame's content and the top and bottom margins.

```
width="length" [CN]
```

Defines the width of the inline frame.

```
height="length" [CN]
```

Defines the height of the inline frame.
    The `align` attribute is deprecated in favor of using style sheets.
Common attributes: `id`, `class`, `title`, and `style`.

Context

Can contain the following:

```
text, a, abbr, acronym, address, applet, b, basefont, bdo, big, blockquote, br,
cite, code, dfn, dir, div, dl, em, fieldset, font, form, hr, i, iframe, img,
isindex, kbd, map, menu, noframes, noscript, object, ol, p, pre, q, s, samp,
script, small, span, strike, strong, sub, sup, table, tt, u, ul, var
```

Can be used in the following:

a, abbr, acronym, applet, b, basefont, bdo, big, blockquote, body, button, caption, center, cite, code, dd, dfn, div, dt, em, fieldset, font, form, i, iframe, kbd, label, legend, li, noframes, noscript, object, p, pre, q, s, samp, small, span, strike, strong, sub, sup, td, th, tt, u, var

Example

```
<html xmlns="http://www.w3.org/1999/xhtml">
<head>
<title>Document Title</title>
</head>
<body>
    <h1>An Inline Frame</h1>
    <hr />
    <iframe src="frame1.htm" name="inline"
            width="100" height="100">
    You can add text here.
    </iframe>
    <hr />
</body>
</html>
```

img (Empty)

When rendered, the img element inserts, or embeds, an object into the XHTML document.

Attributes

Specific attributes:

alt="*text*" [CS]

Specifies alternative text to be displayed for nonvisual browsers. This is an important attribute for accessibility reasons. The language of the alternative text can be set using the lang attribute.

src="*uri*" [CT]

Specifies the location of the image. Most browsers only support these graphics formats: Graphics Interchange Format (GIF), Joint Photographic Experts Group (JPEG), and Portable Network Graphics (PNG).

longdesc="*uri*" [CT]

Specifies a link to a long description of the image. This attribute should be used as a supplement to the alt attribute.

name="*cdata*" [CI]

Provides the element with a name so it can be referred to by scripts and/or style sheets. Although this element is not deprecated, it's better practice to use the `id` attribute to identify elements.

```
width="length" [CN]
```

Specifies the width of the object. This value will override the image's or object's original width.

```
height="length" [CN]
```

Specifies the width of the object. This value will override the image's or object's original width.

The `align`, `border`, `hspace`, and `vspace` attributes have been deprecated in favor of using style sheets.

Common attributes: `id`, `class`, `lang`, `dir`, `title`, `style`, and all intrinsic events.

Context

Can contain the following:

```
Empty
```

Can be used in the following:

```
a, abbr, acronym, applet, b, basefont, bdo, big, blockquote, body, button,
caption, center, cite, code, dd, dfn, div, dt, em, fieldset, font, form, i,
iframe, kbd, label, legend, li, noframes, noscript, object, p, pre, q, s, samp,
small, span, strike, strong, sub, sup, td, th, tt, u, var
```

Example

```
<body>
<p><img src="file.gif" />The image will be inserted before the text</p>
</body>
```

input (Empty)

The `input` element defines form objects. There are several types of input controls: text field, password field, checkbox, radio button, submit button, reset button, file, hidden control, and a graphical submit button. All of these form controls are defined using the same `input` element, but with different `type` attribute values.

Attributes

Specific attributes:

```
type="text|password|checkbox|radio|submit|reset|file|hidden|
image|button" [CI]
```

Specifies the type of control. Each control type can accept different accompanying attributes. The following are the possible values:

- **text** generates field with a single line text entry.
- **password** generates a field with a single line text entry that obscures the data as it is entered.
- **checkbox** generates a field with a checkbox used for a Boolean choice, or for attributes that can accept multiple values. When the user checks the checkbox, the data is sent as name="on"; otherwise, it will be ignored.
- **radio** generates a field with a radio button. Radio buttons occur in groups and radio buttons in the same group should have the same name attribute, but different value attributes.
- **submit** generates a button that, when triggered, sends the form data to the server. It's legal to have multiple submit buttons; however, you should be sure that each one has a different name.
- **reset** generates a button that restores the form to its original state.
- **file** enables the user to upload a file to the server. You might want to provide users with a list of acceptable file types. You can do this with the accept attribute.
- **hidden** enables the author to create a form field that users do not interact with and does not appear in the document.
- **image** creates an image that functions much like a submit button; however, with the image input type, the coordinates of the image are sent to the server as well.
- **button** generates a button that can use scripting to make the button perform some action.

accesskey="*text*" [CN]

Identifies the character to be used as a keyboard shortcut. The value can be any alphanumeric character from a browser's character set.

accept="*content-type-list*" [CI]

Specifies the MIME types separated by commas that the form processing server and script recognize.

name="*cdata*" [CI]

Specifies the control name.

value="*cdata*" [CI]

Specifies the initial value of a control. It's a required attribute when the type attribute has the value of radio or checkbox.

size="*cdata*" [CI]

Specifies the width of the input window. The width is represented in pixels, except when the type attribute has the value of text or password, and then the width is represented by the number of characters.

maxlength="*number*" [CN]

Used when the `type` attribute is set to `text` or `password` to limit the user to a specified number of characters. For example, if the value is set to **8**, the user is allowed to enter only eight characters in the text field.

> `checked="checked"` [CI]

Used when the `type` attribute is set to `radio` or `checkbox` to turn on the button. Browsers ignore this attribute when `type` is set to any other control type.

> `src="uri"` [CT]

Used when the `type` attribute is set to `image` to specify the location of the image to be used.

> `alt="text"` [CS]

Specifies alternative text that is displayed as a substitute for nonvisual browsers. This is an important attribute for accessibility reasons. The language of the alternative text is set using the `lang` attribute.

> `readonly="readonly"` [CI]

Prohibits the user from modifying the control; therefore, any information contained in the form will automatically be sent with the form.

> `disabled="disabled"` [CI]

When used, this attribute disables the control for user input.

> `tabindex="number"` [CN]

Tabbing allows the author to give focus or access to an element by using a standard keyboard sequence. The sequence order is normally defined by the order of the elements. The `tabindex` attribute enables the author to establish a different order by identifying the position of the current element in the tabbing order. The value must be a number between 0 and 32767. The tabbing order specifies the order of attention for elements when navigated by the user.

> `usemap="uri"` [CT]

Associates an image map with the element. The value must match the value assigned to the `name` attribute in the corresponding `map` element.

The `align` attribute is deprecated in favor of using style sheets.

Common attributes: `id`, `class`, `lang`, `dir`, `title`, `style`, and all intrinsic events.

Context

Can contain the following:

> `Empty`

Can be used in the following:

> `a, abbr, acronym, applet, b, basefont, bdo, big, blockquote, body, button,`
> `caption, center, cite, code, dd, dfn, div, dt, em, fieldset, font, form, i,`
> `iframe, kbd, label, legend, li, noframes, noscript, object, p, pre, q, s, samp,`
> `small, span, strike, strong, sub, sup, td, th, tt, u, var`

Example

```
<form action="..." method="post">
Name: <input type="text" name="name" value="name" /><br />
Password: <input type="password" name="pswd" maxlength="8" /><br />
Now tell us your favorite band:<br />
<input type="radio" name="band" value="0" checked="checked" />Pajamacus<br />
<input type="radio" name="band" value="1" checked="checked" />Ratt<br />
<input type="radio" name="band" value="2" checked="checked" />Adult Rodeo<br />
<p>
<input type="sumbit" value="ok" />
</p>
</form>
```

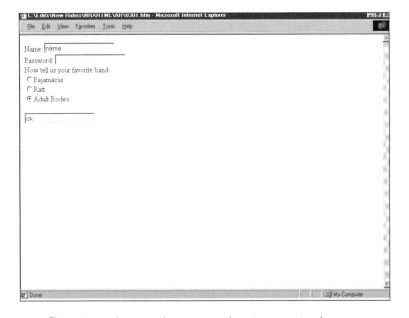

Figure 3.1   The form element example as it appears in a browser.

ins

The ins element is used in conjunction with the del element. It specifies when an author has inserted text into a document.

Attributes
Specific attributes:

```
cite="uri" [CT]
```

Identifies a source document or message.

```
datetime="datetime" [CS]
```

Specifies the date and time when the change was made. The values can be as follows:

```
YYYY-MM-DDThh:mm:ssTZD
```

- **YYYY.** Four-digit year
- **MM.** Two-digit month
- **DD.** Two-digit day of the month
- **hh.** Two-digit hour
- **mm.** Two-digit minutes
- **ss.** Two-digit seconds
- **TZD.** Time zone designator

Common attributes: id, class, lang, dir, title, style, and all intrinsic events.

Context

Can contain the following:

```
text, a, abbr, acronym, address, applet, b, basefont, bdo, big, blockquote, br,
cite, code, dfn, dir, div, dl, em, fieldset, font, form, hr, i, iframe, img,
isindex, kbd, map, menu, noframes, noscript, object, ol, p, pre, q, s, samp,
script, small, span, strike, strong, sub, sup, table, tt, u, ul, var
```

Can be used in the following:

```
body
```

Example

```
<body>
<ins>Inserted text goes here</ins>
</body>
```

isindex (Empty) (Deprecated)

This element is deprecated in favor of using the input element to create text controls.

kbd

kbd is an inline style element that renders monospaced text (for example, typewriter text).

Attributes

Specific attributes: None.
Common attributes: id, class, lang, dir, title, style, and all intrinsic events.

Context

Can contain the following:

```
a, abbr, acronym, b, bdo, big, br, button, cite, code, dfn, em, i, img, input,
kbd, label, map, object, q, samp, script, select, small, span, strong, sub, sup,
textarea, tt, var
```

Can be used in the following:

```
a, abbr, acronym, applet, b, basefont, bdo, big, blockquote, body, button,
caption, center, cite, code, dd, dfn, div, dt, em, fieldset, font, form, i,
iframe, kbd, label, legend, li, noframes, noscript, object, p, pre, q, s, samp,
small, span, strike, strong, sub, sup, td, th, tt, u, var
```

Example

```
<p>Sometimes you want text to render as <kbd>monospaced</kbd>.</p>
```

label

Specifies a label, such as a description, for a form control or element. This element is recommended for accessibility reasons.

Attributes

Specific attributes:

```
for="idref" [CS]
```

Specifies which form control the label is attached to. If this attribute is not used, the label is associated with the contained text.

```
accesskey="text" [CN]
```

Identifies the character to be used as a keyboard shortcut. The value can be any alphanumeric character from a browser's character set.

Common attributes: id, class, lang, dir, title, style, and all intrinsic events.

Context

Can contain the following:

```
text, a, abbr, acronym, applet, b, bdo, big, br, cite, code, dfn, em, font, i,
img, iframe, kbd, map, object, q, s, samp, script, small, span, strike, strong,
sub, sup, tt, u, var
```

Can be used in the following:

```
a, abbr, acronym, applet, b, basefont, bdo, big, blockquote, body, button,
caption, center, cite, code, dd, dfn, div, dt, em, fieldset, font, form, i,
iframe, kbd, label, legend, li, noframes, noscript, object, p, pre, q, s, samp,
small, span, strike, strong, sub, sup, td, th, tt, u, var
```

Example

```
<form action="..." method="post">
<label for="name">Name</label>
<input type="text" name="fullname" id="name" />
<label for="email">Email Address</label>
<input type="text" name="emailaddress" id="email" />
</form>
```

legend

Assigns a caption to the `fieldset`, increasing accessibility.

Attributes

Specific attributes:

```
accesskey="text" [CN]
```

Identifies the character to be used as a keyboard shortcut. The value can be any alphanumeric character from a browser's character set.

The `align` attribute is deprecated in favor of using style sheets.

Common attributes: `id`, `class`, `lang`, `dir`, `title`, `style`, and all intrinsic events.

Context

Can contain the following:

```
text, a, abbr, acronym, applet, b, bdo, big, br, cite, code, dfn, em, font, i,
img, iframe, kbd, map, object, q, s, samp, script, small, span, strike, strong,
sub, sup, tt, u, var
```

Can be used in the following:

```
fieldset
```

Example

```
<form action="..." method="post">
<fieldset>
<legend>Customer Information</legend>
Customer name:<input type="text" name="fullname" value="name" />
<button type="submit" name="sub1" value="sub1">
<img src="file.gif" />
</button>
</fieldset>
</form>
```

li

As the child of the ul and ol elements, li identifies list items.

Attributes

Specific attributes: The type, start, value, and compact attributes are deprecated.
Common attributes: id, class, lang, dir, title, style, and all intrinsic events.

Context

Can contain the following:

```
text, a, abbr, acronym, address, applet, b, basefont, bdo, big, blockquote, br,
cite, code, dfn, dir, div, dl, em, fieldset, font, form, hr, i, iframe, img,
isindex, kbd, map, menu, noframes, noscript, object, ol, p, pre, q, s, samp,
script, small, span, strike, strong, sub, sup, table, tt, u, ul, var
```

Can be used in the following:

```
dir, menu, ol, ul
```

Example

```
<body>
<ul>
<li>List item</li>
<li>List item</li>
<li>List item</li>
</ul>
</body>
```

link (Empty)

This element defines a link. The link element functions much like the a element, and even uses some of the same attributes. This element is the child of the head element.

Attributes
Specific attributes:

```
charset="character-encoding" [CI]
```

Identifies the character encoding of the linked Web resource. The default is
ISO-8859-1.

```
href="uri" [CT]
```

Identifies the URI that is loaded when the hyperlink is triggered. You can also reference an email address using the following as the value: mailto:name@domain.com.

```
hreflang="language-code" [CI]
```

Identifies the base language of the resource identified by the `href` attribute.

```
rel="text" [CI]
```

Defines the relationship between the current document and the resource specified by the `href` attribute. This attribute is not widely used.

```
rev="text" [CI]
```

Defines a reverse link from the resource specified by the `href` attribute to the current document. This attribute is not widely used.

```
shape="rect|circle|poly|default" [CI]
```

Specifies the shape of a region.

```
target="window|_blank|_parent|_self|_top" [CI]
```

Used within a frameset where a frame is named as an attribute of the `frame` element. Defines how the resource should be loaded. Here's what each of the values means:

- **window** loads the resource into the named targeted window.

- **_blank** loads the resource into a new window.

- **_parent** loads the resource into the parent of the current document.

- **_self** loads the resource into the same window.

- **_top** loads the resource into the body of the window.

```
type="content-type" [CI]
```

Provides the MIME type of the URL, or resource.

```
media="screen|print|projection|braille|speech|all" [CI]
```

Uses a keyword to specify the desired rendering destination for the referenced style sheet. The `screen` value is the default.

Common attributes: id, class, lang, dir, title, style, and all intrinsic events.

Context

Can contain the following:

```
Empty
```

Can be used in the following:

```
head
```

Example

```
<head>
<title>Document Title</title>
<link rel="stylesheet" type="text/css" href="stylefile.css" />
</head>
```

map

The `map` element is used in conjunction with the `area` element to define hot spots, which are hyperlink destinations attached to geometric regions on an image, for a client-side image map. A client-side image map stores the hot spot definitions within the XHTML document itself or in a map file on the server.

Attributes

Specific attributes:

```
name="cdata" [CI]
```

Assigns a name to the map.
Common attributes: `id`, `class`, `lang`, `dir`, `title`, `style`, and all intrinsic events.

Context

Can contain the following:

```
text, a, abbr, acronym, address, applet, area, b, basefont, bdo, big, blockquote,
br, cite, code, dfn, dir, div, dl, em, fieldset, font, form, hr, i, iframe, img,
isindex, kbd, map, menu, noframes, noscript, object, ol, p, pre, q, s, samp,
script, small, span, strike, strong, sub, sup, table, tt, u, ul, var
```

Can be used in the following:

```
a, abbr, acronym, applet, b, basefont, bdo, big, blockquote, body, button,
caption, center, cite, code, dd, dfn, div, dt, em, fieldset, font, form, i,
iframe, kbd, label, legend, li, noframes, noscript, object, p, pre, q, s, samp,
small, span, strike, strong, sub, sup, td, th, tt, u, var
```

Example

```
<body>
<map name="map1">
<area coords="0,0,100,100" href="file.html" />
<area coords="0,142,28,285" href="file2.html />
</map>
</body>
```

menu (Deprecated)

The `menu` element is deprecated in favor of using an unordered list (`ul`).

meta (Empty)

A child of the `head` element, the `meta` element is used to embed document meta-information (information about the contents of the document). This information is commonly used by servers and clients to aid in identifying, searching, indexing, and cataloging document meta-information.

Attributes

Specific attributes:

```
content="cdata" [CS]
```

Specifies a value for a named property.

```
http-equiv="name" [CI]
```

Binds the meta element to a Hypertext Transfer Protocol (HTTP) response header field. When a Web page is requested from a server, the content portion of the element will be attached to the document header that is passed to the browser first, before the rest of the document content. May be used in place of the name attribute.

```
name="name" [CS]
```

Defines a property name such as author, publication date, and so on.

```
scheme="cdata" [CS]
```

Specifies a scheme to be used to interpret the content attribute value.

Common attributes: lang and dir.

Context

Can contain the following:

```
Empty
```

Can be used in the following:

```
head
```

Example

```
<head>
<meta name="creation_date" content="Mon, 17 Jul, 2000 17:44:00 GMT" />
<meta http-equiv="expires" content="Wed, 06 September 2000 21:22:00 GMT" />
<meta http-equiv="keywords" content="SGML, HTML, markup" />
<meta http-equiv="reply-to" content="name@mydomain.com" />
<meta name="author" content="First Lastname" />
<meta http-equiv="distribution" content="global" />
<meta http-equiv="copyright" content="LANWrights, Inc. — 2000" />
<title>LANWrights, Inc.</title>
</head>
```

noframes

The noframes element is used to include alternate content for browsers that cannot render frames. Note that the frame, frameset, and noframes elements will not be supported in XTHML 1.1.

Attributes

Specific attributes: None

Common attributes: id, class, lang, dir, title, style, and all intrinsic events.

Context

Can contain the following:

> *text,* a, abbr, acronym, address, applet, b, basefont, bdo, big, blockquote, body, br, cite, code, dfn, dir, div, dl, em, fieldset, font, form, hr, i, iframe, img, isindex, kbd, map, menu, noframes, noscript, object, ol, p, pre, q, s, samp, script, small, span, strike, strong, sub, sup, table, tt, u, ul, var

Can be used in the following:

> applet, basefont, blockquote, body, center dd, div, fieldset, form, frameset, iframe, li, noframes, noscript, object, pre, td, th

Example

```
<html>
<head>
   <title>Document Title</title>
</head>
<frameset cols="20%,*">
   <frame src="frame1.html" name="frame1" />
<frameset rows="50%,*">
   <frame src="frame3.html" name="frame2" />
   <frame src="frame4.html" name="frame3" />
</frameset>
<noframes>
   <body>
           This text will appear if the browser does not support frames.
   </body>
</noframes>
</frameset>
</html>
```

noscript

This element is an alternate content container for browsers that do not support the scripting language used.

Attributes

Common attributes: id, class, lang, dir, title, style, and all intrinsic events.

Context

Can contain the following:

> *text,* a, abbr, acronym, address, applet, b, basefont, bdo, big, blockquote, br, cite, code, dfn, dir, div, dl, em, fieldset, font, form, hr, i, iframe, img, isindex, kbd, map, menu, noframes, noscript, object, ol, p, pre, q, s, samp, script, small, span, strike, strong, sub, sup, table, tt, u, ul, var

Can be used in the following:

> applet, basefont, blockquote, body, center dd, div, fieldset, form, iframe, li, noframes, noscript, object, pre, td, th

Example

```
<script type="text/javascript">
...
</script>
<noscript>
Your browser does not support our scripting. Please see our
<a href="www.mydomain.com/text.html">text only page</a>.
</noscript>
```

object

The object element inserts an object, such as an applet, document, or image.

Attributes

Specific attributes:

```
archive="uri-list" [CT]
```

Specifies a space-separated list of locations (URLs) for archives that contain resources relevant to the object.

```
classid="uri" [CT]
```

Identifies the resource to be used for object rendering.

```
codebase="uri" [CT]
```

Identifies the code base or the location of the programming code for the object.

```
codetype="codetype" [CI]
```

Specifies the Internet Media Type (MIMETYPE) for code. For details, see ftp://ftp.isi.edu/in-notes/iana/assignments/media-types/.

```
data="uri" [CT]
```

Specifies a location for the object data.

```
declare="declare" [CI]
```

Defines the object without activating it. Indicates an object that is not instantiated until it's needed by something that references it. Each occasion typically results in a separate copy of the object.

`height="`*`number`*`" [CN]`

Specifies a height for the object.

`name="`*`cdata`*`" [CI]`

Defines the name of the object when submitted as part of a form.

`standby="`*`message`*`" [CS]`

Identifies a message to show while the object is loading.

`tabindex="`*`number`*`" [CN]`

Tabbing allows the author to give focus or access to an element by using a standard keyboard sequence. The sequence order is normally defined by the order of the elements. The `tabindex` attribute allows the author to establish a different order by identifying the position of the current element in the tabbing order. The value must be a number between 0 and 32767. The tabbing order specifies the order of attention for elements when navigated by the user.

`type="`*`type`*`" [CI]`

Specifies the Internet Media Type (MIMETYPE) for data.

`usemap="`*`URL`*`" [CT]`

Associates an `imagemap` to use with the object.

`width="`*`number`*`" [CN]`

Specifies the width of the object.

The `align`, `border`, `hspace`, and `vspace` attributes are deprecated in favor of using style sheets.

Common attributes: `id`, `class`, `lang`, `dir`, `title`, `style`, and all intrinsic events.

Context

Can contain the following:

> *text,* `a, abbr, acronym, address, applet, b, basefont, bdo, big, blockquote, br, cite, code, dfn, dir, div, dl, em, fieldset, font, form, hr, i, iframe, img, isindex, kbd, map, menu, noframes, noscript, object, ol, p, param, pre, q, s, samp, script, small, span, strike, strong, sub, sup, table, tt, u, ul, var`

Can be used in the following:

> `a, abbr, acronym, applet, b, basefont, bdo, big, blockquote, body, button, caption, center, cite, code, dd, dfn, div, dt, em, fieldset, font, form, head, i, iframe, kbd, label, legend, li, noframes, noscript, object, p, pre, q, s, samp, small, span, strike, strong, sub, sup, td, th, tt, u, var`

Example

```
<body>
<object src="file.mov" width="100" height="150">A movie.
</object>
</body>
```

ol

The ol element presents a numbered list of items. This element automatically attaches numbers in order of occurrence.

Attributes

Specific attributes: The type, start, value, and compact attributes are deprecated.
Common attributes: id, class, lang, dir, title, style, and all intrinsic events.

Context

Can contain the following:

```
li
```

Can be used in the following:

```
applet, basefont, blockquote, body, center dd, div, fieldset, form, iframe, li,
noframes, noscript, object, pre, td, th
```

Example

```
<ol>
   <li>List item 1</li>
   <li>List item 2</li>
   <li>List item 3</li>
</ol>
```

optgroup

This element represents an option group.

Attributes
Specific attributes:

```
disabled="disabled" [CI]
```

When used, disables the control for user input.

```
label="text" [CS]
```

Specifies a label for the option group.
Common attributes: id, class, lang, dir, title, style, and all intrinsic events.

Context

Can contain the following:

    optgroup, option

Can be used in the following:

    select, optgroup

Example

```
<p>
Favorite People:
<select name="Favoritepeople">
<option label="Sam" value="sam">Sam Williams</option>
<option label="Mary" value="mary">Mary Burmeister</option>
<optgroup label="Family">
    <option value="mom">Suzy Valentine McElroy</option>
    <option value="dad">Tom Valentine</option>
    <option value="brother">Austin Valentine</option>
</optgroup>
</select>
</p>
```

option

Defined within the `select` element, the `option` element indicates a choice within a selection list.

Attributes

Specific attributes:

    label="*text*" [CS]

Allows a shorter label for the option to be used.

    selected="selected" [CI]

Specifies that this option is initially selected.

    value="*cdata*" [CS]

Specifies the value for a specific `select` option.

    disabled="disabled" [CI]

When used, disables the control for user input.
Common attributes: `id`, `class`, `lang`, `dir`, `title`, `style`, and all intrinsic events.

Context

Can contain the following:

    text

Can be used in the following:

```
optgroup, select
```

Example

```
Favorite People:
<select name="Favoritepeople">
<option label="Sam" value="sam">Sam Williams</option>
<option label="Mary" value="mary">Mary Burmeister</option>
<optgroup label="Family">
   <option value="mom">Suzy Valentine McElroy</option>
   <option value="dad">Tom Valentine</option>
   <option value="brother">Austin Valentine</option>
</optgroup>
</select>
```

p

The p element identifies a block of text as a paragraph. Most browsers insert a line break and carriage return around this element.

Attributes

Specific attributes: The align attribute is deprecated in favor of using style sheets.
Common attributes: id, class, lang, dir, title, style, and all intrinsic events.

Context

Can contain the following:

```
text, a, abbr, acronym, applet, b, bdo, big, br, cite, code, dfn, em, font, i,
img, iframe, kbd, map, object, q, s, samp, script, small, span, strike, strong,
sub, sup, tt, u, var
```

Can be used in the following:

```
applet, basefont, blockquote, body, center dd, div, fieldset, form, iframe, li,
noframes, noscript, object, pre, td, th
```

Example

```
<body>
<h1>This is a heading</h1>
<p>This is a paragraph</p>
<p>This is another paragraph</p>
<p class="special">This paragraph has a class that allows the author to attach CSS
style rules for the section.</p>
</body>
```

param **(Empty)**

This element passes values to an embedded object or Java applet.

Attributes
Specific attributes:

```
name="cdata"
```

Specifies a name of a runtime parameter. Case sensitivity is determined by the object.

```
type="content-type" [CI]
```

Specifies the Internet Media Type (MIMETYPE).

```
value="cdata" [CI]
```

Specifies the value of a runtime parameter identified by the `name` attribute.

```
valuetype="data|ref|object" [CI]
```

Provides information about the type of value that is found in the `value` attribute. The values are as follows:

- **data**. The value identifies data and the value will be passed directly the object as a string.
- **ref**. The value identifies a URL where runtime values are stored.
- **object**. The value identifies the URL of an object.

Common attributes: None.

Context

Can contain the following:

```
Empty
```

Can be used in the following:

```
applet, object
```

Example

```
<applet codebase="http://www.url.com" code="News" width="110" height="165">
<param name="delay" value="28" />
<param name="pause1" value="18" />
<param name="pause2" value="44" />
<param name="scroll" value="5" />
<param name="area" value="0 23 110 119" />
</applet>
```

pre

The pre element displays its contents as is and reserves all formatting, meaning white-space. This element is most commonly used to create quick and easy tables of data.

Attributes

Specific attributes: The width attribute is deprecated in favor of using style sheets.
Common attributes: id, class, lang, dir, title, style, and all intrinsic events.

Context

Can contain the following:

> text, a, abbr, acronym, b, bdo, br, cite, code, dfn, em, i, kbd, map, q, s, samp, script, span, strike, strong, tt, u, var

Can be used in the following:

> applet, basefont, blockquote, body, center dd, div, fieldset, form, iframe, li, noframes, noscript, object, pre, td, th

Example

```
<pre>
This is a table

Name    Age
Sam     12
Mary    10
Ed      16
</pre>
```

q

The q element highlights short quotations.

Attributes

Specific attributes:

> cite="*uri*" [CT]

Defines a source document or message that provides information about the quotation source.
Common attributes: id, class, lang, dir, title, style, and all intrinsic events.

Context

Can contain the following:

> text, a, abbr, acronym, applet, b, bdo, big, br, cite, code, dfn, em, font, i, img, iframe, kbd, map, object, q, s, samp, script, small, span, strike, strong, sub, sup, tt, u, var

Can be used in the following:

```
a, abbr, acronym, applet, b, basefont, bdo, big, blockquote, body, button,
caption, center, cite, code, dd, dfn, div, dt, em, fieldset, font, form, i,
iframe, kbd, label, legend, li, noframes, noscript, object, p, pre, q, s, samp,
small, span, strike, strong, sub, sup, td, th, tt, u, var
```

Example

```
<body>
<p>
Sam Williams said,
<q cite="http://www.sam.com/sourcefile.htm">&quot;Let there be macaroni and cheese
please.&quot;</q>
</p>
</body>
```

s (Deprecated)

This element produces strikethrough text. It's deprecated in favor of using style sheets.

samp

The samp element indicates a sequence of literal characters or output from a program
or script.

Attributes

Specific attributes: None.
Common attributes: id, class, lang, dir, title, style, and all intrinsic events.

Context

Can contain the following:

```
a, abbr, acronym, b, bdo, big, br, button, cite, code, dfn, em, i, img, input,
kbd, label, map, object, q, samp, script, select, small, span, strong, sub, sup,
textarea, tt, var
```

Can be used in the following:

```
a, abbr, acronym, applet, b, basefont, bdo, big, blockquote, body, button,
caption, center, cite, code, dd, dfn, div, dt, em, fieldset, font, form, i,
iframe, kbd, label, legend, li, noframes, noscript, object, p, pre, q, s, samp,
small, span, strike, strong, sub, sup, td, th, tt, u, var
```

Example

```
<samp>script output</samp>
```

script

Instructs browsers that the enclosed content is part of a scripting language. For more information on scripting, see Chapter 9, "Calling Scripts and Other Objects."

Attributes
Specific attributes:

```
charset="character-encoding" [CI]
```

Identifies the character encoding of the linked Web resource. The default is ISO-8859-1.

```
defer="defer" [CI]
```

Specifies that the script is not going to generate document content, and therefore, allows the browser to continue parsing and rendering.

```
src="uri" [CT]
```

Identifies an external script source.

```
type="content-type" [CI]
```

Specifies the MIME type of the script.

The language attribute is deprecated.

Common attributes: None.

Context

Can contain the following:

```
text, comments
```

Can be used in the following:

```
a, abbr, acronym, applet, b, basefont, bdo, big, blockquote, body, button,
caption, center, cite, code, dd, dfn, div, dt, em, fieldset, font, form, head, i,
iframe, kbd, label, legend, li, noframes, noscript, object, p, pre, q, s, samp,
small, span, strike, strong, sub, sup, td, th, tt, u, var
```

Example

```
<html xmlns="http://www.w3.org/1999/xhtml">
<head>
   <script language="JavaScript">
      <!-- hide script from old browsers
      function getname(str) {
      alert("Hi, "+ str + "!");
      }
      // end hiding contents <!-- and -->
   </script>
</head>
<body>
```

```
    Please enter your name:
    <form>
      <input type="text" name="name" onBlur="getname(this.value)" value="" />
    </form>
  </body>
</html>
```

select

This element enables users to choose one or more options from a list of possible values found in the input form.

Attributes
Specific attributes:

```
disabled="disabled" [CI]
```

When used, disables the control for user input.

```
multiple="multiple" [CI]
```

Allows for multiple selections.

```
name="cdata" [CI]
```

Assigns a control name.

```
size="number" [CN]
```

Specifies the number of visible rows in the list.

```
tabindex="number" [CN]
```

Tabbing allows the author to give focus or access to an element by using a standard keyboard sequence. The sequence order is normally defined by the order of the elements. The `tabindex` attribute allows the author to establish a different order by identifying the position of the current element in the tabbing order. The value must be a number between 0 and 32767. The tabbing order specifies the order of attention for elements when navigated by the user.

Common attributes: id, class, lang, dir, title, style, and all intrinsic events.

Context

Can contain the following:

```
optgroup, option
```

Can be used in the following:

```
a, abbr, acronym, applet, b, basefont, bdo, big, blockquote, body, button,
caption, center,, cite, code, dd, dfn, div, dt, em, fieldset, font, form, i,
iframe, kbd, label, legend, li, noframes, noscript, object, p, pre, q, s, samp,
small, span, strike, strong, sub, sup, td, th, tt, u, var
```

Example

```
Favorite People:
<select name="Favoritepeople">
<option label="Sam" value="sam">Sam Williams</option>
<option label="Mary" value="mary">Mary Burmeister</option>
<optgroup label="Family">
    <option value="mom">Suzy Valentine McElroy</option>
    <option value="dad">Tom Valentine</option>
    <option value="brother">Austin Valentine</option>
</optgroup>
</select>
```

small

This element produces text that is rendered one size smaller than the default size.

Attributes

Specific attributes: None.
Common attributes: id, class, lang, dir, title, style, and all intrinsic events.

Context

Can contain the following:

> *text*, a, abbr, acronym, applet, b, bdo, big, br, cite, code, dfn, em, font, i,
> img, iframe, kbd, map, object, q, s, samp, script, small, span, strike, strong,
> sub, sup, tt, u, var

Can be used in the following:

> a, abbr, acronym, applet, b, basefont, bdo, big, blockquote, body, button,
> caption, center, cite, code, dd, dfn, div, dt, em, fieldset, font, form, i,
> iframe, kbd, label, legend, li, noframes, noscript, object, p, pre, q, s, samp,
> small, span, strike, strong, sub, sup, td, th, tt, u, var

Example

```
<p>Sometimes you want text to be <small>smaller</small> than the rest.</p>
```

span

This element allows authors to apply CSS style rules to text within a document. Note that the span element is inline by default, and the div element is a block element.

Attributes

Specific attributes: The align attribute is deprecated in favor of using style sheets.
Common attributes: id, class, lang, dir, title, style, and all intrinsic events.

Context

Can contain the following:

> text, a, abbr, acronym, applet, b, bdo, big, br, cite, code, dfn, em, font, i, img, iframe, kbd, map, object, q, s, samp, script, small, span, strike, strong, sub, sup, tt, u, var

Can be used in the following:

> a, abbr, acronym, applet, b, basefont, bdo, big, blockquote, body, button, caption, center, cite, code, dd, dfn, div, dt, em, fieldset, font, form, i, iframe, kbd, label, legend, li, noframes, noscript, object, p, pre, q, s, samp, small, span, strike, strong, sub, sup, td, th, tt, u, var

Example

```
<body>
<p>This text has no specific style information.</p>
<p><span style="font-size:15pt">This text is formatted with 15 point font
size.</span></p>
</body>
```

strike (Deprecated)

This element produces strikethrough text and is deprecated in favor of using style sheets.

strong

The strong element displays contained text with a strong emphasis.

Attributes

Specific attributes: None.
Common attributes: id, class, lang, dir, title, style, and all intrinsic events.

Context

Can contain the following:

> a, abbr, acronym, b, bdo, big, br, button, cite, code, dfn, em, i, img, input, kbd, label, map, object, q, samp, script, select, small, span, strong, sub, sup, textarea, tt, var

Can be used in the following:

> a, abbr, acronym, applet, b, basefont, bdo, big, blockquote, body, button, caption, center, cite, code, dd, dfn, div, dt, em, fieldset, font, form, i, iframe, kbd, label, legend, li, noframes, noscript, object, p, pre, q, s, samp, small, span, strike, strong, sub, sup, td, th, tt, u, var

Example

```
<p>Some words need to have a <strong>strong emphasis</strong>.</p>
```

style

This element contains internal style sheet information.

Attributes

Specific attributes:

```
type="content-type" [CI]
```

Provides the MIME type of the URL, or resource.

```
media="screen|print|projection|braille|speech|all" [CI]
```

Uses a keyword to specify the desired rendering destination for the referenced style sheet. The default is `screen`.

Common attributes: `lang`, `dir`, and `title`.

Context

Can contain the following:

```
text (style sheet information), comments
```

Can be used in the following:

```
head
```

Example

```
<head>
<title>Document Title</title>
<style type="text/css">
  body {font-size:12pt}
  h1 {font-size:18pt; color:blue;}
</style>
</head>
```

sub

The `sub` element renders the contained text as a subscript.

Attributes

Specific attributes: None.
Common attributes: `id`, `class`, `lang`, `dir`, `title`, `style`, and all intrinsic events.

Context

Can contain the following:

> *text*, a, abbr, acronym, applet, b, bdo, big, br, cite, code, dfn, em, font, i,
> img, iframe, kbd, map, object, q, s, samp, script, small, span, strike, strong,
> sub, sup, tt, u, var

Can be used in the following:

> a, abbr, acronym, applet, b, basefont, bdo, big, blockquote, body, button,
> caption, center, cite, code, dd, dfn, div, dt, em, fieldset, font, form, i,
> iframe, kbd, label, legend, li, noframes, noscript, object, p, pre, q, s, samp,
> small, span, strike, strong, sub, sup, td, th, tt, u, var

Example

> `<p>You should drink eight glasses of H<sub>2</sub>0 a day.</p>`

sup

This element renders the contained text as a superscript.

Attributes

Specific attributes: None.
Common attributes: id, class, lang, dir, title, style, and all intrinsic events.

Context

Can contain the following:

> *text*, a, abbr, acronym, applet, b, bdo, big, br, cite, code, dfn, em, font, i,
> img, iframe, kbd, map, object, q, s, samp, script, small, span, strike, strong,
> sub, sup, tt, u, var

Can be used in the following:

> a, abbr, acronym, applet, b, basefont, bdo, big, blockquote, body, button,
> caption, center, cite, code, dd, dfn, div, dt, em, fieldset, font, form, i,
> iframe, kbd, label, legend, li, noframes, noscript, object, p, pre, q, s, samp,
> small, span, strike, strong, sub, sup, td, th, tt, u, var

Example

> `<p>I won 1<sup>st</sup> place.</p>`

table

The `table` element is the parent container for all table-related elements. You use this element to create a table; however, without `tr`, `td`, or `th` elements, the table has no content.

Attributes

Specific attributes:

```
border="pixels" [CN]
```

Specifies the width, in pixels, of the table border. To create a table with no borders, you can set this attribute to `0`.

```
cellpadding="length" [CN]
```

Identifies the amount of space between the contents and the sides of a cell. The value is in pixels or a percentage; the value is most commonly defined in pixels.

```
cellspacing="length" [CN]
```

Identifies the amount of space that should be between the cells themselves, and between the frame of the table and the cells. The value is in pixels or a percentage; the value is most commonly defined in pixels.

```
frame="void|above|below|hsides|lhs|rhs|vsides|box|border" [CI]
```

Defines which sides of a frame should be visible in a browser. The values are as follows:

- **void** is the default value and displays no sides.
- **above** displays the top side only.
- **below** displays the bottom side only.
- **hsides** displays the top and bottom sides only.
- **vsides** displays the right and left sides only.
- **lhs** displays the left-hand side only.
- **rhs** displays the right-hand side only.
- **box** displays all four sides.
- **border** displays all four sides.

```
rules="none|groups|rows|cols|all" [CI]
```

Specifies which rules occur between table-data cells within a given table. The values are as follows:

- **none** applies no rules.
- **groups** applies rules between row groups and column groups only.
- **rows** applies rules between rows only.

- **cols** applies rules between columns only.
- **all** applies rules between all rows and columns.

`summary="text" [CS]`

Provides a summary of the table's purpose and contents for nonvisual browsers (for accessibility reasons).

`width="length" [CN]`

Defines the width for the entire table. The value can be a percentage or pixels.

The `align` and `bgcolor` attributes are deprecated in favor of using style sheets.

Common attributes: id, class, lang, dir, title, style, and all intrinsic events.

Context

Can contain the following:

`caption, col, colgroup, thead, tfoot, tbody`

Can be used in the following:

`applet, basefont, blockquote, body, center dd, div, fieldset, form, iframe, li, noframes, noscript, object, pre, td, th`

Example

```
<table border="1" cellpadding="5" width="75%">
<caption>Table Caption</caption>
<thead>
  <tr>
   <th>cell</th>
   <th>cell</th>
   <th>cell</th>
   <th>cell</th>
  </tr>
</thead>
<tfoot>
  <tr>
   <td>cell</td>
   <td>cell</td>
   <td>cell</td>
   <td>cell</td>
  </tr>
</tfoot>
<tbody>
  <tr>
   <td>cell</td>
   <td>cell</td>
   <td>cell</td>
   <td>cell</td>
  </tr>
  <tr>
   <td>cell</td>
```

```
      <td>cell</td>
      <td>cell</td>
      <td>cell</td>
    </tr>
  </tbody>
</table>
```

tbody

Table rows (`tr`) can be grouped into three sections in a table: table head, table foot, and table body. The table body (`tbody`) element contains the table data. The table header (`thead`) and table footer (`tfoot`) elements contain information about the columns. The `tfoot` element comes before the `tbody` element to allow browsers to render the footer before rendering the possibly numerous table-data cells.

Attributes

Specific attributes:

```
align="left|center|right|justify|char" [CI]
```

Specifies the alignment of data in a cell. The values are as follows:

- **left** specifies that the data is left-justified. This is the default value for table data.
- **center** specifies that the data is centered in the cell. This is the default value for table headers.
- **right** specifies that the data is right-justified.
- **justify** specifies that the data is double-justified.
- **char** specifies that the text aligns around a specific character.

```
char="character" [CN]
```

You use this attribute to designate a specific character that is used as a point to which to align data from each cell in the column.

```
charoff="length" [CN]
```

Sets the offset within the cell where the alignment character will be placed.

```
valign="top|middle|bottom|baseline" [CI]
```

Specifies the vertical alignment of data within a cell. The values are as follows:

- **top** specifies that the cell data should align with the top of the cell.
- **middle** specifies that the cell data should be centered vertically within the cell. This is the default value.
- **bottom** specifies that the cell data is aligned with the bottom of the cell.
- **baseline** specifies that all cells in the same row should have their data positioned so that the first text line occurs on a common baseline.

Common attributes: id, class, lang, dir, title, style, and all intrinsic events.

Context
Can contain the following:

    tr

Can be used in the following:

    table

Example
See table example.

td
The td element contains the data for each table-data cell.

Attributes
Specific attributes:

    abbr="text" [CS]

Defines an abbreviated name for a header cell. When not defined, the default abbreviation is the cell content.

    align="left|center|right|justify|char" [CI]

Specifies the alignment of data in a cell. The values are as follows:

- **left** specifies that the data is left-justified. This is the default value for table data.
- **center** specifies that the data is centered in the cell. This is the default value for table headers.
- **right** specifies that the data is right-justified.
- **justify** specifies that the data is double-justified.
- **char** specifies that the text aligns around a specific character.

    axis="text" [CI]

Provides the user with an abbreviated description of a cell's contents.

    char="character" [CN]

You use this attribute to designate a specific character that will be used as a point to which to align data from each cell in the column.

    charoff="length" [CN]

Sets the offset within the cell that the alignment character will be placed.

    colspan="number" [CN]

Specifies the number of columns spanned by the particular cell. The default value is 1.

```
headers="idrefs" [CS]
```

Specifies a space-separated list of cell names that provide header information for the current data cell.

```
rowspan="number" [CN]
```

Specifies the number of rows spanned by the particular cell. The default value is 1.

```
scope="row|col|rowgroup|colgroup" [CI]
```

Can be used instead of the `headers` attribute. This attribute marks off the cells that contain header information. The values are as follows:

- **row** indicates that the current cell provides header information for the row that contains it.
- **col** indicates that the current cell provides header information for the column that is specified for it.
- **rowgroup** indicates that the current cell provides header information for the rest of the row group that contains it.
- **colgroup** indicates that the current cell provides header information for the rest of the column group that contains it.

```
valign="top|middle|bottom|baseline" [CI]
```

Specifies the vertical alignment of data within a cell. The values are as follows:

- **top** specifies that the cell data should align with the top of the cell.
- **middle** specifies that the cell data should be centered vertically within the cell. This is the default value.
- **bottom** specifies that the cell data is aligned with the bottom of the cell.
- **baseline** specifies that all cells in the same row should have their data positioned so that the first text line occurs on a common baseline.

The `bgcolor`, `nowrap`, `width`, and `height` attributes are deprecated in favor of using style sheets.

Common attributes: `id`, `class`, `lang`, `dir`, `title`, `style`, and all intrinsic events.

Context

Can contain the following:

```
text, a, abbr, acronym, address, applet, b, basefont, bdo, big, blockquote, br,
cite, code, dfn, dir, div, dl, em, fieldset, font, form, hr, i, iframe, img,
isindex, kbd, map, menu, noframes, noscript, object, ol, p, pre, q, s, samp,
script, small, span, strike, strong, sub, sup, table, tt, u, ul, var
```

Can be used in the following:

```
tr
```

Example

See table example.

textarea

This element creates a text input area for a form.

Attributes

Specific attributes:

```
accesskey="text" [CN]
```

Identifies the character to be used as a keyboard shortcut. The value can be any alphanumeric character from a browser's character set.

```
cols="number" [CN]
```

Specifies the number of columns for the textarea field.

```
disabled="disabled" [CI]
```

When used, the attribute disables the control for user input.

```
name="cdata" [CI]
```

This is a required attribute that defines a name for the form field.

```
readonly="readonly" [CI]
```

Specifies that the text content cannot be modified by the user.

```
rows="number" [CN]
```

Specifies the number of lines, or rows, for the textarea field.

```
tabindex="number" [CN]
```

Tabbing allows the author to give focus or access to an element by using a standard keyboard sequence. The sequence order is normally defined by the order of the elements. The tabindex attribute allows the author to establish a different order by identifying the position of the current element in the tabbing order. The value must be a number between 0 and 32767. The tabbing order specifies the order of attention for elements when navigated by the user.

Common attributes: id, class, lang, dir, title, style, and all intrinsic events.

Context

Can contain the following:

```
text
```

Can be used in the following:

```
a, abbr, acronym, applet, b, basefont, bdo, big, blockquote, body, button,
caption, center, cite, code, dd, dfn, div, dt, em, fieldset, font, form, i,
iframe, kbd, label, legend, li, noframes, noscript, object, p, pre, q, s, samp,
small, span, strike, strong, sub, sup, td, th, tt, u, var
```

Example

```
<form action="..." method="post">
  <textarea name="input" rows="15" cols="100">
  </textarea>
<p>
<input type="submit" value="ok" />
<input type="reset" value="reset" />
</p>
</form>
```

tfoot

Table rows (tr) can be grouped into three sections in a table: table head, table foot, and table body. The table body (tbody) element contains the table data. The table header (thead) and table footer (tfoot) elements contain information about the columns. The tfoot element comes before the tbody element to allow browsers to render the footer before rendering the possibly numerous table-data cells.

Attributes
Specific attributes:

```
align="left|center|right|justify|char" [CI]
```

Specifies the alignment of data in a cell. The values are as follows:

- **left** specifies that the data is left-justified. This is the default value for table data.
- **center** specifies that the data is centered in the cell. This is the default value for table headers.
- **right** specifies that the data is right-justified.
- **justify** specifies that the data is double-justified.
- **char** specifies that the text aligns around a specific character.

```
char="character" [CN]
```

You use this attribute to designate a specific character that will be used as a point to which to align data from each cell in the column.

```
charoff="length" [CN]
```

Sets the offset within the cell where the alignment character will be placed.

```
valign="top|middle|bottom|baseline" [CI]
```

Specifies the vertical alignment of data within a cell. The values are as follows:

- **top** specifies that the cell data should align with the top of the cell.
- **middle** specifies that the cell data should be centered vertically within the cell. This is the default value.
- **bottom** specifies that the cell data is aligned with the bottom of the cell.
- **baseline** specifies that all cells in the same row should have their data positioned so that the first text line occurs on a common baseline.

Common attributes: id, class, lang, dir, title, style, and all intrinsic events.

Context

Can contain the following:

```
tr
```

Can be used in the following:

```
table
```

Example

See table example.

th

This element is identical to the td element, except that it contains the headers for a given column. Most browsers display the contents of a th element in bold.

Attributes

Specific attributes:

```
align="left|center|right|justify|char" [CI]
```

Specifies the alignment of data in a cell. The values are as follows:

- **left** specifies that the data is left-justified. This is the default value for table data.
- **center** specifies that the data is centered in the cell. This is the default value for table headers.
- **right** specifies that the data is right-justified.
- **justify** specifies that the data is double-justified.
- **char** specifies that the text aligns around a specific character.

```
abbr="text" [CS]
```

Defines an abbreviated name for a header cell. When not defined, the default abbreviation is the cell content.

```
axis="text" [CI]
```

Provides the user with an abbreviated description of a cell's contents.

```
char="character" [CN]
```

You use this attribute to designate a specific character that is used as a point to which to align data from each cell in the column.

```
charoff="length" [CN]
```

Sets the offset within the cell where the alignment character will be placed.

```
colspan="number" [CN]
```

Specifies the number of columns spanned by the particular cell. The default value is 1.

```
headers="idrefs" [CS]
```

Specifies a space-separated list of cell names that provide header information for the current data cell.

```
rowspan="number" [CN]
```

Specifies the number of rows spanned by the particular cell. The default value is 1.

```
scope="row|col|rowgroup|colgroup" [CI]
```

Is used instead of the `headers` attribute. This attribute marks off the cells that contain header information. The values are as follows:

- **row** indicates that the current cell provides header information for the row that contains it.
- **col** indicates that the current cell provides header information for the column specified for it.
- **rowgroup** indicates that the current cell provides header information for the rest of the row group that contains it.
- **colgroup** indicates that the current cell provides header information for the rest of the column group that contains it.

```
valign="top|middle|bottom|baseline" [CI]
```

Specifies the vertical alignment of data within a cell. The values are as follows:

- **top** specifies that the cell data should align with the top of the cell.
- **middle** specifies that the cell data should be centered vertically within the cell. This is the default value.
- **bottom** specifies that the cell data is aligned with the bottom of the cell.
- **baseline** specifies that all cells in the same row should have their data positioned so that the first text line occurs on a common baseline.

The `bgcolor`, `nowrap`, `width`, and `height` attributes are deprecated in favor of using style sheets.

Common attributes: `id`, `class`, `lang`, `dir`, `title`, `style`, and all intrinsic events.

Context

Can contain the following:

```
text, a, abbr, acronym, address, applet, b, basefont, bdo, big, blockquote, br,
cite, code, dfn, dir, div, dl, em, fieldset, font, form, hr, i, iframe, img,
isindex, kbd, map, menu, noframes, noscript, object, ol, p, pre, q, s, samp,
script, small, span, strike, strong, sub, sup, table, tt, u, ul, var
```

Can be used in the following:

```
tr
```

Example

See `table` example.

thead

Table rows (`tr`) can be grouped into three sections in a table: table head, table foot, and table body. The table body (`tbody`) element contains the table data. The table header (`thead`) and table footer (`tfoot`) elements contain information about the columns. The `tfoot` element comes before the `tbody` element to allow browsers to render the footer before rendering the possibly numerous table-data cells.

Attributes

Specific attributes:

```
align="left|center|right|justify|char" [CI]
```

Specifies the alignment of data in a cell. The values are as follows:

- **left** specifies that the data is left-justified. This is the default value for table data.
- **center** specifies that the data is centered in the cell. This is the default value for table headers.
- **right** specifies that the data is right-justified.
- **justify** specifies that the data is double-justified.
- **char** specifies that the text aligns around a specific character.

```
char="character" [CN]
```

You use this attribute to designate a specific character that will be used as a point to which to align data from each cell in the column.

```
charoff="length" [CN]
```

Sets the offset within the cell where the alignment character will be placed.

```
valign="top|middle|bottom|baseline" [CI]
```

Specifies the vertical alignment of data within a cell. The values are as follows:

- **top** specifies that the cell data should align with the top of the cell.
- **middle** specifies that the cell data should be centered vertically within the cell. This is the default value.
- **bottom** specifies that the cell data is aligned with the bottom of the cell.
- **baseline** specifies that all cells in the same row should have their data positioned so that the first text line occurs on a common baseline.

Common attributes: id, class, lang, dir, title, style, and all intrinsic events.

Context

Can contain the following:

```
tr
```

Can be used in the following:

```
table
```

Example

See table example.

title

This element defines the title for an XHTML document. The contents of the title element are most often rendered at the very top of the browser window. The title element must be a child of the head element.

Attributes

Specific attributes: None.
Common attributes: lang and dir.

Context

Can contain the following:

```
text
```

Can be used in the following:

```
head
```

Example

```
<html xmlns="http://www.w3.org/1999/xhtml">
<head>
<title>Document Title</title>
</head>
<body>
...
</body>
</html>
```

tr

The tr element is part of the table body and identifies a table row. Each table row element contains table-data cells (td elements).

Attributes

Specific attributes:

```
align="left|center|right|justify|char" [CI]
```

Specifies the alignment of data in a cell. The values are as follows:

- **left** specifies that the data is left-justified. This is the default value for table data.

- **center** specifies that the data is centered in the cell. This is the default value for table headers.

- **right** specifies that the data is right-justified.

- **justify** specifies that the data is double-justified.

- **char** specifies that the text aligns around a specific character.

```
char="character" [CN]
```

You use this attribute to designate a specific character that is used as a point to which to align data from each cell in the column.

```
charoff="length" [CN]
```

Sets the offset within the cell that the alignment character will be placed.

```
valign="top|middle|bottom|baseline" [CI]
```

Specifies the vertical alignment of data within a cell. The values are as follows:

- **top** specifies that the cell data should align with the top of the cell.

- **middle** specifies that the cell data should be centered vertically within the cell. This is the default value.

- **bottom** specifies that the cell data is aligned with the bottom of the cell.

- **baseline** specifies that all cells in the same row should have their data positioned so that the first text line occurs on a common baseline.

The `bgcolor` attribute is deprecated in favor of using style sheets.
Common attributes: `id`, `class`, `lang`, `dir`, `title`, `style`, and all intrinsic events.

Attributes

Specific attributes: None.
Common attributes: `id`, `class`, `lang`, `dir`, `title`, `style`, and all intrinsic events.

Context

Can contain the following:

```
td, th
```

Can be used in the following:

```
table, tbody, tfoot, thead
```

Example

See `table` example.

tt

This element applies teletype or monospaced text style to contained text.

Attributes

Specific attributes: None.
Common attributes: `id`, `class`, `lang`, `dir`, `title`, `style`, and all intrinsic events.

Context

Can contain the following:

```
a, abbr, acronym, b, bdo, big, br, button, cite, code, dfn, em, i, img, input,
kbd, label, map, object, q, samp, script, select, small, span, strong, sub, sup,
textarea, tt, var
```

Can be used in the following:

```
a, abbr, acronym, applet, b, basefont, bdo, big, blockquote, body, button,
caption, center, cite, code, dd, dfn, div, dt, em, fieldset, font, form, i,
iframe, kbd, label, legend, li, noframes, noscript, object, p, pre, q, s, samp,
small, span, strike, strong, sub, sup, td, th, tt, u, var
```

Example

```
<p>Type <tt>My name is George</tt>.</p>
```

u (Deprecated)

The u element underlines text and is deprecated in favor of using style sheets.

ul

This element creates an unordered list and contains `li` (list item) elements.

Attributes
Specific attributes:
The `type`, `start`, `value`, and `compact` attributes are deprecated.
Common attributes: `id`, `class`, `lang`, `dir`, `title`, `style`, and all intrinsic events.

Context
Can contain the following:

```
li
```

Can be used in the following:

```
text, a, abbr, acronym, applet, b, bdo, big, br, button, caption, cite, code, dfn,
dt, em, font, i, iframe, img, kbd, label, legend, map, object, p, q, s, samp,
script, small, span, strike, strong, sub, sup, tt, u, var
```

Example

```
<body>
<ul>
<li>List item</li>
<li>List item</li>
<li>List item</li>
</ul>
</body>
```

var

This element is used to represent a variable name or program argument. This text contained in the variable element is usually rendered in italics.

Attributes
Specific attributes: None.
Common attributes: `id`, `class`, `lang`, `dir`, `title`, `style`, and all intrinsic events.

Context

Can contain the following:

```
a, abbr, acronym, b, bdo, big, br, button, cite, code, dfn, em, i, img, input,
kbd, label, map, object, q, samp, script, select, small, span, strong, sub, sup,
textarea, tt, var
```

Can be used in the following:

```
a, abbr, acronym, applet, b, basefont, bdo, big, blockquote, body, button,
caption, center, cite, code, dd, dfn, div, dt, em, fieldset, font, form, i,
iframe, kbd, label, legend, li, noframes, noscript, object, p, pre, q, s, samp,
small, span, strike, strong, sub, sup, td, th, tt, u, var
```

Example

```
<p>When the login dialog box appears and says <tt>Logon to Network:</tt> enter
your <var>username</var> to logon.</p>
```

For More Information

Several resources have similar information to this chapter in them. However, some of them may not have the most updated information, such as which elements are deprecated and so on. Some useful sites are as follows:

- **The W3C HTML 4.01 list of elements.** www.w3.org/TR/html4/index/elements.html

- **ZDNet Tag Developer Library.**
  www.zdnet.com/devhead/resources/tag_library/

- **webreview.com.** http://webreview.com/

- **ProjectCool Developer.** www.projectcool.com/developer/

4

Converting HTML to XHTML

U NLESS YOU'VE NEVER CREATED A WEB PAGE BEFORE, you're probably interested in how to convert an existing HTML page to XHTML. The Web has expanded to consist of an overwhelming number of Web pages—most of which are created with HTML. Undoubtedly, many Web developers will make the switch to XHTML before long. If you're one of these developers, this chapter prepares you for the task.

Differences Between HTML and XHTML

To convert an HTML document to XHTML, you must first identify the differences between the two languages. When it comes to these differences, there are two funda-mental truths that any Web developer must understand:

- HTML will not be developed any further. XHTML 1.0 is what you need to learn.
- XHTML is a reformulation of HTML 4 in XML 1.0.

This section focuses on the differences between HTML and XHTML, but as this dis-cussion progresses, keep in mind that XHTML is just the next evolutionary step in the HTML family. The elements used to create an HTML Web page are the very same elements used to create an XHTML Web page. XHTML is just a restatement of HTML goals in the form of an open, extensible markup language based on XML.

Since late 1998, there has been a migration toward XML-related technologies. The XML hype is no surprise. After all, XML gives authors the capability to deliver standardized markup while separating display from structure, which makes maintenance and parsing much easier. In addition, XML allows you to define custom vocabularies (in other words, create your own element tags). Who wouldn't be chomping at the bit?

With the influx of portable Web-enabled browsers, there is another reason authors are ready to tackle XML: strict, clean, standardized code.

In the past, HTML did what was needed, but it's outlived its usefulness. Most HTML documents are bloated with unnecessary code, which makes it difficult to create pages compatible with nonconventional platforms, such as handheld devices. Who wants to force the user to mess with bloated—and yes, slow—pages? Bloated code is just one of the many current limitations of HTML.

Limitations of HTML

HTML was never designed to do what we expect of it today. You can look at HTML markup and the various iterations of the language itself, and see how it has evolved as a way to keep up with the Web's demands. What began as a simple structural language has evolved to include stylistic markup that affects display and not structure. As Netscape and Internet Explorer fought for market share, they too introduced their own HTML elements, which forced Web designers to learn different nonstandard elements. Why has HTML fallen behind in the rat race? Here are a few limitations to working with HTML today:

- Lack of large amounts of semantic markup leads to difficulty in describing and exchanging data.
- Proprietary and stylistic elements create sloppy, bloated code that is difficult to maintain—not to mention slow to download.
- The predefined element set (as well as the way developers use the element set) does not work well with nonconventional platforms, such as handheld devices.

These are some of the reasons HTML has seen its day. To learn more about why XHTML will make any Web designer grin from ear to ear, see Chapter 2, "All About Markup."

Viewing Web Pages

According to the Web gods, by 2002 over 75 percent of desktop users will view Web pages on platforms other than your average desktop machine, for example, mobile phones, refrigerators, and Palm Pilots.

Major Differences

The major differences between HTML and XHTML can be broken into two groups: syntactical and functional. Once browsers get up to speed, XHTML will not be as forgiving as HTML. We use the future tense here because right now, XHTML functions much like HTML in older browsers. To understand how XHTML can render in non-XML-compatible browsers, see the section titled "Compatibility Issues and Browser Requirements" later in this chapter. If you're familiar with the HTML-browser debate, you probably know two things:

- Not all browsers are alike: Different browsers support different elements and some proprietary elements of their own. Until recently, browser developers were not concerned with standards.

- Browsers let authors get away with murder, theoretically anyway.

If you want to test the previous theories, do a quick test. Create the following XHTML document in a text editor and save it on your hard drive with a .htm extension:

```
<html>
<body>
<h4>This is a heading 4</h4>
<p>Here is our paragraph</p>
</html>
```

Right off the bat, you *should* notice a couple mistakes. First, there's not a head element or a title element (which are both required for a valid HTML document). Second, the closing body tag is not present.

After you save the document on your hard drive, open it in your browser. To open an (X)HTML document in your browser, select File, Open, click the Browse button, select the document name, and then click Open. The document should render in your browser without a hitch, as shown in Figure 4.1.

With XHTML, all bets are off. When you create an XHTML document, you're instructing the browser to follow XML rules. If you make a mistake, such as omitting a closing tag or typing element names in uppercase, your page will not be well formed or valid, and the result will be an ugly error message. The terms *well formed* and *valid* are essential to XHTML. If you do not know what they mean, see Chapter 2, "All About Markup."

As mentioned earlier in this section, there are two categories of differences between XHTML and HTML: syntactical and functional. The syntactical differences have to do with the structure of the document (its syntax). As you become well versed in XML (and you will because XHTML is an XML application), syntax becomes increasingly important. When we mention XML rules, we're talking about XML syntax rules. One of the advantages of XML is its standardized—and yes, strict—markup. This means that the first significant difference between HTML and XHTML is syntax.

Figure 4.1 The HTML document is displayed, even with mistakes.

HTML follows its own syntax rules based on a predefined set of elements (most of which define style or structure), whereas XHTML must adhere to the syntax rules defined by the XML specification. (We identify each rule in detail later in this chapter in the "XML Syntax Rules" section.) With the capability to create your own elements in XML, minus the capability to manipulate style, XML allows only for elements that define the meaning and structure of their content. That alone doesn't do more than HTML. To really take advantage of the XHTML benefits, you should read Chapter 12, "The Benefits of Extensibility," and Chapter 13, "Where the Future Leads, XHTML Follows," and learn more about extending your markup.

The next set of major differences is driven by function. As discussed earlier, HTML has outlived its usefulness, and XHTML intends to pick up where HTML left off. Most advantages found in XHTML actually come from XML. Because XHTML is an application of XML (which means it follows the rules of XML), it reaps the rewards of extensibility and portability.

When someone from the XHTML community says *extensible*, he or she means that XHTML can be extended beyond its predefined core elements. With extensibility, other XML applications, such as Scalable Vector Graphics (SVG) and your very own XML creations, can be incorporated in XHTML documents.

The second XML advantage is *portability*. With XML, a single page can result in multiple outputs. After the markup and content is compiled into an XML (or in our case, an XHTML) document, various style sheets can be applied that control different outputs. And, who's to say that output is only for display. Maybe the data needs to be sent to a database at another company, with XML. This type of data transfer is now an option. The idea is to only write and modify the content once. (Now that is a media we can get behind!) However, remember that you can't just write an XHTML document and expect it to start calling up other companies and sharing information; there is some work involved. The key is that it's possible.

Compatibility Issues and Browser Requirements

Good news: XHTML documents will render in older browsers. There are a few glitches, but there are simple workarounds that fix the problems. Here they are, one by one:

- Empty elements should include a trailing space after the element name and before /> (for example, `<br />`).

- Do not minimize elements that are not defined as empty, even if they do not appear to contain content. For example, sometimes the p element is used alone with no content. If this occurs, be sure to write it as `<p></p>` and not `<p />`.

- Avoid using multiple spaces or line breaks within an element's tag(s). In XML, using line breaks is common practice. For example:

```
<book  type="paperback"
       isbn="99-9999-999-9"
            year="1972">
```

In XHTML, do not include line breaks, for example:

```
<link type="text/css" rel="stylesheet" href="style.css" />
```

Note that throughout this book, we insert spaces in markup for readability purposes only. When you write your markup, be sure to follow the spacing rules outlined in this section.

This is by no means an exhaustive list. For more information on compatibility, visit `www.w3.org/TR/xhtml1/#guidelines` or flip to Appendix A "XHTML 1.0: The Extensible HyperText Marlkup Language," which contains the entire XHTML Specification, including the HTML Compatibility Guidelines.

XML-Compatible Browsers

There are many XML-compatible browsers that render XHTML documents perfectly, such as Amaya, Mozilla, and Internet Explorer 5.

- Amaya is offered by the W3C and boasts support for most W3C standards, including heavy-duty CSS support. (We like it here at the office.) As far as popularity goes, however, Amaya is only used by a fraction of the Web-browsing community.

- Mozilla was created as an open-source venture, and is incorporated into the most recent version of Netscape 6. It too boasts support for the most common Web standards, such as HTML and XML (and therefore XHTML). Mozilla also includes heavy-duty CSS support.

- Internet Explorer 5 is Microsoft's premier browser. Although not perfect, Internet Explorer 5 does support XML. One word of warning, however: it does not support the full CSS specification, and CSS is important to XHTML display. The next version of Internet Explorer should include better CSS support.

For a complete listing of XML-compatible browsers, see `www.xmlsoftware.com/browsers/`.

Mechanical Translation from HTML to XHTML

Translation from HTML to XHTML is truly a breeze. Instead of thinking of it as a full-blown conversion process, think of it as cleaning up your HTML document. XHTML uses the same elements—the only difference is syntax and rules. We break them down for you in the following sections.

XML Syntax Rules

All XML documents have something in common: syntax. There are a few, easy rules to remember when you work with XML documents. Here they are, one by one:

- All elements must be contained by a root element (also called a document element). For XHTML, the `html` element is the root element: `<html>...</html>` contains all other elements

- If your document adheres to a Document Type Definition (DTD), the document must include a document type declaration. For XHTML, the document type declaration is formed as follows:

      <!DOCTYPE html PUBLIC "-//W3C//DTD XHTML 1.0 Strict//EN"
      "http://www.w3.org/TR/xhtml1/DTD/xhtml1-strict.dtd">

  The `DOCTYPE` declaration is not an element; it's a declaration and has its own syntax. All `DOCTYPE` declarations begin with an exclamation point and uppercase keyword (for example, `<!DOCTYPE>`). This is not negotiable. If you're new to the term DTD, please read Chapter 2.

- All element and attribute names must be lowercase (for example, `<head>` not `<HEAD>`).

- All nonempty elements must have a closing tag (for example, `<p>...</p>`).

- All empty elements must use the following syntax: `<img />`. (For backward-compatibility reasons, although it's not required, be sure to include a space between the element name and `/>`.)

- Elements must be nested correctly (for example, `<p><b>This is correct</b></p>` and `<p><b>This is not correct</p></b>`).

- All attributes must have values and those values must be contained by single or double quotation marks. This means that the standalone attributes used in HTML (such as `<td nowrap>`) are no longer valid). The correct form is `<td nowrap="nowrap">`.

The main syntax rules end there. However, there are a few XHTML-specific rules you have to follow as you convert your documents.

XHTML-Specific Rules

To become familiar with the XHTML-specific rules, let's go through an HTML document from top to bottom and identify the necessary changes and additions to required elements.

The first item on an HTML page is normally the `html` element. This is no longer the case. There are a few pieces of markup that must come at the beginning of any XHTML document.

First, you must include a `DOCTYPE` declaration (also known as a document type declaration). You may also include XML version and encoding information (which is optional) in the XML declaration right before the `DOCTYPE` declaration. We strongly recommend that you include the XML declaration. For more on the XML declaration, see Chapter 2. The correct markup takes the form:

```
<?xml version="1.0"?>
<!DOCTYPE html PUBLIC
      "-//W3C//DTD XHTML 1.0 Strict//EN"
      "http://www.w3.org/TR/xhtml1/DTD/xhtml1-strict.dtd">
```

The next item on the list is the `html` element. In XHTML, this element is called the root element. The *root element* contains all other elements. To read more on including a root element, see Chapter 3, "Overview of Element Structures." Not only is the `html` element required, but it must also contain a predefined attribute-value pair. This specific required attribute is called an *XML namespace*. XML namespaces are commonly used in XML documents. The specific namespace used for XHTML documents is often referred to as the *XHTML namespace* and is a way to uniquely identify the set of elements as XHTML elements. The correct XHTML namespace is as follows:

```
<html xmlns="http://www.w3.org/1999/xhtml">
```

Imagine that you're in the world of XML and you want to combine your XHTML document with some elements you made from scratch. In the list of elements you named, you decided to use a `title` element type to represent the title of a book. This means that your combined document now has two `title` element types with two completely different meanings.

How do you tell the XML processor (a browser is one type of processor) that the XHTML `title` element is the title of the document and your `title` element represents the title of a book? You use a namespace to uniquely separate the two.

Namespaces are like surnames. Defining a namespace in the root element means that all elements contained by the `html` element belong to the XHTML element set. Any elements that are not contained by the `html` element or that have their own namespaces attached will belong to a different set of elements. The namespace debate is not yet settled at the W3C—for a while, there was an argument about how and when to use namespaces. To learn more about namespaces, see Chapter 2 or check out the W3C site at www.w3.org/TR/REC-xml-names/.

Next, you must include the `head`, `title`, and `body` structural elements, which are required in XHTML. The one exception is if you're creating a frameset document. In this case, you have to replace the `body` element with the `frameset` element.

Now that you know the differences between XHTML and HTML, it's time to convert an HTML document to an XHTML document.

Step-by-Step Examples

If you're following along at your computer, go to the Chapter 4 examples on the CD and look for Example 4.1. For this exercise, we're going to take this fairly unattractive code and clean it up by hand. The markup behind the page is shown in Example 4.1.

Example 4.1   **This Markup Needs to Be Cleaned Up**

```
<html>
<head>
<title>Picasso, Pablo</title>
</head>
<body>
<h1>Pablo Picasso</H1>

<ul>
<li>
<img src="http://www.artic.edu/aic/collections/modern/pictures/E31631.jpg"
alt="Picasso's The Old Guitarist">
<cite>Picasso's The Old Guitarist
</cite>
<br>
Oil on panel, 1903;
Helen Birch Bartlett Memorial Collection, 1926.253
```

```
<li>
<img src="http://www.nga.gov/image/a00022/a00022bd.jpg" alt="Picasso's The
Tragedy">
<cite>The Tragedy</cite>
<br>
Oil on panel, 1903; Chester Dale Collection, 1963.10.196
<li>
<img src="http://www.diamondial.org/limage/70.190.JPEG" alt="Picasso's Melancholy
Woman">
<cite>Melancholy Woman</cite>
<br>
Oil on canvas, 1902; Bequest of Robert H. Tannahill, 70.190
</ul>
</body>
</html>
```

If you want to make the changes as we do in this book, save the file from the CD in a folder on your hard drive, and open it in a text editor.

When converting a document by hand, first look for syntax differences. For example:

- Change all element and attribute names to lowercase.

- Add quotation marks to all attribute values.

- Add appropriate closing tags.

- Add trailing space and forward slash (/) to all empty elements.

After you make the necessary syntax changes, you need to add a few XHTML-specific pieces of information:

- **Add the XML declaration.** To do this, add the following markup as the first line of the document:

    ```
    <?xml version="1.0"?>
    ```

- **Add a DOCTYPE declaration.** To do this, you have three options to choose from (to learn more about these options, see Chapter 2). To add this markup correctly, insert the following markup as the second line of the document:

    ```
    <!DOCTYPE html PUBLIC
           "-//W3C//DTD XHTML 1.0 Strict//EN"
           "http://www.w3.org/TR/xhtml1/DTD/xhtml1-strict.dtd">
    ```

- **Add the XHTML namespace to the root element.** To do this, simply add the following attribute-value pair to the html element:

    ```
    <html xmlns="http://www.w3.org/1999/xhtml">
    ```

After you make the previous changes, the resulting code should look like Example 4.2.

Example 4.2   **This XHTML Document Is Syntactically Correct**

```
<?xml version="1.0"?>
<!DOCTYPE html PUBLIC
        "-//W3C//DTD XHTML 1.0 Strict//EN"
        "http://www.w3.org/TR/xhtml1/DTD/xhtml1-strict.dtd">
<html xmlns="http://www.w3.org/1999/xhtml">
<head>
<title>Picasso, Pablo</title>
</head>
<body>
<h1>Pablo Picasso</h1>

<ul>
<li>
<img src="http://www.artic.edu/aic/collections/modern/pictures/E31631.jpg"
alt="Picasso's The Old Guitarist" />
<cite>Picasso's The Old Guitarist</cite>
</li>
<br />
Oil on panel, 1903;
Helen Birch Bartlett Memorial Collection, 1926.253
<li>
<img src="http://www.nga.gov/image/a00022/a00022bd.jpg" alt="Picasso's The
Tragedy" />
<cite>The Tragedy</cite>
</li>
<br />
Oil on panel, 1903; Chester Dale Collection, 1963.10.196
<li>
<img src="http://www.diamondial.org/limage/70.190.JPEG" alt="Picasso's Melancholy
Woman" />
<cite>Melancholy Woman</cite>
</li>
<br />
Oil on canvas, 1902; Bequest of Robert H. Tannahill, 70.190
</ul>
</body>
</html>
```

You may notice that we avoided using too much stylistic markup to format the page. Using stylistic markup is a big no-no in the XML world. Achieve style using style sheets (see Chapter 6, "Adding Style," or Chapter 7, "Adding Style with XSL"). It's almost impossible to omit all stylistic markup when using XHTML 1.0 as your markup language of choice because most XHTML elements are style oriented. However, keep in mind that many style elements will be omitted from the next generation of XHTML. Therefore, try to stick to the structural and semantic elements if you can—more on this in Chapter 6.

Working with HTML Tidy

We know the answer to all of your prayers is automation. If you have only a couple HTML pages to your credit, manually converting your documents is a snap. However, if you're a veteran of the Web-design field and went public with your pages years ago (or even months ago), you probably have many HTML documents to convert. There must be an easier way to tackle converting them, and there is.

If you're familiar with the W3C site, you might be familiar with Dave Raggett. He's the Tom Cruise of Web design—well, one of them anyway—and has been hard at work to make your life easier. For anyone searching for a good tool to convert those HTML pages to XHTML, Dave Raggett has created one with your interests in mind: HTML Tidy. You can choose from three different interfaces from which to work with HTML Tidy: a DOS-based interface, a Web-based one, and graphical user interface (GUI) form. It gets better—all three versions of this tool are free!

HTML Tidy from a Command Line

In the past, Windows users could use only HTML Tidy from the command line (and you still can). Therefore, if you used computers in the 80s and early 90s, you're familiar with the command line, and you really want to use it, read the this section.

Before Windows and the ease of drag and drop, PCs were run from a DOS prompt. From the DOS prompt, a PC user could do most of what you do today in a Windows environment. Except the user had to use commands to tell the computer what to do. Some diehards still work from the DOS prompt, but we make the assumption that most of you out there have adopted the wonderful world of Windows. So, to start with, download this version of HTML Tidy from `www.w3.org/People/Raggett/tidy/`.

Next, you need to see the DOS prompt in action. Go to Start, Programs, MS-DOS Prompt. A window with a black background opens with a prompt at the folder `C:\Windows`.

HTML Tidy for the MAC

If you use a Mac, the GUI version was available long ago. Mac users can find out more at `www.geocities.com/SiliconValley/1057/tidy.html`.

Now you can experiment with HTML Tidy. To get started, you do the same as demonstrated previously. Go to Start, Programs, MS-DOS Prompt. Find the folder that contains HTML Tidy. For this example, the folder is `C:\tidy`. To locate this folder, we typed the following at the command line:

```
cd ..\tidy
```

Use the `cd` command to change the folder and then use `..\` to navigate back to the root folder. The last code is `tidy` and it opens the tidy folder. Be sure to include a space between `cd` and `..\` but no space between `..\` and `tidy`.

After you do that, you're ready to use HTML Tidy. If you decided that you're brave enough to tackle HTML Tidy from the DOS prompt, the next step is to convert the nasty HTML document shown in Example 4.3 to clean XHTML.

Example 4.3   **This Document Needs to Be Converted to Clean XHTML, Which You Do with HTML Tidy**

```
<HTML>
<Title>Sloppy Code at Play</Title>
<H1>HTML Document with Mistakes<h1>
<P>This document does not adhere to XHTML rules.
<p>Take a second to see all the mistakes.
<ul>
<li>All element names are not lowercase.
<li>Many elements do not contain the required closing tags.
<li>The XHTML namespace is not used.
<li>The document is missing some required elements.
<li>The document lacks the required DOCTYPE declaration.
</UL>
</html>
```

On our machine, the previous HTML file is located in the following directory:

```
c:\XHTML\tidy.html
```

To convert this document on your computer, you need to do a few things first:

- Create a folder on your hard drive called XHTML. (The name is not important, but if you decided to choose your own filename, be sure to change the name in all the right places.)
- Find Example 4.3 on the CD in the Chapter 4 examples folder and save it in the XHTML folder on your hard drive with the name `tidy.html`.

Now, back to the example. To clean up this file with HTML Tidy, enter the following code at the command prompt:

```
tidy -asxml -m  c:\XHTML\tidy.htm
```

The spaces are important and so is every consonant. What does all that code mean? First, `tidy` identifies the program to use. `-asxml` instructs Tidy to convert the HTML document to XHTML. `-m` tells the program to modify the document in its current location, and `c:\XHTML\tidy.htm` is the location of the messy document to be converted.

After you enter this line and press Enter, the next time your open your document (tidy.html), you'll find an XHTML document instead. The resulting code is shown in Example 4.4.

Example 4.4   **The Result of Running the Code in Example 4.3 Through HTML Tidy**

```
<?xml version="1.0"?>
<!DOCTYPE html PUBLIC "-//W3C//DTD XHTML 1.0 Strict//EN"
    "http://www.w3.org/TR/xhtml1/DTD/xhtml1-strict.dtd">
<html xmlns="http://www.w3.org/1999/xhtml">
<head>
<meta name="generator" content="HTML Tidy, see www.w3.org" />
<title>Sloppy Code at Play</title>
</head>
<body>
<h1> HTML Document with Mistakes</h1>
<p>This document does not adhere to XHTML rules.</p>
<p>Take a second to see all the mistakes.</p>
<ul>
  <li>All element names are not lowercase.</li>
  <li>Many elements do not contain the required closing tags.</li>
  <li>The XHTML namespace is not used.</li>
  <li>The document is missing some required elements.</li>
  <li>The document lacks the required DOCTYPE declaration.</li>
</ul>

</body>
</html>
```

If you want to, save the XHTML document in a separate location to keep the HTML document intact.

You can also personalize the experience and affect only one conversion rule (for example, convert all element names to lowercase), leaving the other XHTML rules alone. Both of these cases, as well as many more, have been taken into consideration. All it takes to perform these tasks is a different code word or two. For a complete listing of commands to work with, see `www.w3.org/People/Raggett/tidy/#help`.

HTML Tidy Online

If you're like many people, you might want to avoid the whole DOS experience. For those of us who are addicted to the Web, WebReview has published a Web-friendly version of HTML Tidy that has an easy-to-use interface. All you have to do is type the URL for the HTML Web page that you want converted and click a button. The new XHTML page is displayed for you online. Keep in mind that when the new page is displayed, you have to select File, Save to save it to your computer. To view the code before saving it, you can always view the source code (View, Source). View the HTML Tidy, Web-friendly front end at `www.webreview.com/1999/07/16/feature/xhtml.cgi`.

TidyGUI

For those of us who don't enjoy a DOS-dominated interface and feel more comfortable doing the conversion on our own machines, André Blavier has created a Windows interface for HTML Tidy. TidyGUI provides all the options of HTML Tidy, with all the ease of a Windows interface that you can customize. For a snapshot of this new Tidy facelift, see Figure 4.2. Enter the desired file to be converted into the field titled, Source File, and then select the Tidy button. If you want to customize the conversion process, select the Configuration button and make any changes you like. It is that easy!

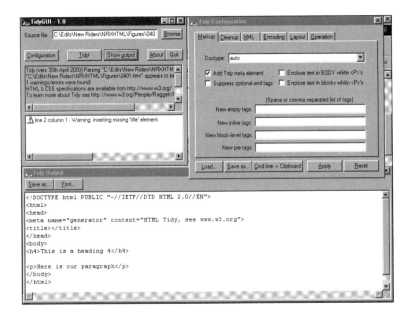

Figure 4.2   The three windows of the TidyGUI utility.

For More Information

By no means does the buck stop here. The W3C is already working the next generation of XHTML and there are some anticipated changes on the horizon (see Chapter 13, "Where the Future Leads, XHTML Follows," for a complete breakdown of the next version of XHTML). In addition, we expect that additional tools will be introduced as the demand for HTML to XHTML conversion increases. To keep up to date on both manual and automated conversion techniques, keep an eye on the following Web sites:

- `http://wdvl.com/Authoring/Languages/XML/XHTML/`
- `www.hwg.org/opcenter/gutenberg/markupXHTML.html`
- `www.xhtml.org/`
- `www.w3.org/MarkUp/Activity.html`
- `www.xmlsoftware.com`

5

Working with Web Development Tools

IN THIS CHAPTER, YOU FIND OUT WHICH TOOLS you can use to help you create new XHTML documents and convert existing HTML documents to XHTML.

Dancing on the Bleeding Edge

There are many tools to choose from if you want to create an HTML document. Because XHTML is relatively new to the scene, it's definitely a bleeding-edge technology. Therefore, there aren't a lot of tools available to help you create or convert your XHTML documents; so you'll probably spend a lot of time looking for XHTML tools. For the most part, you'll have to use an HTML editor, such as Dreamweaver; or an XML editor, such as XMetal. However, we've done the dirty work and found a couple tools you can use to help you with you XHMTL documents.

What does this mean for you as a developer? Well, for the time being you have three options:

- Use an XML tool to create your XHTML documents. This means that WYSI-WYG is out of the question. XML editors will make sure that your document is well formed (follows all of XML's syntax rules), but they won't support the XHTML vocabulary. According to an XML editor, the `title` element is the same thing as a `tightrope` element. All it recognizes is that both are indeed elements.

- Use an HTML editor and then run your document through HTML Tidy. There are a few HTML editors on the market that will create fairly clean markup. When we say clean, we mean that they follow HTML syntax standards well. But, because XHTML follows XML's syntax standards, there are a few changes that will need to be made to every document. HTML-Kit is a tool that will take a clean (or messy) HTML document and convert it to XHTML in the matter of seconds. This is most likely the way most Web developers will go.
- Use an XHTML editor. As of the writing of this book (October 2000), there's only one pure XHTML editor: Mozquito.

As you can see, XHTML editors are sparse. But, that does not mean that you have to wait for the tool developers to catch up. Just because XHTML is on the bleeding edge, doesn't mean you are!

Who's Hip to XHTML?

As mentioned in the previous section "Dancing on the Bleeding Edge," you're likely to discover that there aren't that many editors that support XHTML. Therefore, you just might have to use an XML editor to get the job done—after all, XHTML is XML. What does this mean for you? It means that you aren't going to find a program that has a predefined HTML vocabulary that you can use in a WYSIWYG environment. No, you're going to have to code a lot of your pages by hand.

There is one way around this conundrum. You can create your pages in Dreamweaver, or your editor of choice, and then use HTML-Kit to convert those pages to well-formed and valid XHTML.

But first, we're going to show you the easy way. One company is ahead of everyone else and already has an XHTML tool for you: the company, Mozquito Technologies; the product, Mozquito Factory.

In addition to covering Mozquito, a true XHTML editor, we will show you how to create that page in Dreamweaver and then convert it with HTML-Kit.

Moving with Mozquito

Mozquito has cornered the XHTML-authoring market. Mozquito is one of the only commercial XHTML editors available, and creating XHTML documents is a breeze with this product.

Installing

You can download Mozquito at www.mozquito.com. Note that a Java Runtime Environment (JRE) is required for Mozquito. Mozquito supports Windows, MacOS, and Linux/UNIX platforms. Some additional information for the platforms follows:

- **Windows.** A JRE from Microsoft is installed automatically when you install Internet Explorer 5. However, the folks at Mozquito recommend downloading and installing the JRE 1.1.7 or higher from either IBM at www6.software.ibm.com/dl/dkw/dkre-p or Sun Microsystems at http://java.sun.com/products/jdk/1.1/jre/download-jre-windows.html.

- **MacOS.** Mozquito for Mac runs with MacOS Runtime for Java (MRJ) 2.1.4 or higher. MRJ should already be installed on your system; but if you need to download it, you can find it at www.apple.com/java.

- **Linux/UNIX.** There are no additional requirements for the Linux/UNIX platform.

After you download Mozquito and open the program for the first time, you see the window displayed in Figure 5.1.

Figure 5.1 What you see the first time you launch Mozquito.

From that window, you have the options to launch a tutorial reference guide or close (select OK) the Help window. We recommend that you take a trip through the tutorial before jumping in; but because the Mozquito interface is so easy, the tutorial is not absolutely necessary.

Creating Your First Document

To create your first XHTML document with Mozquito, select File, New. At this time, you're asked to choose from a list of four different document types:

- XHTML Transitional
- XHTML Frameset
- XHTML Strict
- XHTML-FML

We don't cover XHTML-FML 1.0 because that is Mozquito's proprietary Forms Markup Language (FML). Note that XForms is partially based on Mozquito's FML work. See Chapter 8, "Understanding XForms," for more information on XForms.

The other three types of XHTML refer to the flavors of DTDs to which your document will adhere. For a refresher on the various flavors of DTDs, see Chapter 2, "All About Markup."

In this example, we choose XHTML Transitional. Lucky for us, when you choose the transitional DTD—or any of the other three choices—you're automatically presented with the building blocks of a well-formed XHTML document, as you can see in Figure 5.2.

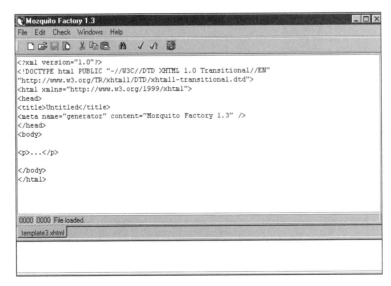

Figure 5.2 Mozquito opens a page with everything from the XML declaration to the XHTML namespace.

The document that comes up is a template document that is precoded with the appropriate document type declaration, namespace, and XML declaration. It even includes the head and body elements. This saves you from having to type this information every time you create a new document.

The wonderful thing about Mozquito is that it checks for well formedness and validity. Although this new document contains no data (that is, content), we can still check for validity by clicking on the two check marks in the toolbar. The first check mark checks for well formedness alone, and the second check mark checks for well formedness and validity.

Note that if you're in a hurry, you can always use keyword commands and select Ctrl+w to check for well formedness and Ctrl+t to check for both well formedness and validity.

After you click one of the check marks, text appears in the message dialog window at the bottom that informs you whether your document has passed the test and is indeed well formed and valid (see Figure 5.3).

What do you do if your document isn't well formed and/or valid? If you've already downloaded the software and are following along, go ahead and remove one of the closing tags from your document (the </body> closing tag, for example). Now when you check for well formedness and validity, you see that Mozquito correctly identifies that the </body> closing tag is missing. From there, you can double-click the error message and your mouse pointer is taken directly to the error in your document. Talk about time saving! No more searching your markup for that one little mistake.

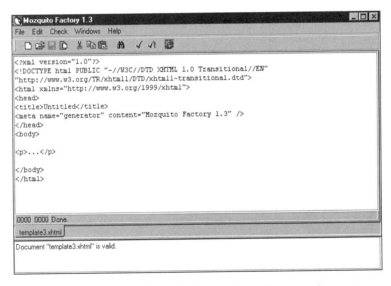

Figure 5.3   The dialog box at the bottom signs off on your document.

Note that Mozquito documents must be well formed, but they don't have to be valid. However, we recommend that you adhere to validity constraints as well.

If you take the time to play with Mozquito, you'll realize that the product interface is easy. Each of the toolbar icons looks and feels like you're looking at your favorite word processing program. The toolbar consists of the following icons:

 • Opens a new file

 • Opens a preexisting file

 • Saves your file

 • Generates and exports an XHTML-FML document as an HTML file with the Mozquito engine

 • Cuts the selected text

 • Copies the selected text

 • Pastes the selected text

 • Triggers the Find and Replace dialog box

 • Checks for well formedness

 • Checks for well formedness and validity

 • Opens the file in your default browser (Note that the icon will differ according to your default browser.)

Everything on the toolbar is what you expect, right? The menu options are familiar as well, but there are some that might look a little new (look at the top of Figure 5.1, 5.2, or 5.3 to see the menu bar).

The menu bar contains much of the same functionality as the icons described in the previous list:

- **File.** Contains all the options you would expect: New, Open, Save, Save As, Export, Close, Close All, Print, and Quit.

- **Edit.** Contains the Cut- and Paste-related options, as well as Find and Replace options.

- **Check.** Checks for wellformedness and validity, as well as enables you to preview your document in your default browser.

- **Window.** Enables you to toggle between open documents.

- **Help.** Provides you with information about the program and version number, as well as access to Help files.

For all Macintosh and Linux/UNIX users, the menu bar is a little different on these platforms. But the options are the same.

When you're ready to save your document, you have to save it with an .xhtml extension. If you want to use your XHTML document on your Web site and are worried about backward compatibility, you can select File, Export to export your document with an .html or .htm extension.

To read more about working with Mozquito, go to their Web site at `www.mozquito.com`.

What We Found

If you want to create a new XHTML document, Mozquito is the way to go. It saves time and checks your document for errors (that by itself is worth its weight in gold). It's the only editor that is solely dedicated to XHTML.

However, if you have older HTML documents that need to be converted, try HTML-Kit instead. When we used a large—and syntactically challenged—document in Mozquito, and then checked it for well-formedness, Mozquito began to process and list our errors at the bottom of the dialog box. But before it could finish, Mozquito displayed the words "too many errors!" To make matters more challenging, Mozquito refused to open our large HTML document because it had an .htm extension, and Mozquito wants documents to have a .xhtml extension.

But, as far as drawbacks go, those were the only ones we could find. Mozquito has a very easy-to-use interface and offers only the necessary functionality that an editor needs—no fluff here.

You can download a 30-day trial version of Mozquito Factory at `https://www.stackoverflow.com/download.html` (which is what we used for our examples) or you can purchase it for $149 at `https://www.stackoverflow.com /purchase.html`.

This software, as all products mentioned in this chapter, comes highly recommended for those who are out to change the face of the Web with XHTML.

Working with Dreamweaver 3

We must start by saying that Dreamweaver 3 does not inherently support XHTML. What it does is create clean HTML, and that gets you pretty close to XHTML. After you create an HTML document with Dreamweaver, the only thing left to do is convert that page to XHTML with HTML-Kit. But first, you need to download and install Dreamweaver.

Installing

Dreamweaver is easy to install. You can purchase the product online and download it straight for Macromedia, or you can order the product, and have the CD (and manuals) delivered to your doorstep. You can also download a 30-day evaluation copy of Dreamweaver. (More about the cost and URLs to download the product in the "What We Found" section at the end of this chapter.) Either way you decide to do it, the process is simple and easy.

Whether you're working in a Windows or MacOS environment, the download process is basically the same. If you decide to download the product from Macromedia, they provide quick-and-easy instructions to guide you through the process. We help you out a little by providing these steps to the installation process:

1. After you begin the download process, a Save As window appears. At this time, save the file to your desktop by choosing Desktop from the pull-down menu.

2. After the file is downloaded, you see a product download icon somewhere on your desktop. To begin downloading Dreamweaver, double-click the product download icon to launch the Preview Download Manager.

3. This triggers the downloading process. Follow the windows and when the download process is complete, you see a "Thank You for Your Purchase" message.

4. Click the Launch button to trigger the installation process.

5. Again, follow the instructions.

6. You're prompted to enter the serial number that is provided in an email sent to you when you purchase the product.

This means that if you're completing this process all at once (instead of registering later), you need to check your email right after you complete your purchase.

We know this sounds like a long process, but it only takes a matter of minutes. After you've downloaded and installed Dreamweaver, you're ready to create your first clean HTML document.

Creating Your First HTML Document

Dreamweaver can do a lot. Truly, there's almost nothing that this little program can't do. The first time you open the program, you see a blank window with a white background.

Remember, Dreamweaver is a WYSIWYG editor. You don't have to see any of the markup if you don't want to. But take a second to look at the source code Dreamweaver starts with; select Window, HTML Source. Figure 5.4 shows this source code.

Now, you can either add your text to the source code directly or you can close that window and use the WYSIWYG interface. The following example uses a little bit of both:

1. With the HTML Source window still open, type a title for your document in between the title tags. We're going to type My Document.

2. Close the HTML Source window and type a heading for your document.

3. Highlight the text and choose Text, Format, Heading 1.

4. Press Enter and select Text, Format, Paragraph and type the body of your document.

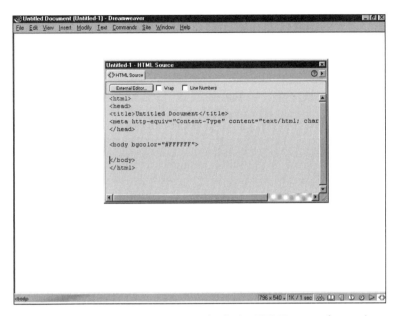

Figure 5.4 In Dreamweaver, you can view and edit the HTML source for any document.

5. Choose File, Save As and type `testdoc.htm`. Figure 5.5 shows our example.

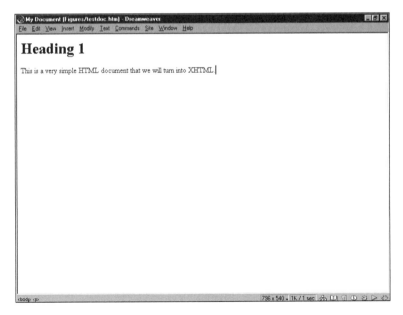

Figure 5.5 Our HTML document.

You see that the title of the document appears at the top of the Dreamweaver window along with the path and filename of your document. For our purposes, this is all we're going to do now.

Dreamweaver has so many capabilities and functions that we could write an entire book about them. For more information on Dreamweaver's capabilities, visit the Macromedia Dreamweaver site at `www.macromedia.com/software/dreamweaver/`. We suggest you take the feature tour to get the full effect.

What We Found

If you want to use a WYSIWYG editor, we highly recommend Dreamweaver. It produces the cleanest code we can find and its interface is easy to navigate. The many benefits of Dreamweaver—too many to list in this chapter—allow you to create dynamic and exciting pages with ease.

With all that said, remember that the current version of Dreamweaver does not create XHTML. If you're interested in creating well-formed and valid XHTML documents, you'll have to convert your pages with a tool (HTML-Kit, which we cover next) or by hand. See the step-by-step example in Chapter 4, "Converting HTML to XHTML," for an example of converting your pages by hand.

You can download the trial version of Dreamweaver from the Macromedia site at `www.macromedia.com/software/dreamweaver/trial/` or you can purchase it for $299 from `www.macromedia.com/software/dreamweaver/download/`. The price may seem a little steep, but it's worth it.

Using HTML-Kit

HTML-Kit doesn't have the sleekest package, but it gets the job done—and for free! HTML-Kit is created by the brightest minds in the Web business. You can use HTML-Kit to fix and create your HTML, XML, and XHTML documents. It comes with HTML Tidy, which is the part of the program that allows you to create such a variety of documents. HTML-Kit is available for Windows 95, 98, NT, ME, and 2000. So, enough of the hype, let's get down to business.

Installing

You download HTML-Kit from `www.chami.com/html-kit/`. It's as easy as every other download on the Internet these days. You find the download link, click it, pick the desired download site, and you're off. Here are the steps to install HTML-Kit:

1. You download the proper EXE file, save it to your desktop or hard drive, and then double-click it.
2. A dialog box appears that asks if you want to install HTML-Kit. Click Yes.
3. After it puts a bunch of files on your system, the Setup screen appears and takes you through the usual: accepting the license, picking a location, and so on.

4. Then, you get the Setup Complete screen that asks if you want to view the Readme file and launch the program. Go ahead and launch the program.

5. It asks if you want to download links to Internet help files. We're going to choose Yes. You can always change this later in the preferences.

6. Next, you can choose whether you want HTML-Kit to associate HTML files with the program. Make your choice.

7. Now you're asked if you want HTML-Kit to check for new versions of the program.

That's it for the installation. You're presented with the Open File Wizard (covered in the next section).

Converting Your HTML Document to an XHTML Document

So, you've installed HTML-Kit and you're ready to go. You should see the Open File Wizard shown in Figure 5.6. Instead of showing you how to create a new document in HTML-Kit, we're going to convert the document you created in Dreamweaver (refer to the section, "Creating Your First HTML Document") to a valid XHTML document. Follow these steps:

1. Choose the Open Existing File radio button and find the document you created in Dreamweaver titled testdoc.htm. Click Open. You should see something similar to Figure 5.7.

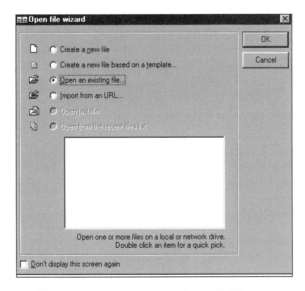

Figure 5.6 The HTML-Kit Open File Wizard

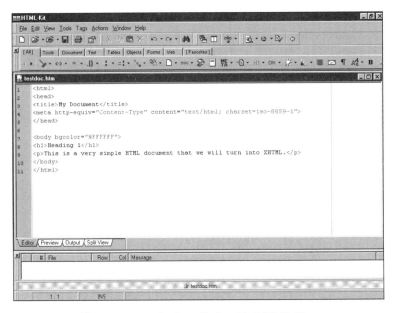

Figure 5.7 testdoc.htm displayed in HTML-Kit.

2. As you can see, this is still just a "plain-Jane" HTML document. To convert it to XHTML, choose Actions, Tools, HTML Tidy, Convert to XHTML.

3. Now your screen should look like Figure 5.8. Notice that on the right side of the screen, you have a well-formed XHTML document! Also look at the bottom of the screen. You should see some messages regarding your document. If there were any errors, they would be listed here.

4. Now, to save the new document as your own, just right-click the right side of the screen and select Copy All to Editor from the pop-up menu. The contents from the right side are transferred to the left side and you now have a well-formed XHTML document.

5. Switch to the Editor tab, make any changes you need to, and choose File, Save. That's it. Your HTML document is now a well-formed XHTML document.

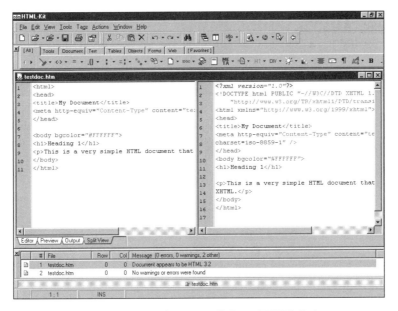

Figure 5.8   HTML-Kit displaying a well-formed XHTML document.

Again, the features of this program are numerous. See `www.chami.com/html-kit/` `#features` for more information.

What We Found

We found that HTML-Kit is one of the best, not to mention cheapest (free), utilities out there for converting your HTML documents to well-formed XHTML. It's not the best interface to use for document creation, which is why we suggest that you create your documents in Dreamweaver and convert them using HTML-Kit. Using these two tools together, you really can't go wrong. Again, you can download HTML-Kit from `www.chami.com/html-kit/`.

Note: You might be one of those people who have an affinity for the command line. If you want (or need) to use the DOS command prompt, HTML Tidy (the HTML to XHTML conversion tool that is a part of HTML Kit) is available as a Windows 95/98/NT/2000 executable. Be sure to read all the documentation before diving in. You can read more and download a copy of this program at `www.w3.org/` `People/Raggett/tidy/`.

Other Tools, Other Rules

We've detailed just a few of the tools you can use to create your XHTML pages, but that doesn't mean that the toolbox must stop here. XML tools can also help you create any XHTML document. Therefore, in theory, you could use almost any XML tool on the market to create your XHTML document. For a complete listing of other XML editors to choose from, visit `www.xmlsoftware.com`.

As for XHTML (and HTML) editors, keep your eyes peeled. We have heard rumors that several HTML editors plan to release future generations with XHTML support. That is the next logical step, and we doubt any tool developers want to get left behind.

For More Information

As always, there's a wealth of information available on the Web. Always check HTML authoring-tool vendor sites regularly to see if they've updated their support to include XHTML. The following list details the Web sites of the tools covered in this chapter:

- **Mozquito.** `www.mozquito.com`
- **Dreamweaver.** `www.macromedia.com/software/dreamweaver/`
- **HTML-Kit.** `www.chami.com/html-kit/`

6

Adding Style with CSS

In THIS CHAPTER, YOU FIND OUT ABOUT THE FIRST METHOD you can use to add style to your XHTML pages: *Cascading Style Sheets* (CSS). You find out why you should use CSS, learn about the different versions of CSS available, and finally, learn the basics of CSS to get you started.

Why Use CSS?

If you're familiar with XHTML elements, then you probably know that those same elements can add style to your Web pages. However, there's another way you can add style to your Web pages: Cascading Style Sheets. Currently, most of the Web pages depend on HTML for their formatting needs instead of using CSS. Using CSS will do more than make your life easier. Using CSS for style capitalizes on the benefits of separating form from function.

To begin with, HTML was not designed to create the graphical monsters you currently find on the Web. Figure 6.1 shows a fictitious Web page styled with HTML. The markup used to produce it is shown in Example 6.1 (The formatting elements are bolded so that you can see them easily.) Example 6.2 demonstrates how fewer lines of style markup can achieve the same results.

Figure 6.1   This Web page can be created with markup from Example 6.1 or 6.2.

Example 6.1   **The Formatting Elements Are Everywhere, Making the Markup Hard to Follow**

```
<?xml version="1.0"?>
<!DOCTYPE html
     PUBLIC "-//W3C//DTD XHTML 1.0 Transitional//EN"
     "http://www.w3.org/TR/xhtml1/DTD/xhtml1-transitional.dtd">
<html xmlns="http://www.w3.org/1999/xhtml">
  <head>
    <title>
      Untitled Document
    </title>
  </head>
  <body bgcolor="#FFFFFF">
    <table border="0" cellpadding="7" cellspacing="0" width="78%">
      <tr>
        <td align="justify" colspan="3" valign="top" bgcolor="#000066">
          <p>
            <font color="#FFFFFF" size="7" face="Helvetica, sans-serif,
            Arial">mymovies.com</font>
          </p>
        </td>
      </tr>
        <tr>
```

```
<td rowspan="4" valign="top" bgcolor="#000066" width="20%">
  <p>
    <b><font face="Helvetica, sans-serif, Arial" color="#FFFFFF">Quotes
    from:</font></b>
  </p>
  <p>
    <a href="airplane.htm"><font color="#FFFFFF" face="Helvetica, sans-
    serif, Arial">Airplane!</font></a>
  </p>
  <p>
    <a href="thejerk.htm"><font color="#FFFFFF" face="Helvetica, sans-
    serif, Arial">The Jerk</font></a>
  </p>
  <p>
    <a href="monty.htm"><font color="#FFFFFF" face="Helvetica, sans-
    serif, Arial">Monty Python and the Holy Grail</font></a>
  </p>
  <p>
    <a href="revenge.htm"><font color="#FFFFFF" face="Helvetica, sans-
    serif, Arial">Revenge of the Nerds</font></a>
  </p>
  <p>
    <a href="crazy.htm"><font color="#FFFFFF" face="Helvetica, sans-
    serif, Arial">The Gods Must Be Crazy</font></a>
  </p>
  <p>
    <a href="mary.htm"><font color="#FFFFFF" face="Helvetica, sans-
    serif, Arial">There Is Something About Mary</font></a>
  </p>
  <p>
    <a href="texas.htm"><font color="#FFFFFF" face="Helvetica, sans-
    serif, Arial">Happy Texas</font></a>
  </p>
</td>
<td colspan="2" valign="top">
  <p>
    <b><font color="#ff0000" face="Helvetica, sans-serif, Arial"
    size="3">Quote of the Day</font></b>
  </p>
  <p>
    <b>Elaine Dickinson</b>: You got a telegram from headquarters
    today.
  </p>
  <p>
    <b>Ted Striker</b>: Headquarters—what is it?
  </p>
  <p>
    <b>Elaine Dickinson</b>: Well, it&#39;s a big building where
    generals meet, but that&#39;s not important right now.
  </p>
</td>
```

continues

Example 6.1 **Continued**

```
      </tr>
      <tr>
        <td colspan="2" valign="top" height="61">
          <b><font face="Helvetica, sans-serif, Arial">Upcoming
          Movies</font></b><br />
           <a href="roadtrip.htm">Road Trip</a><br />
           <a href="upcoming-movies.htm"><b>More Movies. . .</b></a>
        </td>
      </tr>
      <tr>
        <td colspan="2" valign="top" height="73">
          <b><font face="Helvetica, sans-serif, Arial">Columns</font></b><br />
          <a href="column1.htm">Quotes That Keep You Laughing</a><br />
           <a href="columns.htm"><b>More Columns. . .</b></a>
        </td>
      </tr>
      <tr>
        <td valign="top" colspan="2">
          <b><font face="Helvetica, sans-serif, Arial">Movie Review
          Archive</font></b><br />
          <a href="texas.htm">Happy Texas</a><br />
          <a href="mary.htm">There Is Something About Mary</a><br />
           <a href="review-archive.htm"><b>More Reviews. . .</b></a>
        </td>
      </tr>
    </table>
  </body>
</html>
```

Example 6.2 **Replacing Most of the Formatting Elements with CSS Separates Form from Function**

```
<?xml version="1.0"?>
<!DOCTYPE html
    PUBLIC "-//W3C//DTD XHTML 1.0 Transitional//EN"
    "http://www.w3.org/TR/xhtml1/DTD/xhtml1-transitional.dtd">
<html xmlns="http://www.w3.org/1999/xhtml">
  <head>
    <title>
      My Movie Page
    </title>
    <style type="text/css">
     body {background-color:#FFFFFF}
     .logo {color:#FFFFFF;font-size:46pt;font-family:helvetica, sans-serif,
```

```
          arial;}
          .heading1,.link {color:#FFFFFF;font-family:helvetica, sans-serif, arial;}
          .heading2 {color:#FF0000;font-family:helvetica, sans-serif, arial;font-
          weight:bold;}
          .heading3 {font-family:helvetica, sans-serif, arial;font-weight:bold;}
          .blue {background-color:#000066;}
        </style>
</head>
  <body>
     <table border="0" cellpadding="7" cellspacing="0" width="78%">
       <tr>
         <td align="justify" colspan="3" valign="top" class="blue">
           <p>
              <span class="logo">mymovies.com</span>
           </p>
         </td>
       </tr>
         <tr>
           <td rowspan="4" valign="top" width="20%" class="blue">
             <p>
                <span class="heading1">Quotes from:</span>
             </p>
             <p>
                <a href="airplane.htm" class="link">Airplane!</a>
             </p>
             <p>
                <a href="thejerk.htm" class="link">The Jerk</a>
             </p>
             <p>
                <a href="monty.htm" class="link">Monty Python and the Holy
                Grail</a>
             </p>
             <p>
                <a href="revenge.htm" class="link">Revenge of the Nerds</a>
                </p>
             <p>
                <a href="crazy.htm" class="link">The Gods Must Be Crazy</a>
                </p>
             <p>
                <a href="mary.htm" class="link">There Is Something About Mary</a>
                </p>
             <p>
                <a href="texas.htm" class="link">Happy Texas</a>
             </p>
           </td>
           <td colspan="2" valign="top">
```

continues

Example 6.2 **Continued**

```
<p>
    <span class="heading2">Quote of the Day</span>
</p>
<p>
    <b>Elaine Dickinson</b>: You got a telegram from headquarters
    today.
</p>
<p>
    <b>Ted Striker</b>: Headquarters—what is it?
</p>
<p>
    <b>Elaine Dickinson</b>: Well, it&#39;s a big building where
    generals meet, but that&#39;s not important right now.
</p>
    </td>
</tr>
<tr>
  <td colspan="2" valign="top" height="61">
    <span class="heading3">Upcoming Movies</span><br />
    <a href="roadtrip.htm">Road Trip</a><br />
    <a href="upcoming-movies.htm"><b>More Movies. . .</b></a>
  </td>
</tr>
<tr>
  <td colspan="2" valign="top" height="73">
    <span class="heading3">Columns</span><br />
    <a href="column1.htm">Quotes That Keep You Laughing</a><br />
    <a href="columns.htm"><b>More Columns. . .</b></a>
  </td>
</tr>
<tr>
  <td valign="top" colspan="2">
    <span class="heading3">Movie Review Archive</span><br />
    <a href="texas.htm">Happy Texas</a><br />
    <a href="mary.htm">There Is Something About Mary</a><br />
    <a href="review-archive.htm"><b>More Reviews. . .</b></a>
  </td>
</tr>
    </table>
  </body>
</html>
```

In the beginning, HTML was a simple markup language that didn't include formatting elements. Instead, the language focused on structure. This did not last long.

Soon after HTML was introduced, developers began cooking up ways to manipulate Web-page display. Nothing fancy, just a few elements here and there to format text. Over time, developers found that the easiest way to add formatting features to HTML was to expand the element set. With each generation of HTML, developers introduced an increasing number of elements dedicated to style. However, an element set can expand only so far. Finally, in 1998, the W3C decided enough is enough.

CSS enables HTML (and hence XHTML) to get back to its original goal: content. By separating content from display, CSS creates a whole new way to make developers' lives easier. Therefore, you should become familiar with using XHTML to describe your data (and what it means) and using a style sheet to control display. Another good reason to use style sheets to control display is that the next generation of XHTML (1.1) will eliminate many of the formatting elements.

Separating Style from Content

Most veteran Web gurus—and we use that in the loosest sense—are used to thinking of style as content. Because of browser-compatibility issues, many Web developers use HTML style elements to render the style of their documents. However, with the introduction of XML (the parent, metalanguage of XHTML), describing data becomes the sole function and display is left to style sheets. This is not to say that form is not important. But the separation of form and content is essential. Keeping the two separate enables developers to tightly control their Web pages.

Readability

It's easier to maintain your Web site when you use style sheets. The most common scenario is that you, as a Web developer, have an unwieldy Web site to maintain. When this happens, the simplicity and readability of your style sheets always help—design notes don't hurt either.

Separating form from function enables pages to do what they were meant to do, deal with the content. Less markup means less confusion for the author, not to mention the next Web developer that comes along to help maintain that page.

Write Once

The same style sheet can be used to format multiple XHTML documents. (*Translation*: less time spent typing.) Not only do you save time by using one style sheet to drive the style of your entire Web site, but you also standardize the look and feel of your Web site (one of the primary design goals for most developers).

The idea of writing once can be seen another way. If you create an XHTML document, you can then apply multiple style sheets to provide formatting for various outputs. This comes in handy when you have to create a Web page that can be viewed on the Web, printed from the Web, and displayed on unconventional platforms (such as most handheld devices). In this case, you would create one XHTML document and associate three different style sheets tailored for the different outputs. Again, this saves time because the content is centralized in one document.

Either way, you save some time and improve the consistency and efficiency of your Web site.

CSS for Today

Until recently, the future did not appear bright for CSS supporters. However, it seems that browsers are finally making the move toward creating standard, compliant browsers, which means that CSS support is just around the corner.

But this is not the case yet. If you create Web pages for the public at large, you're undoubtedly forced to create pages that render correctly in both Netscape Navigator and Microsoft Internet Explorer. As some of you may know, this is not a small task.

CSS1 or CSS2?

The CSS standard is currently in its second generation. The 1 and 2 trailings of the CSS acronym stand for level 1 and level 2, respectively. CSS2 adds functionality that is not available with CSS1. (Note that CSS3 is a "work in progress"; in other words, it's only in the Working Draft stage. Go to `www.w3.org/Style/CSS/current-work` to keep up with the current CSS happenings.)

In the beginning, CSS1 covered basic formatting. Much of what is covered in this chapter comes from the CSS1 standard. This chapter focuses on the building blocks of CSS to help you understand how to create style sheets and why you should be doing just that.

When CSS2 was introduced, so were some welcome additions to the CSS property family. The main strides were in the ideas of absolute positioning and output. CSS2 is not a complete departure from CSS1, but rather a welcomed addition. The following is a list of some of the new aspects brought to the CSS standard by CSS2:

- **Media types.** CSS2 enables authors to tailor their output to various mediums, such as print or handheld devices.

- **Printing options.** CSS2 enables authors to define extensive formatting for printed documents.

- **Generate content.** CSS2 enables authors to introduce content to the document.

- **Positioning.** CSS2 enables authors to define exactly where element content should appear on the page, using x and y coordinates.

Browser Compatibility

Ever since CSS hit the market, Web developers have been poised and ready to let style sheets guide their Web sites. You too may be hoping to make the switch as soon as possible. CSS support in most major browsers has not been as good as many of us hoped. As a matter of fact, browser vendors only released browsers that fully support CSS1 in mid-2000.

However, this book assumes that you cannot wait for the browsers to catch up to the CSS2 specification. If you're creating Web pages today and need a handy guide to individual property browser support, you should see Eric Meyer's CSS Master List, which is found at the Webreview.com Web site at `http://webreview.com/pub/guides/style/style.html`.

Editors

You may not have time to learn every CSS property, and with that in mind, it's time to introduce some of the finest CSS editors:

- **Amaya**—`www.w3.org`. This editor can do almost anything you want. Created by the W3C, it supports most standards and is used for testing purposes at the W3C. Amaya is not just an XML editor; it's also a browser.

- **Mozquito**—`www.mozquito.com`. As the first commercial XHTML editor on the market, it has won the heart of many Web developers. It too supports CSS. For a more detailed look at Mozquito, see Chapter 5, "Working with Web Development Tools."

- **XMetaL**—`www.softquad.com`. XMetaL is actually an XML editor that supports CSS. However, because XHTML is XML, it also creates XHTML pages. One word of warning, however, it's not designed solely for XHTML. Therefore, if you're not familiar with XML, you might want to try one of the other editors listed.

- **Dreamweaver**—`www.macromedia.com`. Although the current version of Dreamweaver does not support XHTML explicitly, it does create clean HTML. After a couple of manual tweaks, that HTML is ready for the XHTML name. Dreamweaver provides excellent support for CSS with an easy-to-use interface.

CSS Basics

Creating style rules to format your Web pages is quite simple. In the following sections, we show you how to create style rules for your Web pages.

Syntax

Creating CSS syntax is easy and easy to understand. A style sheet is a collection of style rules. Before we show you how to create style rules, we should start by examining a very minimal XHTML document (see Example 6.3).

Example 6.3 **A Very Minimal XHTML Document**

```
<?xml version="1.0"?>
<!DOCTYPE html
     PUBLIC "-//W3C//DTD XHTML 1.0 Strict//EN"
     "http://www.w3.org/TR/xhtml1/DTD/xhtml1-strict.dtd">
<html xmlns="http://www.w3.org/1999/xhtml" xml:lang="en" lang="en">
  <head>
    <title>A Minimal XHTML Document</title>
  </head>
  <body>
    <p>The first and only sentence in our very MINIMAL document</p>
  </body>
</html>
```

Figure 6.2 shows how our minimal document would be viewed in Internet Explorer 5. But what if you want to change the text color to red? There are two ways you can achieve it.

Figure 6.2 A minimal document with no style information attached.

The first way—also the *wrong way*—to change the font color is to use XHTML formatting elements, namely the `font` element with the `color` attribute. But beware: The next generation of XHTML eliminates the `font` element. In other words, if you format your page with the `font` element and attributes, your page will soon be obsolete.

The second way—also the one of the *correct ways*—to change the text color is to use a CSS style rule. To do this, all you need is this tiny string of text:

```
p { color:red }
```

Note that the whitespace before `color` and after `red` is optional. We use whitespace to increase human readability; a processor, however, doesn't care.

The previous piece of markup is called a style rule. A *style rule* is comprised of a selector (most commonly an element name) and its declaration. The style rule tells the processor how to format a given element. You'll also hear style rules referred to as *instructions* or *statements*.

The first piece of a style rule is the selector. In our example, `p` is the selector. The *selector* identifies an XHTML element, and the processor uses this information to attach formatting. Selectors are case sensitive, which makes sense because CSS is designed to work with XML, where case is an issue as well. There are several classifications of selectors, which are covered in the following sections.

The declaration is everything between the { and }. In our example, { `color:red` } is the declaration. A *declaration* consists of a property, followed by a colon (:), followed by a value. In this case, `color` is the property and `red` if the given value. A *property* can be one of 104 predefined keywords, each one representing formatting for a given element(s). Different properties can take different values. Most values fall within one of the following main categories:

- Length
- Percentage
- Color
- URL
- Keyword

We discuss these categories in the following sections.

Which Properties Are Supported?

CSS2—the second generation of CSS—boasts 104 properties to choose from. (CSS1 allowed for about 50.) Even though an author has 104 properties to choose from, most browsers only support about 70 of them. To see a chart outlining property-specific browser compatibility, visit Webreview's Master Compatibility Chart at `http://webreview.com/wr/pub/guides/style/mastergrid.html`.

In addition, you'll notice various punctuation marks within style declarations. They have the following meanings:

- **Period (.).** Used as part of a selector to identify context
- **Comma (,).** Used a connector to separate selectors when grouping them in one style rule
- **Semicolon (;).** Used as part of the declaration to signal the end of the declaration and to separate multiple declarations in a style rule
- **Colon (:).** Used as part of the declaration to separate a property from its value

That's all there is to it—sort of. After all, a style sheet is only a collection of style rules. After you master the art of style-rule creation, you're ready to add style to all your XHTML Web pages. In the following sections, we take a closer look at creating style rules.

Class and ID Selectors

What if you wanted to create a specific style rule that applies only to a few instances of a specific element types? For example, we created an XHTML file that contains multiple instances of the p element. Half of the p elements contain descriptions, and the other half of the p elements contain URLs. For this Web page, we want set off the URLs with a gray box. Before adding CSS, our markup is as shown in Example 6.4.

Example 6.4 **Markup That Shows Multiple Instances of the *p* Element Before Implementing CSS**

```
<?xml version="1.0"?>
<!DOCTYPE html
    PUBLIC "-//W3C//DTD XHTML 1.0 Strict//EN"
    "http://www.w3.org/TR/xhtml1/DTD/xhtml1-strict.dtd">
<html xmlns="http://www.w3.org/1999/xhtml" xml:lang="en" lang="en">
  <head>
    <title>XHTML Examples</title>
  </head>
  <body>
    <p>
      Webreview's CSS Master List: Lists all aspects of the CSS Specification and
      browser compatability.
    </p>
    <p>
      http://webreview.com/wr/pub/guides/style/mastergrid.html
    </p>
    <p>
      Webreview's CSS2 Selectors Support Chart: Lists browser support for advanced
      CSS2 selectors.
    </p>
    <p>
```

```
        http://webreview.com/pub/guides/style/css2select.html
    </p>
  </body>
</html>
```

To set a style rule for only two of the four p elements, we have to use a class selector.
A *class selector* creates multiple instances of a style rule. This is how a class selector
works.

In 1998, the W3C introduced the HTML 4.0 Specification. The new version of the
specification included the `class` attribute. The `class` attribute is used in XHTML
markup in conjunction with the `class` selector in the CSS style rule. Take a look at
Example 6.5.

Example 6.5   **How to Use the *class* Attribute in the CSS Style Rule**

```
<?xml version="1.0"?>
<!DOCTYPE html
      PUBLIC "-//W3C//DTD XHTML 1.0 Strict//EN"
      "http://www.w3.org/TR/xhtml1/DTD/xhtml1-strict.dtd">
<html xmlns="http://www.w3.org/1999/xhtml" xml:lang="en" lang="en">
  <head>
    <title>XHTML Examples</title>
    <style type="text/css">
      p.url { background-color:gray }
    </style>
  </head>
  <body>
    <p>
      Webreview's CSS Master List: Lists all aspects of the CSS Specification and
      browser compatability.
    </p>
    <p class="url">
      http://webreview.com/wr/pub/guides/style/mastergrid.html
    </p>
    <p>
      Webreview's CSS2 Selectors Support Chart: Lists browser support for advanced
      CSS2 selectors.
    </p>
    <p class="url">
      http://webreview.com/pub/guides/style/css2select.html
    </p>
  </body>
</html>
```

Figure 6.3 shows how the previous markup renders in a browser.

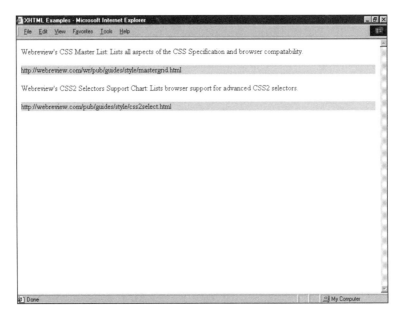

Figure 6.3   Every *p* element with a ***url*** class renders with a gray background.

With the advent of the `class` attribute, authors can use a period and class name to label different classes, as follows:

```
selector.class { property:value }
```

The `selector` is an XHTML element, the `class` is the name of your creation. You follow those by the declaration (remember, that includes the `property` and `value` pair).

Grouping

Style sheets are just collections of style rules. There are many times that you'll want the same formatting to apply to multiple XHTML elements. CSS enables you to create one single rule and then apply that rule to multiple selectors. This function is called *grouping*.

The following is an example that doesn't use grouping:

```
h1 {color:red }
h2 {color:red }
h3 {color:red }
```

However, because CSS supports grouping, you can create one style rule in place of the previous three lines. It looks like this:

```
h1, h2, h3 { color:red }
```

In addition to selectors, declarations can also be grouped, for example:

```
h1 { font-weight : bolder }
h1 { font-size : 12pt }
h1 { font-family : helvetica }
h1 { color : red }
```

The previous markup can be also be written as the following:

```
h1 {
   font-weight : bolder;
   font-size : 12pt;
   font-family : helvetica;
   color : red;
   }
```

As you read through this chapter, you'll notice that most of the examples use grouping. We use grouping because it saves time.

Inheritance

In addition to grouping elements, there's another shortcut you can use. Elements inherit style from their parents, which means that the elements take on the characteristics of their parent elements. For example, consider the following XHTML snippet:

```
<head>
  <title>XHTML Examples</title>
  <style type="text/css">
  body { color:red }
  </style>
</head>
<body>
  <p>This text is contained by the <code>p</code> element.</p>
</body>
```

The style rule in the previous markup (body { color:red }) defines the body element as red. However, the content of the p and code elements both appear in red text. This occurs because the p and code elements inherit the style from the body element.

If you introduce new elements within the body element, their content will also be displayed in red because once a style rule is established for an element, that rule applies to all its descendants. However, this doesn't mean that once you define a style rule for a container (or parent) element, all descendant elements are stuck with that style too. To override a style rule, you just have to introduce a new style rule for the element in question.

In the previous code, for example, if you add the markup code {color:blue} under the body element declaration, the letter *p* between the code tags will be blue.

Cascade

Style sheets can come from one of three different places: the author, the user, or the browser (or other user agent). If you are creating a style sheet, you're creating a style sheet as the author. If you're viewing pages on the Internet, as the user, you can specify your own style sheet. And finally, the browsers can have their say by applying default formatting that functions much like a default style sheet.

The term *cascading* refers to the capability to apply multiple style sheets to a document. Style sheets function under the idea of precedence. Different style sheets have different levels of importance, and therefore, precedence.

As you can see, there are three different origins for style, all of which can overlap in purpose. According to the CSS standard, these three different types of style sheets can interact according to "the cascade." Each style rule carries a weight predefined by the CSS standard. Therefore, when multiple rules apply to the same element, the one that carries the heaviest weight wins.

To read more about the cascading order, see `www.w3.org/TR/REC-CSS2/cascade.html#cascading-order`.

Value and Units

The style-rule declaration is made up of a property and a value. This section focuses on the values attached to properties. Value options are predefined for each property, which means that you cannot create your own color or metric unit.

If you're curious about individual property values, each property and its possible values are listed alphabetically in Appendix C, "CSS Properties Listed Alphabetically."

There are five basic value categories: color units, length units (relative and absolute), percentage units, keywords, and URLs. They are defined as follows:

- **Color units.** Background, text, and color properties can sometimes take a color value. This value can be one of three types. First, the author can use one of the 16 color names. An author can also choose to use the hexadecimal red, green, blue (RGB) color combination. Finally, an author can choose to reference an RGB color by using numbers or percentages. For example, `green`, `#00FF00`, `#0F0`, `rgb(0, 255, 0)`, and `rgb(0%, 100%, 0%)` are all synonyms.

- **Length units.** Many properties use length units as values. This value can be positive or negative; however, some properties place restrictions on negative values. The value is written as a number followed by a unit of measurement (for example, `12pt` or `2px`—12 points and 2 pixels, respectively).

- **Percentage units.** An author can decide to use a percentage instead of an absolute length. For example, if you specify that a `table` element has the width of 75%, it's the same as saying that it will span across 75% of its parent element. If `body` is the parent element, then the table would span across 75% of the browser window.

- **Keywords.** A few properties can take keywords that have predefined meaning. For example, the font-weight property can take one of the following keyword values: bold, bolder, lighter, or normal.

- **URLs.** Properties that deal with images can take URLs as their values. The URL can be an absolute (the full URL: http://www.lanw.com/graphics/file.gif) or a relative path (file.gif).

Lengths and Colors Keywords

The color value has 16 predefined color keywords that an author can choose from: aqua, black, blue, fuchsia, gray, green, lime, maroon, navy, olive, purple, red, silver, teal, white, and yellow.

Length also uses predefined—and hopefully familiar—units. They are listed in Table 6.1.

Table 6.1 **Length Units**

Name	Abbreviation
Em	em
Ex	ex
Pica	pc
Point	pt
Pixel	px
Millimeter	mm
Centimeter	cm
Inch	in

Property Categories

CSS groups its properties into general categories. In this chapter, we don't cover each individual element, but we do show you some examples for each general category. For a complete listing of all CSS properties, see Appendix C.

Colors and Backgrounds

Some of the most common proprieties reside in this category. Many of our examples so far have focused on text color using the color property. Another trick is to use the background-color property. Take a look at the markup in Example 6.6. (Note that this example is only part of an XHTML document.)

Example 6.6 **Assigning a Background Color to the** *body* **Element Using the** *background-color* **Property**

```
<head>
  <title>XHTML Examples</title>
  <style type="text/css">
      body {
      color:white;
      background-color:black;
          }
  </style>
  </head>
  <body>
    <p>This text is contained by the <code>p</code> element.</p>
  </body>
```

In the previous example, the body element is assigned a black background. Because the body element is the parent for all the content, and CSS allows for inheritance, the entire document displays with a black background. See Figure 6.4 for the output.

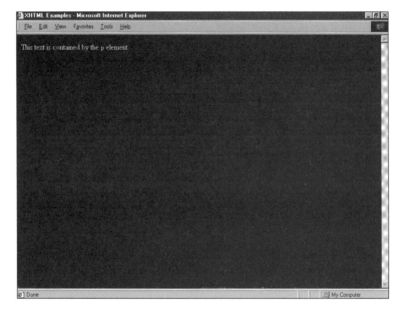

Figure 6.4   The background-color element in action.

However, what happens if you assign a background-color property to the p element, as shown in Example 6.7?

Example 6.7   **Assigning a Background Color to the *p* Element Using the**
             ***background-color* Property**

```
<head>
    <title>XHTML Examples</title>
    <style type="text/css">
    body {
         color:white;
    background-color:black
      }
  p { background-color:red }
    </style>
    </head>
    <body>
      <p>This text is contained by the <code>p</code> element.</p>
    </body>
```

Now, the p element has its own style rule and the text, This text is contained by the
p element. through the end of the paragraph will appear with a red background. The
rest of the page will still have a black background.

   If you would like to learn more about manipulating color and background, the following properties can do just that: color, background-color, background-image,
background-repeat, background-attachment, background-position, and background.
See Appendix C for the details.

Fonts

The XHTML font element is perhaps the most overused formatting element in Web
history. (To see this element at work, take a look at the partial XHTML document in
Example 6.8.) The font element is also deprecated, which means that the next version
of XHTML will ask that you use style sheets to achieve this effect. So, instead of clut-
tering your XHTML pages with font elements, opt for a more practical solution and
use CSS instead.

Example 6.8   **Using the *font* Element Makes for Bloated and Confusing Markup**

```
<html>
  <head>
    <title>Examples</title>
  </head>

<!-- Plain Jane HTML Example  -->

  <body>
    <p><font color="red">The text is red</font></p>
    <p><font color="blue">The blue text is now
    <font color="green">green</font></font></p>
  </body>
</html>
```

The following properties can manipulate font display: `color`, `font-family`, `font-size`, `font-style`, `font-variant`, `font-weight`, `line-height`, and `font`.

For example, let's say you wanted to display the following with a little more pizzazz:

Airplane!

Ted: My orders came through. My squadron ships out tomorrow. We're bombing the storage depots at Daiquiri at 18:00 hours. We're coming in from the North, below their radar.

Elaine: When will you be back?

Ted: I can't tell you that. It's classified.

You only have to use a few CSS style rules to add some style. To try this out at home, type the markup in Example 6.9 into a text editor (or access it on the CD), save it with an .htm extension, and open it in a Web browser that supports CSS.

Example 6.9   **Using Various CSS Font Properties to Add Some Flair**

```
<?xml version="1.0"?>
<!DOCTYPE html
     PUBLIC "-//W3C//DTD XHTML 1.0 Strict//EN"
     "http://www.w3.org/TR/xhtml1/DTD/xhtml1-strict.dtd">
<html xmlns="http://www.w3.org/1999/xhtml" xml:lang="en" lang="en">
  <head>
    <title>XHTML Examples</title>
    <style type="text/css">
      body { color:lime; font-family:Arial, Verdana; font-size:12pt; font-
      weight:bold;}
      h1 { color:gray; font-size:16pt; }
    </style>
  </head>
  <body>
    <h1>Airplane!</h1>
    <p>
Ted: My orders came through. My squadron ships out tomorrow. We're bombing the
storage depots at Daiquiri at 1800 hours. We're coming in from the north, below
their radar.<br />
Elaine: When will you be back?<br />
Ted: I can't tell you that. It's classified.
    </p>
  </body>
</html>
```

The results are shown in Figure 6.5.

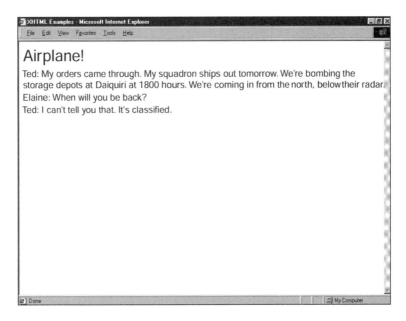

Figure 6.5 By adding CSS style rules, the quote from *Airplane!* has a little more flair.

The bolded sections contain formatting information for the browser. Internal style information is used to convey this information. The first style rule uses body as the selector. This sets default information for the entire page because most elements follow the rules of inheritance. (For more information on inheritance, read the section "Inheritance" earlier in this chapter.) In this style rule, the text of the body of the document is set to Arial, size 12pt font with a color of lime. The second style rule sets the h1 element to gray and font size to 16pt. Because the p element is a child of the body element and there are no style rules to override the default, the content of the p element will follow the rules defined for its parent, the body element.

Text Properties

There are tons of properties dedicated to the basic formatting of document content. The following properties can manipulate text formatting: vertical-align, text-align, text-decoration, text-indent, text-transform, word-spacing, letter-spacing, and white-space. In addition to these CSS1 properties, the following were introduced by CSS2: text-shadow, font-size-adjust, and font-stretch. In addition, there are two new properties for controlling the direction of text: direction and unicode-bidi.

In Example 6.10, you look at textual layout and increase the letter- and word-spacing in an XHTML snippet.

Example 6.10   **Using Various Text Properties to Add Some Flair**

```
<head>
    <title>XHTML Examples</title>
    <style type="text/css">
    p {
      letter-spacing:1em }
       word-spacing:1em
       }
    </style>
</head>
<body>
    <p>This text is longer than usual.</p>
</body>
```

To see this markup in action, see Figure 6.6.

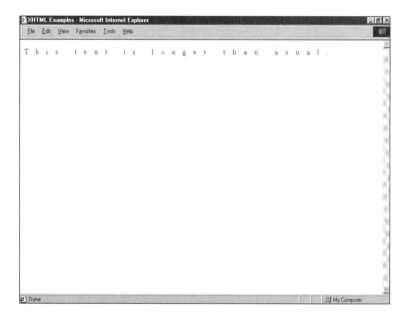

Figure 6.6   The word-spacing and letter-spacing properties stretch the text.

Boxes and Borders

The following properties can be used to manipulate the display of boxes and borders:
display, height, width, float, clear, border-top-width, border-right-width,
border-bottom-width, border-left-width, border-color, border-style, border-top,
border-bottom, border-left, border-right, border, margin-top, margin-left,
margin-bottom, margin-right, margin, padding-top, padding-left, padding-bottom,
padding-right, and padding.

Take a look at Example 6.11.

Example 6.11 **Boxes and Borders in Action**

```
<head>
  <title>XHTML Document</title>
  <style type="text/css">
    ul {
      background: aqua;
      margin: 10px 10px 10px 10px;
      padding: 3px 3px 3px 3px;
    }
    li {
      color: black;
      margin: 10px 10px 10px 10px;
      padding: 12px 0px 12px 12px;
      list-style: none;
    }
    li.border {
      border-style: dashed;
      border-width: medium;
      border-color: black;
    }
  </style>
</head>
<body>
  <ul>
    <li>list item</li>
    <li class="border">list item</li>
  </ul>
</body>
```

The output is shown in Figure 6.7. This example illustrates different ways to manipulate the margin, border, and padding of elements.

More on CSS

This chapter cannot possibly cover the entire CSS standard. There are many books out there on CSS, and we urge you to buy one. Not only is CSS useful for XHTML, but it can also be used with XML.

We suggest *Cascading Style Sheets: The Definitive Guide*, by Eric Meyer (O'Reilly and Associates, 2000, ISBN 1-5659-2622-6).

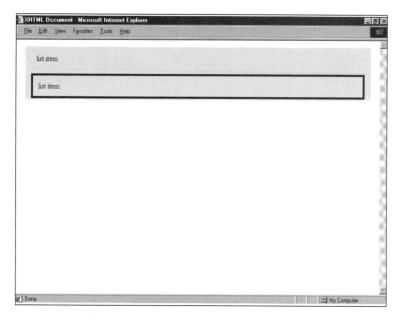

Figure 6.7   Seeing boxes and borders in action.

Adding CSS to XHTML Documents

There are four ways you can add style to your pages:

- Use the `link` element to reference an external style sheet.
- Include style rules in the `head` element, contained by the `style` element.
- Import a style sheet using `@import` keyword.
- Include style rules in the body of the XHTML document.

Example 6.12 illustrates how to add style each of the four ways. We inserted and bolded comments introducing each method so they're easier to see.

Example 6.12   **Using the Four Different Methods to Include Style in an XHMTL Document**

```
<?xml version="1.0"?>
<!DOCTYPE html
    PUBLIC "-//W3C//DTD XHTML 1.0 Strict//EN"
    "http://www.w3.org/TR/xhtml1/DTD/xhtml1-strict.dtd">
<html xmlns="http://www.w3.org/1999/xhtml" xml:lang="en" lang="en">
<head>
 <title>Style Sheets</title>
```

```
<!--The following markup references an external style sheet. For more information
on the link element, see Chapter 3, "Overview of Element Structure." -->
 <link rel="stylesheet" type="text/css" href="file.css" />

<!-- The following markup contains an import function and internal style rules.
For more information on the style element, see Chapter 3. -->
 <style type="text/css">
 @import "file.css"
 body {
        color:green;
        font-weight:bold;
        }
 </style>
</head>
<body>
 <p>This text is bold and green.</p>

<!--The last way to introduce style is by using an inline style element. For more
information on the style element, see Chapter 3. -->
 <p style="color: red">This text is red.</p>
</body>
</html>
```

The first instance uses the `link` element to reference an external style sheet. In this case, the style rules are housed in a separate document that is saved with a .css extension (*file.css*). The following is an example external CSS file:

```
body { background-color:black }
h1, h2, h3 { font-size:12pt }
p { color:red }
```

Nothing is needed to start the document, and nothing is needed to signify the end of it. All that you need to include are style rules. After you do that, you save the document with a .css extension and reference it in your XHTML document. When the browser goes to render the XHTML document, it detects the `link` element, grabs the style information from the style sheet, and renders the document as a complete Web page.

The second instance uses the `@import` directive to reference an external CSS file. Like the `link` element, the `@import` directive loads an external style sheet to add style to a Web page. The `link` element and the `@import` directive are very similar. The syntax is the only significant difference. In Example 6.12, you can see how to use this directive. It always begins with an `@import` followed by the keyword `url` and then the filename in parenthesis. For example, `@import url(file.css)`. One word of warning: This is not supported by all browsers.

The third instance of including style information is done in the head of the XHTML document. This is a very common way to include style information that is specific to an individual document. Most examples in this chapter use this method. To read more about the `style` element, see Chapter 3.

Finally, the last instance of incorporating style rules is an inline style declaration. This allows an author some flexibility when he or she needs to affect one individual element. Inline style rules only apply style to the element to which they are attached. The rule is attached using an XHTML `style` attribute. For more information on the XHTML `style` attribute, see Chapter 3.

Adding CSS to XML Documents

You might think that because XHTML is XML, attaching a CSS style sheet to any XML document would be the same. That is not the case. As a matter of fact, attaching style sheets to XML documents has its own W3C recommendation.

To see the complete recommendation—it's only a few pages long—visit `www.w3.org/TR/xml-stylesheet/`.

Now, for a quick tutorial on adding style to XML pages. Because XML documents don't adhere to the XHTML vocabulary, it makes sense that they can't use XHTML elements. For XML documents, the syntax will look familiar:

```
<?xml-stylesheet type="text/css" href="file.css"?>
```

The previous markup is a processing instruction. The first part of the processing instruction tells the processor to look for a style sheet named `file.css`. For more information on style sheet processing instructions, see Chapter 7, "Adding Style with XSL."

For More Information

As mentioned, this chapter by no means covers everything you can do with CSS. Many online resources are free and exhaustive. We find the following resources to be particularly helpful:

- **The W3C's CSS pages.** `www.w3.org/style/css`
- **WebMonkey's CSS tutorials and resources.** `http://hotwired.lycos.com/ webmonkey/authoring/stylesheets/index.html`
- **Webreview's CSS articles.** `http://webreview.com/wr/pub/Style_Sheets` (and don't forget the browser-compatibility chart at the same site)
- **Western Civilisation's Style Master Web site.** `www.westciv.com/`

7

Adding Style with XSL

As you may have already learned, XHTML is a fairly easy standard to master. One of the advantages to upgrading from HTML 4 of XHTML is that you can utilize all the standards that XML can. This means that now, instead of having just two tools in your arsenal—XHTML and CSS—you've increased that number exponentially. Not only can you extend XHTML to include elements of your own creation, but you can also work with other XML infrastructures, such as the Extensible Stylesheet Language (XSL) and XSL Transformations (XSLT).

Specifications Covered in This Chapter

This chapter is based on the following specifications (note the version dates):

- Extensible Stylesheet Language 1.0 Working Draft: March 27, 2000

- Extensible Stylesheet Language Transformations 1.0 Recommendation: November 16, 1999

- XML Path Language version 1.0 Recommendation: November 16, 1999

What Is XSL

XSL, the *other* style sheet language from the W3C, is one of the many XML vocabularies to hit the streets. Unlike Cascading Style Sheets (CSS), XSL allows for complex, or simple, document transformation, as well as formatting.

What you probably already know is that XSL is a language for creating style sheets. What you might not know is that unlike CSS, it consists of two stages:

1. A transformation process outlined in the XSLT specification.

2. A formatting process defined in the main XSL specification.

When XSL was first introduced, both parts—the transformation and the formatting stages—were defined in the same parent XSL specification; however, the authors of the specification noticed a definitive separation in functions between these stages and decided to represent this separation by creating two different standards that would work together. Figure 7.1 demonstrates this idea.

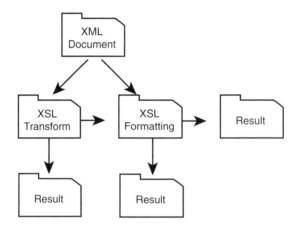

Figure 7.1   XSL is broken into two stages.

An XSL style sheet transforms an XML document into one that uses the XSL formatting vocabulary: first you transform, and then you format. To understand this process, we need to break it down even further.

The first stage of XSL, the transformation stage, is broken down into three steps:

1. The XSLT processor translates the XML document and the XSLT document into trees consisting of nodes. These trees can be referred to as source trees and style sheet trees, respectively.

2. The XSLT processor uses the trees to perform the actual transformation process and outputs a result tree consisting of nodes.

3. The XSLT processor translates the result tree into a result document.

Figure 7.2 illustrates this relationship.

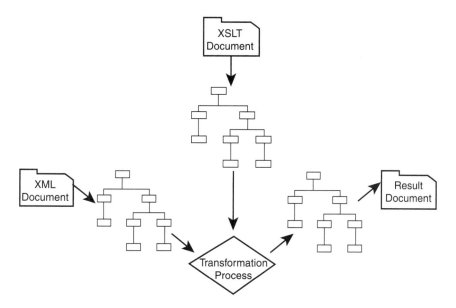

Figure 7.2   XSLT uses trees, similar to those in the Document
Object Model (DOM), to perform the transformation.

XSLT trees consist of nodes that represent seven different types of information found
in an XML document: root node, element node, text node, attribute node, comment
node, processing instruction node, and namespace node. Example 7.1 outlines a simple
XML document, and Figure 7.3 shows an XML document tree as interpreted by an
XSLT processor.

Example 7.1   **A Simple XML Document**

```
<?xml version="1.0"?>
<catalog>
  <book>
    <title>Designing Web Usability</title>
    <keyword>Web Design</keyword>
    <author>Jakob Nielson</author>
  </book>
  <book>
    <title>XHTML</title>
    <keyword>Web Development</keyword>
    <author>Chelsea Valentine</author>
  </book>
</catalog>
```

Every element must be represented by an *element node*, which is also known as a *containing node*. In addition, all the text contained by each element must be represented by a *text node*, which is also called a leaf node.

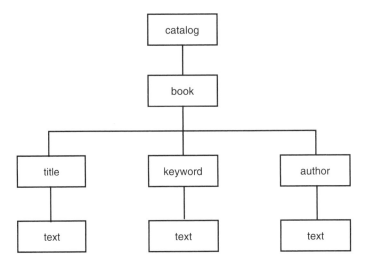

Figure 7.3   An example XML document tree.

Explaining source trees is beyond the scope of this book. Essentially, source trees not only make it easier for the author to locate a particular node (and therefore, reference it in the style sheet), but they also are an important step in the transformation process.

After the XSLT processor completes the transformation process and produces a result document, the formatting stage takes place.

Some individuals refer to the full process of transformation and formatting as XSL; however, many times you'll hear XSLT called by name. You might also come across the name, XSL-FO, where FO stands for *formatting objects*. When used, individuals are referring to the XSL formatting process defined in the parent XSL specification. For clarity in this chapter, we refer to the transformation process as XSLT and the formatting process as XSL-FO. The term XSL style sheet is a general term that can reference either an XSL or XSLT style sheet.

If used, XSL-FO applies formatting to the result document much like CSS does to an XHTML document. This should be more familiar. XSL-FO consists of formatting properties that are associated with given elements in the result document. The processor—most likely a browser—will display the result document with the appropriate formatting defined in the XSL style sheet. Because XSL-FO (defined in the XSL 1.0 Working Draft found at www.w3.org/Style/xsl) is not stable yet, there are no browsers that actually support XSL-FO properties. For more information on when and where you can expect XSL-FO stability, see the sidebar titled "XSL Working Group Charter."

XSL Working Group Charter

The main purpose of the XSL Working Group is to "define a practical style and transformation language capable of supporting the transformation and presentation of, and interaction with, structured information (e.g., XML documents) for use on servers and clients." It's important to understand that XSL is not intended to replace CSS, but rather to support functionality that allows for the transformation of your XML (or XHTML) documents (for example, to reorder document elements).

XSL is made up of three main components: a transformation language (XSLT) that uses an expression language for addressing parts of an XML document (XPath), and a formatting objects vocabulary that contains properties much like those found in CSS (XSL, also known as XSL-FO).

One goal of XSL is to provide a style sheet standard that meets or exceeds the capabilities of CSS and the Document Style Semantics and Specification Language (DSSSL). Much of the work already done is based on these two standards.

The following are deliverables already presented and published by the XSL Working Group:

- Recommendation for XSLT version 1.0 (www.w3.org/TR/xslt)
- Recommendation for XPath version 1.0 (www.w3.org/TR/xpath)
- Last Call Working Draft for XSL version 1.0 (www.w3.org/TR/xsl) (Note that this specification includes the XSL-FO properties)

The following are deliverables to be published by the XSL Working Group in the order that they will appear:

- Requirement documents for XSL version 2.0 and XSLT/XPath Version 2.0
- Candidate Recommendation for XSL version 1.0
- Proposed Recommendation for XSL version 1.0
- Recommendation for XSL version 1.0 (This specification includes the XSL-FO properties.)
- First Working Draft of XSLT 2.0
- First Working Draft of XPath 2.0
- Second Working Draft of XSLT 2.0
- Second Working Draft of XPath 2.0
- Last Call Working Draft of XSLT 2.0
- Last Call Working Draft of XPath 2.0
- First Working Draft for XSL 2.0
- Proposed Recommendation for XSLT 2.0
- Proposed Recommendation for XPath 2.0
- Proposed Recommendation for XSL 2.0
- Recommendation for XSLT 2.0
- Recommendation for XPath 2.0
- Recommendation for XSL 2.0

XSL or CSS

You may wonder why there's a need for a second style sheet language—especially when the W3C isn't even finished with CSS yet. Why can't they just fold all needed enhancements into one language? The fact is that CSS and XSL work really well together. If you're creating Web pages that use only XHTML, you don't really need XSL. You don't need to transform the structure of your document; all you need to do is add some style. CSS is a simple language that allows for quick and simple Web pages to be created for those who don't need to transform their documents.

For example, XSL allows you to transform an XML document's structure to HTML, which can be easily interpreted by any browser. Figure 7.4 demonstrates this idea. For that matter, you can even transform your XHTML document into one with a different element structure. Transforming from one document structure to another means less typing in the end.

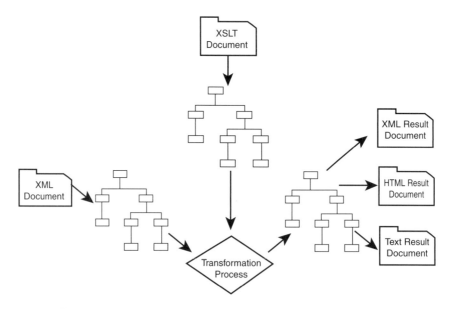

Figure 7.4   An XML document transformed into an HTML document.

The question now is when and where can you use CSS or XSL? Although there's no steadfast rule, Table 7.1 from the W3C shows your options.

Table 7.1 **When and Where to Use CSS and XSL**

	CSS	**XML**
Can be used with HTML	Yes	No
Can be used with XML	Yes	Yes
Transformation language	No	Yes
Syntax	CSS	XML

When deciding which style sheet language to use, remember to weigh all your options. You may even decide to use a little of both!

Later in this chapter, we'll look at two primary examples. In Example 7.2, we use both XSL and CSS to produce the final output: XSLT to transform the document and CSS to add formatting.

Adding Style with Formatting Objects

As noted in the brief discussion of XSL-FO, the formatting objects portion of XSL can be found in the XSL 1.0 Working Draft at www.w3.org/Style/xsl. The goal of XSL-FO is to meet or exceed the same functionality found with CSS and DSSSL. This is a tall order, and XSL-FO is up to task.

XSL (both XSL-FO and XSLT) uses a collection of rules that consist of a pattern and an instruction piece. The instruction provides the action and the pattern locates the node to which to apply that action. And like the overall process itself, the formatting stage can be broken down, as follows:

1. Obtain the result tree (not document) from the XSLT transformation process and build an XSL formatting object tree.

2. Refine the formatting object tree to solve property inheritance issues, remove duplicate properties, and evaluate expressions.

3. Generate an area tree that represents geographical areas on a page and their corresponding position on the page and formatting properties to be associated.

What Can You Do *Now*?

Much of the success of XSL-FO depends on the browsers. This too should sound familiar. If browsers, which would contain the XSL processor, do not support XSL formatting objects, it's less likely that authoring tools will. Without the browser or tool support, XSL-FO might not take off like XSLT has.

This leads us to what you can do now. There are plenty of tools out there that enable authors to create and use XSLT. There are many reasons one would start using XSLT today. For example, if you decide to keep all your data in an XML document, but later decided to use some of that data in your Web page, you can use XSLT to transform that data into an XHTML document ready for the Web. There are many reasons to use XSLT, and some of them don't even involve the Internet, but rather business-to-business data exchange. For more information on why to start using XSLT today, visit the URLs provided at the end of this chapter.

Transforming Your Pages with XSLT

XSLT is one of the few XML vocabularies that has reached the recommendation phase. This means that it has some stability and, therefore, vendors can safely create standard-compliant processors. There are many tools that can process an XSLT document; these are listed toward the end of this chapter. However, before you read about the tools, take a look at the XSLT vocabulary.

XSLT Namespace

It's necessary to include the XSLT namespace to identify the XSLT style sheet. The XSLT namespace is at `http://www.w3.org/1999/XSL/Transform`. The XSLT namespace must always be written as shown. The prefix most commonly attached, `xsl`, is not set by the standard. In theory, you could choose any prefix, as long as you consistently use that prefix, to identify XSLT elements. Although this option is available, it's uncommon.

The XSLT namespace is declared as a part of the `xsl:stylesheet` (or `xsl:transform`) element like so:

```
<xsl:stylesheet version="1.0" xmlns:xsl="http://www.w3.org/1999/XSL/Transform">
...</xsl:stylesheet>
```

All XSLT elements must use the given prefix, or the XSLT processor will not recognize them as XSLT elements. For those of you who don't know what a namespace is, be sure to read Chapter 2, "All About Markup," and Chapter 12, "The Benefits of Extensibility."

XSLT Vocabulary

Like XHTML, XSLT consists of elements that are predefined and, therefore, have predefined behaviors. Table 7.2 lists all XSLT elements and denotes all required attributes with bold. The table assumes that you understand some key terminology. In the content column, the following keywords or descriptions are used:

- **Empty** means that the element cannot contain additional elements or text.
- **Template** means that the element can contain additional instructions and literal result elements.
- **#PCDATA** means that the element can contain parsed character data. For more information on this term, see Chapter 12.

- **DTD syntax** to identify element relationships. For example, `(xsl:param*, template)` means that the element may contain zero or multiple instances of the `xsl:param` element or a template. For more information on DTD syntax, see Chapter 12.

The category column defines the element to be an instruction or top-level element. If no category is listed, the element does not fall into either category and has a specific function.

Most of the XSLT vocabulary can be broken into these two basic categories:

- **Top-level element.** Immediate children of the `xsl:stylesheet` (or `xsl:transform`) element. Table 7.2 identifies all top-level elements.

- **Instruction.** Children of the `xsl:template` element that provide template instructions. Table 7.2 identifies all instruction elements.

Table 7.2 **The XSLT Elements**

Element Name	Section	Description	Possible Attributes	Content	Category
`xsl:apply-imports`	5.6	Allows the overriding template rule to invoke the overridden template rule in the imported module.	None	Empty	Instruction
`xsl:apply-templates`	5.4	Defines a set of nodes to be processed, and instructs the processor to process them by selecting an appropriate template rule.	select mode	`(xsl:sort ¦ xsl:with-param)*`	Instruction
`xsl:attribute`	7.1.3	Outputs an attribute name and value to the output document.	**name** namespace	*template*	Instruction

continues

Table 7.2 **Continued**

Element Name	Section	Description	Possible Attributes	Content	Category
		Used to add attributes to result elements whether created by literal result elements in the style sheet or by instructions such as the `xsl:element`.			
`xsl:attribute-set`	7.1.4	Used to define a named set of attribute names and values. The resulting attribute set can be applied as a whole to any output element, providing a way of defining commonly used sets of attributes in a single plane.	**name** use-attribute-sets	`xsl:attribute*`	Top-level element
`xsl:call-template`	6	Used to invoke a named template.	**name**	`xsl:with-param*`	Instruction
`xsl:choose`	9.2	Defines a choice between a number of alternatives.	None	`(xsl:when+, xsl:otherwise?)`	Instruction
`xsl:comment`	7.4	Used to write a comment to the current output destination.	None	*template*	Instruction

Element Name	Section	Description	Possible Attributes	Content	Category
`xsl:copy`	7.5	Copies the current node in the source document to the output destination. It does not copy children, descendants, or attributes of the current node, only the current node and, if it's an element, its namespace.	`use-attribute-sets`	*template*	Instruction
`xsl:copy-of`	11.3	Used to copy a result tree fragment or a node set to the output destination. It also copies descendants.	**select**	Empty	Instruction
`xsl:decimal-format`	12.3	Used to define the characters and symbols used when converting numbers into strings using the `format-number()` function.	`name` `decimal-separator` `grouping-separator` `infinity` `minus-sign` `NaN` `percent` `per-mile` `zero-digit` `digit` `pattern-separator`	Empty	Top-level element
`xsl:element`	7.1.2	Used to output an element node to the output destination.	**name** `namespace` `use-attribute-sets`	*template*	Instruction

continues

Table 7.2 **Continued**

Element Name	Section	Description	Possible Attributes	Content	Category
xsl: fallback	15	Used to define processing that should occur if no implementation of its parent instruction are available.	None	*template*	Instruction
xsl: for-each	8	Selects a set of nodes using an XPath expression, and performs the same processing for each node in the set.	**select**	(xsl:sort*, *template*)	Instruction
xsl:if	9.1	Encloses a template body that will be instantiated only if a specified condition is true.	**test**	*template*	Instruction
xsl:import	2.6.2	Used to import the contents of one style sheet module into another.	**href**	Empty	Top-level element
xsl:include	2.6.1	Used to include the contents of one style sheet module within another.	**test**	Empty	Top-level element
xsl:key	12.2	Used to declare a named key. For use with the key () function in XPath expressions and paths.	**name** **match** **use**	Empty	Top-level element
xsl:message	13	Defines an output message and may terminate execution of the style sheet.	terminate	*template*	Instruction

Element Name	Section	Description	Possible Attributes	Content	Category
xsl: namespace -alias	7.1.1	Used to declare that one namespace URI is an alias for another namespace URI.	**stylesheet-prefix** **result-prefix**	Empty	Top-level element
xsl:number	7.7	Used to allocate a sequential number to the current node, and/or it can be used to format a number for output.	level count from value format lang letter-value grouping-separator grouping-size	Empty	Instruction
xsl: otherwise	9.2	Used within an xsl:choose instruction to indicate the action that should be taken when none of the xsl:when conditions are satisfied.	None	*template*	
xsl:output	16	Used to control the format of the style sheet output in the result document. (Note the difference between result tree and result document. Remember, the transformation process goes through two stages: the result tree, and then the result document.	method version encoding omit-xml-declaration standalone doctype-public doctype-system cdata-section-elements indent media-type	Empty	Top-level element

continues

Table 7.2 **Continued**

Element Name	Section	Description	Possible Attributes	Content	Category
		This element controls the second stage.)			
xsl:param	11	Used to describe a local parameter to a template. It specifies a name and a default value for the parameter, which is used if the author supplies no value for the parameter.	**name** select	*template*	Top-level element or found as an immediate child of xsl: template
xsl:preserve -space	3.4	Used to control the way in which whitespace nodes in the source handled.	**elements**	Empty	Top-level element
xsl: processing -instruction	7.3	Used to write a processing instruction node to the output.	**name**	*template*	Instruction
xsl:sort	10	Used to define a sort key to specify the order in which nodes selected by xsl:apply -templates or xsl:for-each are processed.	select lang data-type order case-order	Empty	
xsl:strip -space	3.4	Used (along with the xsl:preserve -space) to control the way whitespace nodes in the source document are handled. The xsl:strip-space element identifies	**elements**	Empty	Top-level element

Element Name	Section	Description	Possible Attributes	Content	Category
		elements in which whitespace-only text nodes are considered insignificant, so they can be removed from the source tree.			
xsl: stylesheet	2.2	The outermost element of a style sheet. xsl:transform can be used as a synonym.	id **version** extension-element-prefixes exclude-results-prefixes	(xsl:import*, *top-level-elements*)	Appears as the outermost element of style sheet
xsl:template	5.3	Defines a template for producing output. It may be invoked by either matching nodes against a pattern, or explicitly by name.	match name priority made	(xsl:param*, *template*)	Top-level element
xsl:text	7.2	Used within a template body to output literal text to the output destination.	disable-output-escaping	#PCDATA	Instruction
xsl: transform	2.2	See xsl: stylesheet.	See xsl: stylesheet	See xsl: stylesheet	See xsl: stylesheet
xsl: value-of	7.6.1	Writes the string value of an expression to the result tree.	**select** disable-output-escaping	Empty	Instruction

continues

Table 7.2　**Continued**

Element Name	Section	Description	Possible Attributes	Content	Category
xsl:variable	11	Used to declare a local or global variable in a style sheet, and to give it a value.	**name** select	*template*	Instruction or top-level element
xsl:when	9.2	Defines a condition to be tested and the action to be performed if the condition is true.	**test**	*template*	
xsl: with-param	11.6	Used to set the values of parameters when calling a template, either when using xsl:call-template, or when using xsl:apply-templates.	name select	*template*	

If you look at Table 7.2, you might also notice that there are a few elements that don't fall into either category.

- **xsl:stylesheet and xsl:transform.** Either one can be used as the outermost element of a given style sheet. (Just one of these elements can be used, not both.)

- **xsl:with-param, xsl:sort, xsl:otherwise, and xsl:param.** These elements have unique functions and cannot be used in a template body and occur as children of an instruction, or they are not considered part of the template.

Figure 7.5 illustrates the categorical relationships between XSLT elements.

The order of XSLT elements in an XSLT document

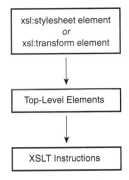

Figure 7.5 XSLT elements work together in a hierarchical relationship.

XSLT *stylesheet* Element

As mentioned, either `xsl:stylesheet` or `xsl:transform` may be used as the outermost element in an XSLT style sheet. There is no distinction between the two elements. They use the same attributes and take on the same meaning. All you have to remember is that if you begin your XSLT document with `xsl:transform`, you must close with it as well! Note that in this book, we use the `xsl:stylesheet` element as the outermost XSLT element for all our examples.

All XSLT style sheets should include one of these two elements (unless you're creating a simplified style sheet, which is one that uses an abbreviated syntax and omits the `xsl:stylesheet` or `xsl:transform` element and all top-level elements).

Table 7.3 defines the `xsl:stylesheet` and `xsl:transform` elements' attributes.

Table 7.3 **The *xsl:stylesheet* and *xsl:transform* Elements' Attributes**

Attribute Name/Value	Attribute Usage
`id="id"`	Identifies a specific `xsl:stylesheet` element.
`version="number"`	Defines XSLT version used by `stylesheet`. Currently, the only valid version number is `"1.0"`. This attribute is required.
`extension-element-prefixes="token"`	Defines namespace used for extension elements (non-XSLT elements used much like instructions).
`exclude-result-prefixes="tokens"`	Defines namespace(s) that are not to be copied to the result tree.

XSLT Top-Level Elements

XSLT elements have a few hierarchical rules that govern their placement in an XSLT document. Top-level elements are defined to occur as immediate children of the `xsl:stylesheet` element.

Providing examples of each top-level element would take up a whole other book. Therefore, this section just focuses on some of the key top-level elements.

The `xsl:template` element is one that you should become very familiar with because it's necessary for creating most XSLT documents. The `xsl:template` element defines a template used to create the result tree, and therefore the result document. Table 7.4 defines the `xsl:template` element's attributes.

Table 7.4   **The *xsl:template* Element's Attributes**

Attribute Name/Value	Attribute Usage
`match="pattern"`	Identifies the nodes to which the template rule will apply. This attribute is required unless a `name` attribute is used.
`name="qname"`	Provides a name for the template. This attribute is required unless a `match` attribute is used. `qname` stands for qualified name and can be any name that can be optionally qualified by a namespace prefix.
`priority="number"`	Any number used to define a priority for a template when several templates match the same node.
`mode="qname"`	Defines the mode. When used, only `xsl:apply-templates` with the same mode are evaluated. (If the `mode` attribute is not used, only templates without a `mode` attribute are considered.)

Example 7.2 demonstrates the `xsl:template` element in action.

Example 7.2   **The *xsl:template* Element in Action**

```
<xsl:stylesheet version="1.0"
xmlns:xsl="http://www.w3.org/1999/XSL/Transform">
<xsl:template match="/">
  <html>
   <head><title>Result Document Title</title></head>
   <body>
<xsl:apply-templates/>
   <table border="1" cellpadding="5" cellspacing="5">
     <tr>
       <th>head1</th>
       <th>head2</th>
     </tr>
<xsl:apply-templates  mode="index"/>
   </table>
```

```
    </body>
    </html>
</xsl:template>

<xsl:template match="book" mode="index">
    <tr>
      <td><xsl:value-of select="title"/></td>
      <td><xsl:value-of select="keyword"/></td>
    </tr>
</xsl:template>
</xsl:stylesheet>
```

In this example, the first instance of the `xsl:apply-templates` is used to evaluate all elements found in the context node. (The `match` attribute value is an XPath expression that denotes the context node. In this case, the value is `"/"` and is shorthand for the root node. When the XSLT template is processed, it will begin with the root node of the XML data document.) The second instance of the `xsl:apply-templates` evaluates those nodes identified in the matching `xsl:template` element. In this instance, only the `title` and `keyword` elements are used.

XSLT Instructions

Instructions are allowed within the template. Table 7.2 provides a complete list of all XSLT instructions. Each instruction provides an action for the processor. For example, if the `xsl:template` element is used to create a template that will contain elements that provide instructions for that template. In Example 7.4, `xsl:value-of` is an instruction.

Literal Result Elements

As you look at an example XSLT document, you may wonder what all those XHTML elements are doing in there. These elements are formally called *literal result elements* and they provide the backbone of the XSLT template. What happens is that the XSLT document creates the structure for the result tree.

In our examples, the desired output structure is created with XHTML. For example, if you have a XML file that contains names and telephone numbers for all your friends, you might want to transform that data into an XHTML document and format it with XHTML list elements. The output would then be a Web page that lists all your friend's names and numbers. The data used for this output is found in the XML document; however, you must create the list structure in the XSLT document and provide instructions to grab the data from the XML document. Figure 7.6 illustrates how you might create a template for this example.

The idea is that you want the XHTML elements used in the XSLT style sheet to be copied directly to the output document as is. If no instruction is attached to these elements, the processor will leave them alone and pass them on. Elements that are left alone and passed to the output as is are the literal result elements.

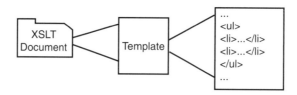

Figure 7.6 The author creates the XHTML list structure as a part of the XSLT style sheet.

XSLT Example

Although we cannot dive into complex XSLT documents, we would like to leave you with simple example that transforms an XML document that contains data to an XHTML document ready for the Web. This takes two documents: one XML document that contains data, and one XSLT style sheet that contains transformation instructions. Examples 7.3 and 7.4 illustrate this process.

Example 7.3 **The XML Document that Will Be Transformed to an XHTML Document**

```
<?xml version="1.0"?>
<catalog>
  <book>
    <title>Designing Web Usability</title>
    <keyword>Web Design</keyword>
    <author>Jakob Nielson</author>
  </book>
  <book>
    <title >XHTML</title>
    <keyword>Web Development</keyword>
    <author>Chelsea Valentine</author>
  </book>
</catalog>
```

After you create the initial XML document that contains your data, save that document with a .xml extension. Then, you're ready to create your XSLT document.

Example 7.4 **The XSL Style Sheet Used to Transform the XML Document in Example 7.3 to XHTML**

```
<?xml version="1.0"?>
<xsl:stylesheet version="1.0"
xmlns:xsl="http://www.w3.org/1999/XSL/Transform">

<xsl:output method="html" indent="yes" />
```

```
<xsl:template match="/">

<html>
<head>
  <title>Your Result Document</title>
</head>

<body>
<table border="0" cellspacing="5" cellpadding="5">
<thead>
  <tr>
    <th>Book Title</th>
    <th>Keyword</th>
    <th>Author</th>
  </tr>
</thead>

<tbody>
  <xsl:apply-templates select="catalog/book" />
</tbody>

</table>
</body>
</html>
</xsl:template>

<xsl:template match="book">
  <tr>
    <td>
      <xsl:value-of select="./title" />
    </td>
    <td>
     <xsl:value-of select="./keyword" />
    </td>
    <td>
    <xsl:value-of select="./author" />
    </td>
  </tr>
</xsl:template>

</xsl:stylesheet>
```

In our style sheet, we use several XSLT top-level and instruction elements, as well as a slew of XHTML elements that are to be processed as literal result elements. The following is a breakdown of what we include in the XSL document and an explanation of what each element actually does:

- **xsl:stylesheet.** This element instructs the processor that the XSLT document adheres to the 1.0 version of the specification and the corresponding namespace.
- **xsl:output.** This element instructs the processor to output the document as an HTML and use indentation when formatting the text.

- **xsl:template.** This element contains the main structure for our HTML output document and identifies the root node as the context node for evaluation. Don't get confused by our use of HTML here. The `xsl:output` element allows for three different types of output: XML, HTML, or text. Because Web support for XHTML is currently limited, we chose HTML. The formatting will still follow XHTML rules; however, it's technically HTML. To output as XHTML, you have to include a DTD declaration in your output and change the method to equal `"xml"`.

- **xsl:apply-templates.** This element instructs the browser to evaluate the template for any `book` element that is a child of the `catalog` element. The processor will find the associated instruction in a template listed later in the style sheet.

- **xsl:template.** This second template element will be inserted into the previous main template between the opening and closing `tbody` tags. This template evaluates the `book` element.

- **xsl:value-of.** This instruction selects the contents of any `title` element that is a child of the context node. The context node for this template is identified by the `xsl:template match` attribute. For this example, the context node is `book`. This instruction will grab the contents of the `title` element and place them as contents of the `td` element in the result tree.

- **xsl:value-of.** This is the second instance of the `xsl:value-of` instruction and it provides the same function as the first instance, except that it evaluates the `keyword` element.

- **xsl:value-of.** This is the third instance of the `xsl:value-of` instruction and it provides the same function as the first instance, except that it evaluates the `author` element.

Associating Style Sheets with Your Documents

Believe it or not, the act of associating style sheets with XML documents has its very own specification. This document is only a few pages long and is worth a look.

The "Associating Style Sheets with XML documents Version 1.0" recommendation dated June 29, 1999 is found at `www.w3.org/TR/xml-stylesheet/`.

Instead of using the XHTML `link` element to associate style sheets, this specification allows style sheets to be associated using one or more processing instructions. The processing instruction must be included in the XML prolog, which means before the root element. Table 7.5 defines the pseudo attributes allowed.

Table 7.5 **XSL Processing Instruction**

Attribute Name/Value	Attribute Usage
href="*uri*"	Identifies the URI of the style sheet to be associated.
type="*media type*"	Provides the media type of the linked resource (for example, `text/css` or `text/xsl`). This attribute is required.
title="*text*"	Provides a title for the processing instruction.
media="*media descriptor*"	Identifies desired output medium (for example, `print`, `screen`, `braille`).
charset="charset"	Specifies character encoding of the style sheet.
alternate="yes ¦ no"	Specifies if an alternative style sheet should be used.

For example, this XSL processing instruction

```
<?xml-stylesheet href="style.css" type="text/css"?>
```

has the same result as this XHTML `link` element:

```
<link rel="stylesheet" type="text/css" href="style.css" />
```

Adding CSS to Your Transformed Documents

Adding CSS does not take much. All you have to do is add the XHTML `link` element as a literal result element to your XSLT document. It will be copied to the output and that is that. To add a CSS style sheet to the previous example, just add the following line of markup to the contents of the `head` element:

```
<link rel="stylesheet" type="text/css" href="style.css" />
```

Once added, it will be copied to the output with all the other literal result elements. Just be sure that you created the CSS document you referenced!

XSLT Tools

As XSL gains popularity and stability, you're sure to see new and improved XSL tools. We have included a list of three XSLT processors that are commonly used by Web developers. To read about additional tools or to keep up to date on the evolution of XSL tools, visit `www.xslinfo.com`.

Michael Kay's Saxon

Saxon is an open-source Java-based XSLT processor created by Michael Kay. You can download a version of Saxon at `http://users.iclway.co.uk/mhkay/saxon/`. If you're running the program on a Windows platform, you can download *Instant Saxon*—the easy installation option.

Once downloaded, Saxon can be invoked from the DOS command prompt or as a Java class. To run a style sheet you have to enter the following command:

```
saxon file.xml file.xsl > output-file.html
```

This command runs file.xsl against file.xml and saves that output to output-file.html. To learn more about Saxon commands, visit the Web site mentioned previously.

James Clark's XT

Similar to Saxon, XT is an open-source Java-based XSLT processor created by James Clark. The functionality is much like Saxon, and the same commands can be used. To download James Clark's XT processor, visit `www.jclark.com/xml/xt.html`.

Microsoft's MSXML processor

Whereas the first two tools we mentioned are run from the DOS prompt, the last tool is actually part of Internet Explorer. This means you can run XSLT style sheets within Internet Explorer. To use the MSXML processor, you should install the latest version of Internet Explorer 5 and the Microsoft MSXML processor. To do this, visit `http://msdn.microsoft.com/xml/default.htm`.

For More Information

There are plenty of reasons a Web developer would want to use XSLT. If you fall into this category, you should visit the following Web sites to learn more:

- **W3C.** `www.w3.org/Style/xsl` (The W3C has an up-to-date Web site that not only houses the XSL, XSLT, and XPath specifications, but also houses a long list of XSL resources and tools.)
- **XML.com.** `www.xml.com` (XML.com publishes a biweekly article titled, "Style Matters." In this article, Didier Martin provides the reader with practical examples and easy to follow explanations.)
- **XSLinfo.** `www.xslinfo.com` (XSLinfo provides readers with a list of XSL resources and tools.)

8

Understanding XForms

IN THIS CHAPTER, WE COVER THE NEWEST TECHNOLOGY in Web forms, XForms. And when we say new, we mean really new. XForms is currently a "work in progress" at the W3C. So, in this chapter, we just provide you with a very brief overview of XForms. For the latest and greatest, visit the W3C site at www.w3.org/MarkUp/Forms/.

The History of Web Forms

Forms provide a portal for electronic commerce (e-commerce) on the Internet. Unless you create scripts to handle user interaction, forms are one of the few ways XHTML Web pages can interact with users—and even then, you're most likely working with scripting to handle that data. Forms were introduced in 1993 as a formal part of HTML, and they haven't changed that much since then. What has changed, however, is their importance on the Web. HTML Web forms are now used by companies worldwide to drive their e-commerce applications. Basically, HTML Web forms are outdated and need a face-lift because they don't provide the functionality needed to fulfill the requirements of complex e-commerce sites.

However, before you dive into the newest proposals for Web forms, namely the W3C's *XML Forms* (XForms), take a second to visit where forms are now.

Why Use Forms at All?

Forms are simply a way to enable users to interact with (pass information to) a Web server. There are many reasons you might choose to use forms.

The simplest of forms are often created to solicit feedback from users. Feedback is a necessary and priceless resource for any Web page and should be used to drive current and future directions of that page—or possibly the entire Web site.

More complicated forms enable users to check their bank account balances, purchase airline tickets, and check their email. Form controls, combined with scripts, enable users to communicate with your server and exchange information. This process drives e-commerce. Think about the last time you purchased something over the Web—for example, an airline ticket. First, you must identify the flight you want to take. To do so, you fill out a form that helps you narrow your search. See Figure 8.1 for an example from Southwest Airlines (www.southwest.com).

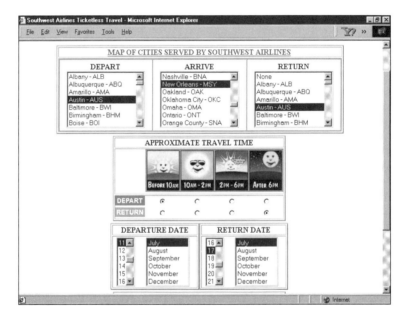

Figure 8.1   The reservations section of Southwest Airlines, where you enter information that narrows down the available flights for your specified preferences[1].

On the page displayed in Figure 8.1, you enter your departure city, arrival city, and desired departure and return dates. That information is sent to a Web server application that evaluates the data and sends you the schedule possibilities. See Figure 8.2 for the results we received when we requested information for flights between Austin, Texas and New Orleans, Louisiana for July 11, 2000.

[1]Note © 2000 Southwest Airlines Co. All content property of Southwest Airlines.

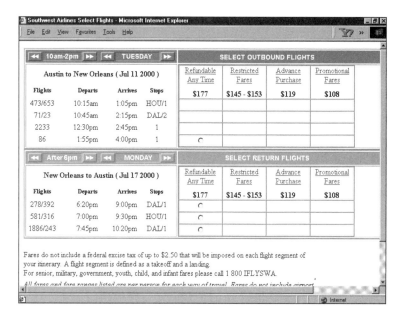

Figure 8.2   The Web server application sends the user all flight possibilities[2].

After that, you're presented with the option of purchasing a ticket. Again, you have to fill out a form. After you complete the form, that data is sent to a server and an appropriate response (hopefully, a purchase confirmation) is sent back to you, the user.

Using Forms Today

This chapter is a primer on XForms; however, it's important that you understand and are able to use current form applications. Table 8.1 lists all XHTML elements and attributes used to create forms. For detailed descriptions of these elements and attributes, see Chapter 3, "Overview of Element Structure."

Table 8.1   **XHTML Form Elements and Attributes**

Element Name	Empty	Description	Possible Attributes
button	No	Creates an input button	disabled, name, tabindex, type, value
fieldset	No	Groups related form controls	None
form	No	Contains form block	accept, accept-charset, action, enctype, method

continues

Table 8.1 **Continued**

Element Name	Empty	Description	Possible Attributes
input	Yes	Defines type and appearance for input objects	accept, align*, alt, checked, disabled, maxlength, name, readonly, size, src, tabindex, type, usemap, value
isindex	Yes	Solicits a single line of input from users	prompt
label	No	Identifies form controls	accesskey, for
legend	No	Provides a caption to a set of related form controls	align*, accesskey
option	No	Assigns a value to an input item	disabled, selected, value, label
optgroup	No	Groups selection choices logically	disabled, label
select	No	Creates a menu or scrolling list of input items	disabled, multiple, name, size, tabindex
textarea	No	Multiple line text area	accesskey, cols, disabled, name, readonly, rows, tabindex

Denotes a deprecated attribute

Example 8.1 is a very simple form that shows some of these elements in action.

Example 8.1 **A Simple XHTML Form Enables Customer Data to Be Sent to a Server**

```
<?xml version="1.0"?>
<!DOCTYPE html
     PUBLIC "-//W3C//DTD XHTML 1.0 Transitional//EN"
     "DTD/xhtml1-transitional.dtd">
<html xmlns="http://www.w3.org/1999/xhtml">
  <head>
    <title>Title of the document.
    </title>
  </head>
  <body>
    <form action="URL" method="post">
      <p>This is a simple form.
      </p>
      <fieldset>
        <legend>Customer Information</legend><br />
        Last Name: <input name="lastname" type="text" tabindex="1"
        /><br />
        First Name: <input name="firstname" type="text" tabindex="2"
        /><br />
```

Example 8.1 **Continued**

```
        E-mail Address: <input name="address" type="text" tabindex="3"
        />
      </fieldset>
    </form>
  </body>
</html>
```

The `input` elements collect data—in text form—from the user. That data is then instructed by the `form` element to be passed to a Uniform Resource Locator (URL) to be processed. That URL points to a server application ready to process the data. It's as easy as that.

To see how this example renders in a browser, see Figure 8.3.

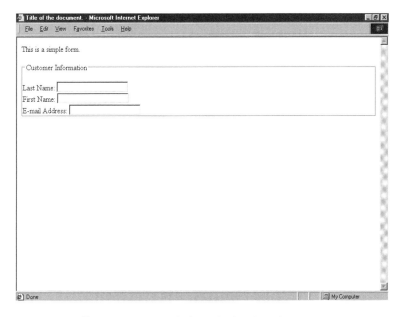

Figure 8.3 A simple form displayed in a browser.

Present-Day Limitations

Currently, Web forms are used as a way to exchange bidirectional data over the Web. However, as e-commerce grows on the Web, so does the need to offer more complex ways to exchange data. For example, Company A might want to place a purchase order with Company B. However, Company A might want to place some conditions on that exchange. Without a common language, namely XML, this process gets difficult and requires serious programming. Even then, many limitations exist.

In addition to the limitations of data exchange, there are other concerns regarding present-day HTML limitations: namely, the capability to separate data from presentation. Current form controls tie presentation closely to the involved data. Although this may not pose a serious problem with simple forms, such as the one in Example 8.1, it does create a mess when complex forms are needed to drive e-commerce for major companies.

After all, forms have not seen the editing block for over seven years!

What Exactly Are XForms?

The goal of XForms resembles the goal we've mentioned for XML throughout this book: to separate display from data. The hope for XForms is that it will separate the user interface from the data and logic, allowing the same form to be completed by users on a computer desktop, personal digital assistant (PDA), or mobile phone.

The following are the goals of XForms as stated by the W3C's XForms Working Group (you can find this list and much more at www.w3.org/MarkUp/Forms/):

- Support for handhelds, television, desktop browsers, printers, and scanners
- Richer user interface to meet the needs of business, consumer, and device control applications
- Decoupled data, logic, and presentation
- Improved internationalization
- Support for structured form data
- Advanced forms logic
- Multiple forms per page, and pages per form
- Suspend and resume support
- Seamless integration with other XML tag sets

The first step to creating a new standard is to identify goals. Next, you need to create a standard to actually achieve those goals. At the time of this writing, the W3C is in the process of mapping out just how to achieve the goals outlined in the previous list.

It's speculated that XForms will be three separate standards: one governing the data module, one governing the user interface, and one defining protocols. The first of the three has already made it to the Working Draft stage at the W3C and is appropriately titled "XForms 1.0: Data Model." (This information is based on the August 15, 2000 Working Draft.) The other two standards are not written yet.

According to the W3C, forms will be split into three layers (which is the reason for the three separate specifications): presentation, logic, and data:

- **Presentation.** The actual markup used with basic form controls. Each form control will be tied to a field in the data model.

- **Logic.** Enables you to define relationships between fields; for example, you might want to require additional fields to be filled in if a particular field is filled in.
- **Data.** Enables you to define a data model for your form. You will be able to use built-in data types or create your own. This layer will also make it easier to validate form information (check that it's a date, a number, and so on) without enormous amounts of scripting.

Now That's Progress!

Just to give you a taste of what's coming, one of the goals of the XForms specification is to enable users to print a form, fill it in by hand, and scan it in!

Who Should Learn XForms?

Anyone interested in creating complex forms, as well as programmers who are used to creating the server-side scripting required to accept, validate, and process incoming data, should look at the next generation of Web forms. For those of us who create Web pages and Web forms, it makes sense to take the next logical step and learn XForms. Because of XForms's e-commerce potential, most companies will expect their Web developers to soon adopt the new XForms capabilities.

Note that application vendors also make up a large piece of the target audience. Until application vendors adopt the XForms data model, Web developers will be unable to capitalize on the new functionality. One vendor is already working on implementing forms: Mozquito. See the "For More Information" section for more details.

As stated previously, programmers who have to deal with server-side scripting that processes the data collected from the Web form will be interested in the new capabilities XForms offers. The hope is that XForms will provide a consistent, XML-based format for incoming data, as well as take advantage of XML's validation framework—both of which will make programmers' lives easier.

Creating XForms

Because XForms is still in its infancy, and the standard is not yet set, you can't start working with XForms just yet. However, you can visit an example cooked up by the W3C's XForms Working Group. Keep in mind that it is an experimental example used by the Working Group to explore different ideas for XForms.

To visit the XForms Working Group example, visit `www.w3.org/MarkUp/Forms/Sample/acme.html`.

For More Information

Because XForms is still in its infancy, not a lot of information is available. However, the W3C, as usual, does have information on XForms on its Web site. Here are some URLs to guide you in your discovery of XForms:

- **The W3C XForms Working Group.** `www.w3.org/MarkUp/Forms/`
- **XForms 1.0: Data Model specification.** `www.w3.org/TR/xforms-datamodel/`
- **Mozquito.** `www.mozquito.com` This is an XHTML editor vendor that not only has a significant role in the creation of XForms, but also has created its own version of Web forms—Forms Markup Language (FML). FML is a collection of new elements for XHTML Web pages. Much of the functionality of XHTML-FML was folded into the W3C's coming version of XForms.

- **W3C's public mailing list subscription.** Send email to `www-forms-request` `@w3.org` with the word *subscribe* as the subject. If you decide you want to be removed from the list, send email to the same address with the word *unsubscribe* as the subject.

9

Calling Scripts and Other Objects

W EB PAGES CAN CONTAIN MUCH MORE THAN MARKUP, style sheets, and forms. This chapter and Chapter 10, "Working with Multimedia and Graphics" explore the plethora of ways available to make your Web sites more useful, more interactive, and more dynamic.

Web pages are often compared to print publications, and many of the best Web sites on the Internet are run by traditional publishing companies. The aspects of the Web that are analogous to any paper-based documents such as magazines, brochures, newspapers, encyclopedias or forms, are only the tip of the iceberg.

To understand the rest of this book and the enormous potential of the Web as a dynamic and interactive environment, we need to change the way we think about Web pages.

A Web page is not just formatted text and images with a beginning and an end. A Web page is actually more like a container. The Web page container can hold a variety of different objects. The possible objects include text, images, audio, multimedia, virtual reality environments, and much more.

Working with Media Types in XHTML

Theoretically, any type of data can be embedded in an XHTML document. In real life, it's impractical to embed a type of file in your document that the majority of your audience can't view because it doesn't have the correct application or plug-in.

One common problem that Web developers run into is that there's no way for a Web developer to control how content is handled by a user's browser. For example, Web developers often ask how they can make sure that the user's browser will play an audio file rather than save it to disk. The answer is that you can't. What a browser does with any one content type depends on how it's configured. Types of media that can be dealt with by the Web browser rarely present any difficulties. You can be sure that common image formats will display in the browser, for example. However, if you use a media type that isn't supported natively by the browser, many more potential problems arise. For this reason, it's important to know the basics of how content types work.

Web browsers and other applications know what to do with files by looking at their content types. When a Web server sends a file to a user, it prefaces the content of the file with a Hypertext Transfer Protocol (HTTP) header. The following markup shows a typical HTTP header:

```
HTTP/1.1 200 OK
Server: Microsoft-IIS/4.0
Date: Tue, 22 Aug 2000 20:50:14 GMT
Content-Type: application/x-shockwave-flash
Accept-Ranges: bytes
Last-Modified: Wed, 05 Jul 2000 15:57:38 GMT
Content-Length: 4262
```

In addition to various other pieces of useful information provided by the HTTP header, it also gives the Web browser the content type of the requested file. Web browsers use the content-type header to decide how to handle a file. If the browser doesn't know how to handle a file type, it will either ask the user how the file should be opened, or it will save the file to disk.

For example, Portable Document Format (PDF) files are viewed using Adobe's Acrobat Reader and Web browsers do not have built-in support for reading PDF files. When you click a link to a PDF file, it's either opened in the Acrobat Reader or in the Acrobat Reader plug-in (provided that either of these are present on your computer).

Today's Web browsers have built-in support for a wide variety of content types. Additional content types can be supported with plug-ins or external applications. Figure 9.1 shows Netscape Navigator's helper application preferences dialog box, which allows you to specify how different content types should be handled.

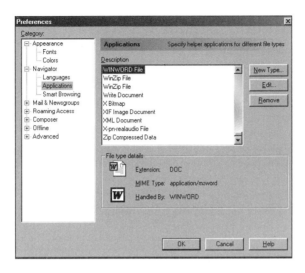

Figure 9.1 Netscape Navigator's helper application Preferences dialog box.

Content type information is specified using standardized Multipurpose Internet Mail Extensions (MIME) types. An HTML page's MIME type is `text/html` and an XML document's MIME type is `text/xml`. MIME types are grouped into categories such as text, audio, video, image, and application. Table 9.1 shows some of the more common MIME types that are used on the Web.

Table 9.1 **Common MIME Types**

MIME Type	Description	File Extension
text/html	HTML text	.html
text/css	Cascading Style Sheets	.css
text/xml	XML text	.xml
Audio/x-wav	Windows WAV audio	.wav
Audio/mp3	MP3 audio	.mp3
Video/quicktime	QuickTime video	.qt, .mov
application/x-shockwave-flash	Flash vector animation	.swf
application/msword	Microsoft Word document	.doc
Image/jpg	JPEG image	.jpg
Image/gif	GIF image	.gif

All these different types of objects can be combined inside the document container to create what we call a Web page.

The Document Object Model

Just as you might have some sort of system to help you find objects that are stored in a physical container (such as a tool box), Web pages also have a system for locating their parts.

The *Document Object Model* (DOM) provides a standard way for programs and scripts to access and manipulate HTML and XML documents. In other words, a DOM is an Application Programming Interface (API) for XML and HTML documents.

A DOM represents a document using a tree structure. DOM trees are made up of *node objects.* The two most common types of node objects are element nodes and text nodes.

Example 9.1 shows a table from an HTML document. Figure 9.2 shows how this table is represented using the DOM. As you can see, a tree view is simply a way to show the hierarchy of data in a document.

Example 9.1 **An HTML Table**

```
<table>
   <tbody>
   <tr>
     <td>John Coltrane</td>
     <td>Blue Train</td>
   </tr>
   <tr>
     <td>Snoop Doggy Dog</td>
     <td>Gin And Juice</td>
   </tr>
   </tbody>
</table>
```

A DOM is created when an HTML or XML document is read by an application, such as a Web browser, that can use the document. The DOM is then stored in memory and is ready for use. The process that a program goes through to find specific nodes is called *tree-walking* or *traversal.*

The Simple API for XML (SAX)

Because the DOM stores a complete model of the document in memory, it's not the most efficient way to programmatically access large documents. For this reason, the members of the XML-DEV mailing list developed the Simplified API for XML, or SAX.

SAX does not generate a tree of nodes like DOM does. Instead, SAX gives the programmer access to XML documents as a sequence of events. The main benefit of using SAX is that it does not require that an application store anything other than the information it needs in memory.

Although it's generally not very useful for dynamic XHTML, SAX may be the better API if you plan to use programs or scripts to access large documents. For more information about SAX and how it compares to the DOM, visit XML.com's DOM vs. SAX resource guide at www.xml.com/pub/Guide/SAX_vs._DOM.

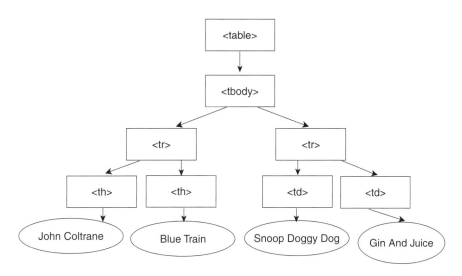

Figure 9.2   DOM representation of an HTML table.

The program that reads an XML document and makes the data in it available to programs is called an *XML parser*. The parsers that you're probably most familiar with are the ones that are built in to Web browsers.

The DOM was originally created by Netscape to enable JavaScript to manipulate the contents of documents. Shortly thereafter, Microsoft created a version of the DOM for its browsers. As so often happens, these two ways of identifying all of the parts of Web pages didn't quite agree, and have been the cause of countless developers' headaches.

As of this writing, there are still serious incompatibilities between Netscape's and Microsoft's browsers. This makes it somewhat difficult to create scripts that work on both browsers.

The W3C DOM is an attempt to standardize the way that programs access parts of documents and to eliminate some of the incompatibilities between browsers. The first version of the W3C DOM was called DOM Level 1 (www.w3.org/TR/REC-DOM-Level-1/). As of this writing, the W3C is about to make DOM Level 2 (www.w3.org/TR/DOM-Level-2/) an official recommendation.

Because the DOM makes it possible to access any part of a document, it also makes it possible for programs or scripts to modify any part of a document at any time. Before the DOM, the only way to have dynamic content in a Web site was to refresh the entire window. Any content that you wanted to change had to be changed on the server. After a document was in your browser, it might as well have been a newspaper.

After browser scripting and the DOM appeared, however, dynamic Web sites became much more common. Perhaps the most widespread examples of the use of the DOM to change the contents of an HTML document are images that change when the user puts his or her mouse pointer over them. These are called *rollovers*. With increased compatibility between the browsers, much more advanced interactivity and dynamic effects will become possible in Web browsers.

The W3C DOM is divided into a set of components, or modules. Each of these modules defines a set of interfaces. DOM Level 1 consists only of the Core and HTML modules.

The Core module represents the functionality used for XML documents. The HTML module defines the DOM interfaces to HTML elements.

DOM Level 2 adds many new features to the DOM. The modules included in DOM Level 2 are as follows:

- Core
- HTML
- Views
- Style sheets
- CSS
- Events
- Traversal
- Range

If the idea of object models seems rather abstract to you at this point, don't worry. The entire purpose of an object model and object-oriented data is to create a layer of abstraction between data and applications. The uses of the DOM, as well as the usefulness of interfaces will become clearer as we move toward specific examples later in this chapter.

Of Events and Objects

Before we talk about specifics of how to manipulate the contents of documents using the DOM, it's important to understand what makes up the DOM itself.

The name says it all. A DOM specification is a blueprint for modeling documents as objects.

Objects

Just as a Web page can be thought of as a container for elements, those elements can also be thought of as containers. These containers are called objects. Similar to real-world objects, DOM objects have characteristics, which are what they can do and what you can do with them.

The top, or *root*, of a DOM tree is the document object and provides the access to the document as a whole. Some examples of objects in a typical XHTML document include link objects, text area objects, paragraph objects, and so forth. Each of these objects corresponds to an element in the document, for example, `a`, `textarea`, and `p`, respectively.

Properties

An object's characteristics are called its properties. For example, the properties of an object that represents a telephone might be as follows:

```
Color="Red"
Weight="1 lb"
```

The properties of an object that represents an HTML input element might look like this:

```
name="City"
value="Long Beach"
size="30"
```

Some properties can be changed dynamically, whereas others are read-only. Examples of some properties of objects that can be changed using the DOM include the following:

- the style (color, font, size, and so forth) of text or other elements
- the position of elements in a document
- the values of input fields
- the image pointed to by an image (img) element

Methods

An object's methods are the tasks that it can perform. In our real-life example, a telephone object would have a method called ring. An example of a method available for XHTML documents is the window object's alert method, which opens an alert box. Other examples of DOM methods that can be used in XHTML documents include the following:

- **document.createElement(*tagNameString*).** Creates a new element in the document with the tag name specified in the parenthesis
- **document.getElementsByTagName(*tagNameString*).** Returns a list of all the elements with the tag name specified in the parenthesis
- **document.createTextNode(*textNode*).** Creates a new text node with the value in the parenthesis as its text

Using DOM methods, you could, for example, dynamically generate and populate an XHTML table from data that is entered into a form on the same page. Or, you could write an in-browser XHTML editor that allows the user to create Web pages by clicking buttons on the screen. Then, those buttons cause XHTML markup to be written and rendered in real-time (even in a separate browser window, if you like).

Events

Events are the things that can be done to an object. Events are generally used to trigger some sort of action. For example, the value of an img object's src property might change when a mouse pointer is over it, or a window element (which represents a browser window) might perform an action every time the document is loaded into a browser (using the document's onload event).

Creating Dynamic XHTML Pages

The collection of technologies that can be used with the DOM to change Web pages dynamically in the Web browsers is called *Dynamic HTML* (DHTML).

We've attempted to stay away from browser-specific DHTML code in this chapter. This is certainly a noble goal, but it's not always possible. At a bare minimum, you'll need either Netscape Communicator 6 or Internet Explorer 4 or greater to run most of the examples in this chapter. We tested the examples in this chapter using Internet Explorer 5 and Netscape Communicator 6, preview release 2, running on Windows 98.

Also, note that you may need to remove the XML declaration (`<?xml version="1.0"?>`) from these examples to get them to work in some Web browsers.

Dynamic HTML isn't a different form of HTML. Dynamic HTML is actually an abstract concept of manipulating objects in an HTML document tree using a scripting language.

The most common choice of scripting languages for creating DHTML pages is JavaScript (or JScript, which is Microsoft's version of Netscape's JavaScript language). JavaScript (or JScript) is used as the language of DHTML because it's the most widely supported browser scripting language.

Netscape first introduced a version of DHTML with version 4.0 of their browser. Netscape's DHTML was limited to the concept of *layers*, or positioning. Microsoft, on the other hand, quickly provided much more comprehensive DHTML support. For a couple years, DHTML authors have struggled with creating code that works on both browsers. The vastly different capabilities of the major browsers have seriously limited the use of DHTML.

With the release of Netscape 6, which features support for the W3C DOM, truly dynamic HTML may finally be ready for prime time.

Calling on Scripts

Scripts that run on the user's browser (also known as client-side scripts) can be included in XHTML documents by using the `script` element. Client-side scripts can be written in any language that the client application (generally a Web browser) can understand.

Java, JavaScript, JScript, Visual Basic Script (VBScript), and ECMAScript

One of the questions that we're asked most frequently by people who are new to Web programming and scripting is, "What is the difference between Java, JavaScript, VBScript, and JScript, and by the way, what in the world is ECMAScript?"

Java is a cross-platform programming language created by Sun Microsystems. Java is similar to C or C++ in that Java source code is compiled into a machine language before it's run. Java can be used to create standalone applications.

JavaScript, on the other hand, is a scripting language that was created by Netscape. Although somewhat similar to Java in syntax, the truth is that they are very different, and JavaScript was named as such primarily for marketing purposes.

The biggest difference between scripting languages and full-fledged programming languages, such as Java, is that scripting languages do not need to be compiled into binary form before they're executed. Instead, scripting languages are stored in plain-text files, and they're interpreted by a separate piece of software (such as a Web browser). Scripting languages are generally easier to use, but more limited in functionality than programming languages.

JScript, by Microsoft, is, for the most part, a JavaScript-compatible scripting language.

VBScript is a scripting language based on Microsoft's Visual Basic programming language. Because it's only supported by Microsoft's Web browser, VBScript is not widely used for client-side scripting.

And finally, *ECMAScript* is an industry-standard scripting language based on JavaScript and JScript.

The `script` element has four optional attributes:

- **src.** This attribute specifies the location of an external script. The `src` attribute is especially useful if you have a script that is on numerous pages of your site.
- **type.** This attribute specifies the content type of the script.
- **language.** This attribute is deprecated. Until `type` is more widely supported, your safest bet is to use both `type` and `language` attributes. The value of this attribute is the language in which the script is written, for example, `javascript`, `jscript`, or `vbscript`.
- **defer.** This is a Boolean attribute. It can be used to tell the browser (or other parser) that the script will not produce any content that needs to be displayed.

The `script` element is typically placed within the header of the document. In HTML documents, script code should be placed inside of HTML comments (`<!-- text here -->`). The reason for this is that if a browser does not understand either the `script` element or the code, it will simply display the code in the browser, which is not what you want at all. Putting the JavaScript code inside of HTML comments doesn't affect the JavaScript, but it does make it invisible to HTML parsers.

In addition, it's common practice to make the HTML comment closing tag invisible to the script code using the scripting language's comment notation. In JavaScript, comments are created by prefacing a line of text with two slashes (//).

In XHTML, if the browser you're using supports it, scripts should be placed inside of *CDATA sections*. An XML CDATA section is specified as follows:

```
<![CDATA[ content goes here ]]>
```

CDATA sections exist for indicating to the XML parser that it should not attempt to find XML markup in the contents of the CDATA section.

The following example shows a piece of JavaScript code inside of a `script` element. This example could be inserted into a well-formed XHTML document.

```
<script type="text/javascript" language="javascript">
//<![CDATA[ hide javascript from old browsers and XML parser
document.write("Client-side JavaScript date:");
document.write(Date());
// ]]>
</script>
```

The result of the execution of this code is that the text `"Client-side JavaScript date:"` will be written to the document followed by the date (or, more specifically, what the user's computer thinks the date is). Let's take a closer look at each line.

```
<script type="text/javascript" language="javascript">
```

This is the opening tag of the `script` element. The `type` attribute's value is specified as a MIME content type. The `language` attribute is included for compatibility with browsers and applications that do not support the `type` attribute.

```
<![CDATA[ hide JavaScript from old browsers and XML parser
```

Placing the code inside of a CDATA section is required for the XHTML document to be well formed. The text that follows the opening of the CDATA section (`"hide JavaScript from old browsers and XML parser"`) is simply a comment that is meant to explain why these lines are commented out to anyone who might modify the document in the future.

```
document.write("Client-side JavaScript date:");
```

This statement is the first of two actual lines of JavaScript code in this `script` element. This is a good example of a simple use of the DOM. What happens is this: When a JavaScript interpreter reads this line, it sends a line of text (`"Client-side JavaScript date:"`) to the `write` method of the `document` object. The `write` method then tells the browser (or other application) to display the line of text.

```
document.write(Date());
```

This line sends a function, namely `Date()`, to the `write` method of the `document` object. A function is simply a prebuilt piece of code that can be reused as needed. The `Date` function requests the current date and time from the user's computer, and the result is displayed in the browser. We'll look briefly at how you can create your own JavaScript function in the next section of this chapter ("Calling JavaScript with Events").

```
// ]]>
</script>
```

These two lines simply close everything. It's a good idea to comment out the closing of the CDATA sections using a JavaScript comment.

Calling JavaScript with Events

The previous example runs immediately when it's read. In the real world, it's common to have scripts run in response to something that is done by the user, by the browser, or by another program.

As you saw in the "The Document Object Model" section earlier in this chapter, these outside stimuli are called events. Table 9.2 shows the list of events that are supported by XHTML 1.0.

Table 9.2 **JavaScript Events Supported in XHTML 1.0**

Event	Description
onblur	The object loses focus.
onchange	The value of an element changes, such as a text input box or a radio button.
ondblclick	The user double-clicks an element.
onfocus	An object gains focus.
onkeydown	The user presses a key.
onkeypress	The user presses and holds a key.
onkeyup	The user releases a key.
onload	An object is loaded into the browser.
onmousedown	The user clicks the mouse button.
onmousemove	The user moves the mouse.
onmouseout	The user moves the mouse off an element.
onmouseover	The user moves the mouse onto an element.
onmouseup	The user releases the mouse button.
onreset	The user resets a form.
onselect	The user selects an element.
onsubmit	The user submits a form.
onunload	The user exits the page.

Most of the events supported by XHTML, such as onkeypress or onmouseover, are self-explanatory. Other events require a little explanation.

The onfocus and onblur events are usually used with form elements, such as input, select, and textarea. When a user makes an object the center of attention by clicking it or tabbing into it, that object is said to have *focus*. When you change focus from one object to another, an onblur event occurs in the object that is losing focus, and an onfocus event occurs in the object that is gaining focus.

Web browsers generally provide some sort of visual clues that an object has focus. Input elements that are in focus will have a visible input cursor. Other elements that are in focus will generally be outlined. For example, in Figure 9.3, the button that is currently in focus has a dotted line inside of it. Only one element in a document may have focus at any one time.

One frequent use of onfocus and onblur events is to trigger a script that performs some sort of calculation when the value of an input field is changed. JavaScript loan calculators or measurement conversion calculators are good examples of places where onfocus and onblur are useful. Example 9.2 shows an example of the use of events to trigger JavaScript.

Figure 9.3 Five buttons, one of which is in focus.

Example 9.2 **Triggering JavaScript with an Event**

```
<?xml version="1.0"?>
<!DOCTYPE html
    PUBLIC "-//W3C//DTD XHTML 1.0 Transitional//EN"
    "DTD/xhtml1-transitional.dtd">
<html xmlns ="http://www.w3.org/1999/xhtml">
  <head>
    <title>Find out the Date</title>
    <script type="text/javascript" language="javascript">
    <![CDATA[ hide javascript from old browsers and XML parser
    function alertDate() {
    alert("The Date and Time are: " + Date());
    }
    // ]]>
    </script>
  </head>
<body>
    <a href="#" onclick="alertDate()">Click here to find out the date
    and time!</a>
</body>
</html>
```

Example 9.2 declares a function called `alertDate`. Functions only run when they're asked to run by other code or by an event such as the `onclick` event in Example 9.2.

Much more dynamic effects are possible than simply displaying an alert box. Example 9.3 shows how JavaScript functions can be used with events and the DOM to create a text rollover effect on a link.

Example 9.3 **Using JavaScript Triggered by Events to Manipulate the DOM**

```
<?xml version="1.0"?>
<!DOCTYPE html
    PUBLIC "-//W3C//DTD XHTML 1.0 Transitional//EN"
    "DTD/xhtml1-transitional.dtd">
<html xmlns ="http://www.w3.org/1999/xhtml">
  <head>
    <title>Find out the Date</title>
```

```
  <script type="text/javascript" language="javascript">
  <![CDATA[ hide JavaScript from old browsers and XML parser
  function alertDate() {
  alert("The Date and Time are: " + Date());
  }
  // ]]>
  </script>
  </head>
<body>
<a href="#" onmouseover="javascript:this.style.color='green'"
           onmouseout="javascript:this.style.color=''"
           onclick="alertDate()">Click here to find out the
           date and time!</a>
</body>
</html>
```

The code in Example 9.3 uses the same `alertDate()` function as Example 9.2 for the action when the link is clicked. Example 9.3 adds `mouseover` and `mouseout` events to the `link` element. The following action is caused by the `mouseover` event:

```
this.style.color='green'
```

This instruction uses the DOM to manipulate the `color` property of the contents of the current object (the link).

As shown in the previous example, JavaScript accesses specific properties of objects in the DOM using *dot syntax*. Dot syntax traverses the DOM tree by specifying nodes in order of increasing specificity, separated by periods (.), until the desired node is reached.

If dot syntax is used inside of the element that you want to locate (as is the case in Example 9.3), you can simply reference the current object by using the keyword `this`.

If you want to reference an object from outside of that object, you need to specify the object as a child node of the document object. In Example 9.3, for instance, the action performed when the mouse is over the `a` element could also have been written as follows:

```
document.links[0].style.color='green';
```

The zero inside of the brackets (`[0]`) specifies that we're referring to the first link to appear in the document. The DOM stores multiple objects with the same name as arrays, or collections of objects. The first link in a document can be accessed using `[0]`, the second can be accessed using `[1]`, and so on.

Using dot syntax, any object can have events that can change the properties of any other object. For example, Example 9.4 shows a `mouseover` event on a link being used to change the contents of an input field.

Example 9.4   **A Link Mouseover Event Changing a Property of a Different Object**

```
<?xml version="1.0"?>
<!DOCTYPE html
     PUBLIC "-//W3C//DTD XHTML 1.0 Transitional//EN"
     "DTD/xhtml1-transitional.dtd">
<html xmlns ="http://www.w3.org/1999/xhtml">
  <head>
    <title>Find out the Date</title>
    <script type="text/javascript" language="javascript">
    <![CDATA[ hide JavaScript from old browsers and XML parser
    function writeDate() {
    myform.myInput.value = Date();
    }
    // ]]> </script>

  </head>
<body>
    <a href="#" onclick="writeDate()">
    Click here to find out the date and time!</a>
    <br />
      <form name="myform">
      The date and time are: <input type="text" name="myInput" />
      </form>
</body>
</html>
```

By manipulating the properties of objects, Dynamic HTML can also be used to create animations, perform calculations, and more. See the end of this chapter for pointers to DHTML resources on the Web.

object Element

The XHTML object element is designed as a generic way to include any type of external data in an XHTML page.

The object element was introduced to HTML in an attempt to simplify the inclusion of images, multimedia, Java applets, and other HTML documents into HTML pages. The idea is that instead of needing to know how to use the img element for images, the embed element for multimedia, and the applet element for Java applets, you can just learn one element, object, and use it any time you want to include an external object in your document.

Unfortunately, the object element is not widely supported by browsers yet, and is therefore not widely used by developers. Web developers prefer to stick to the old ways of embedding objects in documents.

As XHTML picks up steam, and as more people switch to newer, more standards-compliant browsers, use of the `object` element will become much more practical. Until then, be sure to test any use of the `object` element in any browsers in which you can reasonably expect your Web site to be viewed.

Besides simplification, the benefit of switching to use of the `object` element is that it will support types of multimedia that we can't even imagine yet. Whereas the `applet` element only supports Java applets, and the `img` element only supports images, an `object` element could be anything from a simple picture, to an audio file, to a 3D holographic virtual tour of Katmandu.

Attributes

To act as a generic object-inclusion element, `object` needs to have a few more attributes than most elements. The unique attributes of the `object` element are as follows:

- **classid.** This attribute can contain the URI of an application (such as a Java application).

- **codebase.** This attribute is used to specify the base URI that the URIs in the `classid`, `data`, and `archive` attributes are relative to. For example, if a `codebase` attribute has a value of `"http://www.example.com/applets/"` and the `classid` attribute has a value of `"myapplet.class"`, the `object` element would look for a file called `"myapplet.class"` inside the `applets` directory at `http://www.example.com`.

- **codetype.** This attribute is optional. Its value is the content type of the object named by the `classid` attribute. For example, you might use the `codetype` attribute to tell the application reading the `object` element to expect a Java applet.

- **data.** This attribute is used to point to objects that are not applications. For example, `data` would be used in the same way as the `src` attribute of the `img` element.

- **type.** This attribute specifies the HTTP content type of an object that is pointed to by the `data` attribute. The `type` attribute values might include names such as `audio/mpeg` and `image/gif`.

- **archive.** This attribute may contain a space-separated list of URIs for resources that are used by the object pointed to by the `data` attribute or the `classid` attribute. Therefore, the resources needed by the object can be preloaded, which improves overall performance of the object.

- **declare.** This is a Boolean attribute, which means that it doesn't have a value; it's simply either present or it isn't present. If `declare` is present, the `object` element in which it's present will not instantiate the object specified until a subsequent `object` element refers to it.

- **standby.** The value of the `standby` attribute is a message that will be displayed by the browser while the object pointed to by the `classid` or `data` attribute is loading.

Whereas the `img` element only allows you to specify alternative text for images, with the `object` element, you can specify any type of media format as an alternative object, as well as alternative text for objects. Alternative versions of objects are specified by nesting them inside of each other.

The XHTML document in Example 9.5 demonstrates the use of the `object` element to include several different types of media as alternatives to a Java applet. Note that Example 9.5 is a contrived example, not a working example. Therefore, when you open the HTML file on the CD, you will receive an error. Please view the text file instead.

Example 9.5 **Using Alternative Objects**

```
<?xml version="1.0"?>
<!DOCTYPE html
    PUBLIC "-//W3C//DTD XHTML 1.0 Transitional//EN"
    "DTD/xhtml1-transitional.dtd">
<html xmlns ="http://www.w3.org/1999/xhtml">
  <head>
   <title>A Multimedia Extravaganza</title>
  </head>
  <body>
  <!--try the Java applet first-->
        <object codebase="http://www.example.com/multimedia/"
        classid="extravaganza.class"
        type="application/java"
        title="A Multimedia Extravaganza"
        standby="Please wait while the extravaganza is loading."
        width="400"
        height="400">
  <!--If no Java support, try the PNG image-->
        <object codebase="http://www.example.com/multimedia/"
        data="extravaganza_title.png"
        type="image/png"
        width="400"
        height="400">
  <!--If no PNG support, try the GIF-->
        <object codebase="http://www.example.com/multimedia/"
        data="extravaganza_title.gif"
        type="image/gif"
        width="400"
        height="400">
  <!--If no GIF support, display the text-->
         <p>You won't see much of an extravaganza with the browser
         you're using.</p>
         <p><blink>This text might blink on and off, though.</blink></p>
        </object>
        </object>
          </object>
  </body>
  </html>
```

Passing Parameters to Objects

Some objects are islands. They receive no input from the outside world, and simply do the same thing every time they run. Other objects can, or must, receive information from the document in which they're embedded. For example, an embedded program for calculating the volume of a sphere wouldn't be much fun if it always calculated the volume of the same sphere.

Values that can be set by the user (or by you, the Web developer) are called *parameters*. You set parameters using the `param` element. Parameter elements must be nested inside of the element to which they apply. They have two self-explanatory attributes: `name` and `value`. Example 9.6 shows how parameters can be used to set the possible variables that a multimedia game might enable you to change.

Example 9.6 **Setting Object Parameters**

```
<object class="fungame.swf"
        type="application/shockwave"
        width="300"
        height="300"
        standby="Please wait while the fun game is loading...">
   <param name="difficultyLevel" value="easy" />
   <param name="soundVolume" value="High" />
   <param name="players" value="2" />
<p>If you see this text, it's because you don't have the right
plug-in installed to play this game.</p>
</object>
```

The capability to pass parameters to objects makes them much more flexible and reusable.

Using Java Applets

Java applets are programs, written in Sun Microsystems' Java programming language, that can be embedded in Web pages. Because they need to be downloaded the first time they're run (and because they're not as fast as programs written in other programming languages, such as C or C++), Java applets can sometimes cause irritating delays for the average user. With increasingly fast computers and Internet connections, however, the arguments people give for not using Java applets are becoming moot.

Java applets have been used for hundreds of very good purposes, besides the stock tickers and animations that you've probably seen and been annoyed by. Some of the best uses for Java applets that we've seen include the following:

- Browser-based word processors and HTML editors
- In-browser data entry and retrieval applications for internal Web sites
- Applications to monitor scientific data or produce reports from raw data over the Web
- Live tech-support chat applications

Java applets are made up of compiled Java files, which are called Java *class files*. Class files can be run using a Java Virtual Machine (JVM). You can think of a virtual machine as a computer inside of your computer. Most Web browsers come with a JVM built in.

Because Java programs are run by the JVM, rather than your physical computer, Java programs can run on any computer that has a JVM installed on it. This makes Java a perfect programming language for the Web.

Unlike traditional software, for which separate versions must be written for Windows, Macintosh, and Linux, the same Java program can run on all three of these operating systems.

The original, and still best supported, way to embed Java applets in Web pages is to use the `applet` element. Although the `object` element will eventually be supported widely enough for it to replace the `applet` element, this isn't the case yet.

In the most basic form of the `applet` element, you simply use it in the body of the document and the applet appears.

The `applet` element has several attributes:

- **codebase.** Serves the same purpose as the `object` element's `codebase` attribute. Its value is used as the base URI for the other attributes that take addresses as values.

- **code.** Contains the name, or the name and address, of a class file that contains a compiled Java applet.

- **name.** Allows you to give your applet a name, so other applets on the same page can communicate with it.

- **archive.** Has the same purpose as the `object` element's `archive` attribute. Its value is a comma-separated list of resources to be preloaded.

- **object.** The value of this attribute is the address of a serialized representation of an applet's state. In other words, it's possible for applets to save information about what they're doing as a file so the next time the applet is used, it will pick up where it left off—that is, it will have the same *state*. If the `object` attribute is used, the `code` attribute cannot be used, and vice versa.

- **width.** Specifies the initial width of the applet.

- **height.** Specifies the initial height of the applet.

A typical use of the `applet` element looks like this:

```
<applet code="MyApplet.class" width="100" height="140"></applet>
```

The following example shows a more advanced use of a Java applet (even though this particular applet itself is pretty useless):

```
<applet codebase="http://java.sun.com/applets/jdk/1.1/demo/NervousText"
code="NervousText.class" width="400" height="7"5>
  <param name="text" value="Java is fun!" />
  <p>
```

```
    If you are seeing this text, it is because your browser is not
    Java-enabled.
    </p>
</applet>
```

Providing Alternatives

If the script, image, or multimedia element that you embed in a Web page doesn't work on someone's browser for one reason or another, the worst possible thing that could happen is that nothing at all is displayed. A simple fallback message is often all that is required. As demonstrated in the "*object* Element" section of this chapter, much better ways to provide alternative content are often available.

Each element that could have compatibility problems in XHTML has a way to provide information when the element fails. In the case of JavaScript, this fallback is the `noscript` element. The `noscript` element is only shown to a user if the user is using a browser that doesn't understand the `script` element.

The text and markup that you place inside of this element are your chance to apologize and let potential users know what they need to do to make your site work.

The following example executes the script inside of the `script` element if it's read using a browser that supports Microsoft's VBScript. Ideally, in a browser that doesn't understand VBScript, the link inside of the `noscript` element will be shown.

```
<script type="application/vbscript" language="vbscript">
...some vbscript code...
</script>
<noscript>
  <p>You're using a browser that cannot use the VBScript on this page.
  <a href="javascript.html">Click here</a> for the JavaScript version.</p>
</noscript>
```

The reality of browser support for the `noscript` element is not quite so simple. Most browsers will fail to render the text inside of the `noscript` element so long as the browser's scripting capabilities are turned on.

Therefore, if you open the previous markup in a Netscape browser (which doesn't support VBScript), it won't execute the script or display the `noscript` text. As a result, the `noscript` element is currently useful only as a way to provide content for users whose browsers don't have any scripting capabilities at all.

Other methods of making your Dynamic XHTML pages degrade gracefully include the following:

- Use browser detection scripts to provide alternative scripts where there may be compatibility issues.
- Know your audience. Don't use scripts for vital parts of your site (such as navigation) unless you're sure that your audience can use them. Web server log files can be used to find out information about the browsers and computers that visitors to your site use.

- Many elements use the `alt` attribute to specify text alternatives. Use the `alt` attribute wherever possible, and make the value descriptive. Alternative text that gives the name of the file and/or its dimensions (as certain HTML editors generate by default) is useless. If an image is a beautiful picture of a sunset, say so in the `alt` attribute.

Even though Netscape and Microsoft are seemingly rushing full steam ahead toward standards support, there are still plenty of browsers, and plenty of other types of applications, that do not support every cool DHTML effect or other multimedia effects that you might use. For this reason, it's always important to provide alternatives so that your Web pages degrade gracefully, as we say in the business.

As you rush ahead into Chapter 10, and as the Web rushes toward a richer and more dynamic user experience, it's vital that Web developers always remember the variety of ways that Web data can be used. If you write well-formed markup and provide alternatives for multimedia elements, you lessen your chances of losing potential visitors and you still get to use the latest technologies.

For More Information

For more information on the subjects covered in this chapter, visit the following Web sites:

- **The W3C DOM.** www.w3.org/DOM/

- **Dynamic HTML in Netscape Navigator.**
  http://developer.netscape.com/docs/manuals/communicator/dynhtml/

- **Microsoft's DOM.** http://msdn.microsoft.com/workshop/author/dhtml/
  reference/dhtmlrefs.asp

- **DHTML Zone.** www.dhtml-zone.com/

- **Webmonkey's DHTML page.** http://hotwired.lycos.com/webmonkey/
  collections/dynamic_html.html/

- **JavaScript source.** http://javascript.internet.com

- **Sun's Java site.** http://java.sun.com

10

Working with Multimedia and Graphics

IN CHAPTER 9, "CALLING SCRIPTS AND OTHER OBJECTS," you saw various ways to use multimedia, Java applets, and scripts in HTML, XHTML, and XML documents. In this chapter, we take a closer look at some of the currently available types of multimedia, as well as some emerging formats, that you could add to your Web sites.

Using multimedia and graphics on Web sites has always involved compromises. The following are just a few of the issues that Web developers have to think about every time they use graphics or multimedia:

- The number of colors available for graphics must be limited because the color palettes and screen resolutions of different operating systems and computers vary.

- The size of graphics and multimedia files is limited by download times experienced by people browsing the Web with slow connections, such as modems.

- Browser scripting is limited by the lowest common denominator of features supported by most of the Web browsers in use.

- Many multimedia formats require the user to download a plug-in, and people are still highly averse to downloading plug-ins.

- Different combinations of browsers and operating systems support different multimedia plug-ins.

- Download times for multimedia formats vary widely.
- Download time can be reduced or even eliminated by streaming multimedia.
- Streaming multimedia formats generally require both the user and the server to have special software.

The most widely supported type of non-text media used on the Web is static images. Inserting an image into an XHTML document is usually done using the `img` element. For example, the following element inserts the file pointed to by the `src` attribute into the document:

```
<img src="myhouse.jpg" width="300" height="300" alt="This is a picture of my
house." />
```

The two file formats that are likely to be supported by most Web browsers today are Graphics Interchange Format (GIF) and Joint Photographic Experts Group (JPEG) images. These file formats are used for storage of raster images. *Raster images* are commonly created using paint programs, or by scanning pictures. A raster image contains information, such as color and position, for each pixel in the image. Other common raster image file formats include Portable Network Graphics (PNG), Tagged Image File Format (TIFF), and the standard Windows bit-mapped graphics format (BMP).

In many instances, simple raster images are all that a Web site needs to effectively convey the intended message while still looking good. Increasingly, however, a wider variety of multimedia effects are being used on the Web.

Until recently, if you, as a Web developer, chose to use multimedia on your Web site, that part of your site became inaccessible to some group of users—such as people using text-only browsers or handheld computers, or people with disabilities.

The conflict has always been that the client wants flashy graphics and interactive content, but the use of these technologies is limiting to both the client's and the site's potential audience.

Emerging technologies and standards (currently in development) are beginning to eliminate the barriers to using multimedia, high-quality fonts, and high-quality graphics.

One of the most promising new developments from the W3C is an XML-based graphics format called *Scalable Vector Graphics* (SVG).

SVG Takes on Graphics

SVG is a new standard for creating two-dimensional graphics and animations for the Web. Many of the biggest players on the Web have contributed to the SVG standard, and it's highly likely that this standard will have a serious impact on the Web. Some of the companies that have been involved in the creation of SVG include Microsoft, Adobe, Macromedia, IBM, Sun Microsystems, Apple, Xerox, Netscape, Corel, and Kodak. Several products are currently available for working with SVG, and several more are in the works. Web browser support for SVG is currently available through plug-ins, and will soon be built in. A short list of SVG's features and benefits includes the following:

- Can be created and modified with just a text editor
- Can be resized without image degradation
- Capability to use any fonts and styles
- Support for Cascading Style Sheets (CSS)
- Capability to extract text from images
- Can be manipulated using scripts
- Capability to apply sophisticated effects to graphics and text

Using and creating SVG graphics will soon be just as easy as using GIF and JPEG images is today. However, SVG's capabilities are much different from the capabilities of GIFs and JPEGs.

SVG defines a vector graphic format. *Vector graphics* contain information about the curves and lines in a picture, rather than information about the pixels that make up the image. Raster graphic formats, as discussed earlier in this chapter, store information about every pixel in the graphic. Because vector graphic language actually describes only the shapes that a graphic contains, the image will look the same (except, of course, larger) whether it's 50 pixels wide or 850 pixels wide.

Many image creation programs will eventually support SVG (several, such as Adobe Illustrator, already do), and you don't need anything more than a text editor to create SVG graphics. See `www.w3.org/Graphics/SVG/SVG-Implementations` for more information on SVG viewers, editors, and converters.

Writing SVG

SVG is actually an XML application. SVG documents can be either plain text or compressed text files with an .svg extension. Like other XML applications, SVG can also be used in XHTML or other types of XML files. (Note that although software support for SVG is promising, it's still in preliminary stages.) Example 10.1 shows a simple, self-contained SVG document (saved with an .svg extension). This document describes a red circle and a blue rectangle.

Example 10.1 **An SVG Document**

```
<?xml version="1.0" standalone="no"?>
<!DOCTYPE svg PUBLIC "-//W3C//DTD SVG 20000802//EN"
  "http://www.w3.org/TR/2000/CR-SVG-20000802/DTD/svg-20000802.dtd">
<svg width="300" height="300">
  <rect style="stroke:#000000; stroke-width:3; stroke-opacity:1; fill:#ff0000;
  fill-opacity:1"
x="17" y="55" width="119" height="112" />
```

continues

Example 10.1   **Continued**

```
   <circle style="stroke:#000000; stroke-width:3; stroke-opacity:1; fill:#0000ff;
   fill-opacity:1"
cx="232" cy="124" r="60" />
</svg>
```

Viewed using a browser with Adobe's SVG plug-in (which you can download from
`www.adobe.com/svg/viewer/install/`), this SVG file appears as shown in Figure 10.1.

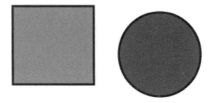

Figure 10.1   Example 10.1 displayed in a browser.

As you can see, SVG is fairly straightforward. Because SVG is an XML vocabulary, it
should be easy for anyone familiar with XML to pick up and start using. Although
there will eventually be plenty of tools available for creating SVG graphics and animations, a basic understanding of its inner workings will give you a greater appreciation
of the power of SVG.

SVG Basics

A document with the extension .svg is called an SVG document. An `svg` element and
its contents (whether they are in a standalone document or not) are called an *SVG
document fragment*. Each element inside of an `svg` element is called a *graphic object*.

SVG document fragments can be embedded in other SVG document fragments.
This is useful, for example, if you want to have separate viewpoints, or documents
inside of documents.

The `svg` element has several important attributes:

- **width.** Specifies the width of the outermost document fragment.

- **height.** Specifies the height of the outermost document fragment.

- **x.** Specifies the horizontal position of an embedded document fragment.

- **y.** specifies the vertical position of an embedded document fragment.

Example 10.2 shows an SVG document with an embedded document fragment.

Example 10.2 **An SVG Document with an Embedded Document Fragment**

```
<?xml version="1.0" standalone="no"?>
<!DOCTYPE svg PUBLIC "-//W3C//DTD SVG 20000802//EN"
  "http://www.w3.org/TR/2000/CR-SVG-20000802/DTD/svg-20000802.dtd">
<svg width="300" height="300">
      <polygon style="stroke:#000000; stroke-width:1; stroke-opacity:1;
      fill:#000000; fill-opacity:1" points="87,40,9,182,164,182"
      transform="matrix(1.7871 0 0 1.55634 -7.08387 -22.2535)" />
<svg x="25" y="25">
      <rect style="stroke:#000000; stroke-width:1; stroke-opacity:1; fill:#ff0000;
      fill-opacity:1" x="109" y="150" width="83" height="68" />
</svg>
</svg>
```

The document shown in Example 10.2 draws a red rectangle inside of a black triangle. By keeping the two in separate document fragments you could, for example, magnify graphics inside of the rectangle while keeping the triangle at the same magnification.

Graphic objects also can be grouped so that they can share attributes. Grouping can be done using the g element. Example 10.3 creates two red rectangles and two blue rectangles.

Example 10.3 **A Portion of an SVG Document That Creates Two Red Rectangles and Two Blue Rectangles**

```
<svg width="5cm" height="5cm">
  <desc>Two groups, each of two rectangles
  </desc>
  <g id="group1" style="fill:red">
    <rect x="1cm" y="1cm" width="1cm" height="1cm" />
    <rect x="3cm" y="1cm" width="1cm" height="1cm" />
  </g>
  <g id="group2" style="fill:blue">
    <rect x="1cm" y="3cm" width="1cm" height="1cm" />
    <rect x="3cm" y="3cm" width="1cm" height="1cm" />
  </g>
</svg>
```

All the SVG examples in this chapter so far have used only vector graphics. However, you can actually include three different kinds of graphic objects in SVG markup: vector graphic shapes, images (for example PNGs or JPEGs), and text.

Using Vector Graphics

Vector graphics are made up of shapes that are drawn using paths. If you've used a vector graphic-based drawing program, such as Adobe Illustrator, you know that paths represent the outline of shapes. Paths are defined by connecting points with lines. For example, a triangle contains three points and three lines. Although SVG enables you to create shapes using paths, the more common method of creating SVG graphics is to use SVG's *basic shapes*. SVG enables you to create six basic shapes:

- **rect.** Rectangles are defined by specifying x and y coordinates and width and length (with x and y both being zero in the upper-left corner of the canvas in which the rectangle is being drawn).

- **circle.** Circles are defined using x and y coordinates of the center and the radius.

- **ellipse.** Ellipses are defined using x and y coordinates of the center and the x-axis and y-axis radii.

- **line.** Lines are defined using starting and ending x and y coordinates.

- **polyline.** A polyline is a set of connected lines. Polyline elements are generally used to define open shapes.

- **polygon.** Polygons describe closed shapes consisting of any number of connected straight lines.

SVG defines an element and attributes that are used to describe each of the basic shapes. Example 10.4 defines one of each of the six basic shapes.

Example 10.4 **An Example That Uses Each of the Basic Shapes**

```
<?xml version="1.0" standalone="no"?>
<!DOCTYPE svg PUBLIC "-//W3C//DTD SVG 20000802//EN"
  "http://www.w3.org/TR/2000/CR-SVG-20000802/DTD/svg-20000802.dtd">
<svg width="300" height="300">
      <rect x="39" y="94" width="196" height="144" />
      <ellipse cx="165" cy="106.5" rx="83" ry="40.5" />
      <circle cx="129.5" cy="235.5" r="50" />
      <polygon points="144,36,180,50,195,86,180,121,144,135,107,121,92,
      86,107,50" />
      <line x1="47" y1="31" x2="260" y2="31" />
      <polyline points="72,275,231,274,273,153,275,252,209,178" />
</svg>
```

Because this example does not contain any style information, the result of this code when viewed using an SVG browser is a set of overlapping black shapes resembling a psychiatrist's inkblot drawing.

Applying Style

Styles such as color, fills, opacity, and so forth can be applied to SVG graphic objects using the `style` attribute. The language for applying styles to SVG objects will look familiar if you've worked with Cascading Style Sheets (CSS) and/or the Extensible Stylesheet Language (XSL). XSL, CSS, and SVG all share the same style properties whenever possible. Because SVG is a graphics format, it has many additional properties that are not available with CSS or XSL. Some of the styles that can be applied to SVG vector graphics that are not included in CSS include the following:

- **Stroke styles**. Stroke styles, such as `stroke-width` and `stroke-opacity`, enable you to specify information about the lines that make up your shapes.

- **Fill styles**. Fill styles enable you to specify information about the interior of a graphical element.

- **Filter effect properties**. Filter effect properties enable you to easily apply commonly used filters such as Gaussian blurs, lighting effects, and drop shadows to graphic elements.

Example 10.5 shows an SVG document with styles applied. Figure 10.2 shows what this SVG document looks like when rendered in a browser that supports SVG.

Example 10.5 **An SVG Document with Styles Applied**

```
<?xml version="1.0" standalone="no"?>
<!DOCTYPE svg PUBLIC "-//W3C//DTD SVG 20000802//EN"
  "http://www.w3.org/TR/2000/CR-SVG-20000802/DTD/svg-20000802.dtd">
<svg width="300" height="300">
    <defs>
        <filter id="drop_shadow">
            <feGaussianBlur result="blurredAlpha" in="SourceAlpha"
            stdDeviation="3"/>
            <feOffset result="offsetBlurredAlpha" in="blurredAlpha" dx="3"
            dy="3"/>
            <feFlood result="flooded" style="flood-color:#000000;
            flood-opacity:0.65"/>
            <feComposite result="coloredShadow" in="flooded" operator="in"
            in2="offsetBlurredAlpha"/>
            <feComposite in="SourceGraphic" operator="over"
            in2="coloredShadow"/>
        </filter>
    </defs>
    <polygon style="filter:url(#drop_shadow); stroke:#dfbfdc; stroke-width:1;
    stroke-opacity:1; fill:#dcc0de; fill-opacity:1"
points="114,61,87,211,140,211"
    transform="matrix(1.69811 0 0 1 -88.7358 -28)" />
    <text style="stroke:#ffffff; stroke-width:1; stroke-opacity:1; font-size:36;
    font-family:Verdana; font-weight:400; fill:#21b11d; fill-opacity:1"
    transform="matrix(1 0 0 1 60 107)">welcome</text>
    <text style="stroke:#da9ede; stroke-width:1; stroke-opacity:1; font-size:48;
    font-family:Garamond; font-weight:400; fill:#b01ea4; fill-opacity:1"
    x="59" y="142">to SVG</text>
</svg>
```

Figure 10.2. An SVG document with styles
applied displayed in a browser that supports SVG.

SVG Text

As you saw in Examples 10.4 and 10.5, you can insert and style text in SVG using the
`text` element. Each `text` element describes a single line of text in your SVG document. So, to create two lines of text, you need to use two `text` elements. Because SVG
text is simply XML text, it can be read by search engines and by browsers for the
visually impaired. In addition, other types of applications can possibly use the textual
content of SVG graphics.

Including Images in SVG

There are times when you may want to include a JPEG graphic (such as a photo-
graph) in an SVG element. This can be done using the `image` element. The `image` element enables you to specify a rectangle into which an entire file is rendered. Example
10.6 is an SVG document fragment that creates a 100×100 pixel rectangle and fills it
with a JPEG image.

Example 10.6 **An SVG Document Fragment That Creates a 100×100 Pixel
Rectangle and Fills It with a JPEG Image**

```
<?xml version="1.0" standalone="no"?>
<!DOCTYPE svg PUBLIC "-//W3C//DTD SVG 20000802//EN"
  "http://www.w3.org/TR/2000/CR-SVG-20000802/DTD/svg-20000802.dtd">
<svg width="4in" height="3in">
  <desc>This graphic links to an external image
  </desc>
  <image x="200" y="200" width="100px" height="100px"
         xlink:href="me.jpg">
    <title>A picture of me</title>
  </image>
</svg>
```

The `image` element can also be used to embed external SVG files in your document.

We've only scratched the surface of SVG's capabilities. Some of the other things that are possible with SVG include linking, interactive graphics, and the capability to use fonts that aren't installed on the user's computer. For more information on SVG, see the W3C site at `www.w3.org/Graphics/SVG/Overview.htm8` or the SVG specification at `www.w3.org/TR/SVG/`.

Moving Beyond Static Images

In this section, you find out about the various available ways to create animation on the Web, including SVG, which was discussed in the previous section. Animation is created when a series of graphics changes over time. Animation has been possible on the Web almost from the beginning. Perhaps the first form of animation, primitive and annoying as it was, was done using Netscape's `blink` element. Fortunately, Web animation has become much more sophisticated since then. Some of the ways to create animation for the Web today are as follows:

- Animated GIFs
- Shockwave
- Flash
- Synchronized Multimedia Integration Language
- SVG

We discuss each of these in more detail in the following sections.

Animated GIFs

Animated GIFs are the simplest and cheapest way to create animation on the Web. Animated GIFs consist of frames. You can control the length of time that each frame displays and the number of times that the animation loops. The benefits of animated GIFs are as follows:

- They're easy to create using free or inexpensive tools.
- They're supported by a larger number of Web browsers than any other animation technology and they don't require a plug-in.

Animated GIFs are not the right solution for every animation need, however. The drawbacks of animated GIFs include the following:

- Frame-based animation usually results in larger file sizes than vector animation.
- It's not possible to create smooth transitions with GIF animation.
- GIF color palettes are limited.
- GIF animation doesn't have any interactive features.

A variety of technologies requiring plug-ins have been introduced to provide the type of features that GIF animations lack. One of the earliest of these was Macromedia's Shockwave.

Shockwave

Macromedia Shockwave was originally designed for creating interactive CD-ROMs. Multimedia created using Shockwave can be viewed in Web browsers using the Shockwave plug-in.

Shockwave multimedia is developed using Macromedia Director and can be scripted using Macromedia's scripting language, Lingo. Using Shockwave, you can create sophisticated, interactive media, such as games and highly interactive presentations that interact with databases and external programs.

The downside to Shockwave is that initial file downloads are typically large and playing Shockwave files requires a plug-in.

Flash

Flash is a vector-based animation format that was created by Macromedia specifically for the Web. The Flash plug-in is a relatively small download and Flash multimedia files also download quickly. The result is that Flash animation is popping up everywhere on the Web.

Although Flash doesn't have all the functionality of Shockwave, the small size of Flash files and the fact that it's a vector graphic format make it great for dynamic Web-site user interfaces, illustrations that can be enlarged and reduced, and long animations.

The downsides to Flash include the fact that it still requires a plug-in, it's a proprietary format, and Web developers have to purchase expensive software to create Flash multimedia.

SMIL

Synchronized Multimedia Integration Language (SMIL, pronounced "smile") enables authoring of television-like multimedia presentations that integrate different types of standalone multimedia elements. Whereas HTML only allows you to describe the layout of elements, SMIL allows you to also describe when multimedia elements should play in relation to each other. For example, you could synchronize a video clip with a separate soundtrack. Or, you could tell an animation to play after a video (or any other multimedia element) has finished playing.

SMIL 1.0 is currently a W3C recommendation and a wide variety of players and authoring tools are available. Find out more about SMIL 1.0 on the W3C site at www.w3.org/TR/REC-smil/.

SVG Animation

In the near future, tools for creating animation and multimedia for the Web (such as Director and Flash) will increasingly be capable of exporting SVG files. As browsers start to have built-in SVG support, SVG will become the preferred animation format on the Web. SVG has five animation elements:

- **animate.** Enables properties and attributes of SVG objects to have different values over time.

- **set.** A shorthand form of animate for changing the value of non-numeric properties and attributes.

- **animateMotion.** Used to move an object along a motion path.

- **animateColor.** Changes the value of color properties or attributes over time.

- **animateTransform.** Modifies SVG transformation attributes over time.

Example 10.7 shows how these elements can be used to animate SVG vector graphics. See the comments to find out what the markup does.

Example 10.7 **How These Elements Can Be Used to Animate SVG Vector Graphics**

```
<?xml version="1.0" standalone="no"?>
<!DOCTYPE svg PUBLIC "-//W3C//DTD SVG 20000802//EN"
  "http://www.w3.org/TR/2000/CR-SVG-20000802/DTD/svg-20000802.dtd">
<svg width="8cm" height="3cm"  viewBox="0 0 800 300">
  <desc>Example anim01 - demonstrate animation elements</desc>

  <!-- The following illustrates the use of the animate element
       to animate a rectangles x, y, and width attributes so
       the rectangle grows to ultimately fill the viewport. -->
  <rect id="RectElement" x="300" y="100" width="300" height="100"
        style="fill:rgb(255,255,0)">
    <animate attributeName="x" attributeType="XML"
          begin="0s" dur="9s" fill="freeze" from="300" to="0" />
    <animate attributeName="y" attributeType="XML"
          begin="0s" dur="9s" fill="freeze" from="100" to="0" />
    <animate attributeName="width" attributeType="XML"
          begin="0s" dur="9s" fill="freeze" from="300" to="800" />
    <animate attributeName="height" attributeType="XML"
          begin="0s" dur="9s" fill="freeze" from="100" to="300" />
  </rect>

  <!-- Set up a new user coordinate system so the
       text string's origin is at (0,0), allowing
       rotation and scale relative to the new origin. -->
  <g transform="translate(100,100)" >
    <!-- The following illustrates the use of the set, animateMotion,
         animateColor, and animateTransform elements. The text element
```

continues

Example 10.7 **Continued**

```
            below starts off hidden (i.e., invisible). At three seconds, it
              * becomes visible
              * continuously moves diagonally across the viewport
              * changes color from blue to dark red
              * rotates from -30 to zero degrees
              * scales by a factor of three. -->
      <text id="TextElement" x="0" y="0"
            style="font-family:Verdana; font-size:35.27; visibility:hidden" >
         It's alive!
         <set attributeName="visibility" attributeType="CSS" to="visible"
              begin="3s" dur="6s" fill="freeze" />
         <animateMotion path="M 0 0 L 100 100"
              begin="3s" dur="6s" fill="freeze" />
         <animateColor attributeName="fill" attributeType="CSS"
              from="rgb(0,0,255)" to="rgb(128,0,0)"
              begin="3s" dur="6s" fill="freeze" />
         <animateTransform attributeName="transform" attributeType="XML"
              type="rotate" from="-30" to="0"
              begin="3s" dur="6s" fill="freeze" />
         <animateTransform attributeName="transform" attributeType="XML"
              type="scale" from="1" to="3" additive="sum"
              begin="3s" dur="6s" fill="freeze" />
      </text>
    </g>
  </svg>
```

Although the details of SVG animation are beyond the scope of this book, you can start getting a feel for how it works by experimenting with this example using a text editor and an SVG browser or browser plug-in.

Working with Audio

As with graphics and animation formats, there are several different ways to create and use audio on the Web. Until recently, the most common options were MIDI and WAV files, which we discuss in the following sections. Then, we discuss the newest audio method: the MP3.

Musical Instrument Digital Interface

Musical Instrument Digital Interface (MIDI) is a digital audio standard that's used to enable electronic instruments and sound processors (sound cards, for example) to talk to each other. MIDI sounds are actually stored on your computer. Because of this, MIDI files only need to contain information about the notes that your sound card should play.

The primary benefit of using MIDI sound is that, because they don't need to contain actual sounds, MIDI files are extremely small. On the other hand, the quality of MIDI audio depends on end user's sound system and the range of sounds is limited to the MIDI set of sounds. Therefore, MIDI can't be used to play your band's CD on your site, but it can be used to play a moving rendition of "The Yellow Rose of Texas" in the background as visitors browse your site—if they can stand it.

Creating MIDI files is easy. All that's needed is a computer with a sound card and MIDI sequencing software. You can use your computer's keyboard to create music, or, you can attach a piano-style MIDI keyboard to your computer.

WAV

WAV is a format developed by IBM and Microsoft for storing audio on PCs. Unlike MIDI files, WAV files do contain the actual information about the sounds. As a result, they can be very large. For example, 1 minute of CD-quality audio takes up about 10MBs when stored as a WAV file. This translates to a transmission time of about 50 minutes over a 28.8 modem.

The two most important factors that determine the size of a sampled audio file are its *sample rate* and its *bit rate*.

Sample Rate

Sound travels through the air in continuous waves. Computers, being digital, are unable to represent continuously variable (or analog) qualities. In order to record waves digitally, then, computers must record (or sample) the frequency and the amplitude of the wave many times per second. The more often the rate of sampling, the better the sound quality.

Bit Rate

Bit rate refers to the amounts of storage space used by each sample. The bit rate determines the dynamic range of a digital recording. An 8-bit recording is equivalent to a cassette tape and a 16-bit recording is audio CD quality.

Until the emergence of the MP3 audio format, adjusting the bit rate and the sample rate were the two most common methods for controlling the size of audio files.

Creating and Using MP3s

MP3 is a compression format. Its full name is MPEG 1 Audio Layer 3. The big deal about MP3 is that it can compress audio files anywhere from 7 to 17 times their original file size. Whereas a typical four-minute song takes up over 40MBs of storage space uncompressed, it takes up less than 4MBs when compressed using MP3.

MP3 uses a variety of techniques to compress audio files. It relies heavily on the fact that the human ear can hear only sounds of certain frequencies, and it hears sounds in some frequencies much better than others. By eliminating information about sounds that we can't hear, the size of audio files is greatly reduced.

MP3 has very quickly become the standard compression format for storing and transmitting high-quality audio on the Internet. You can create your own MP3s and listen to MP3s using one of the many inexpensive tools that are currently available. MP3 files are generally created from audio CDs or from WAV files. The process of compressing the tracks on an audio CD using MP3 is called *ripping* and tools for ripping CDs are called *rippers*. A couple sources for MP3 players and conversion software are listed at the end of this chapter.

Making Movies

Faster downloads, larger images, and higher quality video are coming soon to a browser near you. Film and video producers are beginning to use the Web as an inexpensive video distribution medium.

The leading technologies in Web video are RealNetworks' RealVideo, Apple's QuickTime, and Microsoft Media. All three of these use a technology called *streaming* to reduce or eliminate the wait before you can begin viewing video. A streaming media server feeds compressed data to the user as the file is being viewed by the user. The video that the user sees, or the audio that the user hears, arrives at the user's computer just before it's needed.

The amount of compression determines the quality of the video and audio. Generally, video needs to be heavily compressed to be served over the Internet. Some of the ways that video can be compressed include reducing the following properties:

- The number of frames per minute that are shown to the user (frame rate)
- The quality of the images and the sound
- The size of the image

Streaming video can be used in HTML (and XHTML) pages in the same way as other multimedia elements: You can either link to the streaming video, or you can embed it in the page using the HTML `object` element.

The quality and size of images that can realistically be transmitted over the Internet still prevents your computer from replacing your home entertainment center, but, as with every form of multimedia on the Web, the technology is rapidly improving.

For More Information

As mentioned, Web multimedia is changing rapidly. Recent developments, such as SVG and MP3, point to a future of greater standardization and compatibility. With the amount of excitement surrounding new multimedia technologies, it's important and not very hard to stay up-to-date. The following list provides some starting points:

- **Adobe's SVG site.** `www.adobe.com/svg`

- **The W3C's SVG overview.** `www.w3.org/Graphics/SVG/Overview.htm8`

- **The SMIL 1.0 recommendation.** `www.w3.org/TR/REC-smil/`.

- **Macromedia (proprietor of Shockwave and Director).** `www.macromedia.com`

- **MP3Now.com.** `www.cmj.com/mp3` (contains MP3 news, hardware and software reviews, MP3 related feature articles, and music)

- **MP3.com.** `www.mp3.com` (an enormous library of MP3 audio files, as well as general MP3 news and information and lists of MP3 rippers and players)

- **Streaming Media World.** `http://smw.internet.com` (news, reviews, and information about streaming media)

11

Advanced Linking Techniques

Lᴛɴᴋꜱ ᴀʀᴇ ᴡʜᴀᴛ ᴍᴀᴋᴇ ᴛʜᴇ Wᴇʙ ɢᴏ ᴀʀᴏᴜɴᴅ, so to speak. They enable us to connect to other resources on the Web. Except for a couple of differences, which are noted later in this chapter, XHTML linking works the same way as HTML 4.0 linking. Linking is one of those areas that will be changing dramatically in the near future, however. A W3C standard exists that defines a new, more advanced, way to create links on the Web: XLink, or the Extensible Markup Language (XML) linking language. This chapter covers the following topics:

- The history of linking
- Why we need XLink
- How XLink works

In addition, we cover XPointer and XPath briefly.

History and Theory of Linking

The Web was originally conceived as being similar to a spider's web in structure—without dead-ends and with each page linking to further information. Today, however, we've reached a point where much of the Web is more like islands, or in the case of enormous Web publishers, continents. Whereas the early Web consisted of documents with links and entire pages of links and lists, today's Web is becoming more like television. You can't get anywhere without manually changing the channel. People are afraid to create links because of potential legal problems, because they don't want to help their competition or encourage people to leave their site, because they don't want to risk their users encountering a dead link, or because they just don't think of the Web that way.

This devaluing of linking is partly a result of the commercialization of the Web, but it can't be completely blamed on that. Another contributing factor is that our ability to create links is severely limited. HTML links have the following limitations:

- Links are unidirectional.
- To create links on a document, you have to own it.
- Links can have only one destination.

For those of us who've been around since the beginning of the development of HTML in the early 1990s, these limitations don't seem like limitations, but more like features. In fact, it's hard to imagine how the Web would function or what it would look like without these "features." To get a wider perspective on linking, it's important to know that linking goes back much further than the early 1990s.

Linking Pioneers

The original concept of linking between documents goes back centuries to the creation of the bibliography or cross-reference. However, with the enormous amount of information being produced and published today, a more dynamic type of linking was conceived as a way to manage this information and hopefully make sense of it all. The roots of our current concept of linking are generally traced from several pioneers of the mid-twentieth century, through the development of HTML, to today.

Vannevar Bush

Vannevar Bush coordinated the activities of American scientists in the application of science to warfare during World War II. As the war was drawing to a close, he wrote an article that appeared in *Atlantic Monthly* in July 1945. The article was titled, "As We May Think." This article is widely cited as the origin of modern hyperlinking.

In the article, Dr. Bush imagines a device he called a "Memex," which allows the user to access various types of information in a vast and ever-growing library. He theorizes that the device would allow data to be accessed using an index, as well as through association. He describes the process of adding information to this web of data, as well as the ability of the user to create links or "trails" that imitate and improve on the way that our brains seem to operate.

Douglas Engelbart

Douglas Engelbart did research in the 1960s in augmenting human intellect. In his work, he cites Vannevar Bush's groundbreaking paper, expands on it, and brings the Memex up-to-date with the electric computer technology of the 1960s. Based on this work, Engelbart created a hypermedia-groupware system called oNLine System (NLS). For this system, he also invented what has become the preferred device for using links on the Web, the mouse.

Ted Nelson

Ted Nelson coined the word *hypertext* to describe the text and media in his Xanadu Project, which he began in 1960. In many ways, today's Web can be seen as a dumbed-down version of Ted Nelson's Xanadu. In his writing, Nelson describes bidirectional, overlapping, complex links between content that protect copyright holders while still making information accessible and giving everyone the ability to make links (much like margin notes in a book) wherever they please. Unfortunately, Xanadu has been in development for 40 years and still hasn't been fully realized.

ACM SIGWEB

The Association for Computing Machinery (ACM) Special Interest Group on Hypertext, Hypermedia, and Web (SIGWEB) was formed in 1989 and was known as SIGLINK until 1998. SIGWEB has sponsored conferences on hypertext and hyper-media since its founding. SIGWEB is considered the center of academic research into hypertext systems.

Bill Atkinson

Bill Atkinson is the creator of HyperCard, which was released in 1987. HyperCard is a graphical hypertext system for the Macintosh. It was designed to make creating inter-active applications, called "stacks," easy enough for the average Macintosh user. HyperCard is credited with popularizing hypertext.

Tim Berners-Lee and Robert Caillau

As you no doubt have heard, Tim Berners-Lee and Robert Caillau created the world's first Web browser, the first Web server, and defined HTML, the Hypertext Transfer Protocol (HTTP), and Uniform Resource Locators (URLs) while working at the European Laboratory for Particle Physics (CERN) in 1989. HTML introduced the world to hypertext and linking.

HTML Linking

HTML defines a *link* as "a connection from one Web resource to another." This is a simple and well-stated rule. The things that have been accomplished using the links that are described by this simple definition are astonishing. HTML links are the fundamental backbone of the Web. They make connected collections of pages into Web sites, they have made giant directory Web sites possible and popular, they make every type of data accessible through a Web browser interface, and they have made "Web browsing" into a favorite form of recreation for millions.

HTML's Capabilities

HTML links have two ends, called "anchors," which are defined using either a Uniform Resource Identifier (URI), or an anchor name.

A typical link that uses a URI might look like this:

```
<a href="http://www.lanw.com/">Visit our Web site</a>
```

Specific parts of the same document in which the link resides or a separate document can be accessed by assigning an `id` attribute to the destination resource and using the value of this `id` attribute as a *fragment identifier* in a URI.

A fragment identifier allows you to reference a portion of a document. For example, this is a URI with a fragment identifier that points to an anchor named `the_good_part`.

```
http://www.somesitewithsomestuff.com/long_document.html#the_good_part
```

The section of `long_document.html` where this destination is defined might look like this:

```
<p>And so, in closing, <a id="the_good_part">I propose that everyone be given
an immediate pay raise, which should be retroactive to the beginning of the
year.</a></p>
```

HTML link destinations also can be specified by adding `id` attributes to elements other than `a`. For example, if you want to link to a particular list item in a document, you write the list item as follows:

```
<ul>
<li id="first_thing">The first thing is...</li>
</ul>
```

You can then link to this element using a fragment identifier, as follows:

```
<a href="long_document.html#first_thing">Click Here for the first thing.</a>
```

The use of an `id` attribute to identify the end points of links has been possible in HTML since version 4.0, but the more common way of identifying link endings is by using the `name` attribute of the `a` element. For example, in HTML, it's common to create elements such as the following to identify a part of a document:

```
<a name="second_thing">
```

The biggest difference between HTML and XHTML linking is that XHTML fragment identifiers must use the `id` attribute, even for elements that have traditionally used the `name` attribute.

The HTML `img` element is also a type of link. Like the `a` element, the `img` element is unidirectional and has a starting point and an ending point. The `img` element, however, is usually traversed automatically when an HTML page is loaded. The resource pointed to by the link (usually an image) is then displayed in the browser.

HTML's Limitations

For everything that has been done with HTML linking, the definition and functionality of HTML links are actually quite restrictive. As mentioned earlier, HTML links join only two resources, and they are unidirectional.

Another problem with HTML linking is that it predetermines which elements will be used for linking. In XML, the whole idea is that you can create your own elements. The result we need is a new way (besides the `a` element or the `img` element) to tell a processor what a link is.

Perhaps one of the biggest problems with HTML linking, however, is its ability to maintain links. HTML links are hard-coded into files. As you probably know, this makes it rather difficult to locate all the links in a Web site and make sure they're up-to-date.

XLink combines the best features and some of the simplicity of HTML linking with the best features of several other hypertext systems and standards (especially HyTime, an SGML hyperlink standard) to solve many of the problems of linking on the Web.

XLink Basic Concepts

Like HTML, XLink uses URIs to create links. XLink goes beyond HTML linking to provide advanced features that will help us achieve more of the hypermedia potential that was described by Vannevar Bush and those who came after him.

XLink was developed to provide advanced linking between XML documents and other resources. The XLink specification doesn't specify what these links will look like when they're rendered in a browser or other application, but it does define a language for creating and describing links. Just as with XML, HTML, and XHTML, the actual appearance of the link is up to the application that uses the data.

Envisioning some of the possible uses for XLink can be rather difficult. We're used to thinking about hyperlinks being underlined text or images that say "click me." When clicked, these links will (as long as the resource on the other end exists) open that resource. XLink has capabilities that simply don't make sense when we try to envision them fitting our experiences with hyperlinks. XLink makes the following possible:

- Links with multiple destinations
- Bidirectional links
- Links on resources for which you don't have Write access

- A standard way of attaching roles and descriptive titles to the various ends to which a link attaches, and asserting connections between particular ends
- A standard way of specifying behaviors such as whether a link appears in a new window

Linking Terminology

For Web developers who've been working primarily with HTML, XLink will require you to change your thinking about the nature of links. To better clarify what we're talking about in the rest of this chapter, some definitions are in order.

Link

The XLink specification defines a *link* as "an explicit relationship between resources or portions of resources." This definition, without the directionality or even the word *connection*, which are both in the HTML specification, defines a broader set of functionality than HTML can provide.

A *hyperlink* is a particular kind of link that is intended for human viewing and use (in a browser, for example). Although hyperlinks can be defined using XLink, links created using XLink do not have to be hyperlinks. In fact, you can even create links that will only be used by scripts and programs.

Resources

A *resource* is any addressable unit of information or service. Examples of resources include images, XML documents, XHTML documents, and programs.

Local Resource

A *local resource* is a resource that participates in a link by being inside of an element that is a link, or that is a link itself. As you'll see later in this chapter, local resources provide a way for information to be stored and linked to locally.

Remote Resource

A *remote resource* is a resource that is addressed using a URI. A remote resource may or may not reside outside of the document that links to it. As long as it's addressed using a URI, it's a remote resource.

Traversal and Arc

Traversal is the act of using or traveling across (traversing) a link. Traversal always involves two resources: a starting point (or *starting resource*) and an ending point (or *ending resource*). Information about how to traverse resources (such as the direction of traversal) is called an *arc*.

Outbound, Inbound, and Third-Party Arcs

An arc with a local starting resource and a remote ending resource is called an *outbound arc*. An arc with a remote starting resource and a local ending resource is called an *inbound arc*, and an arc with a remote starting and ending arc is called a *third-party arc*.

Outbound arcs are simple enough to understand. They describe links from a document that you control to some other resource. This is how HTML linking works.

Inbound and third-party arcs present some difficulties, however. The biggest problem is that inbound and third-party arcs may have starting points that are in resources to which you don't have access.

In HTML linking, we put an `a` element in a document that we are able to edit, and it points to a resource that we may or may not have Write access to. In style-style linking, the linking element that you create does not have to be the starting point. Using XLink, you can create a link element that specifies a link from an external resource to it (inbound), or you can specify a link between two remote resources (third party).

This may seem strange at first. Does this mean that your competitors will be able to put links to their site all over your site, or make changes to the links on your site without your permission? No. Remember that XLink only suggests links. It is up to the application that reads the XLink markup to actually interpret it.

Inbound or third-party links that you create may be simply stored on your computer or local network, so when you browse the Web, you'll be able to create relationships between resources. Your browser might create an XML document containing all of these third-party and inbound links. This would be similar to, but much more flexible than, a bookmark file.

A collection of inbound and third-party links is called a *linkbase*. When you're browsing the Web, your browser could check your linkbase and any other linkbase you specify to see if the page you're viewing is part of any link relationships. If it is, the browser would render the links as if they were part of the document.

XLink Namespace

Because XLink allows you to make any element into a link, an application that uses the links needs a method for identifying them. The XLink namespace is this method. The *XLink namespace* is `www.w3.org/1999/xlink`. If you use XLink, you must specify the namespace for elements that contain links or whose descendents contain links. For example:

```
<html xmlns="http://www.w3.org/1999/xhtml"
xmlns:xlink="http://www.w3.org/1999/xlink">
```

If you declare the `xlink` namespace as part of the XHTML start tag (`html`) as shown, you can use XLink elements throughout the document simply by prefacing element names or attribute names with `xlink` and a colon (:). This is an example of a simple link:

```
<xlink:mylink
      type="simple"
      href="linked.html"
      title="A document for you"/>
```

As you'll see in Chapter 12, "The Benefits of Extensibility," XML (and languages created from XML such as XHTML) enables you to use multiple XML vocabularies in one document. By giving each vocabulary a unique namespace, applications that use such a document can avoid potential problems, such as XML vocabularies with elements with the same names. (Note, however, that tools that handle namespaces may not handle XLink in particular.)

Linking Elements with XLink

XLink makes it possible to link from any element to any other element. XLink allows you to create HTML-style links, as well as much more advanced links. Rather than simply defining linking elements like HTML does, XLink defines linking attributes that can be used inside of any element.

XLink Attributes

The XLink `type` attribute is the only required attribute for every element that uses the XLink namespace. The `type` attribute has several possible values: `simple`, `extended`, `locator`, `arc`, `resource`, `title`, and `none`.

Including `type`, XLink defines 10 attributes that may be used to specify information about links. The other nine attributes are `href`, `role`, `arcrole`, `title`, `show`, `actuate`, `label`, `from`, and `to`. XLink's attributes are global attributes, which means that they can be used in elements that are not part of the XLink namespace.

You may use other attributes in an element in addition to XLink attributes. The following is an XHTML document that shows the use of XLink attributes along with XHTML attributes inside of XHTML elements:

```
<html
  xmlns="http://www.w3.org/1999/xhtml"
  xmlns:xlink="http://www.w3.org/1999/xlink">
<head>
  <title>A Link</title>
</head>
  <body>
    <img src="me.gif" width="100" height="100" alt="Me!"
            xlink:type="simple" xlink:href="me.xml">
  </body>
</html>
```

Although you can use XLink attributes with any element, the combination of XLink attributes that may be used in any one element is determined by the value of the `type` attribute. Table 11.1 shows the attributes that may be used with the different types of links.

Table 11.1 **The Possible Attributes for Each Type of Link**

	simple	extended	locator	arc	resource	title
type	Required	Required	Required	Required	Required	Required
href	Optional		Required			
role	Optional	Optional	Optional		Optional	
arcrole	Optional			Optional		
title	Optional	Optional	Optional	Optional	Optional	
show	Optional			Optional		
actuate	Optional			Optional		
label			Optional		Optional	
from				Optional		
to				Optional		

As shown in Table 11.1, there are six possible types of links. These six link types are divided into two groups: simple and extended.

Simple Links

Simple links are HTML-style links, and provide the same functionality as the HTML a element or the img element. Creating simple links is similar to creating HTML links. The difference is that any element in your document can be a link, not just certain elements. Example 11.1 is an example of a simple link.

Example 11.1 **A Simple Link**

```
<employee xmlns:xlink="http://www.w3c.org/2000/XLink"
          xlink:type="simple"
          xlink:href="/employees/jdoe.html"
          xlink:title="John Doe"
          xlink:role="/employees/employees.html">
    John Doe
</employee>
```

xlink:href

The xlink:href attribute is called the locator attribute. The purpose of the xlink:href attribute is the same as the purpose of the HTML href attribute—its value is used to locate a remote resource. The resource it points to is called the *target*. In Example 11.1, the value of href is the relative address /employees/jdoe.html. This creates (or, more accurately, it describes) a connection from the employee element to the document at /employees/jdoe.html.

Semantic Attributes

Example 11.1 also demonstrates the use of the XLink *semantic attributes*. These attributes are named semantic attributes because they describe the meaning of linked resources. The semantic attributes are `xlink:title`, `xlink:role`, and `xlink:arcrole`.

xlink:title

The `xlink:title` attribute has the same purpose as HTML's `title` attribute—it describes the target resource. The use of this information is dependent on the application reading the link. A browser may display the value of the `title` attribute when you put your mouse over a link, for example.

xlink:role and xlink:arcrole

The `xlink:role` and `xlink:arcrole` attributes' values must be URIs. These URIs point to information about a property of the target resource. In the Example 11.1, the `role` attribute might point to information about what an employee's role is in the company. As with `xlink:title` and many other XLink attributes, what an application does with this information is completely up to it.

Behavior Attributes

There are XLink attributes that do provide suggestions on how they should be used by a browser or other application. These attributes are called *behavior attributes*.

In HTML, as you know, not all links behave the same. For example, you can use the `target` attribute of the a element to specify where the target of a link should open (in a new window, in the same window, and so on). Also, Web browsers automatically open HTML `img` elements by default.

These different ways of handling links are called behaviors. You can create the same types of behaviors using XLink. For example, to automatically open an image in an XML document, you could use a simple link similar to the following:

```
<photo xmlns:xlink="http://www.w3.org/2000/XLink"
       xlink:type="simple"
       xlink:actuate="onLoad" xlink:show="embed"
       xlink:href="http://www.example.com/images/jdoe.jpg" />
```

The `xlink:show` and `xlink:actuate` attributes in the previous example are optional XLink behavior attributes.

xlink:show

The value of `xlink:show` must be one of the following: `replace`, `new`, `embed`, `other`, or `none`. If the value of `xlink:show` is `replace`, it causes the browser to replace the current documents with the target of the link when the link is traversed. This is the default behavior of HTML links.

If the value of `xlink:show` is `new`, the browser will open a new window for the target. This behavior is similar to the behavior of HTML browsers when the `target` attribute of a link element has the value `_blank`.

If the value of `xlink:show` is `embed`, the target of the link will be inserted into the current document in place of the link. This is similar to how HTML browsers handle the links created with the `img` element. This can also be used to include any other type of external file in the document. For example, you could create a link that, when traversed, shows a graph inside of the document, plays a song, or inserts external resources into the document.

If the value of `xlink:show` is `other`, the application reading the link should look for other information in the link about what to do with the target of the link.

If the value of `xlink:show` is `none`, the action caused by traversing the link is up to the application.

xlink:actuate

You use the `actuate` attribute to communicate when a link should be traversed. The value of `actuate` must be one of the following: `onLoad`, `onRequest`, `other`, or `none`.

If the value of `actuate` is `onLoad`, the link is automatically traversed when the link is read. For example, a picture or sound file can be automatically embedded in a document, or a separate window can automatically be opened when the document containing a link is opened.

If the value of actuate is `onRequest`, the link will only be traversed when the user (or some other event) performs an action, such as clicking on the linked element.

If the value of actuate is `other`, the application should look for other markup in the link that describes when the link should be traversed.

If the value of actuate is `none`, it's up to the application to decide when the link should be traversed.

Fragment Identifiers in Simple Links

Simple links can also contain fragment identifiers. The following example shows a link to a URI with a simple fragment identifier:

```
<para>Please read about our
<link xmlns:xlink="http://www.w3.org/2000/XLink"
      xlink:type="simple"
      xlink:href="/privacy.html#cookies">
cookie policy
</link>
in our privacy statement.
</para>
```

As you'll see later in this chapter in the "The Role and Reason for XPointer" section, XPointers can be used to provide much more powerful fragment identifiers.

Extended Links

Extended links describe connections between any number of resources in any combination of local or remote. An extended link might look like this:

```
<further_reading xmlns:xlink="http://www.w3.org/2000/xlink"
                 xlink:type="extended"
                 xlink:title="More Linking Fun">
    <web_site xlink:type="locator"
              xlink:href="http://www.theatlantic.com/unbound/
                          flashbks/computer/bushf.htm"
              xlink:title="As We May Think" />
    <web_site xlink:type="locator"
              xlink:href="http://www.xanadu.com"
              xlink:title="Xanadu" />
    <web_site xlink:type="locator"
              xlink:href="http://www.lirmm.fr/ftp/ACMSIGWEB/index.html"
              xlink:title="ACM/SIGWEB" />
</further_reading>
```

This is a rather basic extended `link`. You can see, however, how a single `link` element can link to multiple destinations.

Extended link elements may contain elements with the following values of the `type` attribute:

- `locator`-type elements, which address the remote resources participating in the link
- `arc`-type elements, which provide traversal rules among the link's participating resources
- `title`-type elements, which provide human-readable labels for the link
- `resource`-type elements, which supply local resources that participate in the link

locator- and *resource-*Type Elements

As discussed earlier, XLink divides resources into two categories: local and remote. In extended links, `locator`-type elements are used to link to remote resources, and `resource`-type elements are used to link local resources. Example 11.2 is an extended link that references three remote resources and one local resource.

Example 11.2   **An Extended Link That References Three Remote Resources and One Local Resource**

```
<further_reading xmlns:xlink="http://www.w3.org/2000/xlink"
                 xlink:type="extended"
                 xlink:title="More Linking Fun">
    <topic xlink:type="resource">Linking History</topic>
    <web_site xlink:type="locator"
              xlink:href="http://www.theatlantic.com/unbound/flashbks/
                          computer/bushf.htm"
```

```
            xlink:title="As We May Think" />
    <web_site xlink:type="locator"
            xlink:href="http://www.xanadu.com"
            xlink:title="Xanadu" />
    <web_site xlink:type="locator"
            xlink:href="http://www.lirmm.fr/ftp/ACMSIGWEB/index.html"
            xlink:title="ACM/SIGWEB" />
</further_reading>
```

Note that this extended link does not say anything about how these resources are connected or what should happen when they are traversed. This is where `arc`-type elements come in.

arc-Type Elements

In simple links, the `show` and `actuate` attributes are used to determine how and when links will be traversed. In extended links, the `show` and `actuate` attributes are used with `arc`-type elements to specify traversal information between participating resources.

Extended links can create more kinds of links than simple links can; therefore, additional attributes are necessary to specify the start and end points of the link. `arc`-type elements inside of extended links use attributes called `xlink:from` and `xlink:to` to specify the starting and ending points of links.

Each `arc` has only one starting resource and one ending resource. The values of the `xlink:from` and `xlink:to` attributes must be the values of `xlink:label` attributes from other linking elements inside of an extended link. Example 11.3 demonstrates the use of `arc`-type elements.

Example 11.3 **Use of *arc*-Type Elements**

```
<further_reading xmlns:xlink="http://www.w3.org/2000/xlink"
                xlink:type="extended"
                xlink:title="More Linking Fun">
    <topic xlink:type="resource" label="topic">Linking History</topic>
    <web_site xlink:type="locator"
            xlink:href="http://www.theatlantic.com/unbound/flashbks
                        /computer/bushf.htm"
            xlink:title="As We May Think"
            xlink:label="vbush" />
    <web_site xlink:type="locator"
            xlink:href="http://www.xanadu.com"
            xlink:title="Xanadu"
            xlink:label="tnelson" />
    <web_site xlink:type="locator"
            xlink:href="http://www.lirmm.fr/ftp/ACMSIGWEB/index.html"
            xlink:title="ACM/SIGWEB"
            xlink:label="sigweb" />
    <connection xlink:type="arc" xlink:from="topic"
```

```
                        xlink:to="vbush"     xlink:show="replace"
                        xlink:actuate="onRequest"/>
     <connection xlink:type="arc" xlink:from="topic"
                        xlink:to="tnelson"     xlink:show="replace"
                        xlink:actuate="onRequest"/>
     <connection xlink:type="arc" xlink:from="topic"
                        xlink:to="sigweb"     xlink:show="replace"
                        xlink:actuate="onRequest"/>
     <connection xlink:type="arc" xlink:from="vbush"
                        xlink:to="tnelson"     xlink:show="replace"
                        xlink:actuate="onRequest"/>
  </further_reading>
```

How this code would be rendered in a browser with XLink support (of which there are none at this time) is yet to be determined. You can imagine it as a drop-down (or pop-up) list showing all the relevant connections between the different resources, depending on which resource you're currently viewing.

title-Type Elements

Elements with the xlink:type value of title can be used to provide more detailed human-readable information than an extended link's title attribute can contain. Examples of situations where you might want to include one or more title-type elements in an extended link include the following:

- When a link element requires multiple titles
- When you want to provide titles in multiple languages
- When titles must include XML markup

An xlink:title element may have any content. The following is an example of the use of the title-type element:

```
<web_site xlink:type="locator"
          xlink:href="http://www.theatlantic.com/unbound/flashbks/
                      computer/bushf.htm"
            xlink:title="As We May Think"
            xlink:label="vbush">
<site_info xlink:type="label">
   <owner>The Atlantic Monthly</owner>
   <location>Boston, MA</location>
</site_info>
</web_site>
```

As you can see from this example, title-type elements are the simplest of the six XLink element types—their primary function is to provide information for the human user of the link.

The Role and Reason for XPointer

Yet another way to link documents is to use the XML Pointer Language (XPointer). XPointer is a language that extends the XML Path Language (XPath, which is discussed later in the "Understanding XPath" section) expression language to allow you to locate and create links to any point in an XML document. The portion of an XML document that is addressed by an XPointer is referred to as a *subresource*. The subresource that the XPointer addresses can be one element, a set of elements, or a node. (A *node* is the point at which more than one line meets in a hierarchical document tree structure.) A subresource is, naturally, only a part of the entire XML resource.

XPointer allows you to identify parts of XML documents based on factors such as element types, attribute values, character content, and relative position. After XPointer identifies a structure, it can be used as the target for a link.

XPointers use iterative selections to locate parts of XML documents. This means that each selection operates based on the previous selection. For example, you could use XPointer to locate an element called `moon` with an attribute called `name` with a value of `Ganymede` that is the child of an element called `Jupiter`, which has an attribute called `galaxy` with a value of `Milky Way`. You could then create a link to the information that is contained in this particular element. Because XLink and XPointer don't specify what will happen if this link is traversed, there are a number of uses this link could have besides the typical behavior that we associate with hyperlinks.

One of the main benefits of XPointers is that you don't need to actually have the ability to place anchor elements in a document to be able to link to the exact content that you're referencing. For example, imagine that you want to reference a particular paragraph that is published somewhere on the Web. Using HTML, you have two options: You can either reprint the paragraph on your site, or you can link to the whole document and describe to the reader how he or she can find the paragraph you cite. Unfortunately, reprinting other people's work isn't always possible (or legal), and documents aren't always organized well enough to make the second option feasible.

Using XPointer, you could identify the exact spot in the external resource to which you want to link, and create a link to it. In fact, using XPointer and XLink, you could identify several examples of what you want to point out about the document in question and create one link to all of them.

XPointer and References

XPointer uses expressions in URI references to locate subresources in XML. XPointer expressions are based on the XPath expression language.

The XPointer specification defines three types of XPointer expressions: full XPointers, bare names, and child sequences. Bare names and child sequences are simple, shorthand methods of creating XPointers. We'll discuss these first.

Bare Names

Using bare names is similar to using an `id` or `name` fragment identifier in an HTML link to address an element's `id` attribute. For example, the full syntax for addressing an element with an `id` attribute with the value `intro` is shown in the following markup along with the HTML method and the simplified XPointer expression using just the name. These expressions can all be attached to a URI and used as fragment identifiers for links.

The following is an XPointer expression:

```
xpointer(id('intro'))
```

The following is a `simple` link example that uses the XPointer fragment identifier:

```
<myLink
    xmlns:xlink="http://www.w3.org/2000/xlink"
    xlink:type="simple"
    xlink:href="linked.html#xpointer(id('intro'))"
    xlink:title="The introduction"/>
```

In HTML, this same document fragment can be identified using the following link:

```
<a href="linked.html#intro">The introduction</a>
```

Notice that HTML simply uses the value of the `id` attribute (`intro`) as the fragment identifier. Using the shorthand XPointer expression, you can use the same syntax as HTML to identify fragments by name.

The following is a simple link example with a shorthand XPointer fragment identifier:

```
<myLink
    xmlns:xlink="http://www.w3.org/2000/xlink"
    xlink:type="simple"
    xlink:href="linked.html#intro"
    xlink:title="The introduction"/>
```

Child Sequences

The child sequences form of addressing iterates through a sequence of values separated by slashes to locate an element. For example, to locate the second child of a document's root element, you could use the following expression:

```
/1/2
```

The first part of a child sequence can either be the document root, represented by the string `/1`, as in the previous example, or a bare name that corresponds to the `id` attribute of the element you want to address. For example, the following shows a partial XHTML document from which we want to select elements:

```
<html xmlns=http://www.w3.org/1999/xhtml>
  <head>
```

```
    <title>XHTML</title>
    </head>
     <body>
     <p id="intro">
       . . .
   </html>
```

To select the third child element of the p element with intro as the value of its id attribute, you could use either of the following child sequences:

```
/1/2/3/3
```

or

```
intro/3
```

The following shows how you use these expressions as fragment identifiers in links:

```
<myLink
    xmlns:xlink="http://www.w3.org/2000/xlink"
    xlink:type="simple"
    xlink:href="linked.html#intro/3"
    xlink:title="The introduction"/>
```

The bare names and the child sequences addressing formats can often be useful, and they shield the developer from the complexities of XPath and XPointer. For more sophisticated addressing, you can use full XPointer expressions.

Full XPointers

A full XPointer expression consists of the name of a *scheme*, followed by an *expression* in parentheses. When used for addressing, any number of XPointer expressions with this format may be used together.

Schemes

A *scheme* is simply a way to identify the notation that is used in the XPointer expression. Right now, the only allowed scheme is xpointer. It's anticipated, however, that you'll be able to use different notations to address information in XML documents in the future.

Full XPointer Expressions

XPointer expressions can address any part of the content of an XML document. The expression portion of an XPointer must be enclosed in parentheses and must follow the scheme name.

XPointer Escaping

XPointer expressions rarely exist outside of some other context. Usually, XPointers are used as part of an XLink. When used as part of an XLink, they are subject to not only their own rules of syntax, but also those of XML and URIs. This means that certain characters that are allowed inside of a standalone XPointer expression must be escaped.

When an XPointer expression is used in a URI, characters that aren't allowed in URIs must be escaped using a percent sign (%) followed by the hexadecimal notation of the character's byte code. For example, the following is an XPointer expression that finds an element with an `id` attribute with the value `chapter one`.

```
xpointer(id('chapter one'))
```

Because spaces are not allowed in URIs, you should escape the space character to use this expression in a link, as follows:

```
<myLink
    xmlns:xlink="http://www.w3.org/2000/xlink"
    xlink:type="simple"
    xlink:href="linked.html#xpointer(id('chapter%20one'))"
    xlink:title="The introduction"/>
```

A URI-escaped version of an XPointer expression is called an *XPointer fragment identifier*.

When XPointer expressions appear in XML documents, they must also escape characters that aren't allowed inside XML content; namely, the less-than sign (<) and the ampersand (&). For example, the following XPointer expression locates the first six contact elements:

```
xpointer(addressbook/contact position()<=6)
```

As part of an XLink, the less-than symbol would need to be escaped, as follows:

```
<myLink
    xmlns:xlink="http://www.w3.org/2000/xlink"
    xlink:type="simple"
    xlink:href="doc.xml#xpointer(addressbook/contact position()&lt;=6) />
```

Understanding XPath

The expression language that is used as the basis of XPointer expressions is XPath. XPath is a language for addressing parts of XML documents. XPath also has pattern-matching capabilities. As you saw in Chapter 7, "Adding Style with XSL," the pattern-matching capabilities of XPath are used in Extensible Stylesheet Language Transformations (XSLT).

XPath works by creating a tree of nodes from an XML document. There are several types of nodes, including elements, attributes, and text. The root element is at the top of the tree, each of its subelements is a level below it, and so on. Example 11.4 shows a typical XHTML document. Figure 11.1 shows a graphical representation of how XPath views this document.

Example 11.4   **An XHTML Document**

```
<html xmlns="http://www.w3.org/1999/xhtml">
  <head>
    <title>Chapter 11</title>
  </head>
  <body>
    <h1>Advanced Linking</h1>
      <p id="intro">This chapter will cover the following topics:
      <ul>
        <li>History of Linking</li>
        <li>XLink</li>
        <li>XPointers</li>
        <li>XPath</li>
      </ul>
      </p>
  </body>
</html>
```

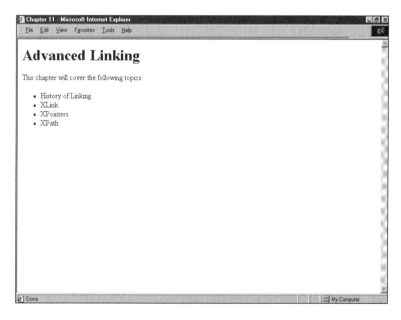

Figure 11.1   A graphical representation of Example 11.4.

XPath is called XPath because it uses URI-like paths to access the different parts of
XML documents. For example, here is one way to address the second li element in
Example 11.4:

```
/html/body/ul/li[2]
```

Expressions

The result of an expression is always an object of one of the following types:

- Node set (an unordered collection of nodes)
- Boolean (yes or no)
- Number
- String (character data)

Although describing all the possible types of XPath expressions is beyond the scope of this book, most XPath expressions are fairly simple.

The most common types of expressions are *location paths*. Location paths locate node sets (collections of nodes) by specifying their relationship to the expression's *context node*. The context node is the current node that the expression is looking at. You've already seen examples of location paths earlier in this chapter as well as in XSLT. XSLT patterns are actually collections of XPath location paths.

The following list details some examples of location paths:

- `child::node()` selects all the children of the context node. Assuming that this expression uses the `html` element as its context node, it would select the `head` element and the `body` element.
- `attribute::name` selects the `name` attribute of the context node.
- `descendant::p` selects the `p` element descendants of the context node. A descendant element is any element lower on the tree than the context node. For example, the descendants of the `p` element in Example 11.4 are the `ul` element and the `li` element.

Like URIs, location paths can be either relative or absolute. *Absolute location paths* always start with a slash (/), which indicates the root element. A slash by itself selects the root element.

Relative location paths do not start with a slash. Both relative and absolute location paths may contain multiple *location steps* joined with slashes. A location step is simply a path that is part of a larger location path. For example, `child::p/child::ul/child::li` selects all of the `li` elements that are children of `ul` elements that are children of `p` elements.

The first part of a location step is called the *axis*. The axis specifies the relationship between the nodes that are selected by the step and the context node. There are 13 possible axes:

- **child.** Contains the children of the context node.
- **descendant.** Contains the descendants (the children, grandchildren, and so on) of the context node.
- **parent.** Contains the node that the context node is a child of—if the context node is not the root node.

- **ancestor.** Contains all of the ancestors (parents, grandparents, and so on) of the context node.

- **following-sibling.** Contains the following siblings of the context node. For example, in an HTML document, the body element is a following sibling of the head element.

- **preceding-sibling.** Contains the preceding siblings of the context node. For example, in an HTML document, the head element is a preceding sibling of the body element.

- **following.** Contains all the nodes that follow the context node in the document, excluding descendants of the context node, attribute nodes, and namespace nodes.

- **preceding.** Contains all the nodes that precede the context node in the document, excluding ancestors of the context node, attribute nodes, and namespace nodes.

- **attribute.** Contains the attributes of the context node.

- **namespace.** Contains the namespace of the context node.

- **self.** Contains just the context node.

- **descendant-or-self.** Contains the context node and its descendants.

- **ancestor-or-self.** Contains the context node and its ancestors.

The second part of a location step is the node test. A *node test* specifies the node type and the name of the nodes to be selected. The node test is separated from the axis by two colons (::). For example, to select the children of the context node named p, you use the following location step:

```
child::p
```

Besides names, there are several other node tests that you can use:

- ***.** True for all nodes of the type specified by the axis. For example, child::* selects all of the children elements of the context node, and attrib::* selects all of the context node's attributes.

- **text(), comment(), processing-instruction(), and so on.** True for all nodes of the type specified. For example, descendant::text() selects the text node descendants of the context node.

- **node().** True for any node type.

The third part of a location step is the *predicates section*. Predicates are optional, and are contained in square brackets after the node test. Predicates filter the set of nodes that is selected by the axis and the node test. For example, if you only wanted to select the third p element in a document, you could specify it as follows:

```
child::p[position()=3]
```

This predicate uses the `position` function to test the `p` elements selected by the node test until it finds the third one. There are several other functions that operate on node sets that you should be aware of. These functions are known as *node set* functions.

Node Set Functions

XPath processors are required to support certain functions for filtering node sets. These functions are listed in Table 11.2. The information from this table was derived from the W3C site at `www.w3.org/TR/xpath#section-Node-Set-Functions`.

Each function returns a number, a node set, a string (character data), or a Boolean value. Some strings allow or require a value to be input into the function. You can input values (called arguments) into functions by putting them inside of the function's parentheses.

If an argument type appears between a function's attributes without any symbol after the type in Table 11.2, the function requires an argument. In cases where an argument is optional, a question mark (?) is shown after the type of the argument. In cases where any number of comma-separated arguments may be entered (including zero), an asterisk (★) follows the argument type. The question mark and the asterisk are called *occurrence operators*. We talk about other occurrence operators, and other ways to use them, in Chapter 12.

Table 11.2 **Node Set Functions**

Function	Return Value Type	Description
`last()`	Number	Returns a number equal to the context size.
`position()`	Number	Returns a number equal to the context position.
`count()`	Number	Returns the number of nodes in the node set.
`id()`	Node set	Selects elements by their unique `id` attribute.
`local-name(node-set?)`	String	Returns the local name (without the namespace) of the first node in the node set.
`namespace-uri(node-set?)`	String	Returns the name of the namespace of the first node in the node set.
`name(node-set?)`	String	Returns the expanded name (with the namespace) of the first node in the node set.
`string(object?)`	String	Converts an object to a string.

Function	Return Value Type	Description
concat(*string*,*string*,*string**)	String	Returns the concatenation of its arguments. For example, concat(Hi,my,name,is) would return Himynameis.
starts-with(*string*,*string*)	Boolean	Returns true if the first string argument starts with the second argument.
contains(*string*,*string*)	Boolean	Returns true if the first string argument contains the second argument.
substring-before(*string*,*string*)	String	Returns the part of the first string that occurs before the first occurrence of the second string.
substring-after(*string*,*string*)	String	Returns the part of the first string that occurs after the first occurrence of the second string.
substring(*string*,*number*,*number*?)	String	Returns the part of the string that starts at the position specified by the first number with the length specified by the second number.
string-length(*string*?)	Number	Returns the number of characters in the string.
normalize-space(*string*?)	String	Returns the string with extra whitespace trimmed.
translate(*string*,*string*,*string*)	String	Replaces characters in the first string that occur in the second string with corresponding characters from the third string. For example, translate(hello,el,ip) returns hippo.
boolean(*object*?)	Boolean	Converts its argument to a Boolean value.
not(*boolean*)	Boolean	Returns true if the Boolean argument is false.
true()	Boolean	Returns a Boolean value of true.
false()	Boolean	Returns a Boolean value of false.

continues

Table 11.2 **Continued**

Function	Return Value Type	Description
lang(*string*)	Boolean	Returns true or false depending on whether the language of the context node is the same as the language of the function's argument. The lang() function uses the xml:lang attribute of the nodes it tests.
number(*object?*)	Number	Converts its argument to a number.
sum(*node-set*)	Number	Returns the sum, for each node in the node set argument, of the result of converting the string values of a node to a number.
floor(*number*)	Number	Returns the largest integer that is not greater than the argument.
ceiling(*number*)	Number	Returns the smallest integer that is not less than the argument.
round(*number*)	Number	Returns the nearest integer to the argument.

Abbreviated Syntax

XPath can be a fairly verbose language. There are a number of ways to abbreviate XPath expressions. Perhaps the most commonly used abbreviation is the omission of child::. Because child is the default axis, intro/p is the same as child::intro/child::p. Additional abbreviations include the following:

- @ can be substituted for attribute::.
- // can be substituted for /descendant-or-self::node()/.
- . is short for self::node().
- .. is short for parent::node().

The following are some examples of abbreviated XPath location steps:

- **p** selects all the p element children of the context node.
- **@name** selects the name attribute of the context node.
- **//li[last()]** selects the last li descendant of the document root.

Bringing XLink, XPointer, and XPath Together

Combining XLink, XPointer, and XPath allows you to create much more dynamic, precise, and useful links. Instead of simply creating a link to an entire resource, XLink allows you to create links to very specific parts of documents. Because XPointer allows you define link endings based on contexts, attribute values, and so forth, it's less likely that links with XPointer fragment identifiers will break when a resource is modified.

Example 11.5 shows how XLink and XPointers might be used inside an XHTML document.

Example 11.5 **Using XLink and XPointers Inside an XHTML Document**

```
<html xmlns="http://www.w3.org/1999/xhtml"
      xmlns:xlink = "http://www.w3.org/1999/xlink">
  <head>
    <title>Chapter 11</title>
  </head>
  <body>
    <h1>Advanced Linking</h1>
      <p id="intro">This chapter covers the following topics:
      <ul>
        <li><go xlink:type="simple"
               xlink:href="/chap11.xml#xpointer(/section%5B@title="History
               %20of%20Linking"%5D)">
            History of Linking
            </go>
        </li>
        <li><go xlink:type="simple"
               xlink:href="/chap11.xml#xpointer(/section%5B@title="XLink"%5D)">
            XLink
            </go>
        </li>
        <li><go xlink:type="simple"
               xlink:href="/chap11.xml#xpointer(/section%5B@title=
               "XPointer"%5D)">
            XPointer
            </go>
        </li>
        <li><go xlink:type="simple"
               xlink:href="/chap11.xml#xpointer(/section%5B@title="XPath"%5D)">
            XPath
            </go>
        </li>
      </ul>
      </p>
  </body>
</html>
```

Note that we escaped the left brackets ([), the right brackets (]), and the spaces in Example 11.4 by using their hexadecimal values (%5B, %5C, and %20, respectively). As noted earlier, this is necessary for XPointer to comply with the syntax of URIs. However, as the use of the Web XLink spreads, you probably won't need to worry about URI escaping. Chances are your XML authoring software will present you with an interface much like many other script- or expression-writing tools. Then, you'll be able to build complex links using a simple interface that shields you from the actual markup.

The State of XLink Today

Although it may be a while before XLink-enabled browsers become common, there are applications available today that can enable you to start working with XLink technologies. Like XML, XLink will become widely used on servers before it shows up on desktop computers.

Perhaps the first widespread application of XLink will be link servers. A *link server* checks every resource that is requested by a user against an XML document containing links (a *linkbase*). If the linkbase contains a link involving the resource being requested, the link server will insert the linking information at the correct point, and the end user will see the document as if it actually contained the link.

For example, you're shopping for a car on the Web and you want to create a bidirectional link between information about two different cars you're considering. In addition, you want to embed the linked information about one of the cars into a page about the other. After that, you could create links from the manufacturer's pages about each car to third-party reviews and pricing information. Then, you could make each type of link using a simple browser add-on.

The information about each type of link would be stored in an XLink linkbase by your link server. The next time you visited one of the sites involved in this series of links you created, your personal or network XLink server could insert HTML links, images, and markup into the document before it gets to your browser. Although the original pages haven't been touched, you'd see them as if you had actually modified the markup of these sites.

XLink will be a great improvement to Web hyperlinking and the way we manage information and connections between resources on the Internet. Inbound, multiple-ended, multidirectional, and third-party linking could also lead to some interesting lawsuits. Eventually, however, we'll be freed from having only the ability to create links on our own sites. XLink will allow us to annotate, cut and paste, and otherwise create the same type of complex associations among resources on the Internet that we currently have the ability to create only in our trains of thought.

For More Information

- **"As We May Think," by Vannevar Bush.** www.theatlantic.com/unbound/ flashbks/computer/bushf.htm
- **Douglas Engelbart's Bootstrap Institute.** www.bootstrap.org
- **Ted Nelson's Project Xanadu.** www.xanadu.com
- **ACM SIGWEB.** www.lirmm.fr/ftp/ACMSIGWEB/index.html
- **HyTime.** www.ornl.gov/sgml/wg8/docs/n1920 (the Hypermedia/Time-based Structuring Language, ISO/IEC10744)

12

The Benefits of Extensibility

WHEN THE W3C GROUP THAT WAS ASSIGNED the task of coming up with a new markup language for the Web was debating names, XML was not the most popular or technically accurate name on the list. Some of the other names that were considered for the markup language we now know as XML include Minimal Generalized Markup Language (MGML), Minimal Architecture for Generalized Markup Applications (MAGMA), and Structured Language for Internet Markup (SLIM). Although each of these names actually describes the language better than Extensible Markup Language, the acronyms weren't quite catchy enough. (MAGMA? SLIM? We thank our lucky stars every day for those losing out.)

In the end, the authors of XML thought that the capability for users to create their own markup languages was the most important aspect of the new standard, so they called it the Extensible Markup Language. In our opinion, this also allowed them (with only a small stretch of the imagination) to use one of the coolest-looking acronyms in computer technology: XML.

Extensibility is the noun form of the adjective extensible, which means capable of being extended. In terms of markup languages, the most common definition of extensible is that the person doing the markup decides how to mark up documents and has the capability to create custom markup languages. In this chapter, you learn how to do just that. You also see how you can use existing XML vocabularies in your XHTML documents. However, first, we need to better define what we mean by extensibility.

When the W3C rewrote HTML using XML, they called the result XHTML, or the Extensible Hypertext Markup Language. This implies that good old HTML isn't extensible. That's not exactly true.

HTML was designed to be simple and easy to learn. The goal was for it to become widespread. In this respect, HTML has been a huge success. The authors of HTML made it clear that HTML parsers should ignore elements or attributes that they don't understand.

Because of this, Web developers also have the capability to create custom HTML elements. There has never been anything stopping Web developers from inserting custom elements into Web pages. The markup in Example 12.1 is not valid HTML (and doesn't contain a picture), but a Web browser won't complain. Go ahead and try it out.

Example 12.1 **This Is Not Valid HTML, But It Will Still Display in a Web Browser**

```
<html>
<head>
<some_stuff_I_just_made_up>
Look Here!
</some_stuff_I_just_made_up>
</head>
<body>
<p>Here is a picture of my best friend, <best_friend>Margaret</best_friend>.</p>
</body>
</html>
```

Even though the elements `some_stuff_I_just_made_up` and `best_friend` aren't valid according to HTML, Web browsers will just ignore them and go on their merry way. If you wanted to, however, you could write a program that would look for these elements and do something with their contents.

It would seem, then, that we don't really need XML at all. So long as HTML browsers just ignore tags they don't understand, we can have our cake and eat it too. Theoretically, we can make custom elements for identifying information like in XML, while not having to learn and follow XML's rules.

However, one of the problems with this argument is that even the following markup displays without a problem in today's HTML browsers. The result might even be exactly the result that the author was aiming for.

```
<html>
<body>
<font face=Arial,Helvetica,Sanssheriff><h1>Welcome to my <b><I>home
page</b></h1>
<b>This</I></b> is my first Web page.<P>
<a href=dog.html>Click Here</a> to see my <h1>dog</h1>.</font>
</html>
```

At this point, a reasonable person might say, "If it ain't broke, don't fix it." The point is that if the markup serves the purpose that the author intended it to serve, who is the W3C to tell this person to write correct markup and to eventually switch to XML?

Believe it or not, this is a good point. Thousands of people, many of them otherwise nontechnical, have learned HTML in the past few years and it has enabled them to publish documents that can be read anywhere where there's Internet access. Many nontechnical people, as well as some who consider themselves to be Web professionals, wouldn't know well-formed HTML if it bit them on the ankle. They write markup that gets the job done. Isn't the W3C running the risk of sabotaging the entire idea of the Web by suddenly forcing writers of HTML markup to stick to strict rules and learn separate languages for formatting text? The answer to this question is, probably not.

Most casual Web page developers do not write HTML by hand anymore. There are plenty of easy-to-use and inexpensive development environments available for novice and nontechnical people. Most of these tools already generate markup that is well on the way to being XHTML compliant. For example, every Web development environment we've ever seen always uses quotes around attribute values, properly nests tags, and sticks to either all uppercase or all lowercase letters for markup. As these HTML writing tools are updated, they will increasingly write correct XHTML.

More and more, Web pages are not being created by tools that are specific to the task of Web design. Word processors, spreadsheets, desktop publishing, and other types of traditional desktop applications are beginning to feature the capability to output HTML. Eventually, people won't even need to bother with knowing any markup language at all. The future of the Web will be one in which XML and XHTML technologies are transparent to everyone but programmers—and they won't even need to be aware of it very often; much like ASCII is today.

So, will this reformulating of HTML and insistence on following rules ruin the Web? Is XHTML the first step in a plot by programmers and markup geeks to take back the Web by frustrating the masses of HTML writers? We don't think so. Rather, XHTML and XML are the first, vital steps required for the programmers and markup geeks to build the applications that will make the Web stronger, more useful, and more transparent.

Flexibility through extensibility is the key to the new and improved Web that will result from XML technologies. As a result of XML, we will see enormous benefits from Web technologies and Internet-enabled devices that we can't even imagine today. By moving toward Web development with an easy-to-use, standardized, and extensible markup language, we will be increasing the possible uses of our markup far beyond the Web browser.

Do We Have to Use XML or XHTML?

No one will force the casual Web-page designer who's still hand-coding markup to use XHTML or XML. If you want to write Web pages using earlier versions of HTML, that's your business. If you don't already, you may need to start specifying the version of HTML you're using in the DOCTYPE declaration at some point in the future, but that's it. Old versions of HTML will continue to be understood by many Web browsers well into the future.

So, what is the problem with HTML? The problem is that it's too closely tied to Web browsers as we know them today. There's no reason for you to trap your data inside of one particular format. XML allows you to free your data. Think of extensibility not only as the capability to create custom elements, but also as the capability to extend the uses of the data that is being marked up.

When Structure Matters Most

For all of its benefits, XHTML is just a start. Eventually, XML documents may be the primary way to transfer data across the Web.

Vast numbers of people have become familiar with markup languages through HTML and the Web. Because of this, XML has the potential to have an impact far beyond the Internet. XML could possibly even become the universal file format that computer standard makers have been trying to come up with for decades.

At the least, XML has raised awareness of the need to have flexible, reusable, standard document types. DTDs to describe documents and data used by various industries are being developed at a mind-boggling pace. Standardized DTDs for entire industries, fields of research, or types of documents or data will enable greater collaboration between organizations, make computer applications more flexible and eliminate many of the headaches of computing that we know so well today.

For example, the DocBook DTD, which is maintained and developed by the DocBook Technical Committee of the Organization for the Advancement of Structured Information Standards (OASIS), is a standard DTD for marking up books and papers. It's especially useful for marking up books and papers about computer software and hardware.

DocBook was originally written in SGML in 1991. However, there's now an XML version.

A number of commercial and free tools are available that feature support for working with DocBook. These tools include popular documentation and markup tools such as Adobe Framemaker+SGML, SoftQuad XMetal, and Arbortext's Epic (formerly, Adept Editor).

In its SGML form, DocBook is already a popular and widely used DTD. As the XML version of DocBook gains popularity, the number of tools that support it out of the box or that can be extended to support it will greatly increase.

Because it has such a broad range of applications, DocBook takes some time to learn and to understand. The end result is that DocBook gives publishers the capability to easily change the formatting of documents, reuse documents easily in multiple formats, and archive documents in a standard, platform-independent format. Like any widely used DTD, DocBook is constantly growing and changing based on user input. In addition, if DocBook doesn't provide exactly the markup that you need, you can modify it to suit your needs. Note that most people who use DocBook use only a subset of it because it's so massive.

Example 12.2 is part of a document that has been marked up using DocBook.

Example 12.2 **Part of a Document That Has Been Marked Up Using DocBook**

```
<!DOCTYPE BOOK PUBLIC "-//Davenport//DTD DocBook V3.0//EN">
<book>
  <bookinfo>
   <bookbiblio>
    <title>Markup Fun for the Whole Family</title>
     <subtitle>DocBook Fun for Everyone</subtitle>
      <authorgroup><corpauthor>New Rider's Publishing</corpauthor>
       <othercredit><authorblurb>
        <para>Indianapolis, IN</para>
        </authorblurb></othercredit>
      </authorgroup>
      <abstract>
       <para>Learn to use DocBook today, and the future will be grand!</para>
      </abstract>
   </bookbiblio>
  </bookinfo>
  <chapter>
   <title>The Benefits of Extensibility</title>
    <para> The DocBook DTD was originally designed and implemented by HaL Computer
Systems and O'Reilly & Associates around 1991. It was developed primarily for the
purpose of holding the results of troff conversion of UNIX documentation, so that
the files could be interchanged. Its design appears to have been based partly on
input from SGML interchange projects being conducted by the UNIX International and
Open Software Foundation consortia.</para>
   </chapter>
</book>
```

This may look complex; but remember, no one expects you to write complex markup by hand. DTDs make it possible for programs to shield you from the nitty-gritty of markup and enable you to apply markup as you currently apply styles in a word processor. For more information on DocBook, see `www.oasis-open.org/docbook/`.

Let the Data Drive Your Development

Data, or rather the desire to manipulate and distribute data, is the reason that people create structured documents. This section spends a little time on what exactly is meant by data in the context of XML (and, of course, XHTML).

Most XML documents consist of nothing but plain text. There are more efficient ways to store information than in text files, and more efficient ways to transmit data than as text files; however, there are not simpler ways. When computing power doubles every 18 months, speed and efficiency really aren't as important as ease of use for most people.

All the text in an XML document can be divided into two categories: character data and markup. Markup consists of start tags, end tags, empty element tags, entity references, character references, comments, CDATA section delimiters, DOCTYPE declarations, and processing instructions. Most forms of markup, such as elements and attributes, are used to specify information about character data and can be defined using a DTD. Markup that does not directly describe character data and is not defined using a DTD can be classified as *instructions*.

XML Instructions

XML instructions provide information that will be used by the XML processor, by applications using the data, or by humans looking at the document. The following types of instructions can be used in XML:

- Processing instructions
- XML declaration
- Document type (DOCTYPE) declaration

Processing Instructions

Processing instructions (PIs) start with <? and end with ?>. The purpose of processing instructions is to provide information for applications that will process the document. Processing instructions are not technically part of the character data of the document; however, XML processors are required to pass the documents to the application that is using the data.

Processing instructions have the following syntax:

```
<?target text?>
```

The *target* of a processing instruction is simply a name that will be recognized by the application using the XML document. You can use any well-formed XML name here, except for the characters xml (in any combination of uppercase and lowercase letters).

If you were writing a document for use by a program called WriteOn, you might create a processing instruction similar to the following:

```
<?writeon data="text" filename="myfirstdocument"?>
```

The text after the target can be anything you want. It's up to the application using the document to know what to do with this data.

XML Declaration

Although it's not required, XML documents generally begin with an XML declaration. Although the XML declaration looks like a processing instruction, it's not. The XML declaration begins with <?xml and ends with ?>. Unlike processing instructions, the attributes of an XML declaration are limited. The attributes that XML declarations can take are as follows:

- version
- encoding
- standalone

The version attribute is the only required attribute. It specifies the version number of XML that the document uses.

The encoding attribute allows you to specify the character encoding that the document uses. A character encoding is a method of converting bytes into characters. In HTML, you could specify the character encoding using something similar to the following tag inside of the head element:

```
<META HTTP-EQUIV="Content-Type" CONTENT="text/html; charset=ISO-8859-1">
```

XML's default encoding is UTF-8. UTF stands for Unicode Transformation Format. Unicode is a specification developed to provide a standard way for computers to implement the Universal Character Set (UCS), which is defined by the International Organization for Standardization (ISO) in ISO/IEC 10646. Unicode contains more than 65,000 characters and is capable of encoding all the characters used for the written languages of the world.

UTF-8 is a way of representing the Unicode characters that uses a variable number of bits in order to minimize the amount of memory needed for standard ASCII characters and to be compatible with ASCII, while still providing support for the entire Unicode character set.

For most of the purposes for which XML is being used today, UTF-8 is ideal. If you plan to use a large number of characters that aren't found in English, or if you're not primarily using ASCII data, you may need to specify a different encoding.

The standalone attribute indicates whether the document uses an external DTD. As previously mentioned, XML documents, unlike SGML documents, do not need to be valid—that is, they don't need to conform to the rules of a DTD—as long as they're well formed. By setting the standalone attribute of the XML declaration to "yes" you can make it clear to any application or person using the document that it does not have an external DTD.

Here are two examples of XML declarations:

```
<?xml version="1.0"?>
<?xml version="1.0" encoding="US-ASCII" standalone="yes"?>
```

Document Type Declaration

The DOCTYPE declaration is used to indicate the DTD (if there is one) that is used by an XML document. For the strict version of XHTML, as you have seen, the DOCTYPE declaration is as follows:

```
<!DOCTYPE html PUBLIC
    "-//W3C//DTD XHTML 1.0 Strict//EN"
    "DTD/xhtml1-strict.dtd">
```

DOCTYPE declarations must appear before the first element in the document. There are two methods an XML processor can use to locate the DTD that is referenced in the DOCTYPE declaration: PUBLIC and SYSTEM.

A SYSTEM identifier is a Uniform Resource Identifier (URI) that points to a copy of the DTD referenced by the DOCTYPE declaration. For a DTD that uses the SYSTEM keyword, an XML processor will locate the DTD using the specified URI. System DOCTYPE declarations use the following format:

```
<!DOCTYPE root-element SYSTEM "URI of DTD">
```

A public identifier provides a way for XML processors to locate a DTD that is not in a specific location. For example, the public identifier for the Strict version of XHTML 1.0 is -//W3C//DTD XHTML 1.0 Strict//EN.

DOCTYPE declarations that use public identifiers use the following format:

```
<!DOCTYPE root-element PUBLIC "name" "URI of DTD">
```

In XML, if you use the PUBLIC keyword in your DOCTYPE declaration, you must also specify a SYSTEM identifier for the XML processor to use as a backup.

Character Data

There are two types of character data: parsed and unparsed.

Parsed character data, or PCDATA, is character data that an XML processor will search for markup. Parsed character data is the actual data in a document. Blocks of parsed character data may not contain the left angle bracket (<) or the ampersand (&). You're probably already familiar with this concept from HTML development. The following markup results in improper display of the Web page in Web browsers, but it will result in fatal processing errors in XHTML processors:

```
<html xmlns="http://www.w3.org/1999/xhtml">
<head>
  <title>Introduction to Logic</title>
</head>
<body>
  <h1>Chapter 4: Less than and less positive</h1>
<p>The < symbol is usually referred to as the less-than symbol. Some suggest that
a more appropriate name for this symbol, which would be more in line with common
usage, is less positive.
</p>
</body>
</html>
```

The < character inside of the p element is interpreted as the beginning of a new tag, not as a literal symbol. To use literal < and/or & characters in parsed character data, you must escape them using numeric character references < and &, respectively, or the strings < or &, respectively.

Unparsed character data, as you may have guessed, is character data in which the XML processor does not look for markup.

If you want to use markup as literal text inside of an XML document, but you don't want to escape every < and & character, you can create special sections, called CDATA sections, in which character data is treated as plain text. CDATA sections begin with <![CDATA[and end with]]>.

Of DTDs and Schemas

A *Document Type Definition* (DTD) is a means for you to explicitly define the structure of a class of XML documents. In other words, DTDs are used to create the rules of a markup language.

Until now, we've mostly talked about DTDs in the abstract. You know that XHTML is defined using an XML DTD. You've also learned to use XML inside of your XHTML documents. Now it's time to get into the specifics of DTDs.

Let's start by looking at an example of a DTD. Example 12.3 shows the declarations in the XHTML Strict DTD that define the anchor (a) element.

Example 12.3 **Excerpt from the XHTML Strict DTD**

```
<!ELEMENT a %a.content;>
<!ATTLIST a
  %attrs;
  charset     %Charset;       #IMPLIED
  type        %ContentType;   #IMPLIED
  name        NMTOKEN         #IMPLIED
  href        %URI;           #IMPLIED
  hreflang     %LanguageCode; #IMPLIED
  rel         %LinkTypes;     #IMPLIED
  rev         %LinkTypes;     #IMPLIED
  accesskey   %Character;     #IMPLIED
  shape       %Shape;         "rect"
  coords      %Coords;        #IMPLIED
  tabindex    %Number;        #IMPLIED
  onfocus     %Script;        #IMPLIED
  onblur      %Script;        #IMPLIED
  >
```

The XHTML DTD is rather complex, so we won't go into much detail about it now. However, by the end of this chapter, you'll be able to read the XHTML DTDs, as well as formally define your own markup languages. For more information on the various types of XHTML DTDs, see www.w3.org/TR/xhtml1/#dtds.

Like style sheets, DTDs are usually saved in external files that can be called from an XML data file. DTD files have the extension .dtd, and are included in an XML file using the DOCTYPE declaration.

You also can write declarations directly inside the `DOCTYPE` declaration. For example:

```
<!DOCTYPE letter SYSTEM "letters.dtd" [
    <!ELEMENT ps (#PCDATA)>
]>
```

In fact, you can include a complete DTD inside of an XML file this way, although that defeats the reusability benefits of using a DTD. More often, internal declarations are used to supplement an external DTD. Internal declarations take precedence over external declarations.

The function and value of a DTD becomes much clearer when you think of it in terms of style sheets. A DTD is to the structure of data what a style sheet is to the format of data. Both specify additional information about raw data and make it possible to reuse data in a variety of situations.

Take, for example, Figure 12.1, which is a typical letter created in a word processing program.

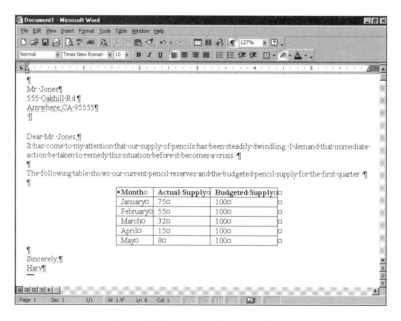

Figure 12.1   A typical business letter.

This letter is clearly human readable. We look at this letter and see an address block, a greeting, the body of the letter, including a table, and a closing. To a computer, however, this is nothing but characters and line breaks. In addition, if this letter were formatted differently, a person might even have a difficult time understanding it, because it might look like the following block of text:

```
Mr. Jones555 Oakhill Rd.Anywhere,CA 95555Dear Mr. Jones,It has come to my
attention that our supply of pencils has been steadily dwindling. I demand that
immediate action be taken to remedy this situation before it becomes a crisis. The
following table shows our current pencil reserves and the budgeted pencil supply
for the first quarter. Month Actual Supply Budgeted Supply January 75 100 February
55 100 March 32 100 April 15 100 May 8 100 Sincerely,Harv
```

At the very least, you probably wouldn't consider the block of text to be a proper letter. Most people still create computer documents as if they're using a typewriter. You might think that you're creating a document with a header, body, and a footer, but you're not. This document has no structure.

By clearly marking up this document, you can eliminate its dependence on formatting for comprehension. Example 12.4 shows one possible way to mark up part of this letter in XML.

Example 12.4 *letter.xml*

```xml
<?xml version="1.0"?>
<letter subject="Dwindling Pencil Supply">
  <head>
    <from><name>Harv</name></from>
    <to><name>Mr. Jones</name>
        <address>555 Oakhill Rd.</address>
        <city>Anywhere,</city>
        <state>CA</state>
        <zipcode>95555</zipcode>
    </to>
  </head>
  <body>
    <greeting>Dear <name>Mr. Jones,</name></greeting>
    <paragraph> It has come to my attention that our supply of pencils has been
steadily dwindling. I demand that immediate action be taken to remedy this
situation before this becomes a crisis.</paragraph>
  </body>
  <footer>Sincerely,<name>Harv</name></footer>
</letter>
```

Marked up, this letter is much more useful. We can easily format the different parts of it, have a program locate the information inside of the to element and add it to our contact database, search parts of the document (for example, only the body), and more.

Now, imagine that you write lots of business letters. Most of these letters have a similar structure, and many even have similar content.

By creating a DTD for the marked up document, you can create a reusable type of document called `letter`. Any program that can read a DTD can then know exactly what you mean by `letter`. Your entire organization could then standardize this definition of `letter`, and be absolutely sure that everyone is writing letters correctly.

Example 12.5 shows a simple DTD for a class of documents called letter.

Example 12.5   *letter.dtd*

```
<!ELEMENT letter (head,body,footer)>
<!ATTLIST letter subject CDATA #IMPLIED>
<!ELEMENT head (from,to)*>
<!ELEMENT from (name,address?,city?,state?,zip?)>
<!ELEMENT name (#PCDATA)*>
<!ELEMENT to (name,address?,city?,state?,zip?)>
<!ELEMENT body (greeting,paragraph*)>
<!ELEMENT greeting (#PCDATA¦name)*>
<!ELEMENT paragraph (#PCDATA)*>
<!ELEMENT footer (#PCDATA¦name)*>
```

Even using this rather basic DTD, the data that makes up this letter becomes much more useful. All the documents that use this letter DTD can be treated as if they make up a huge, distributed database. Because every letter document will be well formed and valid, you can know with absolute certainty that, for example, a `head` element will always contain a `from` element and a `to` element. Then, for example, you could use this information to find all the letters written to a particular person or by (from) a particular person.

Designing and Constructing a DTD

The most common way to begin writing a DTD is to try to look at a representative of the type of documents or data you want to represent in the DTD. For example, if you want to write a DTD for weather-related data, you might start by looking at the current weather and creating markup to describe it, as follows:

```
<weather city="Austin">
    <temperature unit="degrees Fahrenheit">99</temperature>
    <cloud_cover>none</cloud_cover>
    <precipitation>none</precipitation>
</weather>
```

This is a start, but after looking at different examples of weather, you soon discover that additional markup is required. After a few more revisions, you decide that the following document is a representative sample that contains all the elements and attributes that you can imagine needing:

```
<weather city="Detroit">
    <temperature unit="degrees Fahrenheit">45</temperature>
    <cloud_cover>cloudy</cloud_cover>
```

```
    <precipitation>Heavy Rain</precipitation>
    <wind unit="mph" direction="NW">20</wind>
    <humidity>85%</humidity>
</weather>
```

After you've finalized this document, you can start to write the actual DTD. A common problem faced by people trying to create standards is that the disagreements about relatively small matters sometimes threaten the entire project. The solution to this problem (which sounds easier than it actually is) is not to be afraid to create a less-than-perfect DTD. You won't account for everything that might be in a document on your first try, so don't be afraid to agree to come back and revise later.

Element Declarations

The most basic type of markup is the element. The DTD syntax for defining elements is as follows:

```
<!ELEMENT elementname rule>
```

The rule portion, or content model, of an element declaration allows you to specify which elements can be nested inside of this element, the order in which they must appear, and how many times they can appear. Elements that are nested inside of other elements are called its *children*, or *descendants*. For example, a simple name element and its descendants might look like the following:

```
<!ELEMENT name (first,middle*,last)>
<!ELEMENT first #PCDATA;>
<!ELEMENT middle #PCDATA;>
<!ELEMENT last #PCDATA;>
```

The content model of the name element says that first and last elements must occur once (and only once) inside of each name element. The middle element can appear any number of times (including zero), but if it does appear, it must be after first and before last.

Each of the elements, first, middle, and last, may contain parsed character data. See the "Character Data" section earlier for a refresher on PCDATA.

The asterisk (*) after middle in the name element's content model is an *occurrence operator*. Occurrence operators are used to specify how many times an element can appear. If no occurrence operator is specified for an element, the element must occur once. XML has three occurrence operators: ?,+, and *.

- **?.** Means that the element must occur either once or not at all
- **+.** Means that it must occur at least once
- ***.** Means that the element can occur any number of times

The other symbols that can be used in element declarations are the vertical bar (|) to specify an "or" relationship between elements and parentheses to create groups of elements.

Using the three occurrence operators along with grouping element names using parentheses, you can create fairly complex content models. For example:

```
<!ELEMENT car ((door|window)+,engine,sunroof?)>
```

You can also create elements that can contain mixed content, meaning both parsed character data and other elements. Elements with mixed content can be created as follows:

```
<!ELEMENT paragraph (#PCDATA|quote)*>
```

This declaration says that `paragraph` elements can contain parsed character data or the `quote` element any number of times.

To create an empty element, you use the `EMPTY` content model:

```
<!ELEMENT img EMPTY>
```

On the other end of spectrum is the `ANY` content model. `ANY` allows an element to contain general character data as well as elements:

```
<!ELEMENT everything ANY>
```

The `ANY` rule is extremely broad, and therefore almost useless. Avoid creating elements with `ANY` content models unless you absolutely can't think of any other way to accomplish what you need to accomplish.

Attribute Declarations

Attributes enable you to place name/value pairs inside of the starting tag of an element. Attributes are defined using the `<!ATTLIST>` declaration. The syntax of the `<!ATTLIST>` declaration is as follows:

```
<!ATTLIST element_name attribute_name attribute_type default>
```

Multiple attributes for the same element can be declared in one attribute declaration. For example:

```
<!ATTLIST img
          width CDATA #IMPLIED
          height CDATA #IMPLIED
          src CDATA #IMPLIED
          alt CDATA #IMPLIED>
```

In this example, `img` is the target element and `width`, `height`, `src`, and `alt` are attribute names. Each of these attributes has the type CDATA, or character data. Character data is the most common type for attributes, but there are other types as well, which can be divided into three categories:

- String
- Enumerated
- Tokenized

The string category is simply the CDATA type. Attributes with this type can contain anything except markup.

The enumerated type uses a list of possible values, from which one value must be chosen. For example:

```
<!ATTLIST img
          format (gif|jpg|png) #REQUIRED>
```

This declaration says that the format attribute for the img element can have the value "gif", "jpg", or "png". The last part of this declaration, the default value portion, says that this attribute must be specified in every img element.

The category of attributes referred to as tokenized contains eight separate types. These types, and the types of values that attributes can take are shown in Table 12.1.

Table 12.1 **Tokenized Attribute Types**

Value	Description
ID	A unique element identifier
IDREF	A reference to a different ID
IDREFS	Multiple references to IDs, separated by whitespace
ENTITY	An entity declared in the DTD
ENTITIES	Multiple entities declared in the DTD, separated by whitespace
NMTOKEN	An XML name token
NMTOKENS	Multiple name tokens, separated by whitespace
NOTATION	A notation declared in the DTD

Because the values of ID attributes must be unique within a document, attributes of type ID are useful for uniquely identifying elements. Attributes with the IDREF type can then be used to refer to the ID attributes of other elements, thereby providing some rudimentary linking.

The ENTITY and ENTITIES attributes enable you to use the name of an entity that is declared elsewhere in the DTD as the value. The XML processor will expand the value of an attribute with the ENTITY type just as it would with a normal entity reference.

The NMTOKEN and NMTOKENS attributes are used to declare XML name tokens. An XML name token is any valid XML name. Attributes with this type are useful if you want the value of an attribute to be a valid XML name.

Attributes with NOTATION type are used to specify that the value must be a notation that is defined in the DTD. Each possible value must be specified in the attribute declaration. For example:

```
<!ATTLIST img src
          NOTATION (gif|jpg|png) #REQUIRED>
```

The default value section of an attribute declaration can be used to tell the XML processor what the value of the attribute will be if it's not specified, or to tell the XML processor whether the attribute is required.

To give an attribute a default value, you simply put the default value in quotes after the attribute type. For example:

```
<!ATTLIST person number_of_teeth CDATA "32">
```

To make an attribute required, you can use #REQUIRED with the following syntax:

```
<!ATTLIST person eye_color (brown|blue|green|other) #REQUIRED>
```

To make an attribute optional, you use #IMPLIED. For example:

```
<!ATTLIST person tonsils (yes|no) #IMPLIED>
```

To specify a fixed value for an attribute, you use #FIXED. For example:

```
<!ATTLIST person brain CDATA #FIXED "one">
```

Perhaps the oldest and most frequently asked question in the world of markup is, "When should you use attributes and when should you use elements?" For example, the following two pieces of XML mark up the same data, have the same results, and are both well formed. Which one is more efficient?

```
<car>
    <color>Red</color>
<car>
```

or

```
<car color="red"/>
```

The first answer is, "It depends whom you ask." Opinions on attributes versus elements range from, "Attributes should never be used," to, "Attributes should be used everywhere possible." In fact, you can write entire XML documents without using either attributes or elements, and both sides have good arguments for why you would. Most people, however, believe that correct usage of both attributes and elements is beneficial. There are several usage rules that have been generally accepted over the years for deciding when to use attributes and when to use elements. These rules are as follows:

- Use attributes for meta-data or content about an element, rather than the actual content of the element. Therefore, the weight of a book could be considered meta-data, whereas a chapter would clearly be content.

- Use elements where the order of the data is important. There's no way to specify the order in which attributes must appear.

- Use attributes for values that are intended to be read by machines, and elements for values that are intended to be read by humans.

- Use attributes for enumerated values such as unique product IDs.

Entities

General entities (commonly referred to simply as *entities*) can also be declared inside the DTD. Entities enable you to use entity references in your XML document, which can be used as substitutes for other characters. You've probably used entity references while coding HTML. However, XML has only five built-in entity references, as shown in Table 12.2.

Table 12.2 **XML's Built-in Entity References**

Entity Reference	Replacement Text	Character
&amp;	&#38;	&
&lt;	&#60;	<
&gt;	&#62;	>
&apos;	&#39;	'
&quot;	&#34;	"

Any conforming XML processor will enable you to use these five entity references without declaring them first. You may be wondering why XML has so few built-in entity references, when HTML has so many. That's because XML gives you the capability to declare your own entities; it isn't necessary for XML to contain entities that you may never use. (Note that the XHTML DTDs include the declarations for all the entities HTML developers use now.)

Additional entity references are declared using the following syntax:

```
<!ENTITY name "replacement characters">
```

Entities are extremely useful tools for simplifying and making XML markup more readable. They can also be extremely helpful tools for Web-site developers. For example, if you put the same information at the bottom of every page on a site, you could create an entity containing that information, and simply include the entity reference in your documents. An example of an entity declaration for listing copyright information might look like the following:

```
<!ENTITY copyright "&169; 2000 by New Riders Publishing">
```

You can then refer to this entity in an XML document that uses this DTD by using the entity reference &copyright;.

Parameter Entities

Parameter entities function the same as general entities. They enable you to substitute one string of characters for another. The difference is that parameter entities can be used only in DTDs, and not in XML documents.

The primary function of general entities is to make XML documents more readable. The function of parameter entities is to make DTDs more readable. A parameter entity can only be used in the DTD in which it's defined and it must be defined before it's used.

Parameter entities are declared as follows:

```
<!ENTITY % name "replacement_characters">
```

To see how parameter entities can be used, let's take a look at a portion of the XHTML Strict DTD again. The following markup shows the XHTML body element and its attributes.

```
<!ELEMENT body %Block;>
<!ATTLIST body
  %attrs;
  onload          %Script;    #IMPLIED
  onunload        %Script;    #IMPLIED
  >
```

Whereas general entity references use an ampersand before the name of the entity, parameter entity references use a percent sign. Large DTDs, such as the XHTML DTDs, make considerable use of parameter entities to better organize the DTD. In fact, the XHTML DTDs contain parameter entities inside of parameter entities.

The replacement characters for each of the parameter entities in the previous markup can be found at the beginning of the XHTML Strict DTD. Example 12.6 shows XHTML's body element declaration and attribute declarations with the entities fully expanded.

Example 12.6   **XHTML's *body* Element Declaration and Attribute Declarations with the Entities Fully Expanded**

```
<!ELEMENT body (p | h1 | h2 | h3 | h4 | h5 | h6 | div | ul | ol | dl| pre | hr
| blockquote | address | fieldset | table | form | ins | del | script |
noscript)*><!ATTLIST body
  id          ID          #IMPLIED
  class       CDATA       #IMPLIED
  style       CDATA       #IMPLIED
  title       CDATA       #IMPLIED
  lang        NMTOKEN     #IMPLIED
  xml:lang    NMTOKEN     #IMPLIED
  dir         (ltr|rtl)   #IMPLIED
  onclick     CDATA       #IMPLIED
  ondblclick  CDATA       #IMPLIED
  onmousedown CDATA       #IMPLIED
  onmouseup   CDATA       #IMPLIED
  onmouseover CDATA       #IMPLIED
  onmousemove CDATA       #IMPLIED
  onmouseout  CDATA       #IMPLIED
  onkeypress  CDATA       #IMPLIED
  onkeydown   CDATA       #IMPLIED
```

```
onkeyup      CDATA        #IMPLIED
onload       CDATA        #IMPLIED
onunload     CDATA        #IMPLIED
>
```

As you can see, parameter entities can save considerable repetition and confusion.

External Entities

External entities enable you to include external XML data in your document. External entities are defined using the following syntax:

```
<!ENTITY joke SYSTEM "http://my.jokeoftheday.com/todaysjoke.xml">
```

An entity reference can then be used in any document that uses the DTD in which this entity was declared. In this example, the entity reference will replace the entity reference with the content of `todaysjoke.xml`.

Unparsed Entities

An unparsed entity allows you to include non-XML content in an XML document. Unparsed entities are declared with the following syntax:

```
<!ENTITY logo SYSTEM "http://www.lanw.com/lanwlogo.gif" NDATA gif89a>
```

The `NDATA` keyword points to a notation declaration that tells the XML processor what kind of data the unparsed entity represents. It's up to the particular application that is reading the XML to know what to do with an unparsed entity.

Notation Declarations

Notation declarations are used with unparsed entities. They provide additional information about an `NDATA` keyword or point to a viewer application. A typical notation declaration looks like the following:

```
<!NOTATION PNG SYSTEM "/usr/newriders/bin/pngview">
```

XML Schema

Although DTDs are currently the standard way to define the structure of XML documents, they are not the only way.

Unlike SGML, XML is being used extensively for purposes other than marking up documents, including data transmission, data storage, multimedia, and much more. The DTD XML inherited from SGML is actually not a very good fit for the complex data description that XML applications require.

The biggest problem with DTDs is that they don't provide a way to indicate the data type of elements. This is a feature that even the most basic database has. If XML is going to continue to be used for the types of applications it's being used for currently, this capability will become increasingly important.

XML Schema is the top contender for the next generation DTD language for XML. XML Schema divides elements into two types: simple and complex. Simple element types contain data such as strings, integers, and dates. Their equivalents in a DTD are elements that can contain only PCDATA. Elements that can contain other elements are called complex element types.

A detailed discussion of XML Schema is beyond the scope of this book, but you can find more information about XML Schema at `www.w3c.org/XML/Schema`. In addition, Chapter 13, "Where the Future Leads, XHTML Follows," talks a little more about the reasons for paying attention to XML Schema as XHTML and XML move forward.

Adding to the Base Namespace

Until Web browsers mature to the point where using XSL is a viable option for every document, many XML documents will continue to rely either on code that transforms XML into XHTML for display or on XML data embedded in XHTML documents.

Consider a situation in which you're marking up a list of books as an XHTML document. To accomplish this, you can create a document that uses XHTML as well as custom book-related XML markup.

This situation has the potential to present a problem, however. For example, let's say you would like to be able to refer to the titles of the books without running the risk that a browser or other application might confuse book titles with the document title. Such an occurrence (a document containing multiple markup languages that have different elements with the same name) is called a *collision*.

To eliminate collisions between markup languages, the W3C created namespaces. *Namespaces* uniquely identify elements by prefixing them with a namespace ID, which is defined using a unique URI. Because namespaces uniquely identify elements, they also enable a document to be marked up using more than one markup language. Namespaces are defined using the `xmlns` attribute in the root element of a document.

For example, the namespace for XHTML documents is `http://www.w3.org/1999/xhtml` and the root element for an XHMTL document is always `html`. To specify the namespace of an XHTML document, then, you would use the following start tag:

```
<html xmlns="http://www.w3.org/1999/xhtml">
```

The capability to mark up a document with more than one markup language is one of the best reasons to use XHTML rather than HTML. Using namespaces, you can use XHTML elements to define the structure of the document (header, body, paragraphs, and so on) and XML to define the content of the document, without having to worry about the two interfering with each other.

A document's base namespace is one where the element names don't need to be prefixed by the namespace. In an XHTML document, the default namespace is used by XHTML elements. Additional namespaces can be defined and given a name and a unique URI. For example, to create an XHTML document that includes data about books marked up in XML you could specify the namespaces as follows:

```
<html xmlns="http://www.w3.org/1999/xhtml"
xmlns:books="http://www.lanw.com/books">
```

The default namespace in this example is `html`, and the `books` namespace can be used to markup elements about books. Example 12.7 shows how a document that uses these namespaces might look.

Example 12.7 **An Example of a List of Books Marked Up in XHTML and XML**

```
<html xmlns="http://www.w3.org/1999/xhtml"
xmlns:books="http://www.lanw.com/books">
<head>
  <title>A List of Books</title>
</head>
<body>
  <h1>Some of our Books</h1>
<p>Here are some of the books we enjoy.
<ul>
  <books:book>
     <li><books:title>Bleak House</books:title></li>
  </books:book>
  <books:book>
     <li><books:title>Jane Eyre</books:title></li>
  </books:book>
</ul>
</p>
</body>
</html>
```

The previous document displays just fine in a browser, and also takes advantage of the data description capabilities of XML. Using namespaces to put XML and XHTML in the same document is, at least, an excellent short-term solution.

At first glance, the document in Example 12.7 appears to be combining formatting and data, which we have discouraged many times in this book. The truth, however, is that the two namespaces in the document very clearly mark what is data and what is formatting.

You can think of the two namespaces in Example 12.7 as dividing the document into two documents: an XML document and an HTML document. These two documents are shown in Examples 12.8 and 12.9, respectively.

Example 12.8   **The HTML Namespace from Example 12.7**

```
<html xmlns="http://www.w3.org/1999/xhtml">
<head>
  <title>A List of Books</title>
</head>
<body>
  <h1>Some of our Books</h1>
<p>Here are some of the books we enjoy.
<ul>
<li>Bleak House</li>
<li>Jane Eyre</li>
</ul>
</p>
</body>
</html>
```

Example 12.9   **The XML Namespace from Example 12.7**

```
<books xmlns="http://www.lanw.com/books">
  <book>
    <title>Bleak House</title>
  </book>
  <book>
    <title>Jane Eyre</title>
  </book>
</books>
```

Incorporating XML Applications

Namespaces make it possible for one document to contain multiple forms of data. This section will show examples of how to use namespaces to incorporate data into your XHTML documents using various public DTDs.

Imagine that you want to create a document to describe a circle. There are various ways to do this. The first way is to simply describe it in a human-readable format using XHTML, as shown in Example 12.10. Note that this is a contrived example; not a working example; therefore, there is no associated circle.gif file on the CD.

Example 12.10   **Describing a Circle in XHTML**

```
<?xml version="1.0"?>
<!DOCTYPE html PUBLIC "-//W3C//DTD XHTML 1.0 Strict//EN"
  "http://www.w3.org/TR/xhtml1/DTD/strict.dtd">
<html xmlns="http://www.w3.org/TR/xhtml1/strict">
  <head>
```

```
    <title>A Circle</title>
   </head>
   <body>
    <img src="circle.gif" width="50" height="50">
    <p>Here is a circle. It has a radius of 50 pixels.</p>
   </body>
  </html>
```

Another way to describe a circle is mathematically. The Mathematical Markup Language (MathML) is a language for expressing mathematical notation in XML. Using MathML, this circle could be described as shown in Example 12.11.

Example 12.11 **Using MathML to Describe a Circle**

```
<?xml version="1.0"?>
<!DOCTYPE math SYSTEM
"http://www.w3.org/Math/DTD/mathml1/mathml.dtd">
<math xmlns="http://www.w3.org/1998/Math/MathML">
<reln>
   <eq/>
   <apply>
      <plus/>
      <apply>
         <power/>
         <ci>x</ci>
         <cn>2</cn>
      </apply>
      <apply>
         <power/>
         <ci>y</ci>
         <cn>2</cn>
      </apply>
   </apply>
   <cn>1</cn>
</reln>
</math>
```

MathML consists of presentation elements and content elements. Presentation markup specifies how an expression should display in a browser that supports MathML. Content markup provides information about the content of the expression. The previous markup shows the equation for a circle (x2 * y2 = 1) using content markup.

Several browsers, browser plug-ins, and Java applets are currently available for browsing MathML data. It's rare that you would actually need to create a document consisting of nothing but mathematical expressions. MathML is most commonly used to embed mathematical expressions inside of larger documents. Example 12.12 shows the previous example embedded in an XHTML document.

Example 12.12 **MathML Markup Included in an XHTML Document**

```
<html xmlns="http://www.w3.org/TR/xhtml1/strict"
xmlns:mathml="http://www.w3.org/1998/Math/MathML">
  <head>
    <title>A Circle</title>
  </head>
  <body>
   <p>Here is a picture of a circle.</p>
   <img src="circle.gif" width="50" height="50" />
   <p>Here is the mathematical equation for a circle.</p>
   <mathml:math>
    <mathml:reln>
      <mathml:eq/>
       <mathml:apply>
         <mathml:plus/>
          <mathml:apply>
           <mathml:power/>
            <mathml:ci>x</mathml:ci>
            <mathml:cn>2</mathml:cn>
          </mathml:apply>
          <mathml:apply>
           <mathml:power/>
             <mathml:ci>y</mathml:ci>
             <mathml:cn>2</mathml:cn>
           </mathml:apply>
        </mathml:apply>
        <mathml:cn>1</mathml:cn>
    </mathml:reln>
   </mathml:math>
  </body>
</html>
```

If you want, you also can replace the binary representation of the circle with a vector graphic created using Scaleable Vector Graphics (SVG), as shown in Example 12.13. Note that this is a contrived example; not a working example.

Example 12.13 **A Circle Represented Using MathML and SVG, Embedded in an XHTML Document**

```
<html xmlns="http://www.w3.org/TR/xhtml1/strict"
xmlns:mathml="http://www.w3.org/1998/Math/MathML"
xmlns:svg="http://www.w3.org/Graphics/SVG/SVG-19991203.dtd">
  <head>
    <title>A Circle</title>
  </head>
  <body>
   <p>Here is a picture of a circle.</p>
     <svg:svg width="300" height="300">
       <svg:ellipse style="stroke:#000000; stroke-width:3; stroke-opacity:1;
```

```
fill:#000000; fill-opacity:0" cx="150" cy="150" rx="144" ry="144" />
   </svg:svg>
  <p>Here is the mathematical equation for a circle.</p>
  <mathml:math>
   <mathml:reln>
     <mathml:eq/>
      <mathml:apply>
        <mathml:plus/>
        <mathml:apply>
         <mathml:power/>
          <mathml:ci>x</mathml:ci>
          <mathml:cn>2</mathml:cn>
        </mathml:apply>
        <mathml:apply>
         <mathml:power/>
           <mathml:ci>y</mathml:ci>
           <mathml:cn>2</mathml:cn>
        </mathml:apply>
      </mathml:apply>
      <mathml:cn>1</mathml:cn>
   </mathml:reln>
  </mathml:math>
 </body>
</html>
```

With a browser that supports SVG and MathML, or with the proper plug-ins installed on your browser, this document would appear somewhat like Figure 12.2.

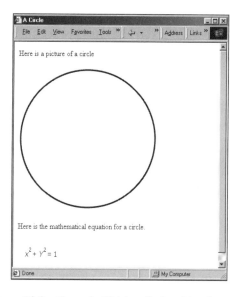

Figure 12.2 Example 12.14 as displayed in a browser.

For More Information

To learn more about the benefits of extensibility, DTDs, and what other Web masters are doing with XHTML and XML, check out the following sites:

- **The W3C XML 1.0 Specification.** www.w3.org/TR/1998/REC-xml-19980210
- **The HTML Writers Guild.** www.hwg.org
- **Internet Explorer Tools for Validating XML and Viewing XSLT Output.** http://msdn.microsoft.com/downloads/ (Expand Web development/ XML and choose Internet Explorer tools for validating XML and viewing XSLT output.)
- **The DocBook Homepage.** www.oasis-open.org/docbook/
- **MathML.** www.w3.org/Math
- **WebEQ MathML browser plug-in.** www.webeq.com/
- **Adobe's SVG browser plug-in.** www.adobe.com/svg/viewer/install/

13

Where the Future Leads, XHTML Follows

DESPITE ALL THE PROGRESS THAT HAS BEEN MADE SINCE its humble beginnings in Switzerland, the Web is still in its infancy. Although these early days of the Web have been exciting, they've also been frustrating for everyone involved in Web development. Many of these frustrations have been caused, at least indirectly, by HTML.

The current HTML limitations found on the Web affect a variety of people. Graphic designers are severely restricted by HTML's limited text-formatting capabilities, the differences in how various Web browsers render HTML, and the requirement that Web pages should not take excessively long to download. Programmers, on the other hand, are frustrated by the difficulty of extracting useful information from HTML, as well as by the limitations of the Hypertext Transfer Protocol (HTTP). In addition, business people become frustrated in their attempts to understand why Web sites sometimes can't achieve the same sort of visuals as print (for example, a consistent layout) or the same functionality and performance as desktop computer applications.

XHTML won't solve all of these problems, but it's a start. The extent to which XHTML succeeds depends largely on how quickly it's adopted by the Web community.

For most developers, the pace of changing standards and languages on the Web has seemingly slowed down a bit since Microsoft won the browser war. The most visible changes happening today are that Cascading Style Sheets (CSS) are starting to catch on and multimedia is becoming more prevalent on the Web.

Underneath the surface, a much bigger and much more important change is taking place: Web development is moving toward becoming much more like programming and less like brochure design.

Software developers have much more of an immediate interest in seeing XML become widely used on the Web than designers do. The main reason for this is that the presentation aspects of XML are not yet fully supported by all the popular Web browsers; however, there are a large number of programming tools that can use XML. Consequently, programmers are leading the push for greater compliance with XML-related standards.

Good programming practices dictate that the user interface, the application (or business logic), and the data should be independent of each other. This practice is called *three-tier computing*, and is the big picture of where Web development is headed. Although it presents unique challenges, the benefits of not combining markup, data, and presentation logic into one file include better maintainability, better accessibility, easier compatibility with different devices and platforms, and increased stability of the final product.

This chapter shows how XHTML fits into this big picture, what the future of the Web is likely to look like, and what you can do today to make sure that you keep up with the changes ahead.

Upcoming Design Trends

As mentioned throughout this book, the purpose of XHTML is to act as a bridge technology between HTML 4 and XML. This move will have an impact on everyone who is involved in the Web. XHTML will help to ease the transition, but it still won't be easy for everyone.

Because rules are strictly enforced in XHTML and XML, and because XHTML and XML allow documents to more easily integrate with applications, Web developers and content creators need to make some adjustments.

Impact on Content Creators and Markup Writers

Content creators and people responsible for marking up text may see their job descriptions change as a result of XHTML and XML. In addition to creating content to be read by people, they may also need to start thinking more about how content will be read by computers.

Example 13.1 shows an excerpt from a press release that is marked up using HTML 4. All that's required of this marked-up text is that a person using a Web browser can read it. It accomplishes this goal just fine. (Note that this is just a portion of an HTML document.)

Example 13.1   **A Press Release Marked Up in HTML**

```
<p>

<a href="http://www.w3.org/">http://www.w3.org/</a> -- 26 January 2000 -

The World Wide Web Consortium (<a href="/">W3C</a>) today releases the
<a href="/TR/2000/REC-xhtml1-20000126">XHTML 1.0</a> specification as a
<a href="/TR/#Recommendations">W3C Recommendation</a>.
This new specification represents cross-industry and expert community
agreement on the importance of XHTML 1.0 as a bridge to the Web of the
future. A W3C Recommendation indicates that a specification is stable,
contributes to Web interoperability, and has been reviewed by the W3C
membership, who favor its adoption by the industry.

</p>
```

As XHTML and XML become more widely used, programmers will start to demand that content creators include markup for the sake of the applications. Example 13.2 shows how you might mark up the blurb in Example 13.1 for use by both people and applications. (Note that Example 13.2 is also just a portion of an XHTML document.)

Example 13.2   **A W3C Press Release Marked Up in XHTML and XML**

```
<press_release>
  <p><a href="http://www.w3.org/">http://www.w3.org/</a> --
    <date>26 January 2000</date> --
      <summary>The
        <who>
           World Wide Web Consortium
           (<a href="http://www.w3.org/">W3C</a>)
        </who>
        <when>
           today
        </when>
           releases the
        <what>
           <a href="/TR/2000/REC-xhtml1-20000126">XHTML 1.0</a>
           specification
        </what>
           as a <a href="/TR/#Recommendations">W3C Recommendation</a>.
        <why>
           This new specification represents cross-industry and expert
           community agreement on the importance of XHTML 1.0 as a
           bridge to the Web of the future.
        </why>
           A W3C Recommendation indicates that a specification is stable,
           contributes to Web interoperability, and has been reviewed by
           the W3C membership, who favor its adoption by the industry.
      </summary>
  </p>
</press_release>
```

Example 13.2 contains much more information about the structure of the press release than Example 13.1. It also requires more work to create. Although XHTML, as XML-compliant markup, has lots of benefits, switching to the more descriptive markup is going to be more difficult (at least at first) for some people.

Much of the work of applying descriptive markup to content can be at least partially automated (using the Extensible Stylesheet Language Transformations, or XSLT, for example). In the near future, XHTML and XML writers will begin to create markup templates for the different types of documents they create. For example, by using tools that exist today, the author of the previous press release could create a template that would allow him or her to apply who, what, where, and when elements in the same way that styles are applied in word processors.

Original content creation will be simplified by word processors that can generate XML and by Web forms. The real challenge for markup writers will be in converting existing documents.

Although old versions of HTML will still be supported by Web browsers as XHTML and XML move forward, many old documents will need to be cleaned up to work with new back-end applications being developed to take advantage of XML. This could be a monumental task for Web sites with lots of static pages. For Web sites that currently generate HTML from databases dynamically, adding XML markup should be easy.

Impact on Graphic Designers and User Interface Designers

Perhaps the biggest impact that XML will have on Web site design is that designers will have many more options as a result of Extensible Stylesheet Language (XSL). Although it may take some practice for designers to adjust to the new possibilities, in the long run, the new options will make Web design more flexible and less frustrating.

One important change that designers may find difficult at first is not creating text images. (Note that this is not an XHTML requirement; it's just good practice to not create text images.) The practice of including text images is a result of the limited capabilities of browsers and HTML; however, it's never been accepted as a good practice. Because of the flexibility and capabilities of XSL, putting text in images will become unnecessary. (See Chapter 7, "Adding Style with XSL," for more information on XSL.)

As browsers and Web developers upgrade their capabilities, sites that are early adopters of XHTML and XML may actually take a step "backward" toward simpler, fast-loading, readable designs. As long as we're reevaluating the languages we use to mark up Web pages, we should also reevaluate our goals in creating documents for the Web.

The goal most Web developers have for their Web pages is that they're read. Extremely complicated design often makes it harder for your audience to read your documents, and in some cases, can actually make it impossible. Background graphics, extremely fragile and complicated tables, hard-coded font sizes, and many other techniques that have developed out of necessity might actually become less prevalent as Web developers begin to think about how content is used and the reasons for separating it from presentation.

Impact on Programmers

Standardization of markup and data exchange languages will increase the use of software components on the Web.

The move toward component-based software is one of the most important trends in the software-development industry today. Although the idea of developing software using flexible, reusable components hasn't been fully realized yet, you can look to another industry, electronics, to get a feel for the potential benefits.

Those in the electronics industry may have never gotten much further than light bulbs if they hadn't figured out that commonly used, complex combinations of transistors, capacitors, and resistors could be integrated. This integration reduces complexity of circuits and increases the speed of circuit design and manufacturing.

As software becomes increasingly complex, the number of bugs, security holes, and failed projects can be greatly decreased through similar means.

For example, most software contains a similar core set of functionalities, including save, function, copy, paste, help, and other commands. These functions are generally provided by the operating system. The software developer doesn't need to touch the code that performs these functions. He or she simply plugs these components into each application.

Besides the core operating system functionality (such as disk access), many applications also contain further similarities. For example, a word processor and a C++ development environment both provide text-editing functionality. Rather than reinventing common functions such as search and replace, software developers can simply plug in a component and specify a couple parameters. This is a much more effective way to create software.

Web development, on the other hand, is still largely dominated by a culture where "quick-and-dirty" hacks generally win out over carefully planned and tested solutions.

The prevalence of chaotic development practices on the Web is partially the result of the lack of formal training among most Web developers. Perhaps more at fault for the sloppy state of affairs, however, is the fast-paced culture of the Web and the unrealistic expectations being put upon developers by project managers who have very little experience and are unable to effectively define requirements and control project scope.

As you'll see in the following section of this chapter, "XHTML 1.1 Goes Modular," componentization is coming to the Web. With increased use of components and standardized markup on the Web will, hopefully, come better development practices and increased flexibility and functionality of Web sites.

XHTML 1.1 Goes Modular

The trend toward greater use of components is also extending to the XHTML specification itself.

Microsoft Internet Explorer for Windows, as of this writing (version 5.5), is typically a 17MB download. The latest version of Netscape Communicator is a 21MB download. Part of the reason that these applications are so huge (and possibly unstable) is that they allow you to do everything from managing your schedule, to FTP'ing files, to participating in Usenet groups. The other contributing factor to browser bloat is the HTML specification itself.

Today's desktop Web browsers must support several different versions of HTML, various custom elements, several scripting languages, and much more. In addition, a huge amount of processing overhead is the result of browsers trying to display poorly written HTML. For today's desktop computers, all the unnecessary processing that goes on behind the scenes in the typical browser and the huge file size of the browser itself isn't much of a problem. For many other Web-enabled devices, however, it is.

There are hundreds of different devices and applications that use or have the potential to use XHTML or HTML markup today. These devices and applications vary in size and functionality—everything from mobile phones to Web browsers to electronic books. Not every device or application that uses HTML needs to use all the features of HTML or XHTML. Memory and processing time can be saved by simply not including the full HTML Document Type Definition (DTD) where it's not needed. More importantly, perhaps, creation of documents for platforms that use a subset of XHTML can be simplified.

For example, a mobile phone that can only display five lines of text has no need for the XHTML `frameset` element. Rather than including the full XHTML DTD along with support for framesets, scripting, and so forth on the mobile phone, it would reduce overhead if the phone could use a subset of XHTML, for example, one that does not include features the device can't support.

Including only a subset of the XHTML DTD is just a start, though. Applications or developers that create markup for use by these applications need to know what is and isn't included in a particular subset or superset of XHTML. To make this possible, the language is broken into standardized parts, or modules.

The W3C document, Modularization of XHTML (`www.w3.org/TR/xhtml -modularization`), breaks XHTML 1.0 into modules and groups of functionality-related modules, as shown in Table 13.1.

XHTML 1.1 (`www.w3.org/TR/xhtml11/`) redefines XHTML using a set of the XHTML 1.0 modules that does not contain any of the deprecated functionality of HTML 4 or XHTML 1.0. The following rather large table shows the XHTML modules. In future versions of XHTML, elements will be added and removed from the specification as modules (or groups) of elements that are related in functionality. It is important, therefore, to see how the different modules are grouped and how they relate to each other. The modules that are not included in XHTML 1.1 are shaded in Table 13.1.

Table 13.1 **Modularization of XHTML 1.0**

Group	Module Name	Module Function	Elements[1]
Basic	Structure	Defines XHTML's major structural elements.	`body`, `head`, `html`, `title`
	Basic Text	Defines the basic text container elements, attributes, and their content models.	`abbr`, `acronym`, `address`, `blockquote`, `br`, `cite`, `code`, `dfn`, `div`, `em`, `h1`, `h2`, `h3`, `h4`, `h5`, `h6`, `kbd`, `p`, `pre`, `q`, `samp`, `span`, `strong`, `var`
	Hypertext	Defines the a element and its attributes.	`a`
	List	Defines the list-oriented elements.	`dl`, `dt`, `dd`, `ol`, `ul`, `li`
	Applet	Defines elements for referencing external applications.	`applet`, `param`
Text Extension	Presentation	Defines simple presentation-related markup.	`b`, `big`, `hr`, `i`, `small`, `sub`, `sup`, `tt`
	Edit	Defines editing-related markup.	`del`, `ins`
	BDO	Defines the element that can be used to declare the bidirectional rules for the element's content.	`bdo`
Forms	Basic Forms	Defines basic form elements for user input. Compatible with HTML 3.2.	`form`, `input`, `select`, `option`, `textarea`
	Forms	Defines all the form elements found in HTML 4.0.	`form`, `input`, `select`, `option`, `textarea`, `button`, `fieldset`, `label`, `legend`, `optgroup`
Table	Basic Tables	Defines a limited form of the table elements.	`caption`, `table`, `td`, `th`, `tr`
	Tables	Defines the complete set of table elements. Designed to provide easier access to using nonvisual user agents.	`caption`, `table`, `td`, `th`, `tr`, `col`, `colgroup`, `tbody`, `thead`, `tfoot`
Image	Image	Defines the `img` element, for basic embedding of images.	`img`

continues

Table 13.1   **Continued**

Group	Module Name	Module Function	Elements
Client-side Image Map	Client-side Image Map	Defines elements for creating client-side image maps. Requires the Image module.	`a&`, `area`, `img&`, `map`, `object&`
Server-side Image Map	Server-side Image Map	Provides support for image-selection and transmission of selection coordinates. Requires the Image module.	`img&`
Object	Object	Provides support for object inclusion.	`object`, `param`
Frames	Frames	Provides support for frames.	`frameset`, `frame`, `noframes`, `a&`, `area&`
Iframe	Iframe	Defines an element for creating inline frames— that is, frames within a block of text.	`iframe`
Intrinsic Events	Intrinsic Events	Defines attributes for elements that can have actions occur as a result of events performed by users.	`a&`, `area&`, `form&`, `body&`, `label&`, `input&`, `select&`, `textarea&`, `button&`
Meta information	Meta information	Defines an element for describing information within the `head` element.	`meta`
Scripting	Scripting	Defines container elements for information pertaining to executable scripts or the lack of support of executable scripts.	`script`, `noscript`
Stylesheet	Stylesheet	Enables style sheet processing.	`style`
Link	Link	Defines an element that can be used to link to external resources.	`link`
Base	Base	Defines an element that can be used to define a base URI.	`base`
Legacy	Legacy	Provides support for elements and attributes that were deprecated in previous version of HTML or XHTML.	`font`, `s`, `strike`, `u`, `body&`, `br&`

---

[1] In cases where a module adds attributes to an element, the element name is listed followed by an ampersand.

Modularizing XHTML makes it possible to create standard combinations of these modules for different applications. The first of these standard XHTML subsets created was *XHTML Basic*.

XHTML Basic includes the minimal set of modules required to still be in the XHTML family of document types. It's designed namely for use with mobile devices, such as personal digital assistants (PDAs), mobile phones, and pagers.

XHTML Basic does not support the following modules:

- Stylesheet
- Scripting
- Events
- Presentation
- Frames
- Tables
- Objects

Because of the limited processing ability and the small screens of the devices XHTML Basic targets, these modules are simply not necessary.

Tracking Key Working Groups and Specifications

At first glance, the world of evolving Web standards can be intimidating. The number of W3C Recommendations, Specifications, Working Drafts, Notes, and Discussion Groups seems limitless. A visit to www.w3.org can leave even an experienced Web developer's head spinning. How do you know what's worth your time and what isn't?

First, understand that you do not need to know everything there is to know about every proposed W3C standard. It's doubtful that anyone does. The reason that the W3C exists is to gather input and brain power from a large number of people with different backgrounds and interests and to try to get them to agree on standards that will be acceptable to the general public (you). Approved standards are called W3C Recommendations.

The process of the creation of a new recommendation starts with a proposal being submitted to the W3C. The W3C then decides if it's going to review a proposal. Then it creates an Activity statement, which specifies the goals, deliverables, and so forth of an Activity. In order to carry out the plan written in an Activity statement, W3C Groups are created. There are three different types of groups:

- Interest Groups
- Coordination Groups
- Working Groups

Interest Groups

An *Interest Group* brings people together who want to evaluate potential Web technologies and policies. Unlike Working Groups, Interest Groups do not have goals or necessarily produce results. A Working Group is sometimes created as a result of the work of an Interest Group.

Coordination Groups

Coordination Groups are created to manage cooperation on issues that involve more than one group. For example, if one Working Group is developing a technology that depends on a technology being developed by a separate Working Group, the two groups could form a Coordination Group.

Working Groups

Working Groups are the W3C groups that you, as a Web professional, need to be especially concerned with. A Working Group's purpose is to study a technical or policy issue involving the Web and to develop proposals for W3C Recommendations.

Each Working Group has a charter that says what the group intends to accomplish. Working Groups have to post intermediate results of their work on a regular basis. These intermediate results are called Working Drafts.

Working Drafts are works in progress. They may change significantly before a final W3C Recommendation is posted. After a Working Group feels that it has fulfilled its charter, it publishes the results of its work as a *Last Call Working Draft*. A Last Call Working Draft is basically a call for feedback and comments from everyone outside of the Working Group.

If a Working Group is not yet in the Last Call Working Draft phase, you probably don't need to pay much attention to it. Once a proposed standard is in this phase, however, it's worth your time to take a look. By this point, things should be fairly well sorted out. Just because something has gotten to this stage does not mean that it will ever become a full recommendation, but this is the point at which you can safely start learning the proposed technolgy in which you have an interest.

After the Last Call Working its Draft phase, the Working Group can either go back to the drawing board or request that their document become a *Candidate Recommendation*. During the Candidate Recommendation phase the document is fine tuned, and small changes are made to it. The Candidate Recommendation phase may result in the document in question being promoted to a *Proposed Recommendation*.

During the Proposed Recommendation phase, which lasts for at least four weeks, the document is reviewed by the W3C Advisory Board. At the end of this review, the director of the W3C may make the candidate a Recommendation. A Recommendation is considered to be a consensus of the W3C and can only be changed by being superceded.

Another term that you may have heard is *W3C Note*. A W3C Note is nothing more than a public record of an idea, comment, or document. Notes are used to publish submission requests or documents that are not created by the W3C.

Notes are not W3C works in progress. Each W3C Note has a status section that specifies whether the note is part of a submission request, whether W3C resources have been allocated to it, and whether the Note was produced by the W3C or by an outside party.

At this point, there are several W3C Working Groups and Notes that have the potential to have an impact on the Web in the near future. These notes are detailed in the following subsections.

Simple Object Access Protocol

As of this writing, Simple Object Access Protocol (SOAP) is only a W3C Note. That said, it's generating quite a bit of interest and debate. SOAP is a protocol for invoking applications remotely using XML messages. For example, a price comparison Web site could use a SOAP message to request product information from an external Web site.

Many people consider SOAP to be the missing link between Web applications and XML data. Others are concerned about the security implications of SOAP's use of the HTTP protocol for remotely invoking applications. If SOAP makes it to Working Draft, this will be a technology to keep an eye on—especially if you're a software developer.

User Agent Accessibility Guidelines 1.0

The idea behind the User Agent Accessibility Guidelines is that it's important that we don't leave anyone out as we move ahead with integrating the Internet into everyday life.

This document specifies guidelines for developers to use to make programs and devices that provide access to Web content (user agents) accessible to people with disabilities.

This specification defines guidelines, checkpoints, and levels of conformance for user agents to follow. The 11 guidelines included in the specification are as follows:

- Support input and output device-independence.
- Ensure user access to all content.
- Allow the user to turn off rendering or stop behavior that may reduce accessibility.
- Ensure user control of styles.
- Observe system conventions and standard interfaces.
- Implement accessible specifications.
- Provide navigation mechanisms.
- Orient the user.

- Notify the user of content and viewport changes.
- Allow configuration and customization.
- Provide accessible product documentation and help.

A side effect of making user agents accessible to people with disabilities is that it also makes the Web more usable for everyone else. For example, if you avoid using images where text could be used, you not only make it possible for voice browsers to read your page, but you also make it possible for people to adjust font sizes to suit their preferences and for search engines to index your site.

W3C Platform for Privacy Preferences Project

The Platform for Privacy Preferences Project (P3P) is being developed to standardize the language of Internet privacy policy statements. Privacy policies developed using P3P will be machine readable as well as human readable. Although Web sites are post-ing privacy policies more frequently, very few users actually take the time to read these policies in detail. Many people would be shocked to find out what some of these so-called privacy policies contain. Web sites regularly sell information gathered through Web sites, rent lists of email addresses, and use personal information to market prod-ucts to you.

Tools developed using P3P will be able to notify you when you visit a Web site that has a privacy policy that doesn't fit with your preferences. P3P will also provide standard language and definitions of terms for privacy policies, so users can be sure of what the language in a policy actually means.

Emerging Development Efforts

As XHTML continues to evolve, there are two future changes to the specification that you should be aware of the following:

- Reformulization of XHTML modules using XML schemas
- XHTML 2.0

Reformulization of XHTML Modules Using XML Schemas

The DTD language used by XHTML 1.0 and XML 1.0 is a simplified version of the language used by Standard Generalized Markup Language (SGML). When XML was first written, it was thought that it, like SGML, it would be used mainly to describe documents. As it turns out, however, XML is most widely used today for data storage and messaging applications. The DTD language that it uses is woefully inadequate for these applications. As a result, several alternative languages for describing XML data have been proposed. The apparent leader today is XML Schemas.

One of the biggest problems of DTDs is that they don't provide a method for specifying data types. For example, there's no easy way to create a rule in a DTD that will say that `<date>11/3/1971</date>` is valid but `<date>cows, pigs, and chickens</date>` is not valid. It was not necessary to be able to define data types in SGML because it was only used to mark up documents. Because XML is so widely used in Web applications, the inability to provide some sort of constraints on the data is becoming a problem.

XHTML uses the XML DTD language. One future goal of the XHTML Working Group is to redefine the language using XML Schema. This change is not likely to alter the way you use XHTML for marking up documents, but it will greatly increase the data description abilities of the language. For more information about XML Schemas, see the W3C site at `www.w3.org/TR/xmlschema-1/`.

XHTML 2.0

The XHTML roadmap states that the XHTML Working Group is aiming for XHTML 2.0 to be a full W3C Recommendation in early 2001. As of this writing, it's not even a Working Draft. The XHTML Working Group states that the functionality of XHTML 2.0 will either be the same or be a superset of XHTML 1.0. This means that documents you create today using XHTML 1.0 probably won't be obsolete when XHTML 2.0 is released.

The main goal of XHTML 2.0 will be to bring HTML more in line with XML so that it conforms to the requirements of related XML standards, such as XML Schema and the XML Linking Language (XLink). XHTML 2.0 will probably contain new modules as well as revisions to existing modules.

Besides the official word on XHTML 2.0, there's quite a bit of discussion about what should and shouldn't be contained in the next major release. It's likely that many of these desired features and changes will make it into the XHTML 2.0 standard at some point. The features and changes being talked about for XHTML 2.0 include the following:

- Support for a more general input model that is not based on the use of the keyboard and mouse. This would allow Web sites to better support alternative input devices such as game controllers, touch screens, and virtual reality-type inputs. This is not just a matter of giving people more of a choice. It's a matter of giving them a more general way of using the Web (one that doesn't always require clicking and typing). This improvement could spawn development of new devices that might make it easier for people with handicaps to use the Web.

- Elimination of HTML-style linking in favor of XLink.

- Elimination of inline style sheets contained in style elements.

- Extensive modifications to the `object` element. Currently, the `object` element has 36 official attributes, and numerous *unofficial* ones that have been added by various vendors. It's clear that the `object` element needs to be simplified.

Other modules that are or have been on the drawing board to be added to XHTML include Extended Forms and Extended Events.

The purpose of the Extended Forms module is to implement a new model for Web forms. Although the original plan was to simply extend the current Forms module, it now appears that the current Forms module will be eliminated. As a result, the work that was to be done by the HTML Working Group has been spun off to a new group and the Extended Forms module has been renamed XForms. See `www.w3.org/MarkUp/Forms/` for more information on XForms.

The reason for this coming major change is that current HTML forms tie presentation too closely to function. For example, an input field created using the `radio` type is expected to be rendered as a radio button. If someone is using a voice browser, there's no such thing as a radio button. The radio button input field is too closely tied to the look of a radio button in a Web browser. A better way to define a `form` element would for it to be defined in terms of the task the user is expected to perform.

Other features that will be included in XForms include client-side calculation abilities, browser-context variables, multi-page forms, and user agent state retention. The addition of these features will be very much welcomed by application developers, as well as content developers because currently, these features require external client-side or server-side code to be implemented.

Incorporating Legacy Web Sites with the Future

With the advent of XHTML, and as XHTML moves forward, a huge amount of Web content is becoming *outlaw code*. There are thousands, if not millions of Web pages today that use code that is not valid according to the XHTML DTD. At this point, you might well be asking yourself if you're going to have to bite the bullet and fix every Web site you've ever created so it will be compatible with XHTML.

Now that beads of sweat are appearing on your brow as you think about all the invalid markup you've written. Let us put your mind at ease. It's a fairly safe bet that HTML, as it has been written since the beginning of the Web, will continue to display correctly in browsers long after the W3C ceases to recognize it. The reason for this is that there are just too many sites that use invalid code. If the next version of a major browser were released tomorrow without support for the `font` element, for example, there would likely be a million-developer march at the corporate headquarters of whichever browser manufacturer dared such a move.

A more likely scenario is that Web development environments will start to phase out old HTML elements, and begin to generate valid XHTML code. For quite some time, most Web sites will be a Frankensteinish/monster-esque combination of HTML and XHTML. Eventually, as old sites die off or are redesigned, the promise of a correctly marked up, extensible Web will be realized. If you want to start taking action today, there are a few things you can do:

- **Learn about XHTML.** If you've made it this far in this book, you've already accomplished this item. Congratulations!

- **Begin using XHTML today.** Existing browsers should parse XHTML correctly and you'll be ahead of the curve when technologies such as XSL and XLink are more widely adopted.

- **Stop using the `font` element.** CSS, although implemented slightly differently in various browsers, will easily do everything that you've been using `font` element to do. Today, more than 90% of the people on the Web are using a browser that supports CSS. If you've been waiting for the audience to reach critical mass before learning CSS, you need not wait any longer. Spend a little time practicing, then just dive into it and see how much easier Web development is when you separate content and presentation.

For More Information

Here are some more sites that you may want to visit to find out more about where XHTML and the Web in general are headed:

- **World Wide Web Consortium.** `www.w3.org/` The W3C will likely be determining, to a great extent, the direction of the Web. If you're involved in the Web at any level, you'd do well to visit their site at least once a month.

- **Electronic Frontier Foundation (EEF).** `www.eff.org/` Founded in 1990, the EFF is dedicated to representing the rights of individuals in the electronic world.

- **OASIS, the Organization for the Advancement of Structured Information Standards.** `www.xml.org/` A nonprofit, international consortium dedicated to accelerating the adoption of product-independent formats based on public standards.

- **XML-DEV mailing list archives.** `http://lists.xml.org/archives/xml-dev/` The XML-DEV mailing list is the most active XML discussion group. The discussion tends to be highly technical, and many of the posters are members of various W3C Working Groups.

XHTML 1.0: The Extensible HyperText Markup Language

IN THIS APPENDIX, WE PROVIDE YOU WITH THE OFFICIAL XHTML recommendation directly from the W3C site at www.w3.org/TR/xhtml1/. Now you can have the specification at your fingertips instead of having to access the Internet every time you want to check something in the specification. Note that this material is copyrighted by the W3C. You can find the copyright notice at www.w3.org/Consortium/Legal/copyright-documents-19990405.

A Reformulation of HTML 4 in XML 1.0 W3C Recommendation 26 January 2000

This version:

http://www.w3.org/TR/2000/REC-xhtml1-20000126
(Postscript version, PDF version, ZIP archive, or Gzip'd TAR archive)

Latest version:

http://www.w3.org/TR/xhtml1

Previous version:

http://www.w3.org/TR/1999/PR-xhtml1-19991210

Authors:

See acknowledgements.

Abstract

This specification defines XHTML 1.0, a reformulation of HTML 4 as an XML 1.0 application, and three DTDs corresponding to the ones defined by HTML 4. The semantics of the elements and their attributes are defined in the W3C Recommendation for HTML 4. These semantics provide the foundation for future extensibility of XHTML. Compatibility with existing HTML user agents is possible by following a small set of guidelines.

Status of This Document

This section describes the status of this document *at the time of its publication*. Other documents may supersede this document. The latest status of this document series is maintained at the W3C.

This document has been reviewed by W3C members and other interested parties and has been endorsed by the Director as a W3C Recommendation. It is a stable document and may be used as reference material or cited as a normative reference from another document. W3C's role in making the Recommendation is to draw attention to the specification and to promote its widespread deployment. This enhances the functionality and interoperability of the Web.

This document has been produced as part of the W3C HTML Activity. The goals of the HTML Working Group (members only) are discussed in the HTML Working Group charter (members only).

A list of current W3C Recommendations and other technical documents can be found at http://www.w3.org/TR.

Public discussion on HTML features takes place on the mailing list www-html@w3.org (archive).

Please report errors in this document to www-html-editor@w3.org.

The list of known errors in this specification is available at http://www.w3.org/2000/01/REC-xhtml1-20000126-errata.

1. What Is XHTML?

XHTML is a family of current and future document types and modules that reproduce, subset, and extend HTML 4. XHTML family document types are XML based and ultimately are designed to work in conjunction with XML-based user agents. The details of this family and its evolution are discussed in more detail in the section Future Directions.

XHTML 1.0 (this specification) is the first document type in the XHTML family. It is a reformulation of the three HTML document types as applications of XML 1.0. It is intended to be used as a language for content that is both XML conforming and, if some simple guidelines are followed, operates in HTML 4-conforming user agents. Developers who migrate their content to XHTML 1.0 will realize the following benefits:

- XHTML documents are XML conforming. As such, they are readily viewed, edited, and validated with standard XML tools.

- XHTML documents can be written to operate as well or better than they did before in existing HTML 4-conforming user agents as well as in new, XHTML 1.0-conforming user agents.

- XHTML documents can utilize applications (for instance, scripts and applets) that rely on either the HTML Document Object Model or the XML Document Object Model (DOM).

- As the XHTML family evolves, documents conforming to XHTML 1.0 will be more likely to interoperate within and among various XHTML environments.

The XHTML family is the next step in the evolution of the Internet. By migrating to XHTML today, content developers can enter the XML world with all of its attendant benefits, while still remaining confident in their content's backward and future compatibility.

1.1 What Is HTML 4?

HTML 4 is an Standard Generalized Markup Language (SGML) application conforming to International Standard ISO 8879, and is widely regarded as the standard publishing language of the World Wide Web.

SGML is a language for describing markup languages, particularly those used in electronic document exchange, document management, and document publishing. HTML is an example of a language defined in SGML.

SGML has been around since the middle 1980s and has remained quite stable. Much of this stability stems from the fact that the language is both feature rich and flexible. This flexibility, however, comes at a price, and that price is a level of complexity that has inhibited its adoption in a diversity of environments, including the World Wide Web.

HTML, as originally conceived, was to be a language for the exchange of scientific and other technical documents, suitable for use by nondocument specialists. HTML addressed the problem of SGML complexity by specifying a small set of structural and semantic tags suitable for authoring relatively simple documents. In addition to simplifying the document structure, HTML added support for hypertext. Multimedia capabilities were added later.

In a remarkably short space of time, HTML became wildly popular and rapidly outgrew its original purpose. Since HTML's inception, there has been rapid invention of new elements for use within HTML (as a standard) and for adapting HTML to vertical, highly specialized, markets. This plethora of new elements has led to compatibility problems for documents across different platforms.

As the heterogeneity of both software and platforms rapidly proliferates, it is clear that the suitability of "classic" HTML 4 for use on these platforms is somewhat limited.

1.2 What Is XML?

XML is the shorthand for Extensible Markup Language, and is an acronym of Extensible Markup Language (XML).

XML was conceived as a means of regaining the power and flexibility of SGML without most of its complexity. Although a restricted form of SGML, XML nonetheless preserves most of SGML's power and richness, and yet still retains all of SGML's commonly used features.

While retaining these beneficial features, XML removes many of the more complex features of SGML that make the authoring and design of suitable software both difficult and costly.

1.3 Why the Need for XHTML?

The benefits of migrating to XHTML 1.0 are described above. Some of the benefits of migrating to XHTML in general are as follows:

- Document developers and user agent designers are constantly discovering new ways to express their ideas through new markup. In XML, it is relatively easy to introduce new elements or additional element attributes. The XHTML family is designed to accommodate these extensions through XHTML modules and techniques for developing new XHTML-conforming modules (described in the forthcoming XHTML Modularization specification). These modules permit the combination of existing and new feature sets when developing content and when designing new user agents.

- Alternative ways of accessing the Internet are constantly being introduced. Some estimates indicate that by the year 2002, 75% of Internet document viewing will be carried out on these alternative platforms. The XHTML family is designed with general user agent interoperability in mind. Through a new user agent and document-profiling mechanism, servers, proxies, and user agents will be able to perform best effort content transformation. Ultimately, it will be possible to develop XHTML-conforming content that is usable by any XHTML-conforming user agent.

2. Definitions

2.1 Terminology

The following terms are used in this specification. These terms extend the definitions in RFC 2119 in ways based upon similar definitions in ISO/IEC 9945-1:1990 (POSIX.1):

- **Implementation defined.** A value or behavior is implementation-defined when it is left to the implementation to define (and document) the corresponding requirements for correct document construction.

- **May.** With respect to implementations, the word may is to be interpreted as an optional feature that is not required in this specification but can be provided. With respect to document conformance, the word may means that the optional feature must not be used. The term optional has the same definition as may.

- **Must.** In this specification, the word must is to be interpreted as a mandatory requirement on the implementation or on strictly conforming XHTML documents, depending on the context. The term shall has the same definition as must.

- **Reserved.** A value or behavior is unspecified, but it is not allowed to be used by conforming documents nor to be supported by conforming user Agents.

- **Should.** With respect to implementations, the word should is to be interpreted as an implementation recommendation, but not a requirement. With respect to documents, the word should is to be interpreted as recommended programming practice for documents and a requirement for strictly conforming XHTML documents.

- **Supported.** Certain facilities in this specification are optional. If a facility is supported, it behaves as specified by this specification.

- **Unspecified.** When a value or behavior is unspecified, the specification defines no portability requirements for a facility on an implementation even when faced with a document that uses the facility. A document that requires specific behavior in such an instance, rather than tolerating any behavior when using that facility, is not a strictly conforming XHTML document.

2.2 General Terms

- **Attribute.** An attribute is a parameter to an element declared in the DTD. An attribute's type and value range, including a possible default value, are defined in the DTD.

- **DTD.** A DTD, or document type definition, is a collection of XML declarations that, as a collection, defines the legal structure, elements, and attributes that are available for use in a document that complies to the DTD.

- **Document.** A document is a stream of data that, after being combined with any other streams it references, is structured such that it holds information contained within elements that are organized as defined in the associated DTD. See Document Conformance for more information.

- **Element.** An element is a document structuring unit declared in the DTD. The element's content model is defined in the DTD, and additional semantics may be defined in the prose description of the element.

- **Facilities.** Functionality includes elements, attributes, and the semantics associated with those elements and attributes. An implementation supporting that functionality is said to provide the necessary facilities.

- **Implementation.** An implementation is a system that provides collection of facilities and services that supports this specification. See User Agent Conformance for more information.

- **Parsing**. Parsing is the act whereby a document is scanned, and the information contained within the document is filtered into the context of the elements in which the information is structured.

- **Rendering.** Rendering is the act whereby the information in a document is presented. This presentation is done in the form most appropriate to the environment (for example, aurally, visually, in print).

- **User Agent.** A user agent is an implementation that retrieves and processes XHTML documents. See User Agent Conformance for more information.

- **Validation.** Validation is a process whereby documents are verified against the associated DTD, ensuring that the structure, use of elements, and use of attributes are consistent with the definitions in the *DTD*.

- **Well formed.** A document is well formed when it is structured according to the rules defined in Section 2.1 of the XML 1.0 Recommendation [XML]. Basically, this definition states that elements, delimited by their start and end tags, are nested properly within one another.

3. Normative Definition of XHTML 1.0

3.1 Document Conformance

This version of XHTML provides a definition of strictly conforming XHTML documents, which are restricted to tags and attributes from the XHTML namespace. See Section 3.1.2 for information on using XHTML with other namespaces (for instance, to include metadata expressed in RDF within XHTML documents).

3.1.1 Strictly Conforming Documents

A Strictly Conforming XHTML document is a document that requires only the facilities described as mandatory in this specification. Such a document must meet all the following criteria:

1. It must validate against one of the three DTDs found in Appendix A, "DTDs," later in this chapter.

2. The root element of the document must be `<html>`.

3. The root element of the document must designate the XHTML namespace using the `xmlns` attribute [XMLNAMES]. The namespace for XHTML is defined to be `http://www.w3.org/1999/xhtml`.

4. There must be a `DOCTYPE` declaration in the document prior to the root element. The public identifier included in the `DOCTYPE` declaration must reference one of the three DTDs found in Appendix A using the respective formal public identifier. The system identifier may be changed to reflect local system conventions.

```
<!DOCTYPE html
    PUBLIC "-//W3C//DTD XHTML 1.0 Strict//EN"
    "DTD/xhtml1-strict.dtd">

<!DOCTYPE html
    PUBLIC "-//W3C//DTD XHTML 1.0 Transitional//EN"
    "DTD/xhtml1-transitional.dtd">

<!DOCTYPE html
    PUBLIC "-//W3C//DTD XHTML 1.0 Frameset//EN"
    "DTD/xhtml1-frameset.dtd">
```

Here is an example of a minimal XHTML document.

```
<?xml version="1.0" encoding="UTF-8"?>
<!DOCTYPE html
    PUBLIC "-//W3C//DTD XHTML 1.0 Strict//EN"
    "DTD/xhtml1-strict.dtd">
<html xmlns="http://www.w3.org/1999/xhtml" xml:lang="en" lang="en">
  <head>
    <title>Virtual Library</title>
  </head>
  <body>
    <p>Moved to <a href="http://vlib.org/">vlib.org</a>.</p>
  </body>
</html>
```

Note that in this example, the XML declaration is included. An XML declaration like the one above is not required in all XML documents. XHTML document authors are strongly encouraged to use XML declarations in all their documents. Such a declaration is required when the character encoding of the document is other than the default UTF-8 or UTF-16.

3.1.2 Using XHTML with Other Namespaces

The XHTML namespace may be used with other XML namespaces as per [XML-NAMES], although such documents are not strictly conforming XHTML 1.0 documents as defined above. Future work by W3C will address ways to specify conformance for documents involving multiple namespaces.

The following example shows the way in which XHTML 1.0 could be used in conjunction with the MathML Recommendation:

```
<html xmlns="http://www.w3.org/1999/xhtml" xml:lang="en" lang="en">
  <head>
    <title>A Math Example</title>
  </head>
  <body>
    <p>The following is MathML markup:</p>
    <math xmlns="http://www.w3.org/1998/Math/MathML">
      <apply> <log/>
        <logbase>
          <cn> 3 </cn>
        </logbase>
        <ci> x </ci>
      </apply>
    </math>
  </body>
</html>
```

The following example shows the way in which XHTML 1.0 markup could be incorporated into another XML namespace:

```
<?xml version="1.0" encoding="UTF-8"?>
<!-- initially, the default namespace is "books" -->
<book xmlns='urn:loc.gov:books'
    xmlns:isbn='urn:ISBN:0-395-36341-6' xml:lang="en" lang="en">
  <title>Cheaper by the Dozen</title>
  <isbn:number>1568491379</isbn:number>
  <notes>
    <!-- make HTML the default namespace for a hypertext commentary -->
    <p xmlns='http://www.w3.org/1999/xhtml'>
        This is also available <a href="http://www.w3.org/">online</a>.
    </p>
  </notes>
</book>
```

3.2 User Agent Conformance

A conforming user agent must meet all of the following criteria:

1. In order to be consistent with the XML 1.0 Recommendation [XML], the user agent must parse and evaluate an XHTML document for well formedness. If the user agent claims to be a validating user agent, it must also validate documents against their referenced DTDs according to [XML].

2. When the user agent claims to support facilities defined within this specification or required by this specification through normative reference, it must do so in ways consistent with the facilities' definition.

3. When a user agent processes an XHTML document as generic XML, it shall only recognize attributes of type ID (for example, the id attribute on most XHTML elements) as fragment identifiers.

4. If a user agent encounters an element it does not recognize, it must render the element's content.

5. If a user agent encounters an attribute it does not recognize, it must ignore the entire attribute specification (for example, the attribute and its value).

6. If a user agent encounters an attribute value it doesn't recognize, it must use the default attribute value.

7. If it encounters an entity reference (other than one of the predefined entities) for which the user agent has processed no declaration (which could happen if the declaration is in the external subset which the user agent hasn't read), the entity reference should be rendered as the characters (starting with the ampersand and ending with the semicolon) that make up the entity reference.

8. When rendering content, user agents that encounter characters or character entity references that are recognized but not renderable should display the document in such a way that it is obvious to the user that normal rendering has not taken place.

9. The following characters are defined in [XML] as whitespace characters:

   - Space ( )
   - Tab (	)
   - Carriage return ()
   - Line feed (
)

The XML processor normalizes different systems' line-end codes into one single line-feed character, that is passed up to the application. The XHTML user agent in addition, must treat the following characters as whitespace:

- Form feed ()
- Zero-width space ()

In elements where the xml:space attribute is set to preserve, the user agent must leave all whitespace characters intact (with the exception of leading and trailing whitespace characters, which should be removed). Otherwise, whitespace is handled according to the following rules:

- All whitespace surrounding block elements should be removed.
- Comments are removed entirely and do not affect whitespace handling. One whitespace character on either side of a comment is treated as two whitespace characters.

- Leading and trailing whitespace inside a block element must be removed.
- Line feed characters within a block element must be converted into a space (except when the `xml:space` attribute is set to `preserve`).
- A sequence of whitespace characters must be reduced to a single space character (except when the `xml:space` attribute is set to `preserve`).
- With regard to rendition, the user agent should render the content in a manner appropriate to the language in which the content is written. In languages whose primary script is Latinate, the ASCII space character is typically used to encode both grammatical word boundaries and typographic whitespace; in languages whose script is related to Nagari (for instance, Sanskrit and Thai), grammatical boundaries may be encoded using the ZW "space" character, but will not typically be represented by typographic whitespace in rendered output; languages using Arabiform scripts may encode typographic whitespace using a space character, but may also use the ZW space character to delimit "internal" grammatical boundaries. (What look like words in Arabic to an English eye frequently encode several words—for example, kitAbuhum = kitAbu-hum = book them = their book); and languages in the Chinese script tradition typically neither encode such delimiters nor use typographic whitespace in this way.

Whitespace in attribute values is processed according to [XML].

4. Differences with HTML 4

Due to the fact that XHTML is an XML application, certain practices that were perfectly legal in SGML-based HTML 4 [HTML] must be changed.

4.1 Documents Must Be Well formed

Well formedness is a new concept introduced by [XML]. Essentially this means that all elements must either have closing tags or be written in a special form (as described below), and that all the elements must nest.

Although overlapping is illegal in SGML, it was widely tolerated in existing browsers.

CORRECT: nested elements

```
<p>here is an emphasized <em>paragraph</em>.</p>
```

INCORRECT: overlapping elements

```
<p>here is an emphasized <em>paragraph.</p></em>
```

4.2 Element and Attribute Names Must Be in Lowercase

XHTML documents must use lowercase for all HTML element and attribute names. This difference is necessary because XML is case sensitive (for instance, `<li>` and `<LI>` are different tags).

4.3 For Non-Empty Elements, End Tags Are Required

In SGML-based HTML 4 certain elements were permitted to omit the end tag; with the elements that followed implying closure. This omission is not permitted in XML-based XHTML. All elements other than those declared in the DTD as EMPTY must have an end tag.

CORRECT: terminated elements

```
<p>here is a paragraph.</p><p>here is another paragraph.</p>
```

INCORRECT: unterminated elements

```
<p>here is a paragraph.<p>here is another paragraph.
```

4.4 Attribute Values Must Always Be Quoted

All attribute values must be quoted, even those which appear to be numeric.

CORRECT: quoted attribute values

```
<table rows="3">
```

INCORRECT: unquoted attribute values

```
<table rows=3>
```

4.5 Attribute Minimization

XML does not support attribute minimization. Attribute-value pairs must be written in full. Attribute names such as compact and checked cannot occur in elements without their value being specified.

CORRECT: unminimized attributes

```
<dl compact="compact">
```

INCORRECT: minimized attributes

```
<dl compact>
```

4.6 Empty Elements

Empty elements must either have an end tag or the start tag must end with /> (for instance, <br/> or <hr></hr>). See the HTML Compatibility Guidelines for information on ways to ensure this is backward compatible with HTML 4 user agents.

CORRECT: terminated empty tags

```
<br/><hr/>
```

INCORRECT: unterminated empty tags

```
<br><hr>
```

4.7 Whitespace Handling in Attribute Values

In attribute values, user agents will strip leading and trailing whitespace from attribute values and map sequences of one or more whitespace characters (including line breaks) to a single interword space (an ASCII space character for western scripts). See Section 3.3.3 of [XML].

4.8 Script and Style Elements

In XHTML, the script and style elements are declared as having #PCDATA content. As a result, < and & will be treated as the start of markup, and entities such as < and & will be recognized as entity references by the XML processor to < and & respectively. Wrapping the content of the script or style element within a CDATA marked section avoids the expansion of these entities.

```
<script>
<![CDATA[
... unescaped script content ...
]]>
</script>
```

CDATA sections are recognized by the XML processor and appear as nodes in the Document Object Model, see Section 1.3 of the DOM Level 1 Recommendation [DOM].

An alternative is to use external script and style documents.

4.9 SGML Exclusions

SGML gives the writer of a DTD the ability to exclude specific elements from being contained within an element. Such prohibitions (called "exclusions") are not possible in XML.

For example, the HTML 4 Strict DTD forbids the nesting of an a element within another a element to any descendant depth. It is not possible to spell out such prohibitions in XML. Even though these prohibitions cannot be defined in the DTD, certain elements should not be nested. A summary of such elements and the elements that should not be nested in them is found in the normative Appendix B, "Element Prohibitions."

4.10 The Elements with *id* and *name* Attributes

HTML 4 defined the name attribute for the elements a, applet, form, frame, iframe, img, and map. HTML 4 also introduced the id attribute. Both of these attributes are designed to be used as fragment identifiers.

In XML, fragment identifiers are of type ID, and there can only be a single attribute of type ID per element. Therefore, in XHTML 1.0 the id attribute is defined to be of type ID. In order to ensure that XHTML 1.0 documents are well-structured XML documents, XHTML 1.0 documents *must* use the `id` attribute when defining fragment identifiers, even on elements that historically have also had a `name` attribute. See the HTML Compatibility Guidelines for information on ensuring such anchors are backwards compatible when serving XHTML documents as media type `text/html`.

Note that in XHTML 1.0, the `name` attribute of these elements is formally deprecated, and will be removed in a subsequent version of XHTML.

5. Compatibility Issues

Although there is no requirement for XHTML 1.0 documents to be compatible with existing user agents, in practice this is easy to accomplish. Guidelines for creating compatible documents can be found in Appendix C, "HTML Compatibility Guidelines."

5.1 Internet Media Type

As of the publication of this recommendation, the general recommended MIME labeling for XML-based applications has yet to be resolved. However, XHTML documents that follow the guidelines set forth in Appendix C may be labeled with the Internet Media Type "text/html", as they are compatible with most HTML browsers. This document makes no recommendation about MIME labeling of other XHTML documents.

6. Future Directions

XHTML 1.0 provides the basis for a family of document types that will extend and subset XHTML, in order to support a wide range of new devices and applications, by defining modules and specifying a mechanism for combining these modules. This mechanism will enable the extension and subsetting of XHTML 1.0 in a uniform way through the definition of new modules.

6.1 Modularizing HTML

As the use of XHTML moves from the traditional desktop user agents to other platforms, it is clear that not all of the XHTML elements will be required on all platforms. For example a handheld device or a cell-phone may only support a subset of XHTML elements.

The process of modularization breaks XHTML up into a series of smaller element sets. These elements can then be recombined to meet the needs of different communities.

These modules will be defined in a later W3C document.

6.2 Subsets and Extensibility

Modularization brings with it several advantages:

- It provides a formal mechanism for subsetting XHTML.
- It provides a formal mechanism for extending XHTML.
- It simplifies the transformation between document types.
- It promotes the reuse of modules in new document types.

6.3 Document Profiles

A document profile specifies the syntax and semantics of a set of documents. Conformance to a document profile provides a basis for interoperability guarantees. The document profile specifies the facilities required to process documents of that type, (for instance, which image formats can be used, levels of scripting, and style sheet).

For product designers this enables various groups to define their own standard profile.

For authors this obviates the need to write several different versions of documents for different clients.

For special groups such as chemists, medical doctors, or mathematicians, this allows a special profile to be built using standard HTML elements plus a group of elements geared to the specialists' needs.

Appendix A: DTDs

This appendix is normative.

These DTDs and entity sets form a normative part of this specification. The complete set of DTD files together with an XML declaration and SGML Open Catalog is included in the Zip file for this specification.

A.1 Document Type Definitions

These DTDs approximate the HTML 4 DTDs. It is likely that when the DTDs are modularized, a method of DTD construction will be employed that corresponds more closely to HTML 4.

- XHTML-1.0-Strict
- XHTML-1.0-Transitional
- XHTML-1.0-Frameset

A.2 Entity Sets

The XHTML entity sets are the same as for HTML 4, but have been modified to be valid XML 1.0 entity declarations. Note the entity for the Euro currency sign (€ or € or €) is defined as part of the special characters.

- Latin-1 characters
- Special characters
- Symbols

Appendix B: Element Prohibitions

This appendix is normative.

The following elements have prohibitions on which elements they can contain (see Section 4.9). This prohibition applies to all depths of nesting, (that is, it contains all the descendant elements).

a

cannot contain other a elements.

pre

cannot contain the img, object, big, small, sub, or sup elements.

button

cannot contain the input, select, textarea, label, button, form, fieldset, iframe, or isindex elements.

label

cannot contain other label elements.

form

cannot contain other form elements.

Appendix C: HTML Compatibility Guidelines

This appendix is informative.

This appendix summarizes design guidelines for authors who want their XHTML documents to render on existing HTML user agents.

C.1 Processing Instructions

Be aware that processing instructions are rendered on some user agents. However, also note that when the XML declaration is not included in a document, the document can only use the default character encodings UTF-8 or UTF-16.

C.2 Empty Elements

Include a space before the trailing / and > of empty elements(for example, `<br />`, `<hr />` and `<img src="karen.jpg" alt="Karen" />`). Also, use the minimized tag syntax for empty elements (for instance, `<br />`), as the alternative syntax `<br></br>` allowed by XML gives uncertain results in many existing user agents.

C.3 Element Minimization and Empty Element Content

Given an empty instance of an element whose content model is not `EMPTY` (for example, an empty title or paragraph) do not use the minimized form (for instance, use `<p></p>` and not `<p />`).

C.4 Embedded Style Sheets and Scripts

Use external style sheets if your style sheet uses `<` or `&` or `]]>` or `--`. Use external scripts if your script uses `<` or `&` or `]]>` or `--`. Note that XML parsers are permitted to silently remove the contents of comments. Therefore, the historical practice of "hiding" scripts and style sheets within comments to make the documents backward compatible is likely to not work as expected in XML-based implementations.

C.5 Line Breaks Within Attribute Values

Avoid line breaks and multiple whitespace characters within attribute values. These are handled inconsistently by user agents.

C.6 *isindex*

Don't include more than one `isindex` element in the document `head`. The `isindex` element is deprecated in favor of the `input` element.

C.7 The *lang* and *xml:lang* Attributes

Use both the `lang` and `xml:lang` attributes when specifying the language of an element. The value of the `xml:lang` attribute takes precedence.

C.8 Fragment Identifiers

In XML, URIs (RFC 2396) that end with fragment identifiers of the form `"#foo"` do not refer to elements with an attribute `name="foo"`; rather, they refer to elements with an attribute defined to be of type `ID`, (for example, the `id` attribute in HTML 4). Many existing HTML clients don't support the use of `ID`-type attributes in this way, so identical values may be supplied for both of these attributes to ensure maximum forward and backward compatibility (for instance, `<a id="foo" name="foo">...</a>`).

Further, since the set of legal values for attributes of type ID is much smaller than for those of type CDATA, the type of the name attribute has been changed to NMTOKEN. This attribute is constrained such that it can only have the same values as type ID, or as the Name production in XML 1.0 Section 2.5, production 5. Unfortunately, this constraint cannot be expressed in the XHTML 1.0 DTDs. Because of this change, care must be taken when converting existing HTML documents. The values of these attributes must be unique within the document, valid, and any references to these fragment identifiers (both internal and external) must be updated should the values be changed during conversion.

Finally, note that XHTML 1.0 has deprecated the name attribute of the a, applet, form, frame, iframe, img, and map elements, and it will be removed from XHTML in subsequent versions.

C.9 Character Encoding

To specify a character encoding in the document, use both the encoding attribute specification on the xml declaration (for example, `<?xml version="1.0" encoding="EUC-JP"?>`) and a `meta http-equiv` statement (for instance, `<meta http-equiv="Content-type" content='text/html; charset="EUC-JP"' />`). The value of the encoding attribute of the XML processing instruction takes precedence.

C.10 Boolean Attributes

Some HTML user agents are unable to interpret Boolean attributes when these appear in their full (nonminimized) form, as required by XML 1.0. Note this problem doesn't affect user agents compliant with HTML 4. The following attributes are involved: compact, nowrap, ismap, declare, noshade, checked, disabled, readonly, multiple, selected, noresize, defer.

C.11 Document Object Model and XHTML

The Document Object Model level 1 Recommendation (DOM) defines document object model interfaces for XML and HTML 4. The HTML 4 document object model specifies that HTML element and attribute names are returned in uppercase. The XML document object model specifies that element and attribute names are returned in the case they are specified. In XHTML 1.0, elements and attributes are specified in lowercase. This apparent difference can be addressed in two ways:

1. Applications that access XHTML documents served as Internet media type text/html via the DOM can use the HTML DOM, and can rely upon element and attribute names being returned in uppercase from those interfaces.

2. Applications that access XHTML documents served as Internet media types `text/xml` or `application/xml` can also use the XML DOM. Elements and attributes will be returned in lowercase. Also, some XHTML elements may or may not appear in the object tree because they are optional in the content model (for instance, the `tbody` element within `table`). This occurs because in HTML 4 some elements were permitted to be minimized such that their start and end tags are both omitted (an SGML feature). This is not possible in XML. Rather than require document authors to insert extraneous elements, XHTML has made the elements optional. Applications need to adapt to this accordingly.

C.12 Using Ampersands in Attribute Values

When an attribute value contains an ampersand, it must be expressed as a character entity reference (for instance, `&amp;`). For example, when the `href` attribute of the `a` element refers to a CGI script that takes parameters, it must be expressed as `http://my.site.dom/cgi-bin/myscript.pl?class=guest&amp;name=user` rather than as `http://my.site.dom/cgi-bin/myscript.pl?class=guest&name=user`.

C.13 Cascading Style Sheets and XHTML

The Cascading Style Sheets level 2 Recommendation (CSS2) defines style properties that are applied to the parse tree of the HTML or XML document. Differences in parsing will produce different visual or aural results, depending on the selectors used. The following hints will reduce this effect for documents which are served without modification as both media types:

1. CSS style sheets for XHTML should use lowercase element and attribute names.

2. In tables, the `tbody` element will be inferred by the parser of an HTML user agent, but not by the parser of an XML user agent. Therefore you should always explicitly add a `tbody` element if it is referred to in a CSS selector.

3. Within the XHTML namespace, user agents are expected to recognize the `"id"` attribute as an attribute of type `ID`. Therefore, style sheets should be able to continue using the shorthand `"#"` selector syntax even if the user agent does not read the DTD.

4. Within the XHTML namespace, user agents are expected to recognize the `"class"` attribute. Therefore, style sheets should be able to continue using the shorthand `"."` selector syntax.

5. CSS defines different conformance rules for HTML and XML documents; be aware that the HTML rules apply to XHTML documents delivered as HTML and the XML rules apply to XHTML documents delivered as XML.

Appendix D: Acknowledgements

This appendix is informative.

This specification was written with the participation of the members of the W3C HTML working group:

Steven Pemberton, CWI (HTML Working Group Chair)
Murray Altheim, Sun Microsystems
Daniel Austin, AskJeeves (CNET: The Computer Network through July 1999)
Frank Boumphrey, HTML Writers Guild
John Burger, Mitre
Andrew W. Donoho, IBM
Sam Dooley, IBM
Klaus Hofrichter, GMD
Philipp Hoschka, W3C
Masayasu Ishikawa, W3C
Warner ten Kate, Philips Electronics
Peter King, Phone.com
Paula Klante, JetForm
Shin'ichi Matsui, Panasonic (W3C visiting engineer through September 1999)
Shane McCarron, Applied Testing and Technology (The Open Group through August 1999)
Ann Navarro, HTML Writers Guild
Zach Nies, Quark
Dave Raggett, W3C/HP (W3C lead for HTML)
Patrick Schmitz, Microsoft
Sebastian Schnitzenbaumer, Stack Overflow
Peter Stark, Phone.com
Chris Wilson, Microsoft
Ted Wugofski, Gateway 2000
Dan Zigmond, WebTV Networks

Appendix E: References

This appendix is informative.

- **CSS2.** "Cascading Style Sheets, level 2 (CSS2) Specification," B. Bos, H. W. Lie, C. Lilley, I. Jacobs, 12 May 1998.

  Latest version available at `http://www.w3.org/TR/REC-CSS2`

- **DOM.** "Document Object Model (DOM) Level 1 Specification," Lauren Wood *et al.*, 1 October 1998.

  Latest version available at `http://www.w3.org/TR/REC-DOM-Level-1`

- **HTML.** "HTML 4.01 Specification,", D. Raggett, A. Le Hors, I. Jacobs, 24 December 1999.

  Latest version available at `http://www.w3.org/TR/html401`

- **POSIX.1** "ISO/IEC 9945-1:1990 Information Technology - Portable Operating System Interface (POSIX) - Part 1: System Application Program Interface (API) [C Language]," Institute of Electrical and Electronics Engineers, Inc, 1990.

- **RFC 2046.** "RFC2046: Multipurpose Internet Mail Extensions (MIME) Part Two: Media Types," N. Freed and N. Borenstein, November 1996.

  Available at `http://www.ietf.org/rfc/rfc2046.txt`. Note that this RFC obsoletes RFC1521, RFC1522, and RFC1590.

- **RFC 2119.** "RFC2119: Key words for use in RFCs to Indicate Requirement Levels", S. Bradner, March 1997.

  Available at `http://www.ietf.org/rfc/rfc2119.txt`

- **RFC 2376.** "RFC2376: XML Media Types," E. Whitehead, M. Murata, July 1998.

  Available at `http://www.ietf.org/rfc/rfc2376.txt`

- **RFC 2396 .** "RFC2396: Uniform Resource Identifiers (URI): Generic Syntax," T. Berners-Lee, R. Fielding, L. Masinter, August 1998.

  This document updates RFC1738 and RFC1808.

  Available at `http://www.ietf.org/rfc/rfc2396.txt`

- **XML.** "Extensible Markup Language (XML) 1.0 Specification," T. Bray, J. Paoli, C. M. Sperberg-McQueen, 10 February 1998.

  Latest version available at `http://www.w3.org/TR/REC-xml`

- **XMLNAMES.** "Namespaces in XML," T. Bray, D. Hollander, A. Layman, 14 January 1999.

XML namespaces provide a simple method for qualifying names used in XML documents by associating them with namespaces identified by URI.

  Latest version available at `http://www.w3.org/TR/REC-xml-names`.

XHTML Elements and Attributes

B

THE TABLES IN THIS APPENDIX CONTAIN A PLETHORA OF INFORMATION that you will find very useful. Note that both of these tables are derived from the W3C Web site, www.w3.org/TR/html4/index/elements.html and www.w3.org/TR/html4/index/attributes.html, respectively.

Table B.1 contains an alphabetical list of all the elements and other information. The information in the table is described as follows:

- **Name.** The element name.

- **Empty.** Elements cited with an E are empty and must use the following syntax: `<element />`.

- **Deprecated.** All elements cited with a D are deprecated, which means that they will be omitted from the next generation of XHTML. (XHTML 1.1 is expected out soon.) This also means that you should not use them unless you absolutely have to. Look to style sheets to achieve the same effects as these elements.

- **DTD.** XHTML documents can use one of three Document Type Definitions: Strict (S), Transitional (T), or Frameset (F). Some elements may only be used when referencing one of the three DTDs. To learn more about DTDs, see Appendix A, "XHTML 1.0: The Extensible HyperText Markup Language."

- **Description.** A description of the element.

Table B.1 **An Alphabetic List of the XHTML Elements**

Name	Empty	Depr.	DTD	Description
a			S	Anchor
abbr			S	Abbreviated form (for example, WWW, HTTP)
acronym			S	Acronym
address			S	Information about author (typically used for a footer)
applet		D	T	Java applet
area	E		S	Client-side image map area
b			S	Bold text style
base	E		S	Document base URI
basefont	E	D	T	Base font size
bdo			S	I18N BiDi override (base direction of the text; left to right or right to left)
big			S	Large text style
blockquote			S	Long quotation
body			S	Document body
br	E		S	Forced line break
button			S	Push button
caption			S	Table caption
center		D	T	Shorthand for DIV align="center"
cite			S	Citation
code			S	Computer code fragment
col	E		S	Table column
colgroup			S	Table column group
dd			S	Definition description
del			S	Deleted text
dfn			S	Instance definition
dir		D	T	Directory list
div			S	Generic language/ style container

Name	Empty	Depr.	DTD	Description
dl			S	Definition list
dt			S	Definition term
em			S	Emphasis
fieldset			S	Form control group
font		D	T	Local change to font
form			S	Interactive form
frame	E		F	Subwindow
frameset			F	Window subdivision
h1			S	Heading 1
h2			S	Heading 2
h3			S	Heading 3
h4			S	Heading 4
h5			S	Heading 5
h6			S	Heading 6
head			S	Document head
hr	E		S	Horizontal rule
html			S	Document root element
i			S	Italic text style
iframe			T	Inline subwindow
img	E		S	Embedded image
input	E		S	Form control
ins			S	Inserted text
isindex	E	D	T	Single line prompt
kbd			S	Text to be entered by the user
label			S	Form field label text
legend			S	Fieldset legend
li			S	List item
link	E		S	A media-independent link
map			S	Client-side image map
menu		D	T	Menu list
meta	E		S	Generic meta–information
noframes			F	Alternate content container for non-frame-based rendering

continues

Table B.1 **Continued**

Name	Empty	Depr.	DTD	Description
noscript			S	Alternate content container for non-script-based rendering
object			S	Generic embedded object
ol			S	Ordered list
optgroup			S	Option group
option			S	Selectable choice
p			S	Paragraph
param	E		S	Named property value
pre			S	Preformatted text
q			S	Short inline quotation
s		D	T	Strike-through text style
samp			S	Sample program output, scripts, and so on
script			S	Script statements
select			S	Option selector
small			S	Small text style
span			S	Generic language/ style container
strike		D	T	Strike-through text
strong			S	Strong emphasis
style			S	Style info
sub			S	Subscript
sup			S	Superscript
table			S	Table
tbody			S	Table body
td			S	Table data cell
textarea			S	Multiline text field
tfoot			S	Table footer
th			S	Table header cell
thead			S	Table header
title			S	Document title
tr			S	Table row
tt			S	Teletype or monospaced text style
u		D	T	Underlined text style

Name	Empty	Depr.	DTD	Description	Page
ul			S	Unordered list	
var			S	Instance of a variable or program argument	

Table B.2 lists XHTML attributes with the following information:

- **Name.** The attribute name.

- **Relevant Elements.** All elements with which the attribute can be used.

- **Type of Value.** Various attributes can take different types of values (for example, "length in pixels"). All possible value types are listed.

- **Deprecated.** Attributes cited with a D are deprecated, which means the attribute will be omitted from the next generation of XHTML (XHTML 1.1).

- **DTD.** XHTML can use one of three DTDs: Strict (S), Transitional (T), or Frameset (F). Some attributes may only be used when referencing one of the three DTDs. To learn more about DTDs, see Appendix A.

- **Description.** A description of the attribute.

Table B.2 **HTML Attributes**

Name	Relevant Elements	Type of Value	Default	Deprecated	DTD	Description
abbr	td, th	Plain text			S	Abbreviation for header cell.
accept-charset	form	Space-delimited list of character encodings from RFC 2045			S	List of supported charsets.
accept	input	Comma-delimited list of media types from RFC 2045			S	List of MIME types for file upload.
accesskey	a, area, button, input, label, legend, textarea	A single character from ISO 10646			S	Accessibility key character.
action	form	URI (RFC 2396)	Required form handler		S	Server side

continues

Table B.2   **Continued**

Name	Relevant Elements	Type of Value	Default	Depre-cated	DTD	Description
align	caption	TOP|BOTTOM|LEFT|RIGHT		D	T	Relative to table
align	applet, iframe, img, input, object	TOP|BOTTOM|LEFT|RIGHT		D	T	Vertical or horizontal alignment
align	legend	TOP|BOTTOM|LEFT|RIGHT		D	T	Relative to fieldset
align	table	LEFT|CENTER|RIGHT		D	T	Table position relative to window
align	hr	LEFT|CENTER|RIGHT		D	T	
align	div, h1, h2, h3, h4, h5, h6, p	LEFT|CENTER|RIGHT|JUSTIFY		D	T	Align, text alignment
align	col, colgroup, tbody, td, tfoot, th, thead, tr	LEFT|CENTER|RIGHT|JUSTIFY|CHAR			S	
alink	body	Color defined by a common color name or a six-digit RGB hex number in the form "#rrggbb"		D	T	Color of selected links
alt	applet	Plain text		D	T	Short description
alt	area, img	Plain text	Required		S	Short description
alt	input	A sequence of characters from the document's character set that can include character entities			S	Short description

Name	Relevant Elements	Type of Value	Default	Depre-cated	DTD	Description
archive	object	URI (RFC 2396)			S	Space-separated archive list
archive	applet	A sequence of characters from the document's character set that can include character entities		D	T	Comma-separated archive list
axis	td, th	A sequence of characters from the document's character set that can include character entities			S	Names groups of related headers
background	body	URI (RFC 2396)		D	T	Texture tile for document background
bgcolor	table	Color defined by a common color name or a six-digit RGB hex number in the form "#rrggbb"		D	T	Background color for cells
bgcolor	tr	Color defined by a common color name or a six-digit RGB hex number in the form "#rrggbb"		D	T	Background color for row
bgcolor	td, th	Color defined by a common color name or a six-digit RGB hex number in the form "#rrggbb"		D	T	Cell back-ground color

continues

Table B.2 **Continued**

Name	Relevant Elements	Type of Value	Default	Deprecated	DTD	Description
bgcolor	body	Color defined by a common color name or a six-digit RGB hex number in the form "#rrggbb"		D	T	Document background color
border width	table	Length in pixels			S	Controls frame around table
border	img, object	Length in pixels		D	T	Link border width
cellpadding	table	Length in pixels as "nn" or in a percentage of available space as "nn%"			S	Spacing within cells
cellspacing	table	Length in pixels as "nn" or in a percentage of available space as "nn%"			S	Spacing between cells
char	col, colgroup, tbody, td, tfoot, th, thead, tr	A single character from ISO 10646			S	Alignment character, (for instance, char=":")
charoff	col, colgroup, tbody, td, tfoot, th, thead, tr	Length in pixels as "nn" or in a percentage of available space as "nn%"			S	Offset for alignment character
charset	a, link, script	Space-delimited list of character encodings from RFC 2045			S	Char encoding of linked resource
checked	input	Checked			S	For radio buttons and check boxes

Name	Relevant Elements	Type of Value	Default	Depre-cated	DTD	Description
cite	block quote, q	URI (RFC 2396)			S	URI for source document or msg
cite	del, ins	URI (RFC 2396)			S	Info on reason for change
class	All elements but base, basefont, head, html, meta, param, script, style, title	A sequence of characters from the document's character set that can include character entities			S	Space-separated list of classes
classid	object	URI (RFC 2396)			S	Identifies an implementation
clear	br	LEFT|ALL| RIGHT|NONE	NONE	D	T	Control of text flow
code	applet	A sequence of characters from the document's character set that can include character entities		D	T	Applet class file
codebase	object	URI (RFC 2396)			S	Base URI for class ID, data, archive
codebase	applet	URI (RFC 2396)		D	T	Optional base URI for applet
codetype	object	Media type (RFC 2045)			S	Content type for code
color	basefont, font	Color defined by a common color name or a six-digit RGB hex number in the form "#rrggbb"		D	T	Text color
cols	frameset	Comma-delimited list of lengths			F	Defines layout of vertical frames
cols	textarea	Number	Required		S	Number of characters per row

continues

Table B.2 **Continued**

Name	Relevant Elements	Type of Value	Default	Depre- cated	DTD	Description
colspan	td, th	Number	1		S	Number of cols spanned by cell
compact	dir, dl, menu, ol, ul	Compact		D	T	Reduced inter-item spacing
content	meta	A sequence of characters from the documents character set that can include character entities	Required		S	Associated information
coords	area	Comma-delimited list of lengths			S	Comma-separated list of length
coords	a	Comma-delimited list of lengths			S	For use with client-side image maps
data	object	URI (RFC 2396)			S	Reference to object's data
datetime	del, ins	Date and time in iso8601 format			S	Date and time of change
declare	object	declare			S	Declare but don't instantiate flag
defer	script	defer			S	UA may defer execution of script
dir	All elements but applet, base, base font, bdo, br, frame, frameset, iframe, param, script	LTR|RTL			S	Direction for weak/neutral text

Name	Relevant Elements	Type of Value	Default	Depre- cated	DTD	Description
dir	bdo	LTR|RTL	Required		S	Direction
disabled	button, input, optgroup, option, select, textarea	Disabled			S	Unavailable in this context
enctype	form	Media type (RFC 2045)	"applica- tion/x-www- form- urlencoded"		S	Defines content type used when submitting a form to the server
face	basefont, font	A sequence of characters from the document's character set that can include character entities	D		T	Comma- separated list of font names
for	label	An ID reference defined by other attributes			S	Matches field ID value
frame	table	VOID|ABOVE| BELOW|HSIDES |LHS|RHS| VSIDES|BOX| BORDER			S	Which parts of frame to render
frameborder	frame, iframe	1|0	1		F	Requests frame borders
headers	td, th	An ID reference defined by other attributes			S	List of ID's for header cells
height	iframe	Length in pixels as "nn" or in a percentage of available space as "nn%"			T	Frame height

continues

Table B.2 **Continued**

Name	Relevant Elements	Type of Value	Default	Depre-cated	DTD	Description
height	img, object	Length in pixels as "*nn*" or in a percentage of available space as "*nn*%"			S	Override height
height	applet	Length in pixels as "*nn*" or in a percentage of available space as "*nn*%"	Required		T	Initial height
height	td, th	Length in pixels		D	T	Height for cell
href	a, area, link	URI (RFC 2396)			S	URI for linked resource
href	base	URI (RFC 2396)			S	URI that acts as base URI
hreflang	a, link	A language code (RFC 1766)			S	Language code
hspace	applet, img, object	Length in pixels		D	T	Horizontal gutter
http-equiv	meta	Name			S	HTTP response header name
id	All elements but base, head, html, meta, script, style, title	ID			S	Document-wide unique ID
ismap	img, input	ismap			S	Use server-side image map
label	option	Plain text			S	For use in hier-archical menus
label	optgroup	Plain text	Required		S	For use in hierarchical menus
lang	All elements but applet, base, basefont, br, frame,	A language code (RFC 1766)			S	Language code

Name	Relevant Elements	Type of Value	Default	Depre-cated	DTD	Description
	frameset, iframe, param, script					
language	script	A sequence of characters from the document's character set that can include character entities		D	T	Predefined script language name
link	body	Color defined by a common color name or a six-digit RGB hex number in the form "#rrggbb"		D	T	Color of links
longdesc	img	URI (RFC 2396)			S	Link to long description (complements alt)
longdesc	frame, iframe	URI (RFC 2396)			F	Link to long description (complements title)
margin-height	frame, iframe	Length in pixels			F	Margin height in pixels
margin-width	frame, iframe	Length in pixels			F	Margin widths in pixels
maxlength	input	Number			S	Max chars for text fields
media	style	A single or comma-delimited list of media descriptors			S	Designed for use with these media

continues

Table B.2 **Continued**

Name	Relevant Elements	Type of Value	Default	Depre- cated	DTD	Description
media	link	A single or comma- delimited list of media descriptors			S	For rendering on these media
method	form	GET | POST	GET		S	HTTP method used to submit the form
multiple	select	multiple			S	Default is single selection
name	button, textarea	A sequence of characters from the document's character set that can include character entities			S	Defines a control name
name	applet	A sequence of characters from the document's character set that can include character entities	D		T	Allows applets to find each other by name
name	select	A sequence of characters from the document's character set that can include character entities			S	Field name
name	form	A sequence of characters from the document's character set that can include character entities			S	Name of form for scripting

Name	Relevant Elements	Type of Value	Default	Depre- cated	DTD	Description
name	frame, iframe	A sequence of characters from the document's character set that can include character entities			F	Name of frame for targeting
name	img	A sequence of characters from the document's character set that can include character entities			S	Name of image for scripting
name	a	A sequence of characters from the document's character set that can include character entities			S	Named link end
name	input, object	A sequence of characters from the document's character set that can include character entities			S	Submit as part of form
name	map	A sequence of characters from the document's character set that can include character entities	Required		S	For reference by usemap
name	param	A sequence of characters from the document's character set that can include character entities	Required		S	Property name

continues

Table B.2 **Continued**

Name	Relevant Elements	Type of Value	Default	Depre-cated	DTD	Description
name	meta	Name			S	Meta-information name
nohref	area	nohref			S	This region has no action
noresize	frame	noresize			F	Users cannot resize frames
noshade	hr	noshade		D	T	Sets the hr element display as a solid color rather than as a two tone rule
nowrap	td, th	nowrap		D	T	Suppress word wrap
object	applet	A sequence of characters from the document's character set that can include character entities		D	T	Serialized applet file
onblur	a, area, button, input, label, select, textarea	A script expression lost the focus			S	The element or code segment
onchange	input, select, textarea	A script expression or code segment			S	The element value was changed
onclick	All elements but applet, base, basefont, bdo, br, font, frame, frameset, head, html, iframe, isindex,	A script expression or code segment			S	A pointer button was clicked

Name	Relevant Elements	Type of Value	Default	Depre-cated	DTD	Description
	`meta`, `param`, `script`, `style`, `title`					
`ondblclick`	All elements but `applet`, `base`, `basefont`, `bdo`, `br`, `font`, `frame`, `frameset`, `head`, `html`, `iframe`, `isindex`, `meta`, `param`, `script`, `style`, `title`	A script expression or code segment			S	A pointer button was double-clicked
`onfocus`	`a`, `area`, `button`, `input`, `label`, `select`, `textarea`	A script expression or code segment			S	The element got the focus
`onkeydown`	All elements but `applet`, `base`, `basefont`, `bdo`, `br`, `font`, `frame`, `frameset`, `head`, `html`, `iframe`, `isindex`, `meta`, `param`, `script`, `style`, `title`	A script expression or code segment			S	A key was pressed
`onkeypress`	All elements but `applet`, `base`, `basefont`, `bdo`, `br`, `font`,	A script expression or code segment			S	A key was pressed and released

continues

Table B.2　**Continued**

Name	Relevant Elements	Type of Value	Default	Depre-cated	DTD	Description
	frame, frameset, head, html, iframe, isindex, meta, param, script, style, title					
onkeyup	All elements but applet, base, basefont, bdo, br, font, frame, frameset, head, html, iframe, isindex, meta, param, script, style, title	A script expression or code segment			S	A key was released
onload	frameset	A script expression or code segment			F	All the frames have been loaded
onload	body	A script expression or code segment			S	The document has been loaded
onmousedown	All elements but applet, base, basefont, bdo, br, font, frame, frameset, head, html, iframe, isindex, meta, param, script, style, title	A script expression or code segment			S	A pointer but-ton was pressed

Name	Relevant Elements	Type of Value	Default	Depre-cated	DTD	Description
onmousemove	All elements but `applet`, `base`, `basefont`, `bdo`, `br`, `font`, `frame`, `frameset`, `head`, `html`, `iframe`, `isindex`, `meta`, `param`, `script`, `style`, `title`	A script expression or code segment			S	A pointer was moved within
onmouseout	All elements but `applet`, `base`, `basefont`, `bdo`, `br`, `font`, `frame`, `frameset`, `head`, `html`, `iframe`, `isindex`, `meta`, `param`, `script`, `style`, `title`	A script expression or code segment			S	A pointer was moved away
onmouseover	All elements but `applet`, `base`, `basefont`, `bdo`, `br`, `font`, `frame`, `frameset`, `head`, `html`, `iframe`, `isindex`, `meta`, `param`, `script`, `style`, `title`	A script expression or code segment			S	A pointer was moved onto

continues

Table B.2 **Continued**

Name	Relevant Elements	Type of Value	Default	Depre-cated	DTD	Description
onmouseup	All elements but `applet`, `base`, `basefont`, `bdo`, `br`, `font`, `frame`, `frameset`, `head`, `html`, `iframe`, `isindex`, `meta`, `param`, `script`, `style`, `title`	A script expression or code segment			S	A pointer button was released
onreset	`form`	A script expression or code segment			S	The form was reset
onselect	`input`, `textarea`	A script expression or code segment			S	Some text was selected
onsubmit	`form`	A script expression or code segment			S	The form was submitted
onunload	`frameset`	A script expression or code segment			F	All the frames have been removed
onunload	`body`	A script expression or code segment			S	The document has been removed
profile	`head`	URI (RFC 2396)			S	Named dictionary of meta info
prompt	`isindex`	Plain text		D	T	Prompt message
readonly	`textarea`	`readonly`			S	When used, prohibits changes to the control
readonly	`input`	`readonly`			S	For text and passwd
rel	`a`, `link`	A comma-delimited list of link types			S	Forward link types

Name	Relevant Elements	Type of Value	Default	Depre-cated	DTD	Description
rev	a, link	A comma-delimited list of link types			S	Reverse link types
rows	frameset	A comma-delimited list of lengths			F	Defines layout of horizontal frames
rows	textarea	Number	Required		S	Defines the number of visible text lines
rowspan	td, th	Number	1		S	Number of rows spanned by cell
rules	table	NONE | GROUPS | NONEROWS | COLS | ALL			S	Rulings between rows and cols
scheme	meta	A sequence of characters from the document's character set that can include character entities			S	Select form of content
scope	td, th	ROW | COL | ROWGROUP | COLGROUP			S	Scope covered by header cells
scrolling	frame, iframe	YES | NO | AUTO	AUTO		F	Scrollbar or none
selected	option	selected			S	When used, defines option as preselected
shape	area	RECT | CIRCLE | POLY | DEFAULT	RECT		S	Controls interpretation of coords
shape	a	RECT | CIRCLE | POLY | DEFAULT	RECT		S	For use with client-side image maps
size	hr	Length in pixels		D	T	Defines the height of the horizontal rule

continues

Table B.2 **Continued**

Name	Relevant Elements	Type of Value	Default	Depre-cated	DTD	Description
size	font	A sequence of characters from the document's character set that can include character entities		D	T	[+|-]*nn* e.g., size="+1", size="4"
size	input	A sequence of characters from the document's character set that can include character entities			S	Specific to each type of field
size	basefont	A sequence of characters from the document's character set that can include character entities	Required		T	Base font size for font elements
size	select	Number			S	Rows visible
span	col	Number	1		S	col attributes affect *n* columns
span	colgroup	Number	1		S	Default number of columns in group
src	script	URI (RFC 2396)			S	URI for an external script
src	input	URI (RFC 2396)			S	For fields with images
src	frame, iframe	URI (RFC 2396)			F	Source of frame content
src	img	URI (RFC 2396)	Required		S	URI of image to embed
standby	object	Plain text			S	Message to show while loading
start	ol	Number		D	T	Starting sequence number

Name	Relevant Elements	Type of Value	Default	Depre-cated	DTD	Description
style	All elements but base, basefont, head, html, meta, param, script, style, title	Style sheet data or markup			S	Associated style info
summary	table	Plain text			S	Purpose/ structure for speech output
tabindex	a, area, button, input, object, select, textarea	Number			S	Position in tabbing order
target	a, area, base, form, link	Frame name or _blank, _parent, _self, or _top			T	Render in this frame
text	body	Color defined by a common color name or a six-digit RGB hex number in the form "#rrggbb"	D		T	Document text color
title	All elements but base, basefont, head, html, meta, param, script, title	Plain text			S	Advisory title
type	a, link	Media type (RFC 2045)			S	Advisory content type
type	object	Media type (RFC 2045)			S	Content type for data
type	param	Media type (RFC 2045)			S	Content type for value when valuetype="ref"

continues

Table B.2 **Continued**

Name	Relevant Elements	Type of Value	Default	Depre-cated	DTD	Description
type	script	Media type (RFC 2045)	Required		S	Content type of script language
type	style	Media type (RFC 2045)	Required		S	Content type of style language
type	input	TEXT | PASSWORD | CHECKBOX | RADIO | SUBMIT | RESET | FILE | HIDDEN | IMAGE | BUTTON	TEXT		S	What kind of widget is needed
type	li	DISC | SQUARE | CIRCLE or 1 | a | A | i | I		D	T	List item style
type	ol	1 | a | A | i | I		D	T	Numbering style
type	ul	DISC | SQUARE | CIRCLE		D	T	Bullet style
type	button	BUTTON | SUBMIT | RESET	SUBMIT		S	For use as form button
usemap	img, input, object	URI (RFC 2396)			S	Use client-side image map
valign	col, colgroup, tbody, td, tfoot, th, thead, tr	TOP | MIDDLE | BOTTOM | BASELINE			S	Vertical align-ment in cells
value	option	A sequence of characters from the document's character set that can include character entities			S	Defaults to element content
value	param	A sequence of characters from the document's character set that can include character entities			S	Property value

Name	Relevant Elements	Type of Value	Default	Deprecated	DTD	Description
value	input	A sequence of characters from the document's character set that can include character entities			S	Required for radio and check boxes
value	button	A sequence of characters from the document's character set that can include character entities			S	Sent to server when submitted
value	li	Number		D	T	Reset sequence number
valuetype	param	DATA|REF| OBJECT	DATA		S	How to interpret value
version	html	A sequence of characters from the document's character set that can include character entities	%HTML. Version;	D	T	Constant
vlink	body	Color defined by a common color name or a six-digit RGB hex number in the form "#rrggbb"		D	T	Color of visited links
vspace	applet, img, object	Length in pixels		D	T	Vertical gutter
width	hr	Length in pixels as "nn" or in a percentage of available space as "nn%"		D	T	Defines the width of the horizontal rule

continues

Table B.2 **Continued**

Name	Relevant Elements	Type of Value	Default	Depre-cated	DTD	Description
width	iframe	Length in pixels as "*nn*" or in a percentage of available space as "*nn*%"			T	Frame width
width	img, object	Length in pixels as "*nn*" or in a percentage of available space as "*nn*%"			S	Override width
width	table	Length in pixels as "*nn*" or in a percentage of available space as "*nn*%"			S	Table width
width	applet	Length in pixels as "*nn*" or in a percentage of available space as "*nn*%"	Required		T	Initial width
width	col	Length in pixels, percentage, or relative			S	Column width specification
width	colgroup	Length in pixels, percentage, or relative			S	Default width for enclosed columns
width	td, th	Length in pixels		D	T	Width for cell
width	pre	Number		D	T	Width of the preformatted area

C

CSS Properties Listed Alphabetically

THIS INFORMATION DERIVED FROM THE W3C INFORMATION found at
www.w3.org/TR/REC-CSS2/propidx.html.
The following demonstrates how the information in this appendix appears:

> **Property Name:** 'Name of property'
> **Possible Values:** Listing of all possible values
> **Initial Value:** Default value
> **Applies to:** All XHTML elements that the property can be applied to
> **Inherited:** (For more information on inheritance, see Chapter 6, "Adding Style.")
> **Media Type:** The type of media—or output—the property can be used with

Property Name: `'azimuth'`
Possible Values: `<angle>` | `[[ left-side | far-left | left | center-left | center | center-right | right | far-right | right-side ] || behind ] | leftwards | rightwards | inherit`
Initial Value: `center`
Applies To: All elements
Inherited: Yes
Media Type: Aural

Property Name: `'background'`
Possible Values: `['background-color'` `||` `'background-image'` `||` `'background-repeat'` `||` `'background-attachment'` `||` `'background-position']` `|` `inherit`
Initial Value: XX
Inherited: No
Media Type: Visual

Property Name: `'background-attachment'`
Possible Values: `scroll` `|` `fixed` `|` `inherit`
Initial Value: `scroll`
Applies To: All elements
Inherited: No
Media Type: Visual

Property Name: `'background-color'`
Possible Values: `<color>` `|` `transparent` `|` `inherit`
Initial Value: `transparent`
Applies To: All elements
Inherited: No
Media Type: Visual

Property Name: `'background-image'`
Possible Values: `<uri>` `|` `none` `|` `inherit`
Initial Value: `none`
Applies To: All elements
Inherited: No
Media Type: Visual

Property Name: `'background-position'`
Possible Values: `[` `[<percentage>` `|` `<length>` `]{1,2}` `|` `[` `[top` `|` `center` `|` `bottom]` `||` `[left` `|` `center` `|` `right]` `]` `]` `|` `inherit`
Initial Value: `0% 0%`
Applies To: Block-level and replaced elements
Inherited: No
Media Type: Visual

Property Name: `'background-repeat'`
Possible Values: `repeat` `|` `repeat-x` `|` `repeat-y` `|` `no-repeat` `|` `inherit`
Initial Value: `repeat`
Applies To: All elements
Inherited: No
Media Type: Visual

Property Name: `'border'`
Possible Values: `[` `'border-width'` `||` `'border-style'` `||` `<color>` `]` `|` `inherit`
Initial Value: see individual properties
Applies To: All elements
Inherited: No
Media Type: Visual

Property Name: 'border-collapse'
Possible Values: collapse | separate | inherit
Initial Value: collapse
Applies To: 'table' and 'inline-table' elements
Inherited: Yes
Media Type: Visual

Property Name: 'border-color'
Possible Values: <color>{1,4} | transparent | inherit
Initial Value: see individual properties
Applies To: All elements
Inherited: No
Media Type: Visual

Property Name: 'border-spacing'
Possible Values: <length> <length>? | inherit
Initial Value: 0
Applies To: 'table' and 'inline-table' elements
Inherited: Yes
Media Type: Visual

Property Name: 'border-style'
Possible Values: <border-style>{1,4} | inherit
Initial Value: see individual properties
Applies To: All elements
Inherited: No
Media Type: Visual

Property Name: 'border-top' 'border-right' 'border-bottom' 'border-left'
Possible Values: ['border-top-width' || 'border-style' || <color>] | inherit
Initial Value: See individual properties
Applies To: All elements
Inherited: No
Media Type: Visual

Property Name: 'border-top-color' 'border-right-color' 'border-bottom-color' 'border-left-color'
Possible Values: <color> | inherit
Initial Value: the value of the 'color' property
Applies To: All elements
Inherited: No
Media Type: Visual

Property Name: 'border-top-style' 'border-right-style'
'border-bottom-style' 'border-left-style'
Possible Values: <border-style> | inherit
Initial Value: none
Applies To: All elements
Inherited: No
Media Type: Visual

Property Name: 'border-top-width' 'border-right-width'
'border-bottom-width' 'border-left-width'
Possible Values: <border-width> | inherit
Initial Value: medium
Applies To: All elements
Inherited: No
Media Type: Visual

Property Name: 'border-width'
Possible Values: <border-width>{1,4} | inherit
Initial Value: See individual properties
Applies To: All elements
Inherited: No
Media Type: Visual

Property Name: 'bottom'
Possible Values: <length> | <percentage> | auto | inherit
Initial Value: auto
Applies To: Positioned elements
Inherited: No
Media Type: Visual

Property Name: 'caption-side'
Possible Values: top | bottom | left | right | inherit
Initial Value: top
Applies To: 'table-caption' elements
Inherited: Yes
Media Type: Visual

Property Name: 'clear'
Possible Values: none | left | right | both | inherit
Initial Value: none
Applies To: Block-level elements
Inherited: No
Media Type: Visual

Property Name: 'clip'
Possible Values: <shape> | auto | inherit
Initial Value: auto
Applies To: Block-level and replaced elements
Inherited: No
Media Type: Visual

Property Name: `'color'`
Possible Values: `<color>` | `inherit`
Initial Value: depends on user agent
Applies To: All elements
Inherited: Yes
Media Type: Visual

Property Name: `'content'`
Possible Values: `[ <string>` | `<uri>` | `<counter>` | `attr(X)` | `open-quote` | `close-quote` | `no-open-quote` | `no-close-quote ]+` | `inherit`
Initial Value: empty string
Applies To: `:Before` and `:after` pseudo–elements
Inherited: No
Media Type: All

Property Name: `'counter-increment'`
Possible Values: `[ <identifier> <integer>? ]+` | `none` | `inherit`
Initial Value: `none`
Applies To: All elements
Inherited: No
Media Type: All

Property Name: `'counter-reset'`
Possible Values: `[ <identifier> <integer>? ]+` | `none` | `inherit`
Initial Value: `none`
Applies To: All elements
Inherited: No
Media Type: All

Property Name: `'cue'`
Possible Values: `[ 'cue-before'` || `'cue-after' ]` | `inherit`
Initial Value: XX
Applies To: All elements
Inherited: No
Media Type: Aural

Property Name: `'cue-after'`
Possible Values: `<uri>` | `none` | `inherit`
Initial Value: `none`
Applies To: All elements
Inherited: No
Media Type: Aural

Property Name: `'cue-before'`
Possible Values: `<uri>` | `none` | `inherit`
Initial Value: `none`
Applies To: All elements
Inherited: No
Media Type: Aural

Property Name: 'cursor'
Possible Values: [[<*uri*> ,]* [auto | crosshair | default | pointer |
move | e-resize | ne-resize | nw-resize | n-resize | se-resize | sw-resize |
s-resize | w-resize| text | wait | help]] | inherit
Initial Value: auto
Applies To: All elements
Inherited: Yes
Media Type: Visual, interactive

Property Name: 'direction'
Possible Values: ltr | rtl | inherit
Initial Value: ltr
Applies To: All elements, but see prose
Inherited: Yes
Media Type: Visual

Property Name: 'display'
Possible Values: inline | block | list-item | run-in | compact | marker |
table | inline-table | table-row-group | table-header-group | table-footer-
group | table-row | table-column-group | table-column | table-cell |
table-caption | none | inherit
Initial Value: inline
Applies To: All elements
Inherited: No
Media Type: All

Property Name: 'elevation'
Possible Values: <*angle*> | below | level | above | higher | lower | inherit
Initial Value: level
Applies To: All elements
Inherited: Yes
Media Type: Aural

Property Name: 'empty-cells'
Possible Values: show | hide | inherit
Initial Value: show
Applies To: 'table-cell' elements
Inherited: Yes
Media Type: Visual

Property Name: 'float'
Possible Values: left | right | none | inherit
Initial Value: none
Applies To: All but positioned elements and generated content
Inherited: No
Media Type: Visual

Property Name: 'font'
Possible Values: [['font-style' || 'font-variant' || 'font-weight']?
'font-size' [/ 'line-height']? 'font-family'] | caption | icon | menu |
message-box | small-caption | status-bar | inherit
Initial Value: See individual properties
Applies To: All elements
Inherited: Yes
Media Type: Visual

Property Name: 'font-family'
Possible Values: [[*<family-name>* | *<generic-family>*],]* [*<family-name>* |
<generic-family>] | inherit
Initial Value: Depends on user agent
Applies To: All elements
Inherited: Yes
Media Type: Visual

Property Name: 'font-size'
Possible Values: *<absolute-size>* | *<relative-size>* | *<length>* | *<percentage>*
| inherit
Initial Value: medium
Applies To: All elements
Inherited: Yes, the computed value is inherited.
Media Type: Visual

Property Name: 'font-size-adjust'
Possible Values: *<number>* | none | inherit
Initial Value: none
Applies To: All elements
Inherited: Yes
Media Type: Visual

Property Name: 'font-stretch'
Possible Values: normal | wider | narrower | ultra-condensed |
extra-condensed | condensed | semi-condensed | semi-expanded | expanded |
extra-expanded | ultra-expanded | inherit
Initial Value: normal
Applies To: All elements
Inherited: Yes
Media Type: Visual

Property Name: 'font-style'
Possible Values: normal | italic | oblique | inherit
Initial Value: normal
Applies To: All elements
Inherited: Yes
Media Type: Visual

Property Name: 'font-variant'
Possible Values: normal | small-caps | inherit
Initial Value: normal
Applies To: All elements
Inherited: Yes
Media Type: Visual

Property Name: 'font-weight'
Possible Values: normal | bold | bolder | lighter | 100 | 200 | 300 | 400 | 500 | 600 | 700 | 800 | 900 | inherit
Initial Value: normal
Applies To: All elements
Inherited: Yes
Media Type: Visual

Property Name: 'height'
Possible Values: <length> | <percentage> | auto | inherit
Initial Value: auto
Applies To: All elements but nonreplaced inline elements, table columns, and column groups
Inherited: No
Media Type: Visual

Property Name: 'left'
Possible Values: <length> | <percentage> | auto | inherit
Initial Value: auto
Applies To: Positioned elements
Inherited: No
Media Type: Visual

Property Name: 'letter-spacing'
Possible Values: normal | <length> | inherit
Initial Value: normal
Applies To: All elements
Inherited: Yes
Media Type: Visual

Property Name: 'line-height'
Possible Values: normal | <number> | <length> | <percentage> | inherit
Initial Value: normal
Applies To: All elements
Inherited: Yes
Media Type: Visual

Property Name: 'list-style'
Possible Values: ['list-style-type' || 'list-style-position' |
| 'list-style-image'] | inherit
Initial Value: XX
Applies To: Elements with 'display: list-item'
Inherited: Yes
Media Type: Visual

Property Name: 'list-style-image'
Possible Values: <uri> | none | inherit
Initial Value: none
Applies To: Elements with 'display: list-item'
Inherited: Yes
Media Type: Visual

Property Name: 'list-style-position'
Possible Values: inside | outside | inherit
Initial Value: outside
Applies To: Elements with 'display: list-item'
Inherited: Yes
Media Type: Visual

Property Name: 'list-style-type'
Possible Values: disc | circle | square | decimal | decimal-leading-zero |
lower-roman | upper-roman | lower-greek | lower-alpha | lower-latin |
upper-alpha | upper-latin | hebrew | armenian | georgian | cjk-ideographic |
hiragana | katakana | hiragana-iroha | katakana-iroha | none | inherit
Initial Value: disc
Applies To: Elements with 'display: list-item'
Inherited: Yes
Media Type: Visual

Property Name: 'margin'
Possible Values: <margin-width>{1,4} | inherit
Initial Value: XX
Applies To: All elements
Inherited: No
Media Type: Visual

Property Name: 'margin-top' 'margin-right' 'margin-bottom' 'margin-left'
Possible Values: <margin-width> | inherit
Initial Value: 0
Applies To: All elements
Inherited: No
Media Type: Visual

Property Name: 'marker-offset'
Possible Values: <length> | auto | inherit
Initial Value: auto
Applies To: Elements with 'display: marker'
Inherited: No
Media Type: Visual

Property Name: 'marks'
Possible Values: [crop || cross] | none | inherit
Initial Value: none
Applies To: Page context
Inherited: N/A
Media Type: Visual, paged

Property Name: 'max-height'
Possible Values: <length> | <percentage> | none | inherit
Initial Value: none
Applies To: All elements except nonreplaced inline elements and table elements
Inherited: No
Media Type: Visual

Property Name: 'max-width'
Possible Values: <length> | <percentage> | none | inherit
Initial Value: none
Applies To: All elements except nonreplaced inline elements and table elements
Inherited: No
Media Type: Visual

Property Name: 'min-height'
Possible Values: <length> | <percentage> | inherit
Initial Value: 0
Applies To: All elements except nonreplaced inline elements and table elements
Inherited: No
Media Type: Visual

Property Name: 'min-width'
Possible Values: <length> | <percentage> | inherit
Initial Value: UA dependent
Applies To: All elements except nonreplaced inline elements and table elements
Inherited: No
Media Type: Visual

Property Name: 'orphans'
Possible Values: <integer> | inherit
Initial Value: 2
Applies To: Block-level elements
Inherited: Yes
Media Type: Visual, paged

Property Name: `'outline'`
Possible Values: [`'outline-color'` || `'outline-style'` || `'outline-width'`]
| `inherit`
Initial Value: See individual properties
Applies To: All elements
Inherited: No
Media Type: Visual, interactive

Property Name: `'outline-color'`
Possible Values: `<color>` | `invert` | `inherit`
Initial Value: `invert`
Applies To: All elements
Inherited: No
Media Type: Visual, interactive

Property Name: `'outline-style'`
Possible Values: `<border-style>` | `inherit`
Initial Value: `none`
Applies To: All elements
Inherited: No
Media Type: Visual, interactive

Property Name: `'outline-width'`
Possible Values: `<border-width>` | `inherit`
Initial Value: `medium`
Applies To: All elements
Inherited: No
Media Type: Visual, interactive

Property Name: `'overflow'`
Possible Values: `visible` | `hidden` | `scroll` | `auto` | `inherit`
Initial Value: `visible`
Applies To: Block–level and replaced elements
Inherited: No
Media Type: Visual

Property Name: `'padding'`
Possible Values: `<padding-width>`{1,4} | `inherit`
Initial Value: XX
Applies To: All elements
Inherited: No
Media Type: Visual

Property Name: `'padding-top'` `'padding-right'` `'padding-bottom'`
`'padding-left'`
Possible Values: `<padding-width>` | `inherit`
Initial Value: `0`
Applies To: All elements
Inherited: No
Media Type: Visual

Property Name: 'page'
Possible Values: <*identifier*> | auto
Initial Value: auto
Applies To: Block-level elements
Inherited: Yes
Media Type: Visual, paged

Property Name: 'page-break-after'
Possible Values: auto | always | avoid | left | right | inherit
Initial Value: auto
Applies To: Block-level elements
Inherited: No
Media Type: Visual, paged

Property Name: 'page-break-before'
Possible Values: auto | always | avoid | left | right | inherit
Initial Value: auto
Applies To: Block-level elements
Inherited: No
Media Type: Visual, paged

Property Name: 'page-break-inside'
Possible Values: avoid | auto | inherit
Initial Value: auto
Applies To: Block-level elements
Inherited: Yes
Media Type: Visual, paged

Property Name: 'pause'
Possible Values: [[<*time*> | <*percentage*>]{1,2}] | inherit
Initial Value: Depends on user agent
Applies To: All elements
Inherited: No
Media Type: Aural

Property Name: 'pause-after'
Possible Values: <*time*> | <*percentage*> | inherit
Initial Value: Depends on user agent
Applies To: All elements
Inherited: No
Media Type: Aural

Property Name: 'pause-before'
Possible Values: <*time*> | <*percentage*> | inherit
Initial Value: Depends on user agent
Applies To: All elements
Inherited: No
Media Type: Aural

Property Name: 'pitch'
Possible Values: <frequency> | x-low | low | medium | high | x-high | inherit
Initial Value: medium
Applies To: All elements
Inherited: Yes
Media Type: Aural

Property Name: 'pitch-range'
Possible Values: <number> | inherit
Initial Value: 50
Applies To: All elements
Inherited: Yes
Media Type: Aural

Property Name: 'play-during'
Possible Values: <uri> mix? repeat? | auto | none | inherit
Initial Value: auto
Applies To: All elements
Inherited: No
Media Type: Aural

Property Name: 'position'
Possible Values: static | relative | absolute | fixed | inherit
Initial Value: static
Applies To: All elements, but not to generated content
Inherited: No
Media Type: Visual

Property Name: 'quotes'
Possible Values: [<string> <string>]+ | none | inherit
Initial Value: Depends on user agent
Applies To: All elements
Inherited: Yes
Media Type: Visual

Property Name: 'richness'
Possible Values: <number> | inherit
Initial Value: 50
Applies To: All elements
Inherited: Yes
Media Type: Aural

Property Name: 'right'
Possible Values: <length> | <percentage> | auto | inherit
Initial Value: auto
Applies To: Positioned elements
Inherited: No
Media Type: Visual

Property Name: 'size'
Possible Values: <length>{1,2} | auto | portrait | landscape | inherit
Initial Value: auto
Applies To: The page context
Inherited: N/A
Media Type: Visual, paged

Property Name: 'speak'
Possible Values: normal | none | spell-out | inherit
Initial Value: normal
Applies To: All elements
Inherited: Yes
Media Type: Aural

Property Name: 'speak-header'
Possible Values: once | always | inherit
Initial Value: once
Applies To: Elements that have table header information
Inherited: Yes
Media Type: Aural

Property Name: 'speak-numeral'
Possible Values: digits | continuous | inherit
Initial Value: continuous
Applies To: All elements
Inherited: Yes
Media Type: Aural

Property Name: 'speak-punctuation'
Possible Values: code | none | inherit
Initial Value: none
Applies To: All elements
Inherited: Yes
Media Type: Aural

Property Name: 'speech-rate'
Possible Values: <number> | x-slow | slow | medium | fast | x-fast | faster | slower | inherit
Initial Value: medium
Applies To: All elements
Inherited: Yes
Media Type: Aural

Property Name: 'stress'
Possible Values: <number> | inherit
Initial Value: 50
Applies To: All elements
Inherited: Yes
Media Type: Aural

Property Name: 'table-layout'
Possible Values: auto | fixed | inherit
Initial Value: auto
Applies To: 'table' and 'inline-table' elements
Inherited: No
Media Type: Visual

Property Name: 'text-align'
Possible Values: left | right | center | justify | *<string>* | inherit
Initial Value: Depends on user agent and writing direction
Applies To: Block-level elements
Inherited: Yes
Media Type: Visual

Property Name: 'text-decoration'
Possible Values: none | [underline || overline || line-through || blink] | inherit
Initial Value: none
Applies To: All elements
Inherited: No (see prose)
Media Type: Visual

Property Name: 'text-indent'
Possible Values: *<length>* | *<percentage>* | inherit
Initial Value: 0
Applies To: Block-level elements
Inherited: Yes
Media Type: Visual

Property Name: 'text-shadow'
Possible Values: none | [*<color>* || *<length>* *<length>* *<length>*? ,]* [*<color>* || *<length>* *<length>* *<length>*?] | inherit
Initial Value: none
Applies To: All elements
Inherited: No (see prose)
Media Type: Visual

Property Name: 'text-transform'
Possible Values: capitalize | uppercase | lowercase | none | inherit
Initial Value: none
Applies To: All elements
Inherited: Yes
Media Type: Visual

Property Name: 'top'
Possible Values: *<length>* | *<percentage>* | auto | inherit
Initial Value: auto
Applies To: Positioned elements
Inherited: No
Media Type: Visual

Property Name: 'unicode-bidi'
Possible Values: normal | embed | bidi-override | inherit
Initial Value: normal
Applies To: All elements, but see prose
Inherited: No
Media Type: Visual

Property Name: 'vertical-align'
Possible Values: baseline | sub | super | top | text-top | middle | bottom |
text-bottom | <percentage> | <length> | inherit
Initial Value: baseline
Applies To: Inline-level and 'table-cell' elements
Inherited: No
Media Type: Visual

Property Name: 'visibility'
Possible Values: visible | hidden | collapse | inherit
Initial Value: inherit
Applies To: All elements
Inherited: No
Media Type: Visual

Property Name: 'voice-family'
Possible Values: [[<specific-voice> | <generic-voice>],]* [<specific-voice>
| <generic-voice>] | inherit
Initial Value: Depends on user agent
Applies To: All elements
Inherited: Yes
Media Type: Aural

Property Name: 'volume'
Possible Values: <number> | <percentage> | silent | x-soft | soft | medium |
loud | x-loud | inherit
Initial Value: medium
Applies To: All elements
Inherited: Yes
Media Type: Aural

Property Name: 'white-space'
Possible Values: normal | pre | nowrap | inherit
Initial Value: normal
Applies To: Block-level elements
Inherited: Yes
Media Type: Visual

Property Name: 'widows'
Possible Values: <*integer*> | inherit
Initial Value: 2
Applies To: Block-level elements
Inherited: Yes
Media Type: Visual, paged

Property Name: 'width'
Possible Values: <*length*> | <*percentage*> | auto | inherit
Initial Value: auto
Applies To: All elements but nonreplaced inline elements, table rows, and row groups
Inherited: No
Media Type: Visual

Property Name: 'word-spacing'
Possible Values: normal | <*length*> | inherit
Initial Value: normal
Applies To: All elements
Inherited: Yes
Media Type: Visual

Property Name: 'z-index'
Possible Values: auto | <*integer*> | inherit
Initial Value: auto
Applies To: Positioned elements
Inherited: No
Media Type: Visual

D

A Compendium of HTML, XML, and XHTML Resources

I<small>N THIS APPENDIX, YOU'LL FIND ALMOST EVERY RESOURCE</small> for HTML, XML, and XHTML imaginable. The information is broken down as follows:

- Standards
- Online Resources
  - Web sites
  - Mailing lists
  - Search engines
- Tools
  - Authoring
  - Browsers
  - Graphics
  - Multimedia
- Books
- Magazines

The Standards

The World Wide Web Consortium was formed in 1994 as a body to govern most Web-related standards. Although not an official standards organization, it does sign off on most Web-related specifications. If you're interested in learning about XHTML, XML, or Web style sheets, you need to be familiar with the following URLs:

- The World Wide Web Consortium Home Page at www.w3.org
- Cascading Style Sheets (CSS) Level 1 Recommendation Specification at www.w3.org/TR/REC-CSS1/
- Cascading Style Sheets (CSS) Level 2 Recommendation Specification at www.w3.org/TR/REC-CSS2/
- Cascading Style Sheets (CSS) Resource Page at www.w3.org/Style/CSS
- Document Object Model (DOM) Level 1 Recommendation Specification at www.w3.org/TR/DOM-Level-1/
- Document Object Model (DOM) Level 2 Recommendation Specification at www.w3.org/TR/DOM-Level-2/
- General Style Sheet Resource Page at www.w3.org/Style
- HTML 4.01 Recommendation Specification at www.w3.org/TR/html4/
- HTML Resource Page at www.w3.org/Markup
- XHTML 1.0 Recommendation Specification at www.w3.org/TR/xhtml1/
- XML 1.0 Recommendation Specification at www.w3.org/TR/REC-xml
- XML Resource Page at www.w3.org/xml
- XSL 1.0 Working Draft Specification at www.w3.org/TR/xsl
- XSL Resource Page at www.w3.org/Style/XSL
- XSLT 1.0 Recommendation Specification at www.w3.org/TR/xslt

Online Resources

If you're a Web developer, or an aspiring Web developer, you need to be sure to keep on the cutting edge of Web technologies. Luckily, there are plenty of online resources that keep up with the latest Web technologies for you. We've listed some of our favorites. Check them out and bookmark them.

Web Sites

The following resources contain tutorials, articles, and various information on Web technologies:

- **BrowserWatch.** www.browserwatch.com
- **CSS Pointer Group.** http://css.nu/

- **Hotwired's Webmonkey.** www.hotwired.com/webmonkey
- **LANWrights.** www.lanw.com
- **Project Cool's Developer Zone.** www.projectcool.com/developer
- **Robin Cover's SGML/XML Pages.** www.oasis-open.org/cover
- **Web Design Group.** www.htmlhelp.com
- **Web Developer's Virtual Library.** www.wdvl.com
- **Web Pages That Suck.** www.webpagesthatsuck.com
- **Webreview.** http://webreview.com
- **<?xmlhack?>.** www.xmlhack.com/
- **XML Info.** www.xmlinfo.com
- **XML Software.** www.xmlsoftware.com
- **XML.com.** www.xml.com
- **XSL Info.** www.xslinfo.com
- **ZDNet Developer Site.** www.zdnet.com/devhead

Mailing Lists

As you probably know, email mailing lists are everywhere. Luckily, there are some you might actually want to get mail from. But first, you have to subscribe to the mailing list(s) of your choice. First, let us offer you a quick tip about mailing lists: Always sign up for the *digest* before signing on for daily messages. Most mailing lists offer a weekly digest that compiles messages for the week into one long email. All the mailing lists mentioned in this appendix can have anywhere from 10 to 40 messages a day—sometimes even more. Therefore, we suggest you sign up for the digest first. After you've decided that the list is for you, you can change your subscription status.

COMP.TEXT.XML Newsgroup

There's plenty covered in this newsgroup and it's worth a look. The topics vary, as does the level of knowledge.

You can join the COMP.TEXT.XML newsgroup from your newsreader software.

XHTML-L

This mailing list is the first mailing list dedicated to XHTML. The mailing list is good for those new to the XHTML world. Topics so far have covered everything from general syntax rules to discussions about the future of XHTML. It is definitely worth a look.

Archives and sign up are found at www.egroups.com/group/XHTML-L.

XML-DEV

If you know more than just the basics, this list may be for you. It's more technical than the others and it's frequented by people with a lot of XML experience, many of whom are W3C members.

Archives are found at `http://lists.xml.org/archives/xml-dev`. Join this list by sending email to `majordomo@xml.org`. Be sure to put "subscribe xml-dev" in the body of the message.

XML-L

If you're new to XML, you might want to start here. Members are responsive to newcomers and you may even find some seasoned XMLers posting to this list.

Archives can be found at `http://listserv.heanet.ie/xml-l.html`. To join, send email to `listserv@listserv.hea.ie`.

XSL-List

This list covers topics relating to XSL, XSL Transformations (XSLT), and XSL Formatting Objects (FOs). This list tends to attract dedicated XMLers who understand the usefulness of XSL(T). You're likely to see messages from Michael Kay, James Clark, and the like. (If you don't recognize those names, they are the ones responsible for two of the most used XSL processors: Saxon, and XT, respectively.) Beginners are welcome and it's a wonderful place to take advantage of the expertise present. However, you might want to check the archives before asking some of the basics. Chances are that someone has already done that for you.

Archives are found at `www.mulberrytech.com/xsl/xsl-list/`. To join, send email to `majordomo@mulberrytech.com`. Be sure to write "subscribe XSL-List" in the body of the message.

Search Engines

The following search engines can lead you to a wealth of information about every Web technology available. Just type your query (such as XHTML, XML, HTML, CSS, or XSL) in the space provided and see what appears. These are some of our favorite search engines:

- Wired Digital, a Lycos Network company, brings us Hotbot, found at `http://hotbot.lycos.com/`.
- You can also just go to the Lycos site directly, which is found at `www.lycos.com`.
- Everyone is familiar with Yahoo, which is found at `www.yahoo.com`.
- AltaVista is the choice for many; it's found at `www.altavista.com`.
- Excite is another popular Web browser; it's found at `www.excite.com`.
- Many of our Web-development friends prefer Google, which is found at `www.google.com`.
- To search them all at once, try 37.com, which is found at `http://37.com`.

Tools

Tools make our lives easier. Although it's important to understand XHTML syntax rules and vocabulary, sometimes it's even more important to get that project done on time. We recommend that you have a good text editor by your side at all times. However, if you need a little more help, there are plenty of *what you see is what you get* (WYSIWYG) editors on the market that will do all the hard work for you.

Authoring

For Web authoring, we recommend the tools discussed in this section. We either own or have test driven all these programs and you won't be disappointed.

Allaire's HomeSite

HomeSite is an easy-to-use HTML editor that can make your Web page creation easier and enable you to deliver DHTML, XML, CSS, JavaScript, and much more. This is probably the most widely used HTML editor. HomeSite is no stranger to Web-development circles. It's only $89 for the download and $99 for the CD. You can find it at www.allaire.com/Products/HomeSite/.

Arachnophilia

Similar to HTML Kit (covered in the following section), this text editor is free. It's not as commonly used as the other editors listed here, but we like its instant view mode that enables you to see your changes as you make them. You can find it at www.arachnoid.com.

HTML-Kit

HTML-Kit is a text editor designed to create HTML and XML. With features allowing authors to edit, format, lookup help, validate, preview, and publish Web pages, this editor is packed with features to help any developer looking to create clean XHTML code. When you download HTML Kit, you also get HTML Tidy (a tool that enables you to convert existing HTML pages to XHTML). The best thing about HTML-Kit is that it's free. You can download it from www.chami.com/html-kit/.

Macromedia's Dreamweaver 3

Most designers prefer Dreamweaver as their HTML authoring tool, and for good reason. Dreamweaver produces good, clean code and even produces CSS style rules and JavaScript. One warning, however: It does not produce XHTML. Although it follows most XHTML rules, such as lowercasing element names and adding quotation marks around all attribute values, it does not add the correct DOCTYPE declaration or use the correct syntax for empty elements. Luckily, Dreamweaver comes with HomeSite, so you can make the necessary changes yourself. You can download the trial version of Dreamweaver from www.macromedia.com/software/dreamweaver/trial/. Or, you can purchase it starting at $299 from www.macromedia.com/software/dreamweaver/.

Mozquito

Mozquito is the first XHTML-specific tool on the market. If you're looking to create quick-and-easy XHTML, this tool is for you. Additionally, if you're looking to work with the next generation of Web forms, Mozquito is definitely the tool to use. You can download a 30-day trial version, or purchase Mozquito for $149 per copy, at www.mozquito.com.

Sausage Software's HotDog Professional

HotDog is a popular text editor that is simple and easy to use. We always suggest that you have access to a text editor; why not choose one that was created with Web development in mind? Download the 30-day trial version, or purchase it for $99.95, from www.sausage.com.

SoftQuad's HoTMetaL Pro

HoTMetal Pro is a WYSIWYG editor that supports both XML and HTML. HoTMetal offers support for CSS, frames, Dynamic HTML, Java, JavaScript, VBScript, Miva, XML, WebTV, Shockwave, Flash, QuickTime, RealAudio, streaming audio and video, and more. This tool even, with the help of HoTMetal's Database Import Wizard, enables you to create database queries, and you don't even have to know the Structured Query Language (SQL). Download the 30-day trial version, or purchase it for $129, from the HoTMetal site at www.hotmetalpro.com/. You can also access it from the SoftQuad site www.softquad.com.

Browsers

Before you decide which browser you want to use, you should do a little reading. Each browser offers very different features and supports different technologies. Here are some of our favorites:

- **Amaya.** Amaya is hosted by the W3C, and it's an authoring tool as well as a browser. And it's free. It supports HTML and CSS1. In addition, you can use it to develop XHTML pages and CSS. Download it from www.w3.org/Amaya/.

- **Microsoft's Internet Explorer.** The newest version of Internet Explorer (5.5) now supports XSLT and structured presentation of XML. You can download it from www.microsoft.com/windows/ie/download/ie55.htm.

- **Mozilla.** In essence, Mozilla is Netscape 6. Mozilla is an open-source Web browser that was designed with portability, performance, and standards in mind—with the cooperation and support of Netscape. Go to www.mozilla.org.

- **Netscape 6.** This current release is simply called Netscape 6 (as opposed to the previous versions, which were called Communicator). This new version supports XML, CSS1, and some XLink. You can download it from www.netscape.com/download/previewrelease.html.

- **Opera.** The latest version of Opera (4.02) has support for CSS1 and 2 and more. You can download it from www.opera.com.

Graphics

In this day and age, you can't really have a Web page without having plenty of images. You might be one of the lucky developers who sits in a meeting with a graphics artist, tells him or her what you want the image to look like, and then you wash your hands of it. However, if you're the one who has to create the images, you should grab a copy of one or more of the following programs.

Adobe Photoshop

Photoshop is a graphics staple. It's one of the most used graphics programs around and has more features than we could ever dream of listing; hence, its hefty price of $609. Photoshop is great for creating graphics intended for the Web, but that's not its only use. Find out more at `http://www.adobe.com/products/photoshop/main.html`.

GIFWorks

GIFWorks is a free, online image editor. It enables you to crop, animate, and manipulate the image of your choice. You can find it at `www.gifworks.com`.

JASC's Paint Shop Pro

Paint Shop Pro is a lighter-weight software program than Photoshop, but don't be fooled by its size. The lack of bells and whistles makes its interface easy to navigate and that is always a plus. This commercial product is also relatively inexpensive. You can download it for $99 or get the CD for $109; there's also an evaluation version available. You can find out more about Paint Shop Pro at `www.jasc.com`.

Macromedia Fireworks

Fireworks is a graphics program designed specifically for creating Web graphics. If you use Dreamweaver, it would be wise to invest in Fireworks. Dreamweaver and Fireworks work hand-in-hand and could make your life easier. You can download the 30-day trial version from `www.macromedia.com/software/fireworks/trial/` or purchase it for $199 from `www.macromedia.com/software/fireworks/download/`.

Multimedia

Multimedia is also something you may want to consider adding to your Web site. We suggest the following products for your multimedia development needs.

Macromedia's Director

You can create movies for the Web, CD-ROM, or DVD-ROM using Director, another Macromedia product. The easy-to-use interface enables you to combine graphics, sound, animation, text, and video to create streaming content. You can download a 30-day trial version, or purchase it for $999, from `www.macromedia.com/software/director/download/`.

Macromedia's Flash

Flash is taking over the Web. And this is yet another contribution from the Web-development software masters, Macromedia. The easy-to-use interface makes creating Flash movies easy as pie. One word of warning, however: Most viewers have to download a Flash player to view a Flash creation. If your target audience is the general public, you should take this accessibility issue into consideration. You can download a 30-day trial version, or buy Flash for $299, from `www.macromedia.com/software/flash/`.

Books

As always, books are a valuable resource. In addition to this one, we suggest you check out the following books:

- Kay, Michael. *XSLT Programmer's Reference.* Wrox Press, 2000. ISBN: 1861003129.
- Meyer, Eric A. *Cascading Style Sheets: The Definitive Guide.* O'Rielly & Associates, 2000. ISBN: 1565926226.
- Nielson, Jakob. *Designing Web Usability: The Practice of Simplicity.* New Riders, 1999. ISBN: 156205810X.
- Tittel, Ed, Chelsea Valentine, and Natanya Pitts. *XHTML For Dummies.* IDG Books Worldwide, 2000. ISBN: 0764507516.

Magazines

There are also some new magazines on the market that will help you keep up to date with the various Web technologies. Keep in mind that these magazines are all young and have seen only a few circulations, but they do have promise.

- **XML Developer.** `www.ashpoint.com.au/XML.html`.
- **XML Journal.** `www.sys-con.com/xml/index2.html`.
- **XML Magazine.** `www.xmlmag.com`.

E

Glossary

attribute   An addition to an XML element that supplies more information about a given instance of an element.

behavior attribute   An XLink attribute that provides suggestions on how the element should be used by a browser or other application.

class selector   An object that creates multiple instances of a style rule.

CML (Chemical Markup Language) A specialized markup language used to represent chemistry-related data, formulae, and the like.

collision   A situation that occurs when a document contains multiple markup languages that have different elements with the same name.

common attribute   An XHTML attribute that can be applied to almost all XHTML elements.

content model   Part of an element's definition in a Document Type Definition (DTD) that includes specific information about how the element can be used with other elements.

CSS (Cascading Style Sheets)   A feature of HTML, developed by W3C, that provides better control over the way a Web page looks on the screen. Cascading refers to more than one style sheet applied to the same Web page.

DocBook DTD   The standard DTD for marking up books and papers, maintained and developed by the DocBook Technical Committee of the Organization for the Advancement of Structured Information Standards (OASIS).

DOCTYPE declaration (document type declaration) An XML declaration used to indicate the DTD (if any) used by an XML document.

document type declaration See DOCTYPE declaration.

DOM (Document Object Model) Provides a standard way for programs and scripts to access and manipulate HTML and XML documents. In other words, a DOM is an application programming interface (API) for XML and HTML documents.

dot syntax A method of traversing the DOM tree by specifying nodes in order of increasing specificity, separated by periods (.), until the desired node is reached.

DSSSL (Document Style Semantics and Specification Language) A standard for a formal language used for document transformation and styles based on SGML.

DTD (Document Type Definition) A document (internal or external) that identifies the elements, attributes, and entities that are part of a markup language vocabulary.

ECMAScript Industry-standard scripting language based on JavaScript and JScript.

e-commerce (electronic commerce) Generic term for running a business on the Web, including sales, funds transfers, and so on.

element The most basic type of markup that describes document content at the most basic level; for example, tags (either a tag pair or an empty element, which only has a start tag with a special closing mark) and their content.

empty element Elements that include information in the document, but don't describe data (in other words, have no content).

entity Virtual storage units that hold everything from multimedia files to information about non-ASCII characters. Entities play a much larger role in XML than they do in HTML.

extensible The capability of being extended beyond predefined core elements.

GedML A specialized markup language for genealogical data.

HTTP (Hypertext Transfer Protocol) The main protocol used on the Internet to connect servers.

Java applet A program written in Sun Microsystems' Java programming language that can be embedded in Web pages.

Java class files Compiled Java files that make up Java applets.

Java Sun Microsystems' object-oriented, cross-platform programming language used extensively on the Web.

JavaScript A scripting language created by Netscape that, although somewhat similar to Java in syntax, is actually very different.

JScript The Microsoft version of Netscape's JavaScript language.

linkbase A collection of inbound and third-party links.

local DTD A DTD that resides on your local computer or network, also called a system DTD.

markup The code that describes the content of a markup language document. Markup consists of start tags, end tags, empty-element tags, entity references, character references, comments, CDATA section delimiters, DOCTYPE declarations, and processing instructions.

MathML (Mathematical Markup Language) A specialized language for expressing mathematical notation in XML.

MIDI (Musical Instrument Digital Interface) A digital audio standard that enables electronic instruments and sound processors to communicate with each other.

MIME (Multipurpose Internet Mail Extensions) A network protocol for the transmission of diverse file types, such as sound, HTML, and graphics.

MP3 (MPEG 1 Audio Layer 3) An audio compression format that can compress audio files anywhere from 7 to 17 times original file size.

namespace A link to a resource that provides more information about a particular XML vocabulary.

node The point at which more than one line meets in a hierarchical document tree structure.

OASIS (Organization for the Advancement of Structured Information Standards) The international consortium for creating cross-platform computer industry specifications based on public standards such as XML.

occurrence operator An operator that is used to specify how many times an element can appear.

OFX (Open Financial Exchange) The specification for the exchange of financial data through the Internet.

OSD (Open Software Description) An XML vocabulary for describing software packages; intended to be used for automatic software distribution.

parameter A value that can be set by the user or Web developer.

PCDATA (parsed character data) Character data that an XML processor searches through for markup; the actual data in a document.

PDA (personal digital assistant) A handheld device that can function as a cellular phone, organizer, and fax, with networking capabilities.

plug-in Software or hardware component that adds functionality to a system or application.

portability In XML, the capability to provide for a single page to result in multiple outputs.

raster graphics Graphic format, such as JPEG, that stores information about every pixel in the graphic.

rollover An image or text in an HTML document that changes when the user puts his or her mouse pointer over it.

semantic attribute An attribute that describes the meaning of linked resources.

streaming media A data transfer method that processes data in a constant flow.

style rule A statement that tells the processor how to format an XML element.

style sheet A kind of template for designating document layout; collections of style rules.

SVG (Scalable Vector Graphics)
A new standard for creating two-dimensional Web graphics and animations written in XML.

tag A formatting command, such as those found in HTML, XHTML, and XML, that designates text layout and appearance.

traversal The process that a program goes through to find specific nodes in a tree structure; also called tree walking.

unparsed entity An entity that enables the inclusion of non-XML content in an XML document.

URI (Uniform Resource Identifier) A generic term for Web addresses and names; for example, the more commonly used URL (Uniform Resource Locator) is a URI.

valid XHTML document A well-formed XML document that also adheres to the rules outlined in the vocabulary.

VBScript (Visual Basic Scripting Edition) A version of the Microsoft Visual Basic language that handles interpretation functions in Web browsers and other applications; used only in Microsoft products.

vector graphics A graphic format that contains information about the curves and lines in a picture, rather than information about the pixels that make up the image.

W3C (World Wide Web Consortium) The international standards organization for the Internet and the Web.

WAV Sound format developed by IBM and Microsoft for storing audio files; unlike MIDI files, WAV files contain actual information about sounds.

well formed An XHTML document that plays by all of XML's rules.

XForms The next generations of Web-based forms; XForms supports better integration with scripting and improves interactivity.

XHTML (Extensible Hypertext Markup Language) A reformulation of HTML 4.01 under the rules of XML.

XHTML Basic A stripped-down version of XHTML designed for use with mobile phones, personal digital assistants (PDAs), and other interfaces that can't reasonably support the full range of XHTML elements.

XHTML Frameset The XHTML DTD that includes the HTML 4.01 elements and is designed to divide a display into one or more frames.

XHTML Modularization A mechanism for extending the functionality of XHTML without building entirely new XML vocabularies.

XHTML Strict The XHTML DTD that defines a markup language in the true sense of the word and does not include any of the elements or attributes in HTML 4.01 that are designed to guide the display of a page in a Web browser.

XHTML Transitional The XHTML DTD that includes all the elements found in HTML 4.01 and is designed to enable developers to take advantage of XML technologies, such as advanced linking and style sheets, while remaining backward compatible with older browsers.

XLink (XML Linking Language) A markup language that implements advanced linking technologies and the best features of several other hypertext systems and standards (especially HyTime, an SGML hyperlink standard).

XML application (XML vocabulary) A set of XML elements designed to describe a particular kind of information.

XML parser The program that reads an XML document and makes the data in it available to programs.

XML Schema A projected replacement for DTDs; schemas are more flexible than DTDs and enable easier document validation based on namespaces.

XSL (Extensible Stylesheet Language) A language for creating style sheets that is used in HTML and XML to separate form from content; sometimes used to refer to XSLT and XSL-FO, where FO stands for formatting objects.

XSLT (Extensible Stylesheet Language Transformations) A language for use in XSL style sheets that converts one XML document to another.

F

Contents on the CD-ROM

THIS APPENDIX DESCRIBES WHAT IS ON THE CD-ROM THAT accompanies this book. Not only is there a large sample of cutting-edge software, but there's also a collection of Web documents to help you navigate the CD.

What You Will Find

The CD-ROM is full of wonderful goodies to get you started working with XHTML: from software to sample XHTML documents. With the info on this CD, you'll be creating your own Web pages with XHTML in no time. A quick peek at what is on the CD follows:

- A Web-friendly front door to the CD's contents
- Sample XHTML documents that you can save to your hard drive and edit
- A copy of the three XHTML DTDs for the looking
- Software for the taking

What You Need to Get Started

You don't need much to access the material on this CD-ROM. To take advantage of what the CD has to offer, make sure your computer meets the following minimum requirements:

- Microsoft Windows 95 or later or Mac OS 7.5 or later.
- 24MB of RAM will ensure the best performance.
- 10MB, minimum, of hard drive space to install the software.
- CD-ROM drive to read the CD.
- A recent-generation Web browser installed on your system. We included both Windows and Mac versions of the two mainstream browsers on the CD.

How to Get Started

To access the CD-ROM contents, follow these steps:

1. Launch your Web browser.
2. Using the Open File command in your browser's File menu, open the INDEX.html file from the CD-ROM.

This file is your front door to the CD-ROM and connects you to all other files. Because the information is stored on a CD-ROM, you will not be able to directly alter any of the example documents. However, if you want to edit any of the files on the CD-ROM, you can save them to your hard drive or floppy disk and then open them in your text editor of choice. Be sure to check out all the great text editors included on the CD!

The easiest way to edit the contents is to copy all the contents of the CD-ROM to your hard drive, which transfers all the Web documents from the CD-ROM to your computer. We recommend saving the contents to your hard drive before you get started.

CD Contents

After you open the INDEX.html file (remember it is a Web-friendly front end, which means it's an XHTML document), you'll find links to individual chapters. However, if you go behind the scenes and take a peek at all the folders on the CD, you will find the following:

- **BookExamples/DTDs.** All three XHTML DTDs (Strict, Transitional, and Frameset) are included. Just open the text file to view the DTD markup in all its glory.

- **Book Examples.** Each chapter default page provides a hyperlink to each example document. That means you select the chapter you're interested in and then select the appropriate example. Each example includes the markup listing from the book and shows the final rendering of the example by a Web browser when possible. If the document is rendered by the Web browser, be sure to select View, Source to view the markup. We've also included text files of all example so that you can view the markup for all examples without opening the file in your Web browser.

- **Graphics.** This folder stores the graphics used to create the lovely default page for the XHTML CD Index. There's no need for you to visit this directory, unless you want to play around with some of our graphics.

- **Web resources.** This folder contains a list of all the URLs from the book in the order in which they appear in the book. So, if you come across a URL in the book that's really long and you don't want to type it in your browser, open the Web Resources folder, find the chapter and the URL, and click the URL to open the resource.

- **3rdparty.** This folder contains all the software included on the CD-ROM. In the following section, we list each tool that you find in this folder.

Software Included

As part of the book, we decided to include some of our favorite—and recommended—software. We regret that we are unable to provide you with free versions of commercial software; however, we do provide evaluation copies that, on average, are good for at least 30 days. Table F.1 lists each piece of included software.

Table F.1 **Included Software**

Tool Name	Developer	Type
Aelfred v1.1	Open Text Corporation	XML Editor
Amaya	W3C	XML-aware Web browser/editor
ColdFusion Express	Allaire Corporation	Web application development environment
ColdFusion Studio	Allaire Corporation	Web application development environment
Dreamweaver 3.0	Macromedia, Inc.	WYSIWYG HTML editor
Expat	James Clark	XML parser
Fireworks 3	Macromedia, Inc.	Web graphics editor
Fusion 5.0	NetObjects	WYSIWYG HTML editor

continues

Table F.1 **Continued**

Tool Name	Developer	Type
GoLive	Adobe	WYSIWYG HTML editor
Homesite 4.5.1	Allaire Corporation	WYSIWYN HTML editor
HotDog Professional v6	Sausage Software	WYSIWYG HTML editor
HTML Tidy	W3C	HTML to XHTML utility
Internet Explorer 5.0	Microsoft Corporation	Web browser
Netscape Communicator 4.7	Netscape Communications	Web browser
XMetal v2.0	SoftQuad	XML editor
XML Authority	Extensibility	XML schema and DTD editor
XML Instance	Extensibility	XML editor
XML Pro v2.01	Vervet Logic	XML editor
XML Spy	Altova	XML editor
XML Style Wizard	Infoteria	XML style sheet editor
XMLwriter	Wattle Software	XML editor
XSL Lint	Norman Walsh	XSL validator
XT	James Clark	XML parser

You might notice that most of the editors we have included on the CD are listed as HTML editors, and not XHTML editors. That is because most editors don't support XHTML authoring, yet. The expectation is that most authoring software will include XHTML support in their next generations, but until then, you have to remember the rules to create well-formed and valid XHTML. If you need a refresher, please refer back to Chapter 2, "All About Markup."

For specific information on many of the listed editors, please see Appendix D, "A Compendium of HTML, XML, and XHTML Resources." For in-depth information on Mozquito, Dreamweaver, XMetaL, and Clip!, see Chapter 5, "Working with Web Development Tools."

Index

Symbols

& (ampersand) character, 22, 264

* (asterisk) character, 269

\ (backslash) character, 248

: (colon) character, 145-146

, (comma) character, 146

< (left angle bracket) character, 264

. (period) character, 146

+ (plus sign) character, 269

? (question mark) character, 269

; (semicolon) character, 22, 146

/ (slash) character, 25

| (vertical bar) character, 269

&# combination, 23

@import directive, 159

<!ATTLIST> declaration, 270-272

#FIXED, 272

#IMPLIED, 272

#REQUIRED, 272

A

a element, 31
   attributes, 32-33
   context, 33
   example, 33

abbr attribute, 92, 97

abbr element, 33
   attributes, 34
   context, 34
   example, 34

absolute location paths (XPath), 248

accept attribute, 54, 64
   context, 55
   example, 55

accept-charset attribute, 54

accesskey attribute, 32, 36, 42, 53, 64, 68-69, 94

ACM SIGWEB (Association for Computing Machinery Special Interest Group on Hypertext, Hypermedia, and Web), 231

acronym element, 34
   attributes, 34
   context, 34
   example, 35

action attribute, 54

address element, 35
   attributes, 35
   context, 35
   example, 35

Adobe Photoshop, 369

align attribute, 45-47, 91-100

Allaire's HomeSite HTML editor, 367

alt attribute, 36, 62-65

Amaya, 109, 143

ampersand (&) character, 22, 264

anchor elements, 31

anchors (HTML), 232

animated GIFs, 221-222

animation, 221
   animated GIFs, 221-222
   Flash, 222
   Macromedia Shockwave, 222
   SMIL, 222
   SVG, 223-224

ANY content model (DTD), 270

applet element, 35, 210-211

applets, 209-210

applications, XML, 3, 278-281

Arachnophilia text editor, 367

arc-type elements (XLink), 241-242

archive attribute, 75

arcs, Web traversal, 234-235

area element, 35

    attributes, 36-37

    context, 37

    example, 37

asterisk (*) character, 269

Atkinson, Bill, 231

<!ATTLIST> declaration, 270-272

attributes, 21-22

    abbr, 92, 97

    accept, 54, 64

        context, 55

        example, 55

    accept-charset, 54

    accesskey, 32, 36, 42, 53, 64, 68-69, 94

    action, 54

    align, 45-47, 91-100

    alphabetic reference, 323-344

    alt, 36, 62, 65

    archive, 75

    axis, 92, 97

    behavior (XLink), 238

    border, 89

    cellpadding, 89

    cellspacing, 89

    char, 45, 47, 91-100

    charoff, 47, 91-100

    charset, 32, 70, 83

    checked, 65

    cite, 40, 49, 67, 81

    class, 30

    classid, 75

    codebase, 75

    codetype, 75

    cols, 57, 94

    colspan, 93, 97

    common, 29-30

    content, 73

    coords, 32, 36

    data, 75

    datetime, 49, 67

    declarations (DTD), 270-272

    declare, 76

    defer, 83

    dir, 30, 39

    disabled, 42, 65, 77-78, 84, 94

    encoding, 263

enctype, 54

ENTITIES type, 271

ENTITY type, 271

for, 68

frame, 89

frameborder, 56, 61

h1-h6, 57

headers, 93, 97

height, 61, 63, 76

href, 32, 36, 38, 70

hreflang, 32, 71

http-equiv, 73

id, 29, 271

    as fragment identifier, 232

IDREF, 271

label, 77-78

lang, 30

length, 45

longdesc, 55, 61-62

marginheight, 56, 61

marginwidth, 56, 61

maxlength, 65

media, 71, 87

method, 54

multiple, 84

name, 32, 42, 54-55, 61-64, 72-80,

    84, 94

NMTOKEN type, 271

NMTOKENS type, 271

nohref, 36

noresize, 55, 61

NOTATION type, 271

profile, 58

readonly, 65, 94

rel, 32, 71

rev, 32, 71

rows, 56, 94

rowspan, 93, 97

rules, 89

scheme, 73

scope, 93, 97

scrolling, 55, 61

selected, 78

shape, 32, 36, 71

size, 64, 84

span, 45, 47

src, 55, 61-65, 83

standalone, 263

standby, 76

style, 30
summary, 90
tabindex, 33, 36, 42, 65, 76, 84, 94
target, 32, 37-38, 54, 71
title, 30
tokenized, 271
type, 33, 42, 63-64, 71, 76-87, 236-237
usemap, 65, 76
valign, 45-47, 91-100
value, 42, 64, 78, 80
valuetype, 80
version, 263
width, 45-47, 61-63, 76, 90
XLink, 236-237
xlink:actuate, 239
xlink:arcrole, 238
xlink:href, 237
xlink:role, 238
xlink:show, 238-239
xlink:title, 238
xmlns, 59, 276

audio, 224
bit rates, 225
MIDI, 224-225
MP3, 225-226
sample rates, 225
WAV, 225

authoring tools, 367
Allaire's HomeSite, 367
Arachnophilia, 367
HotDog Professional, 368
HoTMetal Pro, 368
HTML-Kit, 367
Macromedia Dreamweaver, 367
Mozquito, 368

axes (XPath), 248

axis attribute, 92, 97

azimuth property, 345

B

b element, 37
attributes, 37
context, 37
example, 38

background properties (CSS), 151-153

background property, 346

background-attachment property, 346

background-color property, 346

background-image property, 346

background-position property, 346

background-repeat property, 346

backslash (\) character, 25, 248

bare names (XPointer), 244

base element, 38
attributes, 38
context, 38
example, 38

basefont element, 38

basic shapes (SVG), 218

bdo element, 39
attributes, 39
context, 39
example, 39

behavior attributes (XLink), 238
xlink:actuate, 239
xlink:show, 238-239

Berners-Lee, Tim, 231

big element, 39
attributes, 39
context, 39
example, 40

bit rates (audio files), 225

blockquote element, 40
attributes, 40
context, 40
example, 40

BMP (Windows bit-mapped graphics format), 214

body element, 40
attributes, 40
example, 41

book resources, 370

border attribute, 89

border properties (CSS), 156-158

border property, 346

border-bottom property, 347

border-bottom-color property, 347

border-bottom-style property, 348

border-bottom-width property, 348

border-collapse property, 347

border-color property, 347

border-left property, 347

border-left-color property, 347

border-left-style property, 348

border-left-width property, 348

border-right property, 347

border-right-color property, 347

border-right-style property, 348

border-right-width property, 348

border-spacing property, 347

border-style property, 347

border-top property, 347

border-top-color property, 347

border-top-style property, 348

border-top-width property, 348

border-width property, 348

bottom property, 348

box properties (CSS), 156-158

br element, 41
    attributes, 41
    context, 41
    example, 41

browsers, 368
    backward compatibility, 9
    CSS, support for, 142-143
    media types, 194-195
    opening documents, 107-108
        workarounds for older browsers, 109
    XML compatible, 109-110
        Amaya, 109
        Internet Explorer, 110
        Mozilla, 110

Bush, Vannevar, 230

button element, 42
    attributes, 42
    example, 42

C

Caillau, Robert, 231

Candidate Recommendations (W3C Working Group), 292

caption element, 43
    attributes, 43
    context, 43
    example, 43

caption-side property, 348

Cascading Style Sheets (CSS), 135-142
    adding to documents, 158-160
        XML documents, 160
    browser support, 142-143
    CSS1 versus CSS2, 142
    CSS2, properties, 145
    editors, 143
    fundamentals, 143
    linking to external style sheets, 159
    properties, 345
        azimuth, 345
        background, 346
        background-attachment, 346
        background-color, 346
        background-image, 346
        background-position, 346
        background-repeat, 346
        backgrounds, 151-153
        border, 346
        border-bottom, 347
        border-bottom-color, 347
        border-bottom-style, 348
        border-bottom-width, 348
        border-collapse, 347
        border-color, 347
        border-left, 347
        border-left-color, 347
        border-left-style, 348
        border-left-width, 348
        border-right, 347
        border-right-color, 347
        border-right-style, 348
        border-right-width, 348
        border-spacing, 347
        border-style, 347
        border-top, 347
        border-top-color, 347
        border-top-style, 348
        border-top-width, 348
        border-width, 348
        borders, 156-158
        bottom, 348
        box, 156-158
        caption-side, 348
        clear, 348
        clip, 348
        color, 349
        colors, 151-153
        content, 349

counter-increment, 349
counter-reset, 349
cue, 349
cue-after, 349
cue-before, 349
cursor, 350
direction, 350
display, 350
elevation, 350
empty-cells, 350
float, 350
font, 153-155, 351
font-family, 351
font-size, 351
font-size-adjust, 351
font-stretch, 351
font-style, 351
font-variant, 352
font-weight, 352
height, 352
left, 352
letter-spacing, 352
line-height, 352
list-style, 353
list-style-image, 353
list-style-position, 353
list-style-type, 353
margin, 353
margin-bottom, 353
margin-left, 353
margin-right, 353
margin-top, 353
marker-offset, 354
marks, 354
max-height, 354
max-width, 354
min-height, 354
min-width, 354
orphans, 354
outline, 355
outline-color, 355
outline-style, 355
outline-width, 355
overflow, 355
padding, 355
padding-bottom, 355
padding-left, 355
padding-right, 355
padding-top, 355
page, 356
page-break-after, 356

page-break-before, 356
page-break-inside, 356
pause, 356
pause-after, 356
pause-before, 356
pitch, 357
pitch-range, 357
play-during, 357
position, 357
quotes, 357
richness, 357
right, 357
size, 358
speak, 358
speak-header, 358
speak-numeral, 358
speak-punctuation, 358
speech-rate, 358
stress, 358
table-layout, 359
text, 155-156
text-align, 359
text-decoration, 359
text-indent, 359
text-shadow, 359
text-transform, 359
top, 359
unicode-bidi, 360
vertical-align, 360
visibility, 360
voice-family, 360
volume, 360
white-space, 360
widows, 361
width, 361
word-spacing, 361
z-index, 361
style rules, 143-146
    cascading priority, 150
    class selectors, 146-148
    grouping, 148-149
    inheriting styles, 149
    property values, 150-151
Web resources, 160
versus XSL, 166
XSLT-transformed documents,adding
    to, 183

CDATA sections, 201, 265

cellpadding attribute, 89

cellspacing attribute, 89

center element, 43

char attribute, 45-47, 91-100

character data (XML), 261-265
  parsed, 264

character entities, 22

charoff attribute, 47, 91-100

charset attribute, 32, 70, 83

checked attribute, 65

child sequences (XPointer), 244-245

cite attribute, 40, 49, 67, 81

cite element, 43
  attributes, 43
  context, 43
  example, 44

class attribute, 30, 147-148

class files (Java), 210

class selectors, 147-148

classes, 147-148

classid attribute, 75

clear property, 348

client-side scripts, 200-202
  calling with events, 202-206

clip property, 348

code element, 44
  attributes, 44
  context, 44
  example, 44

codebase attribute, 75

codetype attribute, 75

col element, 45
  attributes, 45
  context, 46
  example, 46

colgroup element, 47
  attributes, 47
  context, 48
  example, 48

colon (:) character, 145-146

color properties (CSS), 151-153

color property, 349

cols attribute, 57, 94

colspan attribute, 93, 97

comma (,) character, 146

comp.text.xml newsgroup, 365

compatibility
  opening documents in older
    broswers, 109
  XML-compatible browsers, 109-110
    Amaya, 109
    Internet Explorer, 110
    Mozilla, 110

componentization of XHTML, 288-291

containing nodes (XSLT), 164

content attribute, 73

content creators, impact of XHTML
  on, 284-286

content models, 21

content property, 349

context nodes (XPath), 248

converting HTML to XHTML, 110-112
  documents, 131-133
  examples, 112-115
  HTML Tidy, 115
    from command line, 115-117
    in Windows (TidyGUI), 118
    on the Web, 118

Coordination Groups (W3C), 292

coords attribute, 32, 36

counter-increment property, 349

counter-reset property, 349

CSS (Cascading Style Sheets)
  adding to documents, 158-160
    XML documents, 160
  browser support, 142-143
  CSS1 versus CSS2, 142
  CSS2, properties, 145
  editors, 143
  fundamentals, 143
  linking to external style sheets, 159
  properties, 345
    azimuth, 345
    background, 346
    background-attachment, 346
    background-color, 346
    background-image, 346
    background-position, 346
    background-repeat, 346
    backgrounds, 151-153

border, 346
border-bottom, 347
border-bottom-color, 347
border-bottom-style, 348
border-bottom-width, 348
border-collapse, 347
border-color, 347
border-left, 347
border-left-color, 347
border-left-style, 348
border-left-width, 348
border-right, 347
border-right-color, 347
border-right-style, 348
border-right-width, 348
border-spacing, 347
border-style, 347
border-top, 347
border-top-color, 347
border-top-style, 348
border-top-width, 348
border-width, 348
borders, 156-158
bottom, 348
box, 156-158
caption-side, 348
clear, 348
clip, 348
color, 349
colors, 151-153
content, 349
counter-increment, 349
counter-reset, 349
cue, 349
cue-after, 349
cue-before, 349
cursor, 350
direction, 350
display, 350
elevation, 350
empty-cells, 350
float, 350
font, 153-155, 351
font-family, 351
font-size, 351
font-size-adjust, 351
font-stretch, 351
font-style, 351
font-variant, 352
font-weight, 352
height, 352

left, 352
letter-spacing, 352
line-height, 352
list-style, 353
list-style-image, 353
list-style-position, 353
list-style-type, 353
margin, 353
margin-bottom, 353
margin-left, 353
margin-right, 353
margin-top, 353
marker-offset, 354
marks, 354
max-height, 354
max-width, 354
min-height, 354
min-width, 354
orphans, 354
outline, 355
outline-color, 355
outline-style, 355
outline-width, 355
overflow, 355
padding, 355
padding-bottom, 355
padding-left, 355
padding-right, 355
padding-top, 355
page, 356
page-break-after, 356
page-break-before, 356
page-break-inside, 356
pause, 356
pause-after, 356
pause-before, 356
pitch, 357
pitch-range, 357
play-during, 357
position, 357
quotes, 357
richness, 357
right, 357
size, 358
speak, 358
speak-header, 358
speak-numeral, 358
speak-punctuation, 358
speech-rate, 358
stress, 358
table-layout, 359

text, 155-156
text-align, 359
text-decoration, 359
text-indent, 359
text-shadow, 359
text-transform, 359
top, 359
unicode-bidi, 360
vertical-align, 360
visibility, 360
voice-family, 360
volume, 360
white-space, 360
widows, 361
width, 361
word-spacing, 361
z-index, 361
style rules, 143-146
cascading priority, 150
class selectors, 146-148
grouping, 148-149
inheriting styles, 149
property values, 150-151
Web resources, 160
versus XSL, 166
XSLT-transformed documents,adding
to, 183

cue property, 349

cue-after property, 349

cue-before property, 349

cursor property, 350

D

data attribute, 75

datetime attribute, 49, 67

dd element, 48
attributes, 48
context, 48
example, 48

declarations (style rules), 145

declare attribute, 76

defer attribute, 83

del element, 49
attributes, 49
context, 49
example, 49

dfn element, 50
attributes, 50
context, 50
example, 50

DHTML (Dynamic HTML), 200
client-side scripts, 200-202
calling with events, 202-206
Web resources, 212

dir attribute, 30, 39

dir element, 50

direction property, 350

Director (Macromedia), 222

disabled attribute, 42, 65, 77-78, 84, 94

display property, 350

div element, 50
attributes, 50
context, 51
example, 51

dl element, 51
attributes, 51
context, 51
example, 51

DocBook DTD, 260

**DOCTYPE declarations, 19, 110-113,
263-264**
PUBLIC identifier, 264
SYSTEM identifier, 264

**Document Object Model (DOM),
196-197**
Dynamic HTML (DHTML), 200
client-side scripts, 200-206
events, 199
methods, 199
modules, 198
objects, 198
properties, 199
tree-walking, 196
Web resources, 212

**document type declarations, 110,
263-264**
PUBLIC identifer, 264
SYSTEM identifier, 264

**Document Type Definitions (DTDs),
19-20, 265-268**
attribute declarations, 270-272
contents models, 21

designing and constructing, 268-269
DocBook, 260
DOCTYPE declarations, 19
element declarations, 269-270
entities, 273
External entities, 275
Notation Declarations, 275
official XHTML recommendation,
   312-313
Parameter Entities, 273-275
standardized, 260-261
unparsed entities, 275
versus XML Schema, 275-276

documents
adding style sheets, 158-160
   XML documents, 160
associating style sheets, 182-183
cascading style priority, 150
conformance, official XHTML recommendation, 304-305
converting from HTML, 121-122,
   131-133
creating, 121-122
   Dreamweaver, 127-130
   Mozquito, 122, 124-127
formatting, 135-143
fragments (SVG), 216
frameset, 112
opening in browsers, 107-108
   work-arounds for older browsers, 109
SVG, 215-216
   JPEG graphics, adding, 220-221
valid, 17-18
well-formed, 17-18
   official XHTML recommendation, 308
XLink, 253-254
XPointer, 253-254
XSL, adding style with, 167
XSLT, adding CSS, 183

**DOM (Document Object Model),
   196-197**
Dynamic HTML (DHTML), 200
   client-side scripts, 200-206
events, 199
methods, 199
modules, 198
objects, 198
properties, 199
tree-walking, 196
Web resources, 212

dot syntax (JavaScript), 205
Dreamweaver, 127-130, 143, 367
drawbacks, 130
installing, 127-128
dt element, 52
context, 52
example, 52
**DTDs (Document Type Definitions),
   19-20, 265-268**
attribute declarations, 270-272
contents models, 21
designing and constructing, 268-269
DocBook, 260
DOCTYPE declarations, 19
element declarations, 269-270
entities, 273
external entities, 275
notation Declarations, 275
official XHTML recommendation,
   312-313
parameter entities, 273-275
standardized, 260-261
unparsed entities, 275
versus XML Schema, 275-276
Dynamic HTML (DHTML), 200
client-side scripts, 200-202
   calling with events, 202-206
Web resources, 212

E

ECMAScript, 201
editors, 134
CSS, 143
Dreamweaver, 127-130, 143, 367
   drawbacks, 130
   installing, 127-128
HTML, Allaire's HomeSite, 367
HTML-Kit, 130, 367
   drawbacks, 133
   HTML documents, converting to
      XHTML, 131-133
   installing, 130-131
image, GIFWorks, 369
Mozquito, 122
   documents, creating, 124-127
   drawbacks, 127
   installing, 123-124

menu bar, 126
toolbar icons, 126
text
   Arachnophilia, 367
   HotDog Professional, 368
   HoTMetal Pro, 368
Web resources, 134

elements, 20-21
a, 31
   attributes, 32-33
   context, 33
   example, 33
abbr, 33
   attributes, 34
   context, 34
   example, 34
acronym, 34
   attributes, 34
   context, 34
   example, 35
address, 35
   attributes, 35
   context, 35
   example, 35
alphabetic reference, 31, 320-323
applet, 35, 210-211
arc-type (XLink), 241-242
area, 35
   attributes, 36-37
   context, 37
   example, 37
b, 37
   attributes, 37
   context, 37
   example, 38
base, 38
   attributes, 38
   context, 38
   example, 38
basefont, 38
bdo, 39
   attributes, 39
   context, 39
   example, 39
big, 39
   attributes, 39
   context, 39
   example, 40
blockquote, 40
   attributes, 40
   context, 40
   example, 40

body, 40
   attributes, 40
   example, 41
br, 41
   attributes, 41
   context, 41
   example, 41
button, 42
   attributes, 42
   example, 42
caption, 43
   attributes, 43
   context, 43
   example, 43
center, 43
cite, 43
   attributes, 43
   context, 43
   example, 44
code, 44
   attributes, 44
   context, 44
   example, 44
col, 45
   attributes, 45
   context, 46
   example, 46
colgroup, 47
   attributes, 47
   context, 48
   example, 48
common attributes, 29-30
dd, 48
   attributes, 48
   context, 48
   example, 48
declarations (DTD), 269-270
del, 49
   attributes, 49
   context, 49
   example, 49
dfn, 50
   attributes, 50
   context, 50
   example, 50
dir, 50
div, 50
   attributes, 50
   context, 51
   example, 51

dl, 51
   attributes, 51
   context, 51
   example, 51
dt, 52
   context, 52
   example, 52
em, 52
   attributes, 52
   context, 52
   example, 52
empty, 20, 270
fieldset, 53
   attributes, 53
   context, 53
   example, 53
font, 53
   attributes, 54
formatting multiple, 148-149
frame, 55
   attributes, 55-56
   context, 56
   example, 56
frameset, 56
   attributes, 56-57
   context, 57
   example, 57
h1–h6
   attributes, 57
   context, 57
   example, 58
head, 58
   attributes, 58
   context, 58
   example, 58
hr, 58
   attributes, 59
   context, 59
   example, 59
html, 59, 111
   attributes, 59-60
   context, 60
   example, 60
i, 60
   attributes, 60
   context, 60
   example, 60
iframe, 61
   attributes, 61
   context, 61
   example, 62

image, 220
img, 62, 214
   attributes, 62-63
   context, 63
   example, 63
inheriting styles, 149
input, 63, 66
   attributes, 63-65
   context, 65
   example, 66
ins, 66
   attributes, 67
   context, 67
   example, 67
isindex, 67
kbd, 67
   attributes, 67
   context, 68
   example, 68
label, 68
   attributes, 68
   context, 68
   example, 69
legend, 69
   attributes, 69
   context, 69
   example, 69
li, 70
   attributes, 70
   context, 70
   example, 70
link, 70
   attributes, 70-71
   context, 71
   example, 71
locator-type (XLink), 240-241
map, 72
   attributes, 72
   context, 72
   example, 72
menu, 72
meta, 72
   attributes, 73
   context, 73
   example, 73
nodes (XSLT), 164
noframes, 73
   attributes, 74
   context, 74
   example, 74

noscript, 74, 211-212
  attributes, 74
  context, 75
  example, 75
object, 75, 206-207
  attributes, 75-76, 207-208
  context, 76
  example, 77
occurrence operators, 269
ol, 77
  attributes, 77
  context, 77
  example, 77
optgroup, 77
  attributes, 77
  context, 78
  example, 78
option, 78
  attributes, 78
  context, 78
  example, 79
p, 79, 264
  attributes, 79
  context, 79
  example, 79
param, 80
  attributes, 80
  context, 80
  example, 80
pre, 81
  attributes, 81
  context, 81
  example, 81
prohibitions, official XHTML
  recommendation, 313
q, 81
  attributes, 81
  context, 81
  example, 82
resource-type (XLink), 240-241
root, 111
s, 82
samp, 82
  attributes, 82
  context, 82
  example, 82
script, 83, 201-202
  attributes, 83
  context, 83
  example, 83

select, 84
  attributes, 84
  context, 84
  example, 85
small, 85
  attributes, 85
  context, 85
  example, 85
span, 85
  attributes, 85
  context, 86
  example, 86
strike, 86
strong, 86
  attributes, 86
  context, 86
  example, 87
style, 87
  attributes, 87
  context, 87
  example, 87
sub, 87
  attributes, 87
  context, 88
  example, 88
sup, 88
  attributes, 88
  context, 88
  example, 88
svg, 216
SVG animation, 223
table, 89
  attributes, 89-90
  context, 90
  example, 90
tbody, 91
  attributes, 91-92
  context, 92
td, 92
  attributes, 92-93
  context, 93
text, 220
textarea, 94
  attributes, 94
  context, 94
  example, 95
tfoot, 95
  attributes, 95-96
  context, 96

th, 96
  attributes, 96-98
  context, 98
thread, 98
  attributes, 98-99
  context, 99
title, 99
  attributes, 99
  context, 99
  example, 100
title-type (XLink), 242
tr, 100
  attributes, 100-101
  context, 101
tt, 101
  attributes, 101
  context, 101
  example, 101
u, 102
ul, 102
  attributes, 102
  context, 102
  example, 102
var, 102
  attributes, 102
  context, 103
  example, 103
Web forms, 187-189
XSLT, predefined, 168-177
  instructions, 179
  literal result elements, 179-180
  top-level elements, 178
  xsl:stylesheet element, 177
  xsl:template element, 178-179
  xsl:transform element, 177
elevation property, 350
em element, 52
  attributes, 52
  context, 52
  example, 52
EMPTY content model (DTD), 270
empty elements, 270
empty-cells property, 350
encoding attribute, 263
encoding information, 24
enctype attribute, 54
Engelbart, Douglas, 231

entities, 22-23, 273
  character, 22
  external, 275
  numeric, 22
  parameter, 273-275
  unparsed, 275
  XML built-in references, 273
ENTITIES type attribute, 271
ENTITY type attribute, 271
event handlers, 30
events
  DOM, 199
  JavaScript, 202-206
  onblur, 203-204
  onfocus, 203-204
extended links (XLink), 240
  arc-type elements, 241-242
  locator-type elements, 240-241
  resource-type elements, 240-241
  title-type elements, 242
extensibility, 108
Extensible Markup Language. *See* **XML**
Extensible Stylesheet Language (XSL), 162
  versus CSS, 166
  documents,
    adding style to, 167
    associating style sheets with, 182-183
    transformed, adding CSS, 183
  formatting with, 167
  tools, 183
    Microsoft MSXML, 184
    Saxon, 183-184
    XT, 184
  Web resources, 184
  XSL Working Group, 165-167
    deliverables, 165
  XSL-FO, 164-167
  XSLT, 162-168
    example, 180-181
    instructions, 179
    literal result elements, 179-180
    namespaces, 168
    predefined elements, 168-177
    tools, 183
    top-level elements, 178
    trees and nodes, 163-164
    Web resources, 184

xsl:apply-templates element, 182
xsl:output element, 181
xsl:stylesheet element, 177-181
xsl:template element, 178-182
xsl:transform elements, 177
xsl:value-of element, 182

External Entities, 275

F

fieldset element, 53
    attributes, 53
    context, 53
    example, 53

#FIXED, 272

Flash (Macromedia), 222

float property, 350

font element, 53
    attributes, 54

font properties (CSS), 153-155
    versus font elements, 153

font property, 351

font-family property, 351

font-size property, 351

font-size-adjust property, 351

font-stretch property, 351

font-style property, 351

font-variant property, 352

font-weight property, 352

for attribute, 68

formatting documents, 135-143

formatting objects, 164
    documents, adding style to, 167

forms, 186-191
    elements and attributes, 187-189
    example XForm, 191
    history, 185
    limitations, 189
    standards, 190
    Web resources, 191

fragment identifiers, 232
    XLink, 239
    XPointer, 245-246

frame attribute, 89

frame element, 55
    attributes, 55-56
    context, 56
    example, 56

frameborder attribute, 56, 61

frameset documents, 112

frameset element, 56
    attributes, 56-57
    context, 57
    example, 57

G

GIF (Graphics Interchange Format), 214
    animated, 221-222

GIFWorks image editor, 369

graphic designers, impact of XHTML on, 286-287

graphic objects (SVG), 216

graphics, 213-214
    file formats, 214
    JPEG, adding to SVG documents, 220-221
    raster images, 214
    SVG, 214-217
        applying style, 219-220
        documents, 215-216
        JPEG graphics, adding, 220-221
        vector graphics, 218
    tools, 369
        Adobe Photoshop, 369
        GIFWorks, 369
        Macromedia Fireworks, 369
        Paint Shop Pro, 369
    vector, 215-218
    Web resources, 227

Graphics Interchange Format (GIF), 214
    animated, 221-222

grouping, 148-149

H

h1–h6 attribute, 57

h1–h6 element
attributes, 57
context, 57
example, 58

head element, 58
attributes, 58
context, 58
example, 58

headers attribute, 93, 97

height attribute, 61-63, 76

height property, 352

HotDog Professional, 368

HoTMetal Pro text editor, 368

hr element, 58
attributes, 59
context, 59
example, 59

href attribute, 32, 36-38, 70

hreflang attribute, 32, 71

HTML
converting to XHTML, 110-112
documents, 121-122, 131-133
examples, 112-115
HTML Tidy, 115-118
documents, creating with Dreamweaver, 128-130
drawbacks, 260
extensibility, 258
HTML 4.01 Specification, 6
legacy code, 296-297
limitations, 106, 283
links, 231-233
anchors, 232
syntax rules, 108
versus XHTML, 10, 25-27, 105-109
XHTML compatibility guidelines, official XHTML recommendation, 313-316
versus XML, 257, 259

html element, 59, 111
attributes, 59-60
context, 60
example, 60

HTML Roadmap, 6

HTML Tidy, 115, 130
from command line, 115-117
on the Web, 118
in Windows (TidyGUI), 118

HTML-Kit, 130
drawbacks, 133
HTML documents, converting to XHTML, 131-133
installing, 130-131
text editor, 367

HTTP headers, 194

http-equiv attribute, 73

hyperlinks
history, 229-230
ACM SIGWEB, 231
Atkinson, Bill, 231
Berners-Lee, Tim, 231
Bush, Vannevar, 230
Caillau, Robert, 231
Engelbart, Douglas, 231
Nelson, Ted, 231
HTML, 231-233
anchors, 232
traversal, 234
XLink, 233-236
attributes, 236-237
behavior attributes, 238
extended links, 240-242
fragment identifiers, 239
namespace, 235-236
semantic attributes, 238
simple links, 237
terminology, 234-235
xlink:actuate attribute, 239
xlink:arcrole attribute, 238
xlink:href attribute, 237
xlink:role attribute, 238
xlink:show attribute, 238-239
xlink:title attribute, 238
XPointer, 243
bare names, 244
child sequences, 244-245
escaping, 245-246
expressions, 243-245
schemes, 245
XPath, 246-247

I

i element, 60
    attributes, 60
    context, 60
    example, 60
id attribute, 29, 271
    as fragment identifier, 232
IDREF attribute, 271
iframe element, 61
    attributes, 61
    context, 61
    example, 62
image element, 220
images, 214
    file formats, 214
    JPEG, adding to SVG documents,
      220-221
    raster, 214
    SVG, 214–217
      applying style, 219-220
      documents, 215-216
      JPEG graphics, adding, 220-221
      vector graphics, 218
    vector graphics, 215–218
    Web resources, 227
img element, 62, 214
    attributes, 62–63
    context, 63
    example, 63
#IMPLIED, 272
inheriting styles, 149
inline style declarations, 160
input element, 63, 66
    attributes, 63–65
    context, 65
    example, 66
ins element, 66
    attributes, 67
    context, 67
    example, 67
instructions (XML), 262
Interest Groups (W3C), 292
Internet Explorer, 110
intrinsic events, 30
isindex element, 67

J-K

Java, 200
    applets, 209-210
      applet element, 210-211
    Web resources, 212
JavaScript, 200-201
    dot syntax, 205
    events, 202-206
    noscript element, 211-212
    Web resources, 212
**JPEG (Joint Photographic Experts
Group), 214**
    adding to SVG documents, 220-221
JScript. *See* **JavaScript**

kbd element, 67
    attributes, 67
    context, 68
    example, 68

L

label attribute, 77–78
label element, 68
    attributes, 68
    context, 68
    example, 69
lang attribute, 30
**Last Call Working Drafts (W3C
Working Group), 292**
left angle bracket (<) character, 264
left property, 352
legend element, 69
    attributes, 69
    context, 69
    example, 69
length attribute, 45
length units, 151
letter-spacing property, 352
li element, 70
    attributes, 70
    context, 70
    example, 70

line-height property, 352

link element, 70, 159
attributes, 70-71
context, 71
example, 71

link servers, 254

links
history, 229-230
ACM SIGWEB, 231
Atkinson, Bill, 231
Berners-Lee, Tim, 231
Bush, Vannevar, 230
Caillau, Robert, 231
Engelbart, Douglas, 231
Nelson, Ted, 231
HTML, 231-233
anchors, 232
traversal, 234
XLink, 233-236
attributes, 236-237
behavior attributes, 238
extended links, 240-242
fragment identifiers, 239
namespace, 235-236
semantic attributes, 238
simple links, 237
terminology, 234-235
xlink:actuate attribute, 239
xlink:arcrole attribute, 238
xlink:href attribute, 237
xlink:role attribute, 238
xlink:show attribute, 238-239
xlink:title attribute, 238
XPointer, 243
bare names, 244
child sequences, 244-245
escaping, 245-246
expressions, 243-245
schemes, 245
XPath, 246-247

list-style property, 353

list-style-image property, 353

list-style-position property, 353

list-style-type property, 353

literal result elements (XSLT), 179-180

local resources, 234

location paths (XPath), 248
absolute, 248
axes, 248
relative, 248

location steps (XPath), 248
abbreviated, 252
node tests, 249
predicates, 249

locator-type elements (XLink), 240-241

longdesc attribute, 55, 61-62

M

Macromedia
Director, 222
Dreamweaver, 127-130, 143, 367
Fireworks, 369
Flash, 222, 370
Shockwave, 222

magazine resources, 370

mailing lists, 365
comp.text.xml newsgroup, 365
XHTML-L, 365
XML-DEV, 366
XML-L, 366
XML-list, 366

map element, 72
attributes, 72
context, 72
example, 72

margin property, 353

margin-bottom property, 353

margin-left property, 353

margin-right property, 353

margin-top property, 353

marginheight attribute, 56, 61

marginwidth attribute, 56, 61

marker-offset property, 354

marks property, 354

markup, 13
collisions, 276
components, 18-19
attributes, 21-22
DTDs, 19-20
elements, 20-21

entities, 22-23
namespaces, 23
XML declarations, 24
overview, 18-19
rules, 16
describing content, 14
formatting elements, 15
style sheets, 14-16
XML, 261
writers, impact of XHTML on, 284-286

MathML (Mathematical Markup Language), 279

max-height property, 354

max-width property, 354

maxlength attribute, 65

media attribute, 71, 87

media types, 194-195

menu element, 72

meta element, 72
attributes, 73
context, 73
example, 73

method attribute, 54

methods (DOM), 199

MIDI (Musical Instrument Digital Interface), 224-225

MIME (Multipurpose Internet Mail Extensions) types, 195

min-height property, 354

min-width property, 354

Modularization of XHTML (W3C document), 288
Web site, 11

modules, 288-291
DOM, 198

Mozilla, 110

Mozquito, 122, 143, 368
documents
checking well formedness, 125
creating, 124-127
drawbacks, 127
installing, 123-124
menu bar, 126
toolbar icons, 126

MP3 (MPEG 1 Audio Layer 3) files, 225-226

MSXML (Microsoft), 184

multimedia, 213-214, 221, 224
animated GIFs, 221-222
Flash, 222
MIDI, 224-225
MP3, 225-226
Shockwave, 222
SMIL, 222
SVG, 214-217
animation, 223-224
documents, 215-216
vector graphics, 218
tools, 369
Macromedia Director, 369
Macromedia Flash, 370
video, 226
WAV, 225
bit rates, 225
sample rates, 225
Web resources, 227

multiple attribute, 84

Multipurpose Internet Mail Extensions (MIME) types, 195

Musical Instrument Digital Interface (MIDI), 224-225

N

name attribute, 32, 42, 54-55, 61-64, 72-84, 94

namespaces, 23, 276-278
official XHTML recommendation, 306
XHTML, 111, 113
XLink, 235-236
XML, 111
XSLT, 168

NDATA keyword, 275

Nelson, Ted, 231

NMTOKEN type attribute, 271

NMTOKENS type attribute, 271

node objects, 196

node sets (XPath), functions, 250-252

node tests (XPath), 249

nodes (XSLT), 163-164

noframes element, 73
  attributes, 74
  context, 74
  example, 74

nohref attribute, 36

noresize attribute, 55, 61

noscript element, 74, 211-212
  attributes, 74
  context, 75
  example, 75

notation declarations, 275

NOTATION type attributes, 271

numeric entities, 22

O

object element, 75, 206-207
  attributes, 75-76, 207-208
  context, 76
  example, 77

objects
  DOM, 198
  passing parameters, 209

occurrence operators, 269

ol element, 77
  attributes, 77
  context, 77
  example, 77

onblur event, 203-204

onfocus event, 203-204

optgroup element, 77
  attributes, 77
  context, 78
  example, 78

option element, 78
  attributes, 78
  context, 78
  example, 79

orphans property, 354

outlaw code, 296

outline property, 355

outline-color property, 355

outline-style property, 355

outline-width property, 355

overflow property, 355

P

p element, 79
  attributes, 79
  context, 79
  example, 79

p elements, 264

P3P (Platform for Privacy Preferences Project), 294

padding property, 355

padding-bottom property, 355

padding-left property, 355

padding-right property, 355

padding-top property, 355

page property, 356

page-break-after property, 356

page-break-before property, 356

page-break-inside property, 356

Paint Shop Pro, 369

param element, 80
  attributes, 80
  context, 80
  example, 80

parameter entities, 273-275

parameters, passing to objects, 209

parsed character data (XML), 264

parsers, 197

pause property, 356

pause-after property, 356

pause-before property, 356

PDF (Portable Document Format) files, 194

period (.) character, 146

PIs (processing instructions), 262

pitch property, 357

pitch-range property, 357

Platform for Privacy Preferences Project (P3P), 294

play-during property, 357

plus sign (+) character, 269

PNG (Portable Network Graphics), 214

portability, 109

Portable Document Format (PDF)
  files, 194

Portable Network Graphics (PNG), 214

position property, 357

pre element, 81
    attributes, 81
    context, 81
    example, 81

predicates (XPath), 249

processing instructions (PIs), 262

profile attribute, 58

programmers, impact of XHTML
  on, 287

properties
    CSS, 345
        azimuth, 345
        background, 346
        background-attachment, 346
        background-color, 346
        background-image, 346
        background-position, 346
        background-repeat, 346
        border, 346
        border-bottom, 347
        border-bottom-color, 347
        border-bottom-style, 348
        border-bottom-width, 348
        border-collapse, 347
        border-color, 347
        border-left, 347
        border-left-color, 347
        border-left-style, 348
        border-left-width, 348
        border-right, 347
        border-right-color, 347
        border-right-style, 348
        border-right-width, 348
        border-spacing, 347
        border-style, 347
        border-top, 347
        border-top-color, 347
        border-top-style, 348
        border-top-width, 348
        border-width, 348

bottom, 348
caption-side, 348
clear, 348
clip, 348
color, 349
content, 349
counter-increment, 349
counter-reset, 349
cue, 349
cue-after, 349
cue-before, 349
cursor, 350
direction, 350
display, 350
elevation, 350
empty-cells, 350
float, 350
font, 351
font-family, 351
font-size, 351
font-size-adjust, 351
font-stretch, 351
font-style, 351
font-variant, 352
font-weight, 352
height, 352
left, 352
letter-spacing, 352
line-height, 352
list-style, 353
list-style-image, 353
list-style-position, 353
list-style-type, 353
margin, 353
margin-bottom, 353
margin-left, 353
margin-right, 353
margin-top, 353
marker-offset, 354
marks, 354
max-height, 354
max-width, 354
min-height, 354
min-width, 354
orphans, 354
outline, 355
outline-color, 355
outline-style, 355
outline-width, 355
overflow, 355
padding, 355

padding-bottom, 355
padding-left, 355
padding-right, 355
padding-top, 355
page, 356
page-break-after, 356
page-break-before, 356
page-break-inside, 356
pause, 356
pause-after, 356
pause-before, 356
pitch, 357
pitch-range, 357
play-during, 357
position, 357
quotes, 357
richness, 357
right, 357
size, 358
speak, 358
speak-header, 358
speak-numeral, 358
speak-punctuation, 358
speech-rate, 358
stress, 358
table-layout, 359
text-align, 359
text-decoration, 359
text-shadow, 359
text-transform, 359
top, 359
unicode-bidi, 360
vertical-align, 360
visibility, 360
voice-family, 360
volume, 360
white-space, 360
widows, 361
width, 361
word-spacing, 361
z-index, 361
DOM, 199
style rules, 145
   box, 156-158
   categories, 151
   colors, 151-153
   font, 153-155
   text, 155-156
   values and units, 150-151

style sheets
   backgrounds, 151-153
   borders, 156-158
Proposed Recommendations (W3C Working Group), 292
PUBLIC identifier, 264

Q-R

q element, 81
   attributes, 81
   context, 81
   example, 82

question mark (?) character, 269

quotes property, 357

raster images, 214

readonly attribute, 65, 94

rel attribute, 32, 71

relative location paths (XPath), 248

remote resources, 234

#REQUIRED, 272

resource-type elements (XLink), 240-241

resources, 234
   books, 370
   local, 234
   magazines, 370
   remote, 234
   XLink
      locator-type elements, 240-241
      resource-type elements, 240-241

rev attribute, 32, 71

richness property, 357

right property, 357

rollovers, 197

root elements, 111

rows attribute, 56, 94

rowspan attribute, 93, 97

rules attribute, 89

S

s element, 82

samp element, 82
  attributes, 82
  context, 82
  example, 82

sample rates (audio files), 225

SAX (Simplified API for XML), 196

Saxon, 183

Scalable Vector Graphics (SVG),
  215-217
  animation, 223-224
  applying style, 219-220
  basic shapes, 218
  document fragments, 216
  graphic objects, 216
  JPEG graphics, adding, 221
  text, 220
  vector graphics, 218

schemas, 294-295

scheme attribute, 73

schemes (XPointer), 245

scope attribute, 93, 97

script element, 83, 201-202
  attributes, 83
  context, 83
  example, 83

scripts, client side, 200-202
  calling with events, 202-206

scrolling attribute, 55, 61

search engines, 366

select element, 84
  attributes, 84
  context, 84
  example, 85

selected attribute, 78

selectors, 145

semantic attributes (XLink), 238

semicolon (;) character, 22, 146

SGML (Standard Generalized Markup
  Language), 294-295, 301

shape attribute, 32, 36, 71

Shockwave (Macromedia), 222

simple links (XLink), 237
  fragment identifiers, 239

Simple Object Access Protocol
  (SOAP), 293

Simplified API for XML (SAX), 196

size attribute, 64, 84

size property, 358

slash (/) character, 25, 248

small element, 85
  attributes, 85
  context, 85
  example, 85

SMIL (Synchronized Multimedia
  Integration Language), 222

SOAP (Simple Object Access
  Protocol), 293

span attribute, 45, 47

span element, 85
  attributes, 85
  context, 86
  example, 86

speak property, 358

speak-header property, 358

speak-numeral property, 358

speak-punctuation property, 358

speech-rate property, 358

src attribute, 55, 61-65, 83

standalone attribute, 263

Standard Generalized Markup
  Language (SGML), 294-295, 301

standby attribute, 76

streaming, 226

stress property, 358

strike element, 86

strong element, 86
  attributes, 86
  context, 86
  example, 87

style attribute, 30

style element, 87
  attributes, 87
  context, 87
  example, 87

style rules, 143-146
  cascading priority, 150
  classes, 147-148
  color keywords, 151
  declarations, 145
    property values, 150-151
    punctuation, 146
  grouping, 148-149
  inheriting styles, 149
  length units, 151
  properties, 145
    backgrounds, 151-153
    borders, 156-158
    box, 156-158
    colors, 151-153
    font, 153-155
    text, 155-156
  selectors, 145
    class, 146-148
style sheets. *See* **Cascading Style
  Sheets; Extensible Stylesheet
  Language**
sub element, 87
  attributes, 87
  context, 88
  example, 88
subresources (XPointer), 243
subsets, 5
summary attribute, 90
sup element, 88
  attributes, 88
  context, 88
  example, 88
**SVG (Scalable Vector Graphics),
  215-217**
  animation, 223-224
  applying style, 219-220
  basic shapes, 218
  document fragments, 216
  graphic objects, 216
  JPEG graphics, adding, 221
  text, 220
  vector graphics, 218
svg element, 216
**Synchronized Multimedia Integration
  Language (SMIL), 222**

syntax rules, 110-112
  CSS, 143-146
    class selectors, 146
    style rules, 145-146
  HTML, 108
SYSTEM identifier, 264

T

**tabindex attribute, 33, 36, 42, 65, 76,
  84, 94**
table element, 89
  attributes, 89-90
  context, 90
  example, 90
table-layout property, 359
Tagged Image File Format (TIFF), 214
tags, uppercase, 21
target attribute, 32, 37-38, 54, 71
tbody element, 91
  attributes, 91-92
  context, 92
td element, 92
  attributes, 92-93
  context, 93
text element, 220
text nodes (XSLT), 164
text properties (CSS), 155-156
text-align property, 359
text-decoration property, 359
text-indent property, 359
text-shadow property, 359
text-transform property, 359
text, SVG, 220
textarea element, 94
  attributes, 94
  context, 94
  example, 95
tfoot element, 95
  attributes, 95-96
  context, 96

th element, 96
   attributes, 96-98
   context, 98

thread element, 98
   attributes, 98-99
   context, 99

three-tier computing, 284

TidyGUI, 118

TIFF (Tagged Image File Format), 214

title attribute, 30

title element, 99
   attributes, 99
   context, 99
   example, 100

title-type elements (XLink), 242

tokenized attributes, 271

tools, 367
   authoring, 367
      Allaire's HomeSite, 367
      Arachnophilia, 367
      HotDog Professional, 368
      HoTMetal Pro, 368
      HTML-Kit, 367
      Macromedia Dreamweaver, 367
      Mozquito, 368
   browsers, 368
   graphics, 369
      Adobe Photoshop, 369
      GIFWorks, 369
      Macromedia Fireworks, 369
      Paint Shop Pro, 369
   multimedia, 369
      Macromedia Director, 369
      Macromedia Flash, 370

top property, 359

top-level elements (XSLT), 178-179

tr element, 100
   attributes, 100-101
   context, 101

transformations. *See* XSLT

translating HTML to XHTML, 110-112
   examples, 112-115
   HTML Tidy, 115
      from command line, 115-117
      on the Web, 118
      in Windows (TidyGUI), 118

tree-walking (DOM), 196

trees
   DOM, 196
   of nodes (XPath), 246
   XSLT, 163-164

tt element, 101
   attributes, 101
   context, 101
   example, 101

type attribute, 33, 42, 63-64, 71, 76, 80-87, 236-237

U

u element, 102

ul element, 102
   attributes, 102
   context, 102
   example, 102

unicode-bidi property, 360

unparsed entities, 275

usemap attribute, 65, 76

User Agent Accessibility Guidelines, 293-294

user agents, conformance, (official XHTML recommendation), 306-308

user interface designers, impact of XHTML on, 286-287

UTF-8 encoding, 263

V

valid documents, 17-18

valign attribute, 45, 47, 91-100

value attribute, 42, 64, 78-80

valuetype attribute, 80

var element, 102
   attributes, 102
   context, 103
   example, 103

VBScript, 201

vector graphics, 215, 218

version attribute, 263

vertical bar (|) character, 269

vertical-align property, 360

video, 226

visibility property, 360

voice-family property, 360

volume property, 360

W

W3C
  groups, 291
    Coordination Groups, 292
    Interest Groups, 292
    Working Groups, 292-293
  Modularization of XHTML
    document, 288
  Notes (W3C Working Group), 293
    Platform for Privacy Preferences Project
     (P3P), 294
    Simple Object Access Protocol
     (SOAP), 293
    User Agent Accessibility Guidelines,
     293-294
  official XHTML recommendation,
    299-302
    acknowledgements, 317
    benefits, 302
    compatibility issues, 311
    document conformance, 304-305
    DTDs, 312-313
    element prohibitions, 313
    future of XHTML, 311-312
    HTML compatibility guidelines,
     313-316
    namespaces, 306
    references, 317-318
    terminology, 303-304
    user agent conformance, 306-308
    well-formed documents, 308
    XHTML versus HTML 4, 308-311
    XML, 302
  recommendations, 291
  Web resources, 364

WAV files, 225
  bit rates, 225
  sample rates, 225

Web forms, 186-191
  elements and attributes, 187-189
  example XForm, 191
  history, 185
  limitations, 189
  standards, 190
  Web resources, 191

Web resources
  mailing lists, 365
    comp.text.xml newsgroup, 365
    XHTML-L, 365
    XML-DEV, 366
    XML-L, 366
    XML-list, 366
  search engines, 366
  Web technologies, 364-365
  World Wide Web Consortium, 364

Web sites
  CSS, 160
  CSS Master List, 143
  DocBook, 261
  DOM versus SAX resource guide, 196
  HTML 4.01 Specification, 6
  HTML Roadmap, 6
  HTML to XHTML conversion, 119
  HTML-Kit, 133
  Macromedia Dreamweaver, 130
  Modularization of XHTML, 11
  Mozquito, 123
  SMIL, 222
  SVG implementations, 215
  Webreview's Master Compatibility
    Chart, 145
  XForms, 11
  XForms Working Group, 191
  XHTML 1.0 Specification, 11
  XHTML 1.1, 11
  XHTML Basic, 11
  XHTML Specification, 27
  XML FAQ, 27
  XML Schema, 276

Webreview's Master Compatibility Chart, 145

well-formed documents, 17-18

white-space property, 360

widows property, 361

width attribute, 45, 47, 61-63, 76, 90

width property, 361

word-spacing property, 361

Working Drafts (W3C Working Groups), 292-293

Candidate Recommendations, 292
Last Call Working Drafts, 292
Proposed Recommendations, 292
W3C Notes, 293

X-Z

XForms, 5, 186-191
elements and attributes, 187-189
example, 191
history, 185
limitations, 189
standards, 190
Web resources, 191
Web site, 11

XHTML
backward compatibility, 9
componentization, 288-291
document criteria, 25
future of, 6, 283-284, 29, 311-312
history, 5
versus HTML, 10, 25-27, 105-109
official W3C recommendation, 299-302
acknowledgements, 317
benefits, 302
compatibility issues, 311
document conformance, 304-305
DTDs, 312-313
element prohibitions, 313
future of XHTML, 311-312
versus HTML 4, 308-311
HTML compatibility guidelines, 313-316
namespaces, 306
references, 317-318
terminology, 303-304
user agent conformance, 306-308
well-formed documents, 308
XML, 302
subsets, 5
versus XML, 4, 259
XHTML 1.0 Specification, 6
overview, 7-8
Web site, 11
XHTML 2.0, 295-296
XHTML Basic, 5, 291
Web site, 11
XHTML Frameset, 15
XHTML Modularization, 5
XHTML Strict, 15

XHTML Transitional, 15
XHTML-L mailing list, 365
XLink, 233-234, 254
attributes, 236-237
behavior attributes, 238
in documents, 253-254
extended links, 240
arc-type elements, 241-242
locator-type elements, 240-241
resource-type elements, 240-241
title-type elements, 242
fragment identifiers, 239
link servers, 254
linking elements, 236
namespace, 235-236
semantic attributes, 238
simple links, 237
terminology, 234-235
xlink:actuate attribute, 239
xlink:arcrole attribute, 238
xlink:href attribute, 237
xlink:role attribute, 238
xlink:show attribute, 238-239
xlink:title attribute, 238

xlink:actuate attribute, 239
xlink:arcrole attribute, 238
xlink:href attribute, 237
xlink:role attribute, 238
xlink:show attribute, 239
xlink:title attribute, 238
xlink:title element, 242
XMetal, 143
XML (Extensible Markup Language), 2-3
adding style sheets, 160
applications, 3, 278-281
adding, 278-281
basic rules, 25-26
built-in entity references, 273
character data, 264-265
parsed, 264
data, 261
declarations, 24, 113, 262-263
DTDs (Document Type Definitions), 265-268
attribute declarations, 270-272
designing and constructing, 268-269
element declarations, 269-270

entities, 273
   external entities, 275
   notation declarations, 275
   parameter entities, 273-275
   unparsed entities, 275
extensibility, 257
versus HTML, 2, 257-259
instructions, 262
   document type declarations, 263-264
   processing instructions (PIs), 262
   XML declarations, 262-263
namespaces, 111
official XHTML recommendation, 302
parsers, 197
schemas, 294-295
standardized DTDs, 260-261
syntax rules, 110-112
Web resources, 3
versus XHTML, 4, 259
XML Forms. *See* XForms
XML Schema, 275-276
XML-compatible browsers, 109-110
   Amaya, 109
   Internet Explorer, 110
   Mozilla, 110
XML-DEV mailing list, 366
XML-L mailing list, 366

xmlns attribute, 59, 276

XPath, 246-247
abbreviated syntax, 252
context nodes, 248
in documents, 253-254
expressions, 248-250
location paths, 248
   absolute, 248
   axes, 248
   relative, 248
location steps, 248
   abbreviated, 252
   node tests, 249
   predicates, 249
node set functions, 250-252
trees of nodes, 246

XPointer, 243
bare names, 244
child sequences, 244-245
in documents, 253-254
escaping, 245-246
expressions, 243, 245
fragment identifiers, 246

schemes, 245
XPath, 246-247
   abbreviated syntax, 252
   expressions, 248-250
   node set functions, 250-252

XSL (Extensible Stylesheet Language), 162
versus CSS, 166
documents,
   adding style to, 167
   associating style sheets with, 182-183
   transformed, adding CSS, 183
formatting with, 167
tools, 183
   Microsoft MSXML, 184
   Saxon, 183-184
   XT, 184
Web resources, 184
XSL Working Group, 165-167
   deliverables, 165
XSL-FO, 164-167
XSLT, 162-168
   example, 180-181
   instructions, 179
   literal result elements, 179-180
   namespaces, 168
   predefined elements, 168-177
   tools, 183
   top-level elements, 178
   trees and nodes, 163-164
   Web resources, 184
   xsl:apply-templates element, 182
   xsl:output element, 181
   xsl:stylesheet element, 177-181
   xsl:template element, 178-182
   xsl:transform elements, 177
   xsl:value-of element, 182

xsl:apply-templates element, 182

xsl:stylesheet element, 177, 181
attributes, 177

xsl:template element, 178-179, 182

xsl:transform element, 177
attributes, 177

xsl:value-of element, 182

XSLT (XSL Transformations), 162-168
example, 180-181
namespaces, 168

predefined elements, 168–177
  example, 180-181
  instructions, 179
  literal result elements, 179-180
  namespaces, 168
  top-level elements, 178
  xsl:apply-templates element, 182
  xsl:output element, 181
  xsl:stylesheet element, 177-181
  xsl:template element, 178-182
  xsl:transform element, 177
  xsl:value-of element, 182
tools, 183
  Microsoft MSXML, 184
  Saxon, 183-184
  XT, 184
trees and nodes, 163–164
Web resources, 184

XT (James Clark), 184

z-index property, 361

Open Source Resource

Master programmer and bestselling author Steve Holzner opens XML up like no other author can, packing *Inside XML* with every major XML topic today and detailing the ways XML is currently used. From using XML in browsers to building standalone Java/XML applications, from working with XPointers and XLinks to XSL style language, from XML namespaces to data binding, it's all here. You get details on creating valid and well-formed XML documents, document type definitions, schemas, the XML DOM, canonical XML, XML and databases, XML with CSS, XSL transformations, XSL formatting objects, converting XML documents to PDF format, server-side XML with JSP, ASP, Java servlets, and Perl. All the XML you need is right here.

ISBN: 0-7357-1020-1

Web Application Development with PHP explains PHP's advanced syntax, including classes, recursive functions, and variables. The authors present software development methodologies and coding conventions which are a must-know for industry quality products and make developing faster and more productive. Included is coverage on Web applications and insight into user and session management, e-commerce systems, XML applications, and WDDX.

ISBN: 0-7357-0997-1

Written by veteran software developer Michael J. Tobler, who has spent more than six years designing and developing multi-tier systems to run under Linux, *Inside Linux* provides comprehensive coverage of the operating system, written so even professionals who are unfamiliar with Linux can understand and use it. The book is filled with up-to-date information on system installation and administration, network and hardware configuration, and the use of services such as email, network file systems, dial-up networking, printing, and Internet news. The book also covers such important issues as merging Linux and Windows through Samba and using the popular Apache Web server. The result is a book that guides you through the process of getting a Linux system up and running.

ISBN: 0-7357-0940-8

Advanced Information on Networking Technologies

New Riders Books Offer Advice and Experience

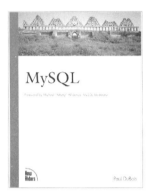

LANDMARK

Rethinking Computer Books

We know how important it is to have access to detailed, solution-oriented information on core technologies. *Landmark* books contain the essential information you need to solve technical problems. Written by experts and subjected to rigorous peer and technical reviews, our *Landmark* books are hard-core resources for practitioners like you.

ESSENTIAL REFERENCE

Smart, Like You

The *Essential Reference* series from New Riders provides answers when you know what you want to do but need to know how to do it. Each title skips extraneous material and assumes a strong base of knowledge. These are indispensable books for the practitioner who wants to find specific features of a technology quickly and efficiently. Avoiding fluff and basic material, these books present solutions in an innovative, clean format—and at a great value.

CIRCLE SERIES

The *Circle Series* is a set of reference guides that meet the needs of the growing community of advanced, technical-level networkers who must architect, develop, and administer operating systems like UNIX, Linux, Windows NT, and Windows 2000. These books provide network designers and programmers with detailed, proven solutions to their problems.

Books for Networking Professionals

Windows NT/2000 Titles

Windows 2000 Professional
By Jerry Honeycutt
1st Edition
350 pages, $34.99
ISBN: 0-7357-0950-5

Windows 2000 Professional explores the power available to the Windows worksta-tion user on the corporate network and Internet. The book is aimed directly at the power user who values the security, stability, and networking capabilities of NT alongside the ease and familiarity of the Windows 9x user interface. This book covers both user and administration top-ics, with a dose of networking content added for connectivity.

Windows 2000 Deployment & Desktop Management
By Jeffrey A. Ferris
1st Ediition
400 pages, $34.99
ISBN: 0-7357-0975-0

More than a simple overview of new features and tools, this solutions-driven book is a thorough reference to deploy-ing Windows 2000 Professional to corporate workstations. The expert real-world advice and detailed exercises make this a one-stop, easy-to-use resource for any system administrator, integrator, engineer, or other IT professional plan-ning rollout of Windows 2000 clients.

Windows 2000 DNS
By Herman Knief, Jeffrey Graham, Andrew Daniels, and Roger Abell
2nd Edition
450 pages, $39.99
ISBN: 0-7357-0973-4

Without proper design and administra-tion of DNS, computers wouldn't be able to locate each other on the network, and applications like email and Web browsing wouldn't be feasible. Administrators need this information to make their networks work. *Windows 2000 DNS* provides a technical overview of DNS and WINS, and how to design and administer them for optimal performance in a Windows 2000 environment.

Planning for Windows 2000

By Eric K. Cone, Jon Boggs, and Sergio Perez
1st Edition
400 pages, $29.99
ISBN: 0-7357-0048-6

Planning for Windows 2000 lets you know what the upgrade hurdles will be, informs you how to clear them, guides you through effective Active Directory design, and presents you with detailed rollout procedures. Eric K. Cone, Jon Boggs, and Sergio Perez give you the benefit of their extensive experiences as Windows 2000 Rapid Deployment Program members by sharing problems and solutions they've encountered on the job.

Inside Windows 2000 Server

By William Boswell
1st Edition
1550 pages, $49.99
ISBN: 1-56205-929-7

Building on the author-driven, no-nonsense approach of our Landmark books, New Riders proudly offers something unique for Windows 2000 administrators—an in-depth, discriminating book on Windows 2000 Server written by someone who can anticipate your situation and give you workarounds that won't leave a system unstable or sluggish.

Windows 2000 Security

By Roberta Bragg
1st Edition
550 pages, $39.99
ISBN: 0-7357-0991-2

No single authoritative reference on security exists for serious network system administrators. The primary goal of this title is to assist the Windows networking professional in understanding and implementing Windows 2000 security in his or her organization. Included are, "Best Practices" sections, which make recommendations for settings and security practices.

Windows 2000 Server Professional Reference

By Karanjit S. Siyan, Ph.D.
3rd Edition
1800 pages, $75.00
ISBN: 0-7357-0952-1

Windows 2000 Server Professional Reference is the benchmark of references available for Windows 2000. Although other titles take you through the setup and implementation phase of the product, no other book provides the user with detailed answers to day-to-day administration problems and tasks. Real-world implementations are key to help administrators discover the most viable solutions for their particular environments. Solid content shows administrators how to manage, troubleshoot, and fix problems that are specific to heterogeneous Windows networks, as well as Internet features and functionality.

Windows 2000 User Management

By Lori Sanders
1st Edition
300 pages, $34.99
ISBN: 1-56205-886-X

With the dawn of Windows 2000, it has become even more difficult to draw a clear line between managing the user and managing the user's environment and desktop. This book, written by a noted trainer and consultant, provides a comprehensive, practical guide to managing users and their desktop environments with Windows 2000.

Windows 2000 Active Directory Design & Deployment

By Gary Olsen
1st Edition
600 pages, $45.00
ISBN: 1-57870-242-9

This book focuses on the design of a Windows 2000 Active Directory environment, and how to develop an effective design and migration plan. The reader is led through the process of developing a design plan by reviewing each pertinent issue, and then provided expert advice on how to evaluate each issue as it applies to the reader's particular environment. Practical examples illustrate all these issues.

Windows 2000 Quality of Service

By David Iseminger
1st Edition
300 pages, $45.00
ISBN: 1-57870-115-5

As the traffic on networks continues to increase, the strain on network infrastructure and available resources has also grown. *Windows 2000 Quality of Service* teaches network engineers and administrators to how to define traffic control patterns and utilize bandwidth in their networks.

Windows 2000 Server: Planning and Migration

By Sean Deuby
1st Edition
450 pages $40.00
ISBN: 1-57870-023-X

Windows 2000 Server: Planning and Migration can quickly save the NT professional thousands of dollars and hundreds of hours. This title includes authoritative information on key features of Windows 2000 and offers recommendations on how to best position your NT network for Windows 2000.

Windows 2000 and Mainframe Integration
By William Zack
1st Edition
400 pages, $40.00
ISBN: 1-57870-200-3

Windows 2000 and Mainframe Integration provides mainframe computing professionals with the practical know-how to build and integrate Windows 2000 technologies into their current environment.

Windows NT/2000 Thin Client Solutions
By Todd Mathers
2nd Edition
750 pages, $45.00
ISBN: 1-57870-239-9

A practical and comprehensive reference to MetaFrame 1.8 and Terminal Services, this book should be the first source for answers to the tough questions on the Terminal Server VCx2/ MetaFrame platform. Building on the quality of the previous edition, additional coverage of installation of Terminal Services and MetaFrame on a Windows 2000 Server is included, as well as chapters on Terminal Server management, remote access, and application integration.

Windows NT/2000 Native API Reference
By Gary Nebbett
1st Edition
500 pages, $50.00
ISBN: 1-57870-199-6

This book is the first complete reference to the API functions native to Windows NT and covers the set of services that are offered by the Windows NT to both kernel- and user-mode programs. Coverage consists of documentation of the 210 routines included in the NT Native API, and the functions that have been be added in Windows 2000. Routines that are either not directly accessible via the Win32 API or offer substantial additional functionality are described in especially great detail. Services offered by the NT kernel, mainly the support for debugging user-mode applications, are also included.

Windows NT/2000 ADSI Scripting for System Administration
By Thomas Eck
1st Edition
700 pages, $45.00
ISBN: 1-57870-219-4

Active Directory Scripting Interfaces (ADSI) enable administrators to automate administrative tasks across their Windows networks. This title fills a gap in the current ADSI documentation by including coverage of its interaction with LDAP and provides administrators with proven code samples that they can adopt to effectively configure and manage user accounts and other usually time-consuming tasks.

Windows 2000 Virtual Private Networking

By Thaddeus Fortenberry
1st Edition
400 pages, $45.00
ISBN 1-57870-246-1
January 2001

Because of the ongoing push for a distributed workforce, administrators must support laptop users, home LAN environments, complex branch offices, and more—all within a secure and effective network design. The way an administrator implements VPNs in Windows 2000 differs from that of any other operating system. In addition to discussions about Windows 2000 tunneling, new VPN features that can affect Active Directory replication and network address translation are also covered.

Windows NT Terminal Server and Citrix MetaFrame

By Ted Harwood
1st Edition
400 pages, $29.99
ISBN: 1-56205-944-0

It's no surprise that most administration headaches revolve around integration with other networks and clients. This book addresses these types of real-world issues on a case-by-case basis, giving tools and advice for solving each problem. The author also offers the real nuts and bolts of thin client administration on multiple systems, covering relevant issues such as installation, configuration, network connection, management, and application distribution.

Windows NT Power Toolkit

By Stu Sjouwerman
and Ed Tittel
1st Edition
800 pages, $49.99
ISBN: 0-7357-0922-X

This book covers the analysis, tuning, optimization, automation, enhancement, maintenance, and troubleshooting of Windows NT Server 4.0 and Windows NT Workstation 4.0. In most cases, the two operating systems overlap completely. Where the two systems diverge, each platform is covered separately. This advanced title comprises a task-oriented treatment of the Windows NT 4 environment. By concentrating on the use of operating system tools and utilities, Resource Kit elements, and selected third-party tuning, analysis, optimization, and productivity tools, this book shows its readers how to carry out everyday and advanced tasks.

Windows NT Performance: Monitoring, Benchmarking, and Tuning

By Mark T. Edmead
and Paul Hinsberg
1st Edition
288 pages, $29.99
ISBN: 1-56205-942-4

Performance monitoring is a little like preventive medicine for the administrator: No one enjoys a checkup, but it's a good thing to do on a regular basis. This book helps you focus on the critical aspects of improving the performance of your NT system by showing you how to monitor the system, implement benchmarking, and tune your network. The book is organized by resource components, which makes it easy to use as a reference tool.

Windows NT Device Driver Development

By Peter Viscarola and
W. Anthony Mason
1st Edition
700 pages, $50.00
ISBN: 1-57870-058-2

This title begins with an introduction to the general Windows NT operating system concepts relevant to drivers, then progresses to more detailed information about the operating system, such as interrupt management, synchronization issues, the I/O subsystem, standard kernel-mode drivers, and more.

Windows NT Shell Scripting

By Tim Hill
1st Edition
350 pages, $32.00
ISBN: 1-57870-047-7

A complete reference for Windows NT scripting, this book guides you through a high-level introduction to the shell language itself and the shell commands that are useful for controlling or managing different components of a network.

Windows Script Host

By Tim Hill
1st Edition
400 pages, $35.00
ISBN: 1-57870-139-2

Windows Script Host is one of the first books published about this powerful tool. The text focuses on system scripting and the VBScript language, using objects, server scriptlets, and provides ready-to-use script solutions.

Internet Information Services Administration

By Kelli Adam
1st Edition
200 pages, $29.99
ISBN: 0-7357-0022-2

Are the new Internet technologies in Internet Information Services giving you headaches? Does providing security on the Web take up all of your time? Then this is the book for you. With hands-on configuration training, advanced study of the new protocols, coverage of the most recent version of IIS, and detailed instructions on authenticating users with the new Certificate Server and implementing and managing the new e-commerce features, *Internet Information Services Administration* gives you the real-life solutions you need. This definitive resource gives you detailed advice on working with Microsoft Management Console, which was first used by IIS.

Win32 Perl Programming: The Standard Extensions

By Dave Roth
1st Edition
600 pages, $40.00
ISBN: 1-57870-067-1

See numerous proven examples and practical uses of Perl in solving every-day Win32 problems. This is the only book available with comprehensive coverage of Win32 extensions, where most of the Perl functionality resides in Windows settings.

SMS 2 Administration

By Michael Lubanski
and Darshan Doshi
1st Edition
350 pages, $39.99
ISBN: 0-7357-0082-6

Microsoft's new version of its Systems
Management Server (SMS) is starting to
turn heads. Although complex, it enables
administrators to lower their total cost of
ownership and more efficiently manage
clients, applications, and support opera-
tions. So if your organization is using or
implementing SMS, you'll need some
expert advice. Michael Lubanski and
Darshan Doshi can help you get the most
bang for your buck with insight, expert
tips, and real-world examples. Michael
and Darshan are consultants specializing
in SMS and have worked with Microsoft
on one of the most complex SMS roll-
outs in the world, involving 32 countries,
15 languages, and thousands of clients.

SQL Server 7 Essential Reference

By Sharon Dooley
1st Edition
400 pages, $35.00 US
ISBN: 0-7357-0864-9

SQL Server 7 Essential Reference is a comprehensive reference of advanced how-tos
and techniques for developing with SQL
Server. In particular, the book addresses
advanced development techniques used in
large application efforts with multiple
users, such as developing Web applications
for intranets, extranets, or the Internet.
Each section includes detail on how each
component is developed and then integrated into a real-life application.

SQL Server System Administration

By Sean Baird,
Chris Miller, et al.
1st Edition
352 pages, $29.99
ISBN: 1-56205-955-6

How often does your SQL Server go
down during the day when everyone
wants to access the data? Do you spend
most of your time being a "report
monkey" for your coworkers and bosses?
SQL Server System Administration helps
you keep data consistently available to
your users. This book omits introductory
information. The authors don't spend
time explaining queries and how they
work. Instead, they focus on the information you can't get anywhere else, like
how to choose the correct replication
topology and achieve high availability of
information.

Networking Titles

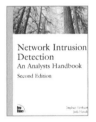

Network Intrusion Detection: An Analyst's Handbook

By Stephen Northcutt
and Judy Novak
2nd Edition
450 pages, $45.00
ISBN: 0-7357-1008-2

Get answers and solutions from someone
who has been in the trenches. Stephen
Northcutt, original developer of the
Shadow intrusion detection system and
former director of the United States
Navy's Information System Security
Office at the Naval Security Warfare
Center, gives his expertise to intrusion
detection specialists, security analysts,
and consultants responsible for setting
up and maintaining an effective defense
against network security attacks.

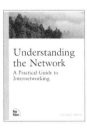

Understanding the Network: A Practical Guide to Internetworking
By Michael Martin
1st Edition
650 pages, $39.99
ISBN: 0-7357-0977-7

Understanding the Network addresses the audience in practical terminology, and describes the most essential information and tools required to build high-availability networks in a step-by-step implementation format. Each chapter could be read as a standalone, but the book builds progressively toward a summary of the essential concepts needed to put together a wide area network.

Understanding Data Communications
By Gilbert Held
6th Edition
600 pages, $39.99
ISBN: 0-7357-0036-2

Updated from the highly successful fifth edition, this book explains how data communications systems and their various hardware and software components work. More than an entry-level book, it approaches the material in text-book format, addressing the complex issues involved in internetworking today. A great reference book for the experienced networking professional that is written by the noted networking authority, Gilbert Held.

Cisco Router Configuration & Troubleshooting
By Mark Tripod
2nd Edition
400 pages, $34.99
ISBN: 0-7357-0999-8

Want the real story on making your Cisco routers run like a dream? Pick up a copy of *Cisco Router Configuration & Troubleshooting* and see what Mark Tripod of Exodus Communications has to say. Exodus is responsible for making some of the largest sites on the Net scream, like Amazon.com, Hotmail, USAToday, Geocities, and Sony. In this book, the author provides advanced configuration issues, sprinkled with advice and preferred practices. By providing real-world insight and examples instead of rehashing Cisco's documentation, Mark gives network administrators information they can start using today.

Understanding Directory Services
By Beth Sheresh and Doug Sheresh
1st Edition
400 pages, $39.99
ISBN: 0-7357-0910-6

Understanding Directory Services provides the reader with a thorough knowledge of the fundamentals of directory services: what DSs are, how they are designed, and what functionality they can provide to an IT infrastructure. This book provides a framework to the exploding market of directory services by placing the technology in context and helping people understand what directories can, and can't, do for their networks.

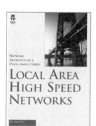

Local Area High Speed Networks

By Dr. Sidnie Feit
1st Edition
650 pages, $50.00
ISBN: 1-57870-113-9

A great deal of change is happening in the technology being used for local area networks. As Web intranets have driven bandwidth needs through the ceiling, inexpensive Ethernet NICs and switches have come into the market. As a result, many network professionals are interested in evaluating these new technologies for implementation. This book provides real-world implementation expertise for these technologies, including traces, so that users can realistically compare and decide how to use them.

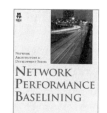

Network Performance Baselining

By Daniel Nassar
1st Edition
700 pages, $50.00
ISBN: 1-57870-240-2

Network Performance Baselining focuses on the real-world implementation of network baselining principles and shows not only how to measure and rate a network's performance, but also how to improve the network's performance. This book includes chapters that give a real "how-to" approach for standard baseline methodologies along with actual steps and processes to perform network baseline measurements. In addition, the proper way to document and build a baseline report is provided.

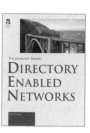

Directory Enabled Networks

By John Strassner
1st Edition
700 pages, $50.00
ISBN: 1-57870-140-6

Directory Enabled Networks is a comprehensive resource on the design and use of DEN. This book provides practical examples side-by-side with a detailed introduction to the theory of building a new class of network-enabled applications that will solve networking problems. It is a critical tool for network architects, administrators, and application developers.

Wide Area High Speed Networks

By Dr. Sidnie Feit
1st Edition
600 pages, $50.00
ISBN:1-57870-114-7

Networking is in a transitional phase between long-standing conventional wide area services and new technologies and services. This book presents current and emerging wide area technologies and services, makes them understandable, and puts them into perspective so that their merits and disadvantages are clear.

Quality of Service in IP Networks

By Grenville Armitage
1st Edition
300 pages, $50.00
ISBN: 1-57870-189-9

Quality of Service in IP Networks presents a clear understanding of the architectural issues surrounding delivering QoS in an IP network, and positions the emerging technologies within a framework of solutions. The motivation for QoS is explained with reference to emerging real-time applications such as Voice/Video over IP, VPN services, and supporting Service Level Agreements.

Intrusion Detection

By Rebecca Bace
1st Edition
300 pages, $50.00
ISBN: 1-57870-185-6

Intrusion detection is a critical new area of technology within network security. This comprehensive guide to the field of intrusion detection covers the foundations of intrusion detection and system audit. *Intrusion Detection* provides a wealth of information, ranging from design considerations to how to evaluate and choose the optimal commercial intrusion detection products for a particular networking environment.

The DHCP Handbook

By Ralph Droms
and Ted Lemon
1st Edition
550 pages, $55.00
ISBN: 1-57870-137-6

The DHCP Handbook is an authoritative overview and expert guide to the setup and management of a DHCP server. This title discusses how DHCP was developed and its interaction with other protocols. Also, learn how DHCP operates, its use in different environments, and the interaction between DHCP servers and clients. Network hardware, inter-server communication, security, SNMP, and IP mobility are also discussed. Included in the book are several appendixes that provide a rich resource for networking professionals working with DHCP.

Solutions from experts you know and trust.

www.informit.com

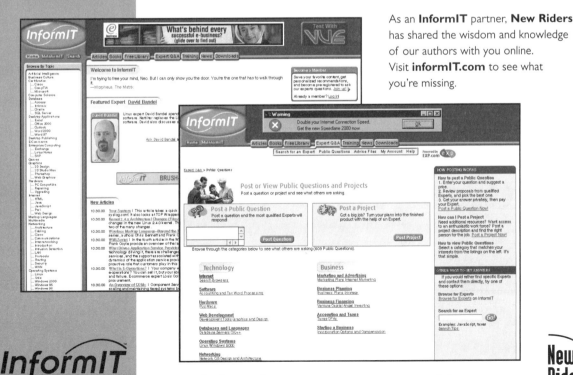

Other Books By New Riders

MICROSOFT TECHNOLOGIES

ADMINISTRATION

Inside Windows 2000 Server
1-56205-929-7 • $49.99 US / $74.95 CAN
Windows Windows 2000 Essential Reference
0-7357-0869-X • $35.00 US / $52.95 CAN
Windows 2000 Active Directory
0-7357-0870-3 • $29.99 US / $44.95 CAN
Windows 2000 Routing and Remote Access Service
0-7357-0951-3 • $34.99 US / $52.95 CAN
Windows 2000 Deployment & Desktop Management
0-7357-0975-0 • $34.99 US / $52.95 CAN
Windows 2000 DNS
0-7357-0973-4 • $39.99 US / $59.95 CAN
Windows 2000 User Management
1-56205-886-X • $34.99 US / $52.95 CAN
Windows 2000 Professional
0-7357-0950-5 • $34.99 US / $52.95 CAN
Planning for Windows 2000
0-7357-0048-6 • $29.99 US / $44.95 CAN
Windows 2000 Server Professional Reference
0-7357-0952-1 • $75.00 US / $111.95 CAN
Windows 2000 Security
0-7357-0991-2 • $39.99 US / $59.95 CAN
Windows 2000 TCP/IP
0-7357-0992-0 • $39.99 US / $59.95 CAN
Windows NT/2000 Network Security
1-57870-253-4 • $45.00 US / $67.95 CAN
Windows NT/2000 Thin Client Solutions
1-57870-239-9 • $45.00 US / $67.95 CAN
Windows 2000 Virtual Private Networking
1-57870-246-1 • $45.00 US / $67.95 CAN
• Available January 2001
Windows 2000 Active Directory Design & Deployment
1-57870-242-9 • $45.00 US / $67.95 CAN
Windows 2000 and Mainframe Integration
1-57870-200-3 • $40.00 US / $59.95 CAN
Windows 2000 Server: Planning and Migration
1-57870-023-X • $40.00 US / $59.95 CAN
Windows 2000 Quality of Service
1-57870-115-5 • $45.00 US / $67.95 CAN
Windows NT Power Toolkit
0-7357-0922-X • $49.99 US / $74.95 CAN
Windows NT Terminal Server and Citrix MetaFrame
1-56205-944-0 • $29.99 US / $44.95 CAN
Windows NT Performance: Monitoring, Benchmarking, and Tuning
1-56205-942-4 • $29.99 US / $44.95 CAN
Windows NT Registry: A Settings Reference
1-56205-941-6 • $29.99 US / $44.95 CAN
Windows NT Domain Architecture
1-57870-112-0 • $38.00 US / $56.95 CAN

SYSTEMS PROGRAMMING

Windows NDIS Miniport Development
1-57870-248-8 • $50.00 US / $74.95 CAN
• Available March 2001
Windows NT/2000 Native API Reference
1-57870-199-6 • $50.00 US / $74.95 CAN
Windows NT Device Driver Development
1-57870-058-2 • $50.00 US / $74.95 CAN
DCE/RPC over SMB: Samba and Windows NT Domain Internals
1-57870-150-3 • $45.00 US / $67.95 CAN

WEB PROGRAMMING

Real World Web Code: Techniques for Structured ASP Programming
0-7357-1033-3 • $39.99 US / $59.95 CAN
• Available March 2001

Exchange & Outlook: Constructing Collaborative Solutions
1-57870-252-6 • $40.00 US / $59.95 CAN

APPLICATION PROGRAMMING

Delphi COM Programming
1-57870-221-6 • $45.00 US / $67.95 CAN
Windows NT Applications: Measuring and Optimizing Performance
1-57870-176-7 • $40.00 US / $59.95 CAN
Applying COM+
0-7357-0978-5 • $49.99 US / $74.95 CAN

SCRIPTING

Windows Script Host
1-57870-139-2 • $35.00 US / $52.95 CAN
Windows NT Shell Scripting
1-57870-047-7 • $32.00 US / $45.95 CAN
Windows NT Win32 Perl Programming: The Standard Extensions
1-57870-067-1 • $40.00 US / $59.95 CAN
Windows NT/2000 ADSI Scripting for System Administration
1-57870-219-4 • $45.00 US / $67.95 CAN
Windows NT Automated Deployment and Customization
1-57870-045-0 • $32.00 US / $45.95 CAN
Win32 Perl Scripting: The Administrator's Handbook
1-57870-215-1 • $35.00 US / $52.95 CAN

BACK OFFICE

SMS 2 Administration
0-7357-0082-6 • $39.99 US / $59.95 CAN
Internet Information Services Administration
0-7357-0022-2 • $29.99 US / $44.95 CAN
SQL Server System Administration
1-56205-955-6 • $29.99 US / $44.95 CAN
SQL Server 7 Essential Reference
0-7357-0864-9 • $35.00 US / $52.95 CAN
Inside Exchange 2000 Server
0-7357-1027-9 • $49.99 US / $74.95 CAN
• Available February 2001

WEB DESIGN & DEVELOPMENT

OPEN SOURCE

MySQL
0-7357-0921-1 • $49.99 US / $74.95 CAN
Web Application Development with PHP 4.0
0-7357-0997-1 • $39.99 US / $59.95 CAN
PHP Functions Essential Reference
0-7357-0970-X • $35.00 US / $52.95 CAN
• Available April 2001
Python Essential Reference
0-7357-0901-7 • $34.95 US / $52.95 CAN
Qt: The Official Documentation
1-57870-209-7 • $50.00 US / $74.95 CAN
Berkeley DB
0-7357-1064-3 • $39.99 US / $59.95 CAN
• Available February 2001
GNU Autoconf, Automake, and Libtool
1-57870-190-2 • $40.00 US / $59.95 CAN

CREATIVE MEDIA

Designing Web Usability
1-56205-810-X • $45.00 US / $67.95 CAN
Designing Web Graphics.3
1-56205-949-1 • $55.00 US / $81.95 CAN
Flash 4 Magic
0-7357-0949-1 • $45.00 US / $67.95 CAN
<creative.html design>
1-56205-704-9 • $39.99 US / $59.95 CAN
Creating Killer Web Sites, Second Edition
1-56830-433-1 • $49.99 US / $74.95 CAN

Secrets of Successful Web Sites
1-56830-382-3 • $49.99 US / $74.95 CAN

XML

Inside XML
0-7357-1020-1 • $49.99 US / $74.95 CAN

LINUX/UNIX

ADMINISTRATION

Networking Linux: A Practical Guide to TCP/IP
0-7357-1031-7 • $39.99 US / $59.95 CAN
• Available February 2001
Inside Linux
0-7357-0940-8 • $39.99 US / $59.95 CAN
Vi iMproved (VIM)
0-7357-1001-5 • $49.99 US / $74.95 CAN
• Available January 2001
Linux System Administration
1-56205-934-3 • $29.99 US / $44.95 CAN
Linux Firewalls
0-7357-0900-9 • $39.99 US / $59.95 CAN
Linux Essential Reference
0-7357-0852-5 • $24.95 US / $37.95 CAN
UnixWare 7 System Administration
1-57870-080-9 • $40.00 US / $59.99 CAN

DEVELOPMENT

Developing Linux Applications with GTK+ and GDK
0-7357-0021-4 • $34.99 US / $52.95 CAN
GTK+/Gnome Application Development
0-7357-0078-8 • $39.99 US / $59.95 CAN
KDE Application Development
1-57870-201-1 • $39.99 US / $59.95 CAN

GIMP

Grokking the GIMP
0-7357-0924-6 • $45.00 US / $59.95 CAN
GIMP Essential Reference
0-7357-0911-4 • $24.95 US / $37.95 CAN

SOLARIS

Solaris Advanced System Administrator's Guide, Second Edition
1-57870-039-6 • $39.99 US / $59.95 CAN
Solaris System Administrator's Guide, Second Edition
1-57870-040-X • $34.99 US / $52.95 CAN
Solaris Essential Reference
0-7357-0023-0 • $24.95 US / $37.95 CAN
Solaris System Management
0-7357-1018-X • $39.99 US / $59.95 CAN
• Available March 2001
Solaris 8 Essential Reference
0-7357-1007-4 • $34.99 US / $52.95 CAN
• Available January 2001

NETWORKING

STANDARDS & PROTOCOLS

Differentiated Services for the Internet
1-57870-132-5 • $50.00 US / $74.95 CAN
Cisco Router Configuration & Troubleshooting, Second Edition
0-7357-0999-8 • $34.99 US / $52.95 CAN
Understanding Directory Services
0-7357-0910-6 • $39.99 US / $59.95 CAN
Understanding the Network: A Practical Guide to Internetworking
0-7357-0977-7 • $39.99 US / $59.95 CAN
Understanding Data Communications, Sixth Edition
0-7357-0036-2 • $39.99 US / $59.95 CAN
LDAP: Programming Directory Enabled Applications
1-57870-000-0 • $44.99 US / $67.95 CAN
Gigabit Ethernet Networking
1-57870-062-0 • $50.00 US / $74.95 CAN

Supporting Service Level Agreements on IP Networks
1-57870-146-5 • $50.00 US / $74.95 CAN
Directory Enabled Networks
1-57870-140-6 • $50.00 US / $74.95 CAN
Policy-Based Networking: Architecture and Algorithms
1-57870-226-7 • $50.00 US / $74.95 CAN
Networking Quality of Service and Windows Operating Systems
1-57870-206-2 • $50.00 US / $74.95 CAN
Policy-Based Management
1-57870-225-9 • $55.00 US / $81.95 CAN
• Available March 2001
Quality of Service on IP Networks
1-57870-189-9 • $50.00 US / $74.95 CAN
Designing Addressing Architectures for Routing and Switching
1-57870-059-0 • $45.00 US / $69.95 CAN
Understanding & Deploying LDAP Directory Services
1-57870-070-1 • $50.00 US / $74.95 CAN
Switched, Fast and Gigabit Ethernet, Third Edition
1-57870-073-6 • $50.00 US / $74.95 CAN
Wireless LANs: Implementing Interoperable Networks
1-57870-081-7 • $40.00 US / $59.95 CAN
Local Area High Speed Networks
1-57870-113-9 • $50.00 US / $74.95 CAN
Wide Area High Speed Networks
1-57870-114-7 • $50.00 US / $74.95 CAN
The DHCP Handbook
1-57870-137-6 • $55.00 US / $81.95 CAN
Designing Routing and Switching Architectures for Enterprise Networks
1-57870-060-4 • $55.00 US / $81.95 CAN
Network Performance Baselining
1-57870-240-2 • $50.00 US / $74.95 CAN
Economics of Electronic Commerce
1-57870-014-0 • $49.99 US / $74.95 CAN

SECURITY

Intrusion Detection
1-57870-185-6 • $50.00 US / $74.95 CAN
Understanding Public-Key Infrastructure
1-57870-166-X • $50.00 US / $74.95 CAN
Network Intrusion Detection: An Analyst's Handbook, 2E
0-7357-1008-2 • $45.00 US / $67.95 CAN
Linux Firewalls
0-7357-0900-9 • $39.99 US / $59.95 CAN
Intrusion Signatures and Analysis
0-7357-1063-5 • $39.99 US / $59.95 CAN
• Available February 2001
Hackers Beware
0-7357-1009-0 • $45.00 US / $67.95 CAN
• Available March 2001

LOTUS NOTES/DOMINO

Domino System Administration
1-56205-948-3 • $49.99 US / $74.95 CAN
Lotus Notes & Domino Essential Reference
0-7357-0007-9 • $45.00 US / $67.95 CAN

PROFESSIONAL CERTIFICATION

TRAINING GUIDES

MCSE Training Guide: Networking Essentials, 2nd Ed.
1-56205-919-X • $49.99 US / $74.95 CAN
MCSE Training Guide: Windows NT Server 4, 2nd Ed.
1-56205-916-5 • $49.99 US / $74.95 CAN
MCSE Training Guide: Windows NT Workstation 4, 2nd Ed.
1-56205-918-1 • $49.99 US / $74.95 CAN
MCSE Training Guide: Windows NT Server 4 Enterprise, 2nd Ed.
1-56205-917-3 • $49.99 US / $74.95 CAN

MCSE Training Guide: Core Exams Bundle, 2nd Ed.
1-56205-926-2 • $149.99 US / $223.95 CAN
MCSE Training Guide: TCP/IP, 2nd Ed.
1-56205-920-3 • $49.99 US / $74.95 CAN
MCSE Training Guide: IIS 4, 2nd Ed.
0-7357-0865-7 • $49.99 US / $74.95 CAN
MCSE Training Guide: SQL Server 7 Administration
0-7357-0003-6 • $49.99 US / $74.95 CAN
MCSE Training Guide: SQL Server 7 Database Design
0-7357-0004-4 • $49.99 US / $74.95 CAN
MCSD Training Guide: Visual Basic 6 Exams
0-7357-0002-8 • $69.99 US / $104.95 CAN
MCSD Training Guide: Solution Architectures
0-7357-0026-5 • $49.99 US / $74.95 CAN
MCSD Training Guide: 4-in-1 Bundle
0-7357-0912-2 • $149.99 US / $223.95 CAN
A+ Certification Training Guide, Second Edition
0-7357-0907-6 • $49.99 US / $74.95 CAN
Network+ Certification Guide
0-7357-0077-X • $49.99 US / $74.95 CAN
Solaris 2.6 Administrator Certification Training Guide, Part I
1-57870-085-X • $40.00 US / $59.95 CAN
Solaris 2.6 Administrator Certification Training Guide, Part II
1-57870-086-8 • $40.00 US / $59.95 CAN
Solaris 7 Administrator Certification Training Guide, Part I and II
1-57870-249-6 • $49.99 US / $74.95 CAN
MCSE Training Guide: Windows 2000 Professional
0-7357-0965-3 • $49.99 US / $74.95 CAN
MCSE Training Guide: Windows 2000 Server
0-7357-0968-8 • $49.99 US / $74.95 CAN
MCSE Training Guide: Windows 2000 Network Infrastructure
0-7357-0966-1 • $49.99 US / $74.95 CAN
MCSE Training Guide: Windows 2000 Network Security Design
0-73570-984X • $49.99 US / $74.95 CAN
MCSE Training Guide: Windows 2000 Network Infrastructure Design
0-73570-982-3 • $49.99 US / $74.95 CAN
MCSE Training Guide: Windows 2000 Directory Svcs. Infrastructure
0-7357-0976-9 • $49.99 US / $74.95 CAN
MCSE Training Guide: Windows 2000 Directory Services Design
0-7357-0983-1 • $49.99 US / $74.95 CAN
MCSE Training Guide: Windows 2000 Accelerated Exam
0-7357-0979-3 • $69.99 US / $104.95 CAN
MCSE Training Guide: Windows 2000 Core Exams Bundle
0-7357-0988-2 • $149.99 US / $223.95 CAN

FAST TRACKS

CLP Fast Track: Lotus Notes/Domino 5 Application Development
0-7357-0877-0 • $39.99 US / $59.95 CAN
CLP Fast Track: Lotus Notes/Domino 5 System Administration
0-7357-0878-9 • $39.99 US / $59.95 CAN
Network+ Fast Track
0-7357-0904-1 • $29.99 US / $44.95 CAN
A+ Fast Track
0-7357-0028-1 • $34.99 US / $52.95 CAN
MCSD Fast Track: Visual Basic 6, Exam #70-175
0-7357-0019-2 • $19.99 US / $29.95 CAN
MCSD FastTrack: Visual Basic 6, Exam #70-175
0-7357-0018-4 • $19.99 US / $29.95 CAN

SOFTWARE ARCHITECTURE & ENGINEERING

Designing for the User with OVID
1-57870-101-5 • $40.00 US / $59.95 CAN
Designing Flexible Object-Oriented Systems with UML
1-57870-098-1 • $40.00 US / $59.95 CAN
Constructing Superior Software
1-57870-147-3 • $40.00 US / $59.95 CAN
A UML Pattern Language
1-57870-118-X • $45.00 US / $67.95 CAN

# How to Contact Us

Visit Our Web Site

`www.newriders.com`

On our Web site you'll find information about our other books, authors, tables of contents, indexes, and book errata.

Email Us

Contact us at this address:

`nrfeedback@newriders.com`

- If you have comments or questions about this book
- To report errors that you have found in this book
- If you have a book proposal to submit or are interested in writing for New Riders
- If you would like to have an author kit sent to you
- If you are an expert in a computer topic or technology and are interested in being a technical editor who reviews manuscripts for technical accuracy
- To find a distributor in your area, please contact our international department at this address.

`nrmedia@newriders.com`

- For instructors from educational institutions who want to preview New Riders books for classroom use. Email should include your name, title, school, department, address, phone number, office days/hours, text in use, and enrollment, along with your request for desk/examination copies and/or additional information.
- For members of the media who are interested in reviewing copies of New Riders books. Send your name, mailing address, and email address, along with the name of the publication or Web site you work for.

Bulk Purchases/Corporate Sales

If you are interested in buying 10 or more copies of a title or want to set up an account for your company to purchase directly from the publisher at a substantial discount, contact us at 800-382-3419 or email your contact information to `corpsales@ pearsontechgroup.com`. A sales representative will contact you with more information.

Write to Us

New Riders Publishing
201 W. 103rd St.
Indianapolis, IN 46290-1097

Call Us

Toll-free (800) 571-5840 + 9 + 7477
If outside U.S. (317) 581-3500. Ask for New Riders.

Fax Us

(317) 581-4663

We Want to Know What You Think

To better serve you, we would like your opinion on the content and quality of this book. Please complete this card and mail it to us or fax it to 317-581-4663.

Name _____

Address _____

City_____State_____Zip _____

Phone _____

Email Address _____

Occupation _____

Operating System(s) that you use _____

What influenced your purchase of this book?
- ❏ Recommendation
- ❏ Table of Contents
- ❏ Magazine Review
- ❏ New Rider's Reputation
- ❏ Cover Design
- ❏ Index
- ❏ Advertisement
- ❏ Author Name

How would you rate the contents of this book?
- ❏ Excellent
- ❏ Good
- ❏ Below Average
- ❏ Very Good
- ❏ Fair
- ❏ Poor

How do you plan to use this book?
- ❏ Quick reference
- ❏ Classroom
- ❏ Self-training
- ❏ Other

What do you like most about this book?
Check all that apply.
- ❏ Content
- ❏ Accuracy
- ❏ Listings
- ❏ Index
- ❏ Price
- ❏ Writing Style
- ❏ Examples
- ❏ Design
- ❏ Page Count
- ❏ Illustrations

What do you like least about this book?
Check all that apply.
- ❏ Content
- ❏ Accuracy
- ❏ Listings
- ❏ Index
- ❏ Price
- ❏ Writing Style
- ❏ Examples
- ❏ Design
- ❏ Page Count
- ❏ Illustrations

What would be a useful follow-up book to this one for you?_____

Where did you purchase this book? _____

_____

Can you name a similar book that you like better than this one, or one that is as good? Why?

_____

_____

How many New Riders books do you own? _____

What are your favorite computer books?_____

_____

What other titles would you like to see us develop? _____

_____

Any comments for us? _____

_____

_____

_____

XHTML, 0-7357-1034-1

www.newriders.com   •   Fax   317-581-4663

Fold here and tape to mail

- -

New Riders Publishing
201 W. 103rd St.
Indianapolis, IN 46290

CD-ROM Licensing Agreement

By opening this package, you are agreeing to be bound by the following agreement:

- You may not copy or redistribute the CD-ROM as a whole. Copying and redistribution of individual software programs on the CD-ROM is governed by terms set by individual copyright holders.

- The installer and code from the authors are copyrighted by the publisher and authors. Individual programs and other items on the CD-ROM are copyrighted by their various authors or other copyright holders. Some of the programs included with this product may be governed by an Open Source license, which allows redistribution; see the license information for each product for more information.

- Other programs are included on the CD-ROM by special permission from their authors.